THE

EIGHTEEN CHRISTIAN CENTURIES.

BY

THE REV. JAMES WHITE,

AUTHOR OF A "HISTORY OF FRANCE."

With a Copious Index.

FROM THE SECOND EDINBURGH EDITION.

NEW YORK:
D. APPLETON AND COMPANY,
346 & 348 BROADWAY.
M DCCC LX.

NOTE BY THE AMERICAN PUBLISHERS.

THIS valuable work, which has been received with much favour in Great Britain, is reprinted without abridgment from the second Edinburgh edition. The lists of names of remarkable persons in the present issue have been somewhat enlarged, and additional dates appended, thereby increasing the value of the book.

CONTENTS.

FIRST CENTURY.

SECOND CENTURY.

THIRD CENTURY.

FOURTH CENTURY.

FIFTH CENTURY.

SIXTH CENTURY.

SEVENTH CENTURY.

EIGHTH CENTURY.

NINTH CENTURY.

TENTH CENTURY.

ELEVENTH CENTURY.

TWELFTH CENTURY.

THIRTEENTH CENTURY.

FOURTEENTH CENTURY.

FIFTEENTH CENTURY.

SIXTEENTH CENTURY.

SEVENTEENTH CENTURY.

EIGHTEENTH CENTURY.

FIRST CENTURY.

Emperors.

A.D.

A.D.	
	Augustus Cæsar.
14.	Tiberius.
37.	Caius Caligula.
41.	Claudius.
54.	Nero. First Persecution of the Christians.
68.	Galba.
69.	Otho.
69.	Vitellius.
69.	Vespasian.
79.	Titus.
81.	Domitian. Second Persecution of the Christians.
96.	Nerva.
98.	Trajan.

Authors.

Livy, Ovid, Tibullus, Strabo, Columella, Quintus Curtius, Seneca, Lucan, Petronius, Silius Italicus, Pliny the Elder, Martial, Quinctilian, Tacitus.

Christian Fathers and Writers.

Barnabas, Clement of Rome, Hermas, Ignatius, Polycarp.

THE

EIGHTEEN CHRISTIAN CENTURIES.

THE FIRST CENTURY.

THE BAD EMPERORS.

NOBODY disputes the usefulness of History. Many prefer it, even for interest and amusement, to the best novels and romances. But the extent of time over which it has stretched its range is appalling to the most laborious of readers. And as History is growing every day, and every nation is engaged in the manufacture of memorable events, it is pitiable to contemplate the fate of the historic student a hundred years hence. He is not allowed to cut off at one end, in proportion as he increases at the other. He is not allowed to forget Marlborough, in consideration of his accurate acquaintance with Wellington. His knowledge of the career of Napoleon is no excuse for ignorance of Julius Cæsar. All must be retained—victories, defeats—battles, sieges—knights in armour, soldiers in red; the charge at Marathon, the struggle at Inkermann—all these things, a thousand other things, at first apparently of no importance, but growing larger and larger as time develops their effects, till men look back in wonder that the acorn escaped their notice which has produced such a majestic oak,—a thousand other things still, for a moment rising in apparently irresistible power, and dying off apparently without cause, must be folded up in niches of the memory, ready to be brought forth when needed, and yet room be left for the future. And who can pretend to be qualified for so great a work? Most of us confess to rather dim recollections of things occurring in our own time,—in our own country—in our own parish; and some, contemplating the vast expanse of human history, its innumerable windings and perplexing variations, are inclined to give it up in despair, and have a sulky sort of gratification in determining to know nothing, since they cannot know all. All kings, they say, are pretty much alike, and whether he is called John in England, or Louis in France, doesn't make much difference. Nobles also are as similar as possible, and peoples are everywhere the same. Now, this, you see, though it ambitiously pretends to be ignorance, is, in fact, something infinitely worse. It is false knowledge. It might be very injurious to liberty, to honour, and to religion itself, if this wretched idea were to become common, for where would be the inducement to noble endeavour? to reform of abuses? to purity of life? Kings and nobles and peoples are not everywhere the same. They are not even *like* each other, or like themselves in the same land at different periods. They are in a perpetual series, not only of change, but of contrast. They are "variable as the sea," —calm and turbulent, brilliant and dark by turns. And it is this which gives us the only chance of attaining clearness and distinctness in our historic views. It is by dissimilarities that things are individualized: now, how pleasant it would be if we could simplify and strengthen our recollections of different times, by getting personal portraits, as it were, of the various centuries, so as to escape the danger of confounding their dress or features. It would be impossible in that case to mistake the Spanish hat and feather of the sixteenth century for the steel helmet and closed vizor of the fourteenth. We should be able, in the same way, to distinguish between the modes of thought and principles of action of the early ages, and those of the present time. We should be able to point out anachronisms of feeling and manners if they occurred in the course of our reading, as well as of dress and language. It is surely worth while, therefore, to make an attempt to individualize the centuries, not by affixing to them any arbitrary marks of one's own, but by taking notice of the distinguishing quality they possess, and grouping round that, as a centre, the incidents which either produce this characteristic or are produced by it. What should we call the present century, for instance? We should at once name it the Century of Invention. The great war with Napoleon ending in 1815, exciting so many passions, and calling forth such energy, was but the natural introduction to the wider efforts and amazing progress of the succeeding forty years. Battles and bulletins, alliances and quarrels, ceased, but the intellect aroused by the struggle dashed into other channels. Commerce spread its humanizing influences over hitherto closed and unexplored regions; the steamboat and railway began their wondrous career. The lightning was trained to be our courier in the electric telegraph, and the sun took our likenesses in the daguerreotype. How changed this century is in all its attributes and tendencies from its predecessor, let any man judge for himself, who compares the reigns of our first Hanoverian kings with that of our gracious queen.

In nothing, indeed, is the course of European history so remarkable as in the immense differences which intervals of a few years introduce. In the old monarchies of Asia, time and the world seem almost to stand still.

The Indian, the Arab, the Chinese of a thousand years ago, wore the same clothes, thought the same thoughts, and led the same life as his successor of to-day. But with us the whole character of a people is changed in a lifetime. In a few years we are whirled out of all our associations. Names perhaps remain unaltered, but the inner life is different; modes of living, states of education, religious sentiments, great national events, foreign wars, or deep internal struggles—all leave such ineffaceable marks on the history of certain periods, that their influence can be traced through all the particulars of the time. The art of printing can be followed, on its first introduction, into the recesses of private life, as well as in the intercourse of nations. The Reformation of religion so entirely altered the relations which the states of the world bore to each other, that it may be said to have put a limit between old history and new, so that human character itself received a new development; and actions, both public and private, were regulated by principles hitherto unknown.

In one respect all the past centuries are alike,—that they have done their part towards the formation of this. We bear the impress, at this hour, of the great thoughts and high aspirations, the struggles, and even the crimes, of our ancestral ages; and yet they have no greater resemblance to the present, except in the unchangeable characteristics of human nature itself, than the remotest forefathers in a long line of ancestry, whose likenesses hang in the galleries of our hereditary nobles, bear to the existing owner of title and estate. The ancestor who fought in the wars of the Roses has a very different expression and dress from the other ancestor who cheated and lied (politically, of course) in the days of the early Georges. Yet from both the present proprietor is descended. He retains the somewhat rusty armour on an ostentatious nail in the hall, and the somewhat insincere memoirs in a secret drawer in the library, and we cannot deny that he is the joint production of the courage of the warrior and the duplicity of the statesman; anxious to defend what he believes to be the right, like the supporter of York or Lancaster—but trammelled by the ties of party, like the patriot of Sir Robert Walpole.

If we could affix to each century as characteristic a presentment as those portraits do of the steel-clad hero of Towton, or the be-wigged, be-buckled courtier of George the Second, our object would be gained. We should see a whole history in a glance at a century's face. If it were peculiarly marked by nature or accident, so much the more easy would it be to recognise the likeness. If the century was a warlike, quarrelsome century, and had scars across its brow; if it was a learned, plodding century, and wore spectacles on nose; if it was a frivolous, gay century, and simpered forever behind bouquets of flowers, or tripped on fantastic toe with a jewelled rapier at its side, there would be no mistaking the resemblance; there would also be no chance of confusing the actions: the legal century would not fight, the dancing century would not depose its king.

Taking our stand at the beginning of our era, there are only eighteen centuries with which we have to do, and how easily any of us get acquainted with the features and expression of eighteen of our friends! Not that we know every particular of their birth and education, or can enter into the minute parts of their character and feelings; but we soon know enough of them to distinguish them from each other. We soon can say of which of the eighteen such or such an action or opinion is characteristic. We shall not mistake the bold deed or eloquent statement of one as proceeding from another.

"Boastful and rough, your first son is a squire.
The next a tradesman, meek, and much a liar:
Tom struts a soldier, open, bold, and brave:
Will sneaks a scrivener, an exceeding knave.
Is he a churchman? then he's fond of power:
A Quaker? sly: a Presbyterian? sour:
A smart free-thinker? all things in an hour."

Now, though it is impossible to put the characteristics of a whole century into such terse and powerful language as this, it cannot be doubted that each century, or considerable period, has its prevailing Thought,—a thought which it works out in almost all the ramifications of its course; which it receives from its predecessor in a totally different shape, and passes on to its successor in a still more altered form. Else why do we find the faith of one generation the ridicule and laughing-stock of the next? How did knighthood rise into the heroic regions of chivalry, and then sink in a succeeding period into the domain of burlesque? How did aristocracy in one age concentrate into kingship in another? And in a third, how did the golden ring of sovereignty lose its controlling power, and republics take their rise? How did the reverence of Europe settle at one time on the sword of Edward the Third, and at another on the periwig of Louis the Fourteenth? These and similar inquiries will lead us to the real principles and motive forces of a particular age, as they distinguished it from other ages. We shall label the centuries, as it were, with their characteristic marks, and know where to look for thoughts and incidents of a particular class and type.

Let us look at the first century.

Throughout the civilized world there is nothing but Rome. Under whatever form of government—under consuls, or triumvirs, or dictators—that wonderful city was mistress of the globe. Her internal dissensions had not weakened her power. While her streets were

running with the blood of her citizens, her eagles were flying triumphant in Farther Asia and on the Rhine. Her old constitution had finally died off almost without a blow, and unconsciously the people, still talking of Cato and Brutus, became accustomed to the yoke. For seven-and-twenty years they had seen all the power of the state concentrated in one man; but the names of the offices of which their ancestors had been so proud were retained; and when Octavius, the nephew of the conqueror Julius Cæsar, placed himself above the law, it was only by uniting in his own person all the authority which the law had created. He was consul, tribune, prætor, pontifex, imperator,—whatever denomination conferred dignity and power; and by the legal exercise of all these trusts he had no rival and no check. He was finally presented by the senate with the lofty title of Augustus, which henceforth had a mysterious significance as the seal of imperial greatness, and his commands were obeyed without a murmur from the Tigris to the Tyne. But whilst in the enjoyment of this pre-eminence, the Roman emperor was unconscious that in a village of Judea, in the lowest rank of life, among the most contemned tribe of his dominions, his Master was
A.D. 1. born. By this event the whole current of the world's history was changed. The great became small and the small great. Rome itself ceased to be the capital of the world, for men's eyes and hearts, when the wonderful story came to be known, were turned to Jerusalem. From her, commissioned emissaries were to proceed with greater powers than those of Roman prætors or governors. From her gates went forth Peter and John to preach the gospel. Down her steep streets rode Paul and his companions, breathing anger against the Church, and ere they reached Damascus, behold, the eyes of the persecutor are blinded with lightning, and

his understanding illuminated with the same flash; and henceforth he proceeds, in lowliness and humility, to convey to others the glad tidings that had been revealed to himself. Away in all directions, but all radiating from Jerusalem, travelled the messengers of the amazing dispensation. Everywhere—in all centuries—in all regions, we shall encounter the results of their ministry; and as we watch the swelling of the mighty tide, first of Christian faith and then of priestly ambition, which overspread the fairest portions of the globe, we shall wonder more and more at the apparent powerlessness of its source, and at the vast effects for good and evil which it has produced upon mankind.

What were they doing at Rome during the thirty-three years of our Saviour's sojourn upon earth? For the first fourteen of them Augustus was gathering round him the wits, and poets, and sages, who have made his reign immortal. After that date his successor, Tiberius, built up by stealthy and slow degrees the most dreadful tyranny the world had ever seen,—a tyranny the results of which lasted long after the founders of it had expired. For from this period mankind had nothing to hope but from the bounty of the emperor. It is humiliating to reflect that the history of the world for so long a period consists of the deeds and dispositions of the successive rulers of Rome. All men, wherever their country, or whatever their position, were dependent, in greater or less degree, for their happiness or misery on the good or bad temper of an individual man. If he was cruel, as so many of them were, he filled the patricians of Rome with fear, and terrified the distant inhabitants of Thrace or Gaul. His benevolence, on the other hand, was felt at the extremities of the earth. No wonder that every one was on the watch for the first glimpse of a new emperor's

A.D. 14.

character and disposition. What rejoicings in Italy and Greece and Africa, and all through Europe, when a trait of goodness was reported! and what a sinking of the heart when the old story was renewed, and a monster of cruelty succeeded to a monster of deceit! For the fearfullest thing in all the descriptions of Tiberius is the duplicity of his behaviour. He withdrew to an island in the sunniest part of the Mediterranean, and covered it with gorgeous buildings, and supplied it with all the implements of luxury and enjoyment. From this magnificent retirement he uttered a whisper, or made a motion with his hand, which displaced an Eastern monarch from his throne, or doomed a senator to death. He was never seen. He lived in the dreadful privacy of some fabled deity, and was only felt at the farthest ends of his empire by the unhappiness he occasioned; by his murders, and imprisonments, and every species of suffering, men's hearts and minds were bowed down beneath this invisible and irresistible oppressor. Self-respect was at an end, and liberty was not even wished for. The emperor had swallowed up the empire, and there was no authority or influence beside. This is the main feature of the first or Imperial Century, that, wherever we look, we see but one,—one gorged and bloated brutalized man, sitting on the throne of earthly power, and all the rest of mankind at his feet. Humanity at its flower had culminated into a Tiberius; and when at last he was slain, and the world began to breathe, the sorrow was speedily deeper than before, for it was found that the Imperial tree had blossomed again, and that its fruit was a Caligula.

A.D. 37.

This was a person with much the same taste for blood as his predecessor, but he was more open in the gratification of this propensity. He did not wait for trial and sentence,—those dim mockeries of justice in which

Tiberius sometimes indulged. He had a peculiar way of nodding with his head or pointing with his finger, and the executioner knew the sign. The man he nodded to died. For the more distinguished of the citizens he kept a box,—not of snuff, like some monarchs of the present day, but of some strong and instantaneous poison. Whoever refused a pinch died as a traitor, and whoever took one died of the fatal drug. Even the degenerate Romans could not endure this long, and
A.D. 41. Chæreas, an officer of his guard, put him to death, after a sanguinary reign of four years.

Still the hideous catalogue goes on. Claudius, a nephew of Tiberius, is forced upon the unwilling senate by the spoilt soldiers of the capital, the Prætorian Guards. Colder, duller, more brutal than the rest, Claudius perhaps increased the misery of his country by the apathy and stupidity of his mind. The other tyrants had some limit to their wickedness, for they kept all the powers of the State in their own hands, but this man enlisted a countless host of favourites and courtiers in his crusade against the happiness of mankind. Badly eminent among these was his wife, the infamous Messalina, whose name has become a symbol of all that is detestable in the female sex. Some people, indeed, in reading the history of this period, shut the book with a shudder, and will not believe it true. They prefer to think that authors of all lands and positions have agreed to paint a fancy picture of depravity and horror, than that such things were. But the facts are too well proved to be doubted. We see a dull, unimpassioned, moody despot; fond of blood, but too indolent to shed it himself, unless at the dictation of his fiendish partner and her friends; so brutalized that nothing amazed or disturbed him; so unobservant that, relying on his blindness, she went through the ostentatious ceremony of a public marriage with one of her paramours during the lifetime, almost under the eyes, of her husband; and yet to this frightful combination of ferocity and stupidity England owes its subjection to the Roman power, and all the blessings which Roman civilization—bringing as it did the lessons of Christianity in its train—was calculated to bestow. In the forty-fourth year of this century, and the third year of the reign of Claudius, Aulus Plautius landed in Britain at the head of a powerful army; and the tide of Victory and Settlement never subsided till the whole country, as far north as the Solway, submitted to the Eagles. The contrast between the central power at Rome, and the officials employed at a distance, continued for a long time the most remarkable circumstance in the history of the empire. Tiberius, Caligula, Claudius, vied with each other in exciting the terror and destroying the happiness of the world; but in the remote extremities of their command, their generals displayed the courage and virtue of an earlier age. They improved as well as conquered. They made roads, and built bridges, and cut down woods. They established military stations, which soon became centres of education and law. They deepened the Thames, and commenced those enormous embankments of the river, to which, in fact, London owes its existence, without being aware of the labour they bestowed upon the work. If by some misfortune a great fissure took place—as has occurred on a small scale once before—in these artificial dikes, it would task the greatest skill of modern engineers to repair the damage. They superseded the blood-stained ceremonies of the Druids with the more refined worship of the heathen deities, making Claudius himself a tutelary god, with priest and temple, in the town of Colchester; and this, though in our eyes the deification of one of the worst of men, was, perhaps, in the estimation of our predecessors, only the visible embodiment of settled government and beneficent power. But murder and treachery, and unspeakable iniquity, went their way as usual in the city of the Cæsars. Messalina was put to death, and another disgrace to womanhood, in the person of Agrippina, took her place beside the phlegmatic tyrant. Thirteen years had passed, when the boundary of human patience was attained, and Rome was startled one morning with the joyful news that her master was no more. The combined cares of his loving spouse and a favourite physician had produced this happy result,—the one presenting him with a dish of deadly mushrooms, and the other painting his throat for a hoarseness with a poisoned feather.

A.D. 54.

Is there no hope for Rome or for mankind? Is there to be a perpetual succession of monster after monster, with no cessation in the dreadful line? It would be pleasant to conceal for a minute or two the name of the next emperor, that we might point to the glorious prospect now opening on the world. But the name has become so descriptive that deception is impossible. When the word Nero is said, little more is required. But it was not so at first; a brilliant sunrise never had so terrible a course, or so dark a setting. We still see in the earlier statues which remain of him the fine outline of his face, and can fancy what its expression must have been before the qualities of his heart had stamped their indelible impression on his features. For the first five years of his reign the world seemed lost as much in surprise as in admiration. Some of his actions were generous; none of them were cruel or revengeful. He was young, and seemed anxious to fulfil the duties of his position. But power and flattery had their usual effect. All that was good in him was turned into evil. He tortured the noblest of the citizens; and degraded the throne to such a degree by the expositions he made of himself, sometimes as a musician on the stage, sometimes as a charioteer in the arena, that if there had been any Romans left they would have despised the tyrant more than they feared him. But there were no Romans left. The senators, the knights, the populace, vied with each other in submission to his power and encouragement of his vices. The rage of the monster, once excited, knew no bounds. He burned the city in the mere wantonness of crime, and fixed the blame on the unoffending Christians. These, regardless of age or condition or sex, he destroyed by every means in his power. He threw young maidens into the amphitheatre, where the hungry tigers leapt out upon them; he exposed the aged professors of the gospel to fight in single combat with the trained murderers of the circus, called the Gladiators; and once, in ferocious mockery of human suffering, he enclosed whole Christian families in a coating of pitch and other inflammable materials, and, setting fire to the covering, pursued his sport all night by the light of these living flambeaux. Some of his actions it is impossible to name. It will be sufficient to say that at the end of thirteen years the purple he disgraced was again reddened with blood. Terrified at the opposition that at last rose against him—deserted, of course, by the confederates of his wickedness —shrinking with unmanly cowardice from a defence which might have put off the evil day, he fled and hid himself from his pursuers. Agonized with fear, howling with repentant horror, he was indebted to one of his attendants for the blow which his own cowardly hand could not administer, and he died the basest, lowest, and most pitiless of all the emperors. And all those hopes he had disappointed, and all those iniquities he had perpetrated, at the age of thirty-two. He was the last of the line of Cæsar; and if that conqueror had foreseen that in so few years after his death the Senate of Rome would have been so debased, and the people of Rome so brutalized, he would have pardoned to Brutus the precautionary blow which was intended to prevent so great a calamity.

A.D. 68. Galba was elected to fill his place, and was murdered in a few months.

The degraded prætorians then elevated one of the companions of Nero's guilty excesses to the throne in the person of Otho, but resistance was made to their
A.D. 69. selection. The forces in Germany nominated Vitellius to the supreme authority; and Otho, either a voluptuary tired of life, or a craven incapable of exertion, committed suicide to save the miseries of civil war. But this calamity was averted by a nobler hand. Vitellius had only time to show that, in addition to the usual vices of the throne, he was addicted to the animal enjoyments of eating and drinking to an almost incredible degree, when he heard a voice from the walls of Jerusalem which hurled him from the seat he had so lately taken; for the legions engaged in that most memorable of sieges had decided on giving the empire of the world to the man who deserved it best, and had proclaimed their general, Flavius Vespasian, Imperator and Master of Rome.

Now we will pause, for we have come to the year
A.D. 70. seventy of this century, and a fit breathing-time to look round us and see what condition mankind has fallen into within a hundred years of the end of the Republic. We leave out of view the great empires of the farther East, where battles were won, and dynasties established on the plains of Hindostan, and within the Chinese Wall. The extent of our knowledge of Oriental

affairs is limited to the circumference of the Roman power. Following that vast circle, we see it on all sides surrounded by tribes and nations who derive their sole illumination from its light, for unless the Roman conquests had extended to the confines of those barbaric states, we should have known nothing of their existence. Beyond that ring of fire it is almost matter of conjecture what must have been going on. Yet we learn from the traditions of many peoples, and can guess with some accuracy from the occurrences of a later period, what was the condition of those "outsiders," and what were their feelings and intentions with regard to the civilized portions of the world. Bend your eyes in any direction you please, and what names, what thoughts, suggest themselves to our minds! We see swarms of wild adventurers with wives and cattle traversing with no definite object the uncultivated districts beyond the Danube; occasionally pitching their tents, or even forming more permanent establishments, around the roots of Caucasus and north of the Caspian Sea, where grass was more plentiful, and hills or marshes formed an easily defended barrier against enemies as uncivilized as themselves. Coming from no certain region—that is, forgetting in a few years of wandering the precise point from which they set out, pushed forward by the advancing waves of great national migrations in their rear—moving onward across the upper fields of Europe, but keeping themselves still cautiously from actual contact with the Roman limits, from those hordes of homeless, lawless savages are derived the most polished and greatest nations of the present day. Forming into newer combinations, and taking different names, their identity is scarcely to be recognised when, three or four centuries after this, they come into the daylight of history; but nobody can doubt that, during these preliminary ages, they were gathering their power together, hereafter, under the impulse of fresh additions, to be hurled like a dammed-up river upon the prostrate realm, carrying ruin and destruction in their course, but no less certainly than the overflowing Nile leaving the germs of future fertility, and enriching with newer vegetation the fields they had so ruthlessly submerged. And year by year the mighty mass goes on accumulating. The northern plains become peopled no one knows how. The vast forests eastward of the Rhine receive new accessions of warriors, who rapidly assimilate with the old. United in one common object of retaining the wild freedom of their tribe, and the possession of the lands they have seized, they have opposed the advance of the Roman legions into the uncultivated districts they call their own; they have even succeeded in destroying the military forces which guarded the Rhine, and have with difficulty been restrained from crossing the great river by a strong line of forts and castles, of which the remains astonish the traveller of the present day, as, with Murray's Guide-Book in his hand, he gazes upon their ruins between Bingen and Aix-la-Chapelle.

Repelled by these barriers, they cluster thicker than ever in the woods and valleys, to which the Romans have no means of penetrating. Southern Gaul submits, and becomes a civilized outpost of the central power; but far up in the wild regions of the north, and even to the eastward of the Gulfs of Bothnia and Finland, the assemblage goes on. Scandinavia itself becomes overcrowded by the perpetual arrival of thousands of these armed and expatriated families, and sends her teeming populations to the east and south. But all these incidents, I must remind you, are occurring in darkness. We only know that the desert is becoming peopled with crowded millions, and that among them all there floats a confused notion of the greatness of the Roman power, the wealth of the cities and plains of Italy; and that, clustering in thicker swarms on the confines of civil government, the watchful eyes of unnumbered savage warriors are fixed on the territories lying rich and beautiful within the protection of the Roman name. So the whole Roman boundary gets gradually surrounded by barbaric hosts. Their trampings may be heard as they marshal their myriads and skirt the upper boundaries of Thrace; but as yet no actual conflict has occurred. A commotion may become observable among some of the farthest distant of the half intimidated of the German tribes; or an enterprising Roman settler beyond the frontier, or travelling merchant, who has penetrated to the neighbourhood of the Baltic, may bring back amazing reports of the fresh accumulations of unknown hordes of strange and threatening aspect; but the luxurious public in Rome receive them merely as interesting anecdotes to amuse their leisure or gratify their curiosity: they have no apprehension of what may be the result of those multitudinous arrivals. They do not foresee the gradual drawing closer to their outward defences—the struggle to get within their guarded lines—the fight that is surely coming between a sated, dull, degraded civilization on the one side, and a hungry, bold, ambitious savagery on the other. They trust every thing to the dignity of the Eternal City, and the watchfulness of the Emperor: for to this, his one idea of irresistible power equally for good or evil, the heart of the Roman was sure to turn. And for the eleven years of the reigns of Vespasian and Titus, the Roman did not appeal for protection against a foreign enemy in vain. Rome itself was compensated by shows and buildings—with a triumph and an arch—for the degradation in which it was held. But prætor and proconsul still pursued their course of oppressing

the lands committed to their defence; and the subject, stripped of his goods, and hopeless of getting his wrongs redressed, had only the satisfaction of feeling that the sword he trembled at was in the hand of a man and not of an incarnate demon. A poor consolation this when the blow was equally fatal. Vespasian, in fact, was fonder of money than of blood, and the empire rejoiced in having exchanged the agony of being murdered
A.D. 79. for the luxury of being fleeced. With Titus, whom the fond gratitude of his subjects named the Delight of the human race, a new age of happiness was about to open on the world; but all the old horrors of the Cæsars were revived and magnified when he was succeeded, after a reign of two years, by his brother, the
A.D. 81. savage and cowardly Domitian. With the exception of the brief period between the years 70 and 81, the whole century was spent in suffering and inflicting pain. The worst excesses of Nero and Caligula were now imitated and surpassed. The bonds of society became rapidly loosened. As in a shipwreck, the law of self-preservation was the only rule. No man could rely upon his neighbour, or his friend, or his nearest of kin. There were spies in every house, and an executioner at every door. An unconsidered word maliciously reported, or an accusation entirely false, brought death to the rich and great. To the unhappy class of men who in other times are called the favourites of fortune, because they are born to the possession of great ancestral names and hereditary estates, there was no escape from the jealous and avaricious hatred of the Emperor. If a patrician of this description lived in the splendour befitting his rank—he was currying favour with the mob! If he lived retired—he was trying to gain reputation by a pretence of giving up the world! If he had great talents—he was dangerous to the state! If he was dull and stupid—oh!

don't believe it—he was only an imitative Brutus, concealing his deep designs under the semblance of fatuity! If a man of distinguished birth was rich, it was not a fitting condition for a subject—if he was poor, he was likely to be seduced into the wildest enterprises. So the prisons were filled by calumny and suspicion, and emptied by the executioner. A dreadful century this—the worst that ever entered into tale or history; for the memory of former glories and comparative freedom was still recent. A man who was sixty years old, in the midst of the terrors of Tiberius, had associated in his youth with the survivors of the Civil War, with men who had embraced Brutus and Cassius; he had seen the mild administration of Augustus, and perhaps had supped with Virgil and Horace in the house of Mæcenas. And now he was tortured till he named a slave or freedman of the Emperor his heir, and then executed to expedite the succession. There was a hideous jocularity in some of these imperial proceedings, which, however, was no laughing-matter at the time. When a senator was very wealthy, it was no unusual thing for Tiberius and his successors to create themselves the rich man's nearest relations by a decree of the Senate. The person so honoured by this graft upon his family tree seldom survived the operation many days. The emperor took possession of the property as heir-at-law and next of kin; and mourned for his uncle or brother—as the case might be—with the most edifying decorum.

But besides giving the general likeness of a period, it is necessary to individualize it still further by introducing, in the background of the picture, some incident by which it is peculiarly known, as we find Nelson generally represented with Trafalgar going on at the horizon, and Wellington sitting thoughtful on horseback in the foreground of the fire of Waterloo. Now, there cannot be a more distinguishing mark than a certain great military achievement which happened in the year 70 of this century, and is brought home to us, not only as a great historical event in itself, but as the commencement of a new era in human affairs, and the completion of a long line of threats and prophecies. This was the capture and destruction of Jerusalem. The accounts given us of this siege transcend in horror all other records of human sorrow. It was at the great annual feast of the Passover, when Jews from all parts of the world flocked to the capital of their nation to worship in the Temple, which to them was the earthly dwelling-place of Jehovah. The time was come, and they did not know it, when God was to be worshipped in spirit and in truth. More than a million strangers were resident within the walls. There was no room in house or hall for so vast a multitude; so they bivouacked in the streets, and lay thick as leaves in the courts of the holy place. Suddenly the Roman trumpets blew. The Jews became inspired with fanatical hatred of the enemy, and insane confidence that some miracle would be wrought for their deliverence. They deliberated, and chose for their leaders the wildest and most enthusiastic of the crowd. They refused the offers of mercy and reconciliation made to them by Titus. They sent back insulting messages to the Roman general, and stood expectant on the walls to see the idolatrous legions smitten by lightning or swallowed up by an earthquake. But Titus advanced his forces and hemmed in the countless multitude of men, and women, and children—few able to resist, but all requiring to be fed. Famine and pestilence came on; but still the mad fanatics of the Temple determined to persevere. They occasionally opened a gate and rushed out with the cry of "The sword of the Lord and of Gideon!" and were slaughtered by the unpitying hatred of the Roman soldiers. Their cruelty to their prisoners, when they succeeded in carrying off a few of their enemies, was great; but the patience of Titus at last gave way, and he soon bettered the instruction they gave him in pitilessness and blood. He drew a line of circumvallation closer round the city, and intercepted every supply; when deserters came over, he crucified them all round the trenches; when the worn-out people came forth, imploring to be suffered to pass through his ranks, he drove them back, that they might increase the scarcity by their lives, or the pestilence by adding to the heaps of unburied dead. Dissensions were raging all this time among the defenders themselves. They fought in the streets, in the houses, and heaped the floor and outcourts of the Temple with thousands of the slain. There was no help either from heaven or earth; eleven hundred thousand people had died of plague and the sword; and the rest were doomed to perish by more lingering torments. Nearest relations—sisters, brothers, fathers, wives—all forgot the ties of natural affection under this great necessity, and fought for a handful of meal, or the possession of some reptile's body if they were lucky enough to trace it to its hiding-place; and at last—the crown of all horrors—the daughter of Eleazer killed her own child and converted it into food. The measure of man's wrong and Heaven's vengeance was now full. The daily sacrifice ceased to be offered; voices were audible to the popular ear uttering in the Holy of Holies, "Let us go hence." The Romans rushed on—climbed over the neglected walls—forced their way into the upper Temple, and the gore flowed in streams so rapid and so deep that it seemed like a purple river! Large conduits had been made for the rapid conveyance away of the blood of bulls and goats offered in sacrifice; they all became choked now with the blood of the slaughtered people. At last the city was taken; the inhabitants were either dead or dying. Many were crushed as they lay expiring in the great tramplings of the triumphant Romans; many were recovered by food and shelter, and sold into slavery. The Temple and walls were levelled with the ground, and not one stone was left upon another. The plough passed over where palace and tower had been, and the Jewish dispensation was brought to a close.

History in ancient days was as exclusive as the court newsman in ours, and never published the movements of anybody below a senator or a consul. All the Browns and Smiths were left out of consideration; and yet to us who live in the days when those families—with the Joneses and Robinsons—form the great majority both in number and influence, it would be very interesting to have any certain intelligence of their predecessors during the first furies of the Empire. We have but faint descriptions even of the aristocracy, but what we hear of them shows, more clearly than any thing else, the frightful effect on morals and manliness of so uncontrolled a power as was vested in the Cæsars, and teaches us that the worst of despotisms is that which is established by the unholy union of the dregs of the population and the ruling power, against the peace and happiness and security of the middle class. You see how this combination of tyrant and mob succeeded in crushing all the layers of society which lay between them, till there were left only two agencies in all the world—the Emperor on his throne, and the millions fed by his bounty. The hereditary nobility—the safest bulwark of a people and least dangerous support of a throne—were extirpated before the end of the century, and impartiality makes us confess that they fell by their own fault. As if the restraints of shame had been thrown off with the last hope of liberty, the whole population broke forth into the most incredible licentiousness. If the luxury of Lucullus had offended the common sense of propriety in the later days of the republic, there were numbers now who looked back upon his feasts as paltry entertainments, and on the wealth of Crœsus as poverty. The last of the Pompeys, in the time of Caligula, had estates so vast, that navigable rivers larger than the Thames performed the whole of their course from their fountain-head to the sea without leaving his domain. There were spendthrifts in the time of Tiberius who lavished thousands of pounds upon a supper. The pillage of the world had fallen into the hands of a few favoured families, and their example had introduced a prodigality and ostentation unheard of before. No one who regarded appearances travelled anywhere without a troop of Numidian horsemen, and outriders to clear the way. He was followed by a train of mules and sumpter-horses loaded with his vases of crystal—his richly-carved cups and dishes of silver and gold. But this profusion had its natural result in debt and degradation. The patricians who had been rivals of the imperial splendour became dependants on the imperial gifts; and the grandson of the conqueror of a kingdom, or the proconsul of the half of Asia, sold his ancestral palace, lived for a while on the contemptuous bounty of his master, and sank in the next generation into the nameless mass. Others, more skilful, preserved or improved their fortunes while they rioted in expense. By threats or promises, they prevailed on the less powerful to constitute them their heirs; they traded on the strength, or talents, or the beauty of their slaves, and lent money at such usurious interest that the borrower tried in vain to escape the shackles of the law, and ended by becoming the bondsman of the kind-hearted gentleman who had induced him to accept the loan.

If these were the habits of the rich, how were the poor treated? The free and penniless citizens of the capital were degraded and gratified at the same time. The wealthy vied with each other in buying the favour of the mob by shows and other entertainments, by gifts of money and donations of food. But when these arts failed, and popularity could no longer be obtained by merely defraying the expense of a combat of gladiators, the descendants of the old patricians—of the men who had bought the land on which the Gauls were encamped outside the gates of Rome—went down into the arena themselves and fought for the public entertainment. Laws indeed were passed even in the reign of Tiberius, and renewed at intervals after that time, against this shameful degradation, and the stage was interdicted to all who were not previously declared infamous by sentence of a court. But all was in vain. Ladies of the highest rank, and the loftiest-born of the nobility, actually petitioned for a decree of defamation, that they might give themselves up undisturbed to their favourite amusement. This perhaps added a zest to their enjoyment, and rapturous applauses must have hailed the entrance of the beautiful grandchild of Anthony or Agrippa, in the character and drapery of a warlike amazon—the louder the applause and greater the admiration. Yet in order to gratify them with such a sight, she had descended to the level of the convict, and received the brand of qualifying disgrace from a legal tribunal. But the faint barrier of this useless prohibition was thrown down by the policy and example of Domitian. The emperor himself appeared in the arena, and all restraint was at an end. Rather, there was a fury of emulation to copy so great a model, and

"Rome's proud dames, whose garments swept the ground," forgot more than ever their rank and sex, and were proud, like their lovers and brothers, not merely to mount the stage in the lascivious costume of nymph or dryad, but to descend into the blood-stained lists of the Coliseum and murder each other with sword and spear. There is something strangely horrible in this transaction, when we read that it occurred for the first time in celebration of the games of Flora—the goddess of flowers and gardens, who, in old times, was worshipped under the blossomed apple-trees in the little orchards surrounding each cottage within the walls, and was propitiated with children's games and chaplets hung upon the boughs. But now the loveliest of the noble daughters of the city lay dead upon the trampled sand. What was the effect upon the populace of these extraordinary shows?

Always stern and cruel, the Roman was now never satisfied unless with the spectacle of death. Sometimes in the midst of a play or pantomime the fierce lust of blood would seize him, and he would cry out for a combat of gladiators or nobles, who instantly obeyed; and after the fight was over, and the corpses removed, the play would go on as if nothing had occurred. The banners of the empire still continued to bear the initial letters of the great words—the Senate and people of Rome. We have now, in this rapid survey, seen what both those great names have come to—the Senate crawling at the feet of the emperor, and the people living on charity and shows. The slaves fared worst of all, for they were despised by rich and poor. The sated voluptuary whose property they were sometimes found an excitement to his jaded spirits by having them tortured in his sight. They were allowed to die of starvation when they grew old, unless they were turned to use, as was done by one of their possessors, Vidius Pollio, who cast the fattest of his domestics into his fish-pond to feed his lampreys. The only other classes were the actors and musicians, the dwarfs and the philosophers. They contributed by their wit, or their uncouth shape, or their oracular sentences, to the amusement of their employers, and were safe. They were licensed characters, and could say what they chose, protected by the long-drawn countenance of the stoic, or the comic grimaces of the buffoon. So early as the time of Nero, the people he tyrannized and flattered were not less ruthless than himself. In his cruelty—in his vanity—in his frivolity, and his entire devotion to the gratification of his passions—he was a true representative of the men over whom he ruled. Emperor and subject had even then become fitted for each other, and flowers, we are credibly told by the historians, were hung for many years upon his tomb.

Humanity itself seemed to be sunk beyond the possibility of restoration; but we see now how necessary it was that our nature should reach its lowest point of depression to give full force to the great reaction which Christianity introduced. Men were slavishly bending at the footstool of a despot, trembling for life, bowed down by fear and misery, when suddenly it was reported that a great teacher had appeared for a while upon earth, and declared that all men were equal in the sight of God, for that God was the Father of all. The slave heard this in the intervals of his torture—the captive in his dungeon—the widow and the orphan. To the poor the gospel, or good news, was preached. It was this which made the trembling courtiers of the worst of the emperors slip out noiselessly from the palace, and hear from Paul of Tarsus or his disciples the new prospect that was opening on mankind. It spread quickly among those oppressed and hopeless multitudes. The subjection of the Roman empire—its misery and degradation—were only a means to an end. The harsher the laws of the tyrant, the more gracious seemed the words of Christ. The two masters were plainly set before them, which to choose. And who could hesitate? One said, "Tremble! suffer! die!" The other said, "Come unto me, all ye that are weary and heavy laden, and I will give you rest!"

SECOND CENTURY.

Emperors.

A.D.	
	TRAJAN—(*continued.*) Third Persecution of the Christians.
117.	ADRIAN. Fourth Persecution of the Christians.
138.	ANTONINUS PIUS.
161.	MARCUS AURELIUS.
180.	COMMODUS.
193.	PERTINAX—DIDIUS, and NIGER—Defeated by
193.	SEPTIMIUS SEVERUS.

Authors.

PLINY THE YOUNGER, PLUTARCH, SUETONIUS, JUVENAL, ARRIAN, ÆLIAN, PTOLEMY, (Geographer,) APPIAN, EPICTETUS, PAUSANIAS, GALEN, (Physician,) ATHENÆUS, TERTULLIAN, JUSTIN MARTYR, TATIAN, IRENÆUS, ATHENAGORAS, THEOPHILUS OF ANTIOCH, CLEMENT OF ALEXANDRIA, MARCION, (Heretic.)

THE SECOND CENTURY.

THE GOOD EMPERORS.

In looking at the second century, we see a total difference in the expression, though the main features continue unchanged. There is still the central power at Rome, the same dependence everywhere else; but the central power is beneficent and wise. As if tired of the hereditary rule of succession which had ended in such a monster as Domitian, the world took refuge in a new system of appointing its chiefs, and perhaps thought it a recommendation of each successive emperor that he had no relationship to the last. We shall accordingly find that, after this period, the hereditary principle is excluded. It was remarked that, of the twelve first Cæsars, only two had died a natural death—for even in the case of Augustus the arts of the poisoner were suspected—and those two were Vespasian and Titus, men who had no claim to such an elevation in right of lofty birth. Birth, indeed, had ceased to be a recommendation. All the great names of the Republic had been carefully rooted out. Few people were inclined to boast of their ancestry when the proof of their pedigree acted as a sentence of death; for there was no surer passport to destruction in the times of the early emperors than a connection with the Julian line, or descent from a historic family. No one, therefore, took the trouble to inquire into the
A.D. 96. genealogy of Nerva, the old and generous man who succeeded the monster Domitian. His nomination to the empire elevated him at once out of the

sphere of these inquiries, for already the same superstitious reverence surrounded the name of Augustus which spreads its inviolable sanctity on the throne of Eastern monarchs. Whoever sits upon that, by whatever title, or however acquired, is the legitimate and unquestioned king. No rival, therefore, started up to contest the position either of Nerva himself, or of the stranger he nominated to succeed him. Men bent in humble acquiescence when they knew, in the third year
A.D. 102. of this century, that their master was named Trajan,—that he was a Spaniard by birth, and the best general of Rome. For eighty years after that date the empire had rest. Life and property were comparatively secure, and society flowed on peaceably in deep and well-ascertained channels. A man might have been born at the end of the reign of Domitian, and die in extreme old age under the sway of the last of the Antonines, and never have known of insecurity or oppression —

> "Malice domestic, foreign levy, nothing
> Could touch him farther!"

No wonder those agreeable years were considered by the fond gratitude of the time, and the unavailing regrets of succeeding generations, the golden age of man. Nerva, Trajan, Adrian, Antoninus Pius, Marcus Aurelius Antoninus—these are still great names, and are everywhere recognised as the most wonderful succession of sovereigns the world has ever seen. They are still called the "Good Emperors," the "Wise Rulers."

It is easy, indeed, to be good in comparison with Nero, and wise in comparison with Claudius; but the effect of the example of those infamous tyrants made it doubly difficult to be either good or wise. The world had become so accustomed to oppression, that it seemed at first surprised at the change that had taken place.

The emperors had to create a knowledge of justice before their just acts could be appreciated. The same opposition other men have experienced in introducing bad and cruel measures was roused by their introduction of wise and salutary laws. What! no more summary executions, nor forfeitures of fortunes, nor banishments to the Danube? All men equal before the dread tribunal of the imperial judge? The world was surely coming to an end, if the emperor did not now and then poison a senator, or stab his brother, or throw half a dozen courtiers to the beasts! It is likely enough that some of the younger Romans at first lamented those days of unlimited license and perpetual excitement; but in the course of time those wilder spirits must have died out, and the world gladly acquiesced in an existence of dull security and uninteresting peace. By the end of the reign of Trajan the records of the miseries of the last century must have been studied as curiosities —as historical students now look back on the extravagances and horrors of the French Revolution. Fortunately, men could not look forward to the times, more pitiable still, when their descendants should fall into greater sorrows than had been inflicted on mankind by the worst of the Cæsars, and they enjoyed their present immunity from suffering without any misgivings about the future. But a government which does every thing for a people renders it unable to do any thing for itself. The subject stood quietly by while the emperor filled all the offices of the State—guarded him, fed him, clothed him, treated him like a child, and reduced him at last to childlike dependence. An unjust proconsul, instead of being supported and encouraged in his exactions, was dismissed from his employment and forced to refund his ill-got gains,—the population, relieved from their oppressor, saw in his punishment the hand of an avenging Providence. The wakeful eye of the governor in Rome saw the hostile preparations of a tribe of barbarians beyond the Danube; and the legions, crossing the river, dispersed and subdued them before they had time to devastate the Roman fields. The peaceful colonist saw, in the suddenness of his deliverance, the foresight and benevolence of a divinity. No words were powerful enough to convey the sentiments of admiration awakened, by such vigour and goodness, in the breast of a luxurious and effeminate people; and accordingly, if we look a little closely into the personal attributes of the five good emperors, we shall see that some part of their glory is due to the exaggerations of love and gratitude.

Nerva reigned but sixteen months, and had no time to do more than display his kindness of disposition, and to name his successor. This was Trajan, a man who was not even a Roman by birth, but who was thought by his patron to have retained, in the distant province of Spain where he was born, the virtues which had disappeared in the centre and capital of the empire. The deficiency of Nerva's character had been its softness and want of force. The stern vigilance of Trajan made ample amends. He was the best-known soldier of his time, and revived once more the terror of the Roman arms. He conquered wherever he appeared; but his warlike impetuosity led him too far. He trod in the footsteps of Alexander the Great, and advanced farther eastward than any of the Roman armies had previously done. But his victories were fruitless: he attached no new country permanently to the empire, and derives all his glory now from the excellence of his internal administration. He began his government by declaring himself as subordinate to the laws as the meanest of the people. His wife, Pompeia Plotina, was worthy of such a husband, and said, on mounting the steps of the palace, that she should descend them unaltered from what she was. The emperor visited his friends on terms of equality, and had the greatness of mind, generally deficient in absolute princes, to bestow his confidence on those who deserved it. Somebody, a member perhaps of the old police who had made such fortunes in the time of Domitian by alarming the tyrant with stories of plots and assassinations, told Trajan one day to beware of his minister, who intended to murder him on the first opportunity. "Come again, and tell me all particulars to-morrow," said the emperor. In the mean time he went unbidden and supped with the accused. He was shaved by his barber—was attended for a mock illness by his surgeon—bathed in his bath—and ate his meat and drank his wine. On the following day the informer came. "Ah!" said Trajan, interrupting him in his accusation of Surenus, "if Surenus had wished to kill me, he would have done it last night."

The emperor died when returning from a distant expedition in the East, and Pompeia declared that he
A.D. 117. had long designated Adrian as his successor. This evidence was believed, and Adrian, also a Spaniard by birth, and eminent as a military commander, began his reign. Trajan had been a general—a conqueror, and had extended for a time the boundaries of the Roman power. But Adrian believed the empire was large enough already. He withdrew the eagles from the half-subdued provinces, and contented himself with the natural limits which it was easy to defend. But within those limits his activity was unexampled. He journeyed from end to end of his immense domain, and for seventeen years never rested in one spot. News did not travel fast in those days—but the emperor did. Long before the inhabitants of Syria and Egypt heard that

he had left Rome on an expedition to Britain, he had rushed through Gaul, crossed the Channel, inquired into the proceedings of the government officers at York, given orders for a wall to keep out the Caledonians, (an attempt which has proved utterly vain at all periods of English history, down to the present day,) and suddenly made his appearance among the bewildered dwellers in Ephesus or Carthage, to call tax-gatherers to order and to inspect the discipline of his troops. The master's eye was everywhere, for nobody knew on what point it was fixed. And such a master no kingdom has been able to boast of since. His talents were universal. He read every thing and forgot nothing. He was a musician, a poet, a philosopher. He studied medicine and mineralogy, and plead causes like Cicero, and sang like a singer at the opera. Perhaps it is difficult to judge impartially of the qualities of a Roman emperor. One day he found fault on a point of grammar with a learned man of the name of Favorinus. Favorinus could have defended himself and justified his language, but continued silent. His friends said to him, "Why didn't you answer the emperor's objections?" "Do you think," said the sensible grammarian, "I am going to enter into disputes with a man who commands thirty legions?" But the greatness of Adrian's character is, that he *did* command those thirty legions. He was severe and just; and Roman discipline was never more exact. The result of this was shown on the grand scale only once during this reign, and that was in the case of the revolted Jews. We have seen the state to which their Temple at Jerusalem was reduced by Titus. Fifty years had now passed, and the passionate love of the people for their native land had congregated them once more within their renovated walls, and raised up another temple on the site of the old. They still expected the

Messiah, for the Messiah to them represented vengeance upon the Romans and triumph over the world. An impostor of the name of Barcho-chebas led three hundred thousand of them into the field. They were mad with national hatred, and inspired with fanatical hope. It took three years of desperate effort to quell this sedition; and then Adrian had his revenge. The country was laid waste. Fifty towns and a thousand villages were sacked and burned. The population, once more nearly exhausted by war and famine, furnished slaves, which were sold all over the East. Jerusalem itself felt the conqueror's hatred most. Its name was blotted out—it was called Ælia Capitolina; and, with ferocious mockery, over the gate of the new capital of Judea was affixed the statue of the unclean beast, the abomination of the Israelite. But nothing could keep the Jews from visiting the land of so many promises and so much glory. Whenever they had it in their power, they crept back from all quarters, if it were only to weep and die amid the ruins of their former power.

Trajan and Adrian had now made the world accustomed to justice in its rulers; and as far as regards their public conduct, this character is not to be denied. Yet in their private relations they were not so faultless. Trajan the great and good was a drunkard. To such a pitch did he carry this vice, that he gave orders that after a certain hour of the day none of his commands were to be obeyed. Adrian was worse: he was regardless of life; he put men to death for very small offences. An architect was asked how he liked a certain series of statues designed by the emperor and ranged in a sitting attitude round a temple which he had built. The architect was a humourist, not a courtier. "If the goddesses," he said, "take it into their heads to rise, they will never be able to get out at the door." A poor criticism, and not a good piece of wit, but not bad enough to justify his being beheaded; yet the answer cost the poor man his life. As Adrian grew older, he grew more reckless of the pain he gave. He had a brother-in-law ninety years of age, and there was a grandson of the old man aged eighteen. He had them both executed on proof or suspicion of a conspiracy. The popular feeling was revolted by the sight of the mingled blood of two sufferers so nearly related, at the opposite extremities of life. The old man, just before he died, protested his innocence, and uttered a revengeful prayer that Adrian might wish to die and find death impossible! This imprecation was fulfilled. The emperor was tortured with disease, and longed for deliverance in vain. He called round him his physicians, and priests, and sorcerers, but they could give him no relief. He begged his slaves to kill him, and stabbed himself with a dagger; but in spite of all he could not die. Lingering on, and with no cessation of his pain, he must have had sad thoughts of the past, and no pleasant anticipations of the future, if, as we learn from the verses attributed to him, he believed in a future state. His lines still remain, but are indebted to Pope, who paraphrased them, for their Christian spirit and lofty aspiration:—

"Vital spark of heavenly flame!
Quit, oh, quit this mortal frame!
Trembling, hoping, lingering, flying,
Oh, the pain, the bliss of dying!
Cease, fond nature, cease thy strife,
And let me languish into life!

"Hark! they whisper! angels say,
Sister spirit, come away!
What is this absorbs me quite,
Steals my senses, shuts my sight,
Drowns my spirits, draws my breath?
Tell me, my soul, can this be death?

"The world recedes; it disappears!
Heaven opens on my eyes! my ears
With sounds seraphic ring:
Lend, lend your wings! I mount! I fly!
O Grave! where is thy victory?
O Death! where is thy sting?"

His wish was at last achieved. He died aged sixty-two, having reigned twenty-one years. In travelling and building his whole time was spent. Temples, theatres, bridges—wherever he went, these evidences of his wisdom or magnificence remained. He persecuted the Christians, but found persecution a useless proceeding against a sect who gloried in martyrdom, and whose martyrdoms were only followed by new conversions. He tried what an opposite course of conduct would do, and is said to have intended to erect a temple to Jesus Christ. "Take care what you do," said one of his counsellors: "if you permit an altar to the God of the Christians, those of the other gods will be deserted."

But now came to supreme authority the good and wise Antoninus Pius, who was as blameless in
A.D. 138. his private conduct as in his public acts. His fame extended farther than the Roman arms had ever reached. Distant kings, in lands of which the names were scarcely known in the Forum, took him as arbiter of their differences. The decision of the great man in Rome gave peace on the banks of the Indus. The barbarians themselves on the outskirts of his dominions were restrained by respect for a character so pure and power so wisely used. An occasional revolt in Britain was quelled by his lieutenants—an occasional conspiracy against his authority was caused by the discontent which turbulent spirits feel when restrained by law. The conspiracies were repressed, and on one occasion two of the ringleaders were put to death. The Senate was for making further inquiry into the plot. "Let us

stop here," said the emperor. "I do not wish to find out how many people I have displeased." Some stories are told of him, which show how little he affected the state of a despotic ruler. A pedantic philosopher at Smyrna, of the name of Polemo, returned from a journey at a late hour, and found the proconsul of Rome lodged in his house. This proconsul was Antonine, who at that time had been appointed to the office by Adrian. Instead of being honoured by such a guest, the philosopher stormed and raged, and made so much noise, that in the middle of the night the sleepless proconsul left the house and found quarters elsewhere. When years passed on, and Antonine was on the throne, Polemo had the audacity to present himself as an old acquaintance. "Ha! I remember him," said the emperor: "let him have a room in the palace, but don't let him leave it night or day." The imprisonment was not long, for we find the same Polemo hero of another anecdote during this visit to Rome. He hissed a performer in the theatre, and stamped and screeched, and made such a disturbance that the unfortunate actor had to leave the stage. He complained of Polemo to the emperor. "Polemo!" exclaimed Antonine; "he forced you off the stage in the middle of the day, but he drove me from his house in the middle of the night, and yet I never appealed." It would be pleasant if we could learn that Polemo did not get off so easily. But the twenty-two years of this reign of mildness and probity were brought to a close, and Marcus Aurelius succeeded in 161.

A.D. 161.

Marcus Aurelius did no dishonour to the discernment of his friend and adoptive father Antoninus Pius. Studying philosophy and practising self-command, he emulated and surpassed the virtues of the self-denying leaders of his sect, and only broke through the rule he imposed on himself of clemency and mildness, when he found philosophy in danger of being counted a vain deceit, and the active duties of human brotherhood preferred to the theoretic rhapsodies on the same subject with which his works were filled. Times began to change. Men were dissatisfied with the unsubstantial dream of Platonist and Stoic. There were symptoms of an approaching alteration in human affairs, which perplexed the thoughtful and gave promise of impunity to the bad. Perhaps a man who, clothed in the imperial purple, bestowed so much study on the intellectual niceties of the Sophists, and endeavoured to keep his mind in a fit state for abstract speculation by scourging and starving his body, was not so fitted for the approaching crisis as a rougher and less contemplative nature would have been. Britain was in commotion, there were tumults on the Rhine, and in Armenia the Parthians cut the Roman legions to pieces. And scarcely were those troubles settled and punished, when a worse calamity befell the Roman empire. Its inviolability became a boast of the past. The fearful passions for conquest and rapine of the border-barbarians were roused. Barbaric cohorts encamped on the fields of Italy, and the hosts of wild men from the forests of the North pillaged the heaped-up treasures of the garden of the world. The emperor flew to the scene of danger, but the fatal word had been said. Italy was accessible from the Alps and from the sea; and, though a bloody defeat at Aquileia flung back the invaders, disordered and dispirited, over the mountains they had descended with such hopes, the struggle was but begun. The barbarians felt their power, and the old institutions of Rome were insufficient to resist future attacks. But to the aid of the old Roman institutions a new institution came, an institution which was destined to repel the barbarians by overcoming barbarism itself, and save the dignity of Rome by giving it the protection of the Cross. But at present —that is, during the reign of the philosophic Marcus Aurelius—a persecution raged against the Christians which seemed to render hopeless all chance of their success. The mild laws of Trajan and Adrian, and the favourable decrees of Antoninus Pius, were set aside by the contemptuous enmity of this explorer of the mysterious heights of virtue, which occasionally carried him out of sight of the lower but more important duties of life. An unsocial tribe the Christians were, who rigorously shut their eyes to the beauties of abstract perfection, and preferred the plain orders of the gospel to the most ambitious periods of the emperor. But the persecution of a sect so small and so obscure as the Christian was at that time, is scarcely perceptible as a diminution of the sum of human happiness secured to the world by the gentleness and equity which regulated all his actions. Here is an example of the way in which he treated rebels against his authority. An insurrection broke out in Syria and the East, headed by a pretended descendant of the patriot Cassius, who had conspired against Julius Cæsar. The emperor hurried to meet him—some say to resign the empire into his hands, to prevent the effusion of blood; but the usurper died in an obscure commotion, and nothing was left but to take vengeance on his adherents. This is the letter the conqueror wrote to the Senate:—"I beseech you, conscript Fathers! not to punish the guilty with too much rigour. Let no Senator be put to death. Let the banished return to their country. I wish I could give back their lives to those who have died in this quarrel. Revenge is unworthy of an emperor. You will pardon, therefore, the children of Cassius, his son-in-law, and his wife. Pardon, did I say? Ah! what crime have they committed? Let them live in safety, let them retain all that Cassius possessed. Let them live in whatever place they choose, to be a monument of your clemency and mine."

In such hands as these the fortune of mankind was safe. A pity that the father's feelings got the better of his judgment in the choice of his successor. It is the one blot on his otherwise perfect disinterestedness. In dying, with such a monster as Commodus ready to leap into his seat, he must have felt how inexpressibly valuable his life would be to the Roman people. He perhaps saw the danger to which he exposed the world; for he committed his son to the care of his wisest counsellors, and begged him to continue the same course of government he had pursued. Perhaps he was tired of life, perhaps he sought refuge in his self-denying philosophy from the prospect he saw before him of a state of perpetual struggle and eventual overthrow. When the Tribune came for the last time to ask the watchword of the day, "Go to the rising sun," he said; "for me, I am just going to set."

And here the history of the Second Century should close. It is painful to go back again to the hideous scenes of anarchy and crime from which we have been delivered so long. What must the sage counsellors, the chosen companions and equals in age of the Antonines, have thought when all at once the face of affairs, which they must have believed eternal, was changed?—when the noblest and wisest in the land were again thrown heedlessly into the arena without trial?—when spies watched every meal, and the ferocious murderer on the throne seemed to gloat over the struggles of his victims? Yet, if they had reflected on the inevitable course of events, they must have seen that a government depending on the character of one man could never be relied on. Where, indeed, could any element of security be found? The very ground-work of society was overthrown. There was no independent body erect amid the general prostration at the footstool of the emperor. Local self-government had ceased except in name. All the towns which hitherto had been subordinate to Rome, but endowed at the same time with privileges which were worth defending, had been absorbed into the great whirlpool of imperial centralization, and were admitted to the rights of Roman citizenship,—now of little value, since it embraced every quarter of the empire. Jupiter and Juno, and the herd of effete gods and goddesses, if they had ever held any practical influence over the minds of men, had long sunk into contempt, except in so far as their rich establishments were defended by persons interested in their maintenance, and the processions and gaudy display of a foul and meretricious worship were pleasing to the depraved taste of the mob. But the religious principle, as a motive of action, or as a point of combination, was at an end. Augurs were still appointed, and laughed at the uselessness of their office; oracles were still uttered, and ridiculed as the offspring of ignorance and imposture; conflicting deities fought for pre-eminence, or compromised their differences by an amalgamation of their altars, and perhaps a division of their estates. It was against this state of society the early Fathers directed their warnings and denunciations. The world did certainly lie in darkness, and it was indispensable to warn the followers of Christ not to be conformed to the fashion of that fleeting time. Some, to escape the contagion of this miserable condition, when men were without hope, and without even the wretched consolation which a belief in a false god would have given them, fled to the wilds and caves. Hermits escaped equally the perils of sin and the hostility of the heathen. Believers were exhorted to flee from contamination, and some took the words in their literal meaning. But not all. Many remained, and fought the good fight in the front of the battle, as became the soldiers of the cross. In the midst of the anarchy and degradation which characterized the last years of the century, a society was surely and steadily advancing towards its full development, bound by rules in the midst of the helplessness of external law, and combined by strong faith, in a world of utter unbelief—an empire within an empire—soon to be the only specimen left either of government or mutual obligation, and finally to absorb into its fresh and still-spreading organization the withered and impotent authority which had at first seen in it its enemy and destroyer, and found it at last its refuge and support. Yet at this very time the empire had never appeared so strong. By a stroke of policy, which the event proved to be injudicious, Marcus Aurelius, in the hope of diminishing the number of his enemies, had converted many thousands of the barbarians into his subjects. They had settlements assigned them within the charmed ring. What they had not been able to obtain by the sword was now assured to them by treaty. But the unity of the Roman empire by this means was destroyed. Men were admitted within the citadel who had no reverence implanted in them from their earliest years for the majesty of the Roman name. They saw the riches contained in the stronghold, and were only anxious to open the gates to their countrymen who were still outside the walls.

But before we enter on the downward course, and since we are now arrived at the period of the greatest apparent force and extent of the Roman empire, let us see what it consisted of, and what was the real amount of its power.

Viewed in comparison with some of the monarchies

of the present day, neither its extent of territory, nor amount of population, nor number of soldiers, is very surprising. The Queen of England reigns over more subjects, and commands far mightier fleets and armies, than any of the Roman emperors. The empire of Russia is more extensive, and yet the historians of a few generations ago are lost in admiration of the power of Rome. The whole military force of the empire amounted to four hundred and fifty thousand men. The total number of vessels did not exceed a thousand. But see what were the advantages Rome possessed in the compactness of its territory and the unity of its government. The great Mediterranean Sea, peopled and cultivated on both its shores, was but a peaceful lake, on which the Roman galley had no enemy to fear, and the merchant-ship dreaded nothing but the winds and waves. There were no fortresses to be garrisoned on what are now the boundaries of jealous or hostile kingdoms. If the great circuit of the Roman State could be protected from barbarian inroads, the internal defence of all that vast enclosure could be left to the civil power. If the Black Sea and the Sea of Azoff could be kept clear of piratical adventurers, the broad highway of the Mediterranean was safe. A squadron near Gibraltar, a squadron at the Dardanelles, and the tribes which might possibly venture in from the ocean—the tribes which, slipping down from the Don or the Dnieper, might thread their way through the Hellespont and emerge into the Egean—were caught at their first appearance; and when the wisdom of the Romans had guarded the mouths of the Danube from the descent, in canoe or coracle, of the wild settlers on its upper banks, the peace and commerce of the whole empire were secured. With modern Europe the case is very different. There are boundaries to be guarded which occupy more soldiers than the territories are worth. Lines are arbitrarily fixed across the centre of a plain, or along the summit of a mountain, which it is a case of war to pass. Belgium defends her flats with a hundred thousand men, and the marshes of Holland are secured by sixty thousand Dutch. The State of Dessau, in Germany, threatens its neighbours with fifteen hundred soldiers, while Reuss guards its dignity and independence with three hundred infantry and fifty horse. But the Great Powers, as they are called, take away from the peaceable and remunerative employments of trade or agriculture an amount of labour which would be an incalculable increase to the riches and happiness of the world. The aggregate soldiery of Europe is upwards of five millions of men,—just eleven times the largest calculation of the Roman legions. The ships of Europe—to the smaller of which the greatest galleys of the ancient world would scarcely serve as tenders—amount to 2113. The number of guns they carry, against which there is nothing we can take as a measure of value in ancient warfare, but which are now the greatest and surest criterions of military power, amounts to 45,367. But this does not give so clear a view of the alteration in relative power as is yielded by an inspection of some of the separate items. Gaul, included within the Rhine, was kept in order by six or seven legions. The French empire has on foot an army of six hundred and fifty thousand men, and a fleet of four hundred sail. Britain, which was garrisoned by thirty thousand men, had, in 1855, an army at home and abroad of six hundred and sixty thousand men, and a fleet of five hundred and ninety-one ships of war, with an armament of seventeen thousand guns. The disjointed States which now constitute the Empire of Austria, and which occupied eight legions in their defence, are now in possession of an army of six hundred thousand men; and

Prussia, whose army exceeds half a million of soldiers, was unheard of except in the discussions of geographers.*

With the death of the excellent Marcus Aurelius the golden age came to a close. Commodus sat on the throne, and renewed the wildest atrocities of the previous century. Nero was not more cruel—

A.D. 181.

* The following is a carefully compiled table of the forces of Europe in the year 1854–55. Since that time the Russian fleet has been destroyed, but the diminution has been more than counterbalanced by the increased navies of the other powers.

MILITARY FORCES OF EUROPE IN 1855.

	Men.	Ships.	Guns.
Austria	650,000	102	752
Bavaria	239,886	...	...
Belgium	100,000	...	...
Denmark	75,169	120	880
France	650,000	407	11,773
Germany	452,473	...	...
Great Britain	265,000[1]	591	17,291
Greece	10,226	25	143
Ionian Isles	3,000	4	...
Modena and Parma	6,302	...	...
Netherlands	58,647	84	2,000
Papal States	11,274	...	...
Portugal	33,000	44	404
Prussia	525,000	50	250
Russia	699,000	207	9,000
Sardinia	48,088	40	900
Sicilies	106,264	29	444
Spain	75,000	410	1,530
Sweden	167,000	...	...
Switzerland	108,000	...	...
Tuscany	16,930	...	...
Turkey	310,970	...	...
	4,611,229	2113	45,367[2]

[1] Indian army 250,000, and militia 145,000, not included; making a total of 660,000.

[2] Taking an average of ten men to each gun, the sailors will be 453,670; which gives a total of fighting-men, 5,064,899 ! ! !

Domitian was not so reckless of human life. He fought in the arena against weakly-armed adversaries, and slew them without remorse. He polluted the whole city with blood, and made money by selling permissions to murder. Thirteen years exhausted the patience of the world, and a justifiable assassination put an end to his life. There was an old man of the name of Pertinax, originally a nickname derived from his obstinate or pertinacious disposition, who now made his appearance on the throne and perished in three months. It chanced that a certain rich man of the name of Didius was giving a supper the night of the murder to some friends. The dishes were rich, and the wine delicious. Inspired by the good cheer, the guests said, "Why don't you buy the empire? The soldiers have proclaimed that they will give it to the highest bidder." Didius knew the amount of his treasure, and was ambitious: he got up from table and hurried to the Prætorian camp. On the way he met the mutilated body of the murdered Pertinax, dragged through the streets with savage exultation. Nothing daunted, he arrived at the soldiers' tents. Another had been before him—Sulpician, the father-in-law and friend of the late emperor. A bribe had been offered to each soldier, so large that they were about to conclude the bargain; but Didius bade many sesterces more. The greedy soldiery looked from one to the other, and shouted with delight, as each new advance was made. At last Sulpician was
A.D. 193. silent, and Didius had purchased the Roman world at the price of upwards of £200 to each soldier of the Prætorian guard. He entered the palace in state, and concluded the supper, which had been interrupted at his own house, on the viands prepared for Pertinax. But the excitement of the auction-room was too pleasant to be left to the troops in Rome. Offers were made to the legions in all the provinces, and Didius was threatened

on every side. Even the distant garrisons of Britain named a candidate for the throne; and Claudius Albinus assumed the imperial purple, and crossed over into Gaul. More irritated still, the army in Syria elected its general, Pescennius Niger, emperor, and he prepared to dispute the prize; but quietly, steadily, with stern face and unrelenting heart, advancing from province to province, keeping his forces in strict subjection, and laying claim to supreme authority by the mere strength of his indomitable will, came forward Septimius Severus, and both the pretenders saw that their fate was sealed. Illyria and Gaul recognised his title at once. Albinus was happy to accept from him the subordinate title of Cæsar, and to rule as his lieutenant. Didius, whose bargain turned out rather ill, besought him to be content with half the empire. Severus slew the messengers who brought this proposition, and advanced in grim silence. The Senate assembled, and, by way of a pleasant reception for the Illyrian chief, requested Didius to prepare for death. The executioners found him clinging to life with unmanly tenacity, and killed him when he had reigned but seventy days. One other competitor remained, the general of the Syrian army—the closest friend of Severus, but now separated from him by the great temptation of an empire in dispute. This was Niger, from whom an obstinate resistance was expected, as he was equally famous for his courage and his skill. But fortune was on the side of Severus. Niger was conquered after a short struggle, and his head presented to the victor. Was Albinus still to live, and approach so near the throne as to have the rank of Cæsar? Assassins were employed to murder him, but he escaped their assault. The treachery of Severus brought many supporters to his rival. The Roman armies were ranged in hostile camps. Severus again was fortunate, and Albinus, dashing towards him to engage in combat, was slain before his eyes. He watched his dying agonies for some time, and then forced his horse to trample on the corpse. A man of harsh, implacable nature—not so much cruel as impenetrable to human feelings, and perhaps forming a just estimate of the favourable effect upon his fortunes of a disposition so calm, and yet so relentless. The Prætorians found they had appointed their master, and put the sword into his hand. He used it without remorse. He terrified the boldest with his imperturbable stillness; he summoned the seditious soldiery to wait on him at his camp. They were to come without arms, without their military dress, almost like suppliants, certainly not like the ferocious libertines they had been when they had sold the empire at the highest price. "Whoever of you wishes to live," said Severus, frowning coldly, "will depart from this, and never come within thirty leagues of Rome. Take their horses," he added to the other troops who had surrounded the Prætorians, "take their accoutrements, and chase them out of my sight." Did the Senate receive a milder treatment? On sending them the head of Albinus, he had written to the Conscript Fathers alarming them with the most dreadful threats. And now the time of execution had come. He made them an oration in praise of the proscriptions of Marius and Sylla, and forced them to deify the tyrant Commodus, who had hated them all his life. He then gave a signal to his train, and the streets ran with blood. All who had borne high office, all who were of distinguished birth, all who were famous for their wealth or popular with the citizens, were put to death. He crossed over to England and repressed a sedition there. His son Caracalla accompanied him, and commenced his career of warlike ardour and frightful ferocity, which can only be explained on the ground of his being mad. He tried even to murder his father, in open day, in the sight of the soldiers. He was stealing upon the old man, when a cry from the legion made him turn round. His inflexible eye fell upon Caracalla—the sword dropped from his unfilial hand—and dreadful anticipations of vengeance filled the assembly. The son was pardoned, but his accomplices, whether truly or falsely accused, perished by cruel deaths. At last the emperor felt his end approach. He summoned his sons Caracalla and Geta into his presence, recommended them to live in unity, and ended by the advice which has become the standing maxim of military despots, "Be generous to the soldiers, and trample on all beside."

With this hideous incarnation of unpitying firmness on the throne—hopeless of the future, and with dangers accumulating on every side, the Second Century came to an end, leaving the amazing contrast between its miserable close and the long period of its prosperity by which it will be remembered in all succeeding time.

THIRD CENTURY.

Emperors.

A.D.	
	Septimius Severus—(*continued.*) Fifth Persecution of the Christians.
211.	Caracalla and Geta.
217.	Macrinus.
218.	Heliogabalus.
222.	Alexander Severus.
235.	Maximin. Sixth Persecution.
238.	Maximus and Balbinus.
238.	Gordian.
244.	Philip the Arabian.
249.	Decius. Seventh Persecution.
251.	Vibius.
251.	Gallus.
254.	Valerian. Eighth Persecution.
260.	Gallien.
268.	Claudius the Second.
270.	Aurelian. Ninth Persecution.
275.	Tacitus.
276.	Florian.
277.	Probus.
278.	Carus.
278.	Carinus and Numerian.
284.	Diocletian and Maximian. Tenth and Last Persecution.

Authors.

Clement of Alexandria, Dion Cassius, Origen, Cyprian, Plotinus, Longinus, Hippolitus Portuensis, Julius Africanus, Celsus, Origen.

THE THIRD CENTURY.

ANARCHY AND CONFUSION—GROWTH OF THE CHRISTIAN CHURCH.

WE are now in the twelfth year of the Third Century. Septimius Severus has died at York, and Caracalla is let loose like a famished tiger upon Rome. He invites his brother Geta to meet him to settle some family feud in the apartment of their mother, and stabs him in her arms. The rest of his reign is worthy of this beginning, and it would be fatiguing and perplexing to the memory to record his other acts. Fortunately it is not required; nor is it necessary to follow minutely the course of his successors. What we require is only a general view of the proceedings of this century, and that can be gained without wading through all the blood and horrors with which the throne of the world is surrounded. Conclusive evidence was obtained in this century that the organization of Roman government was defective in securing the first necessities of civilized life. When we talk of civilization, we are too apt to limit the meaning of the word to its mere embellishments, such as arts and sciences; but the true distinction between it and barbarism is, that the one presents a state of society under the protection of just and well-administered law, and the other is left to the chance government of brute force. There was now great wealth in Rome—great luxury—a high admiration of painting, poetry, and sculpture—much learning, and probably infinite refinement of manners and address. But it was not a civilized state.

Life was of no value—property was not secure. A series of madmen seized supreme authority, and overthrew all the distinctions between right and wrong. Murder was legalized, and rapine openly encouraged. It is a sort of satisfaction to perceive that few of those atrocious malefactors escaped altogether the punishment of their crimes. If Caracalla slays his brother and orders a peaceable province to be destroyed, there is a Macrinus at hand to put the monster to death. But
A.D. 218. Macrinus, relying on the goodness of his intentions, neglects the soldiery, and is supplanted by a boy of seventeen—so handsome that he won the admiration of the rudest of the legionaries, and so gentle and captivating in his manners that he strengthened the effect his beauty had produced. He was priest of the Temple of the Sun at Emesa in Phœnicia; and by the arts of his grandmother, who was sister to one of the former empresses, and the report that she cunningly spread abroad that he was the son of their favourite Caracalla, the affection of the dissolute soldiery knew no bounds. Macrinus was soon slaughtered, and the long-haired priest of Baal seated on the throne of the Cæsars, under the name of Heliogabalus. As might be expected, the sudden alteration in his fortunes was fatal to his character. All the excesses of his predecessors were surpassed. His extravagance rapidly exhausted the resources of the empire. His floors were spread with gold-dust. His dresses, jewels, and golden ornaments were never worn twice, but went to his slaves and parasites. He created his grandmother a member of the Senate, with rank next after the consuls; and established a rival Senate, composed of ladies, presided over by his mother. Their jurisdiction was not very hurtful to the State, for it only extended to dresses and precedence of ranks, and the etiquette to be observed

in visiting each other. But the evil dispositions of the emperor were shown in other ways. He had a cousin of the name of Alexander, and entertained an unbounded jealousy of his popularity with the soldiers. Attempts at poison and direct assassination were resorted to in vain. The public sympathy began to rise in his favour. The Prætorians formally took him under their protection; and when Heliogabalus, reckless of their menaces, again attempted the life of Alexander, the troops revolted, proclaimed death to the infatuated emperor, and slew him and his mother at the same time.

A.D. 222. Alexander was now enthroned—a youth of sixteen; gifted with higher qualities than the debased century in which he lived could altogether appreciate. But the origin of his noblest sentiments is traced to the teaching he had received from his mother, in which the precepts of Christianity were not omitted. When he appointed the governor of a province, he published his name some time before, and requested if any one knew of a disqualification, to have it sent in for his consideration. "It is thus the Christians appoint their pastors," he said, "and I will do the same with my representatives." When his justice, moderation, and equity were fully recognised, the beauty of the quotation, which was continually in his mouth, was admired by all, even though they were ignorant of the book it came from: "Do unto others as you would that they should do unto you." He trusted the wisest of his counsellors, the great legalists of the empire, with the introduction of new laws to curb the wickedness of the time. But the multiplicity of laws proves the decline of states. In the ancient Rome of the kings and earlier consuls, the statutes were contained in forty decisions, which were afterwards enlarged into the laws of the Twelve Tables, consisting of one hundred and fifty texts. The profligacy of some emperors, the vanity of others, had loaded the statute-book with an innumerable mass of edicts, senatus-consultums, prætorial rescripts, and customary laws. It was impossible to extract order or regularity from such a chaos of conflicting rules. The great work was left for a later prince; at present we can only praise the goodness of the emperor's intention. But Alexander, justly called Severus, from the simplicity of his life and manners, has held the throne too long. The Prætorians have been thirteen years without the donation consequent on a new accession.

Among the favourite leaders selected by Alexander for their military qualifications was one Maximin, a Thracian peasant, of whose strength and stature incredible things are told. He was upwards of eight feet high, could tire down a horse at the gallop on foot, could break its leg by a blow of his hand, could overthrow thirty wrestlers without drawing breath, and maintained this prodigious force by eating forty pounds of meat, and drinking an amphora and a half, or twelve quarts, of wine. This giant had the bravery for which his countrymen the Goths have always been celebrated. He rose to high rank in the Roman service; and when at last nothing seemed to stand between him and the throne but his patron and benefactor, ambition blinded him to every thing but his own advancement. He murdered the wise and generous Alexander, and presented for the first time in history the spectacle of a barbarian master of the Roman world. Other emperors had been born in distant portions of the empire; an African had trampled on Roman greatness in the person of Septimius Severus; a Phœnician priest had disgraced the purple in the person of Heliogabalus; Africa, however, was a Roman province, and Emesa a Roman town. But here sat the colossal representative of the terrible Goths of Thrace, speaking a language half Getic, half Latin, which no one could easily understand; fierce, haughty, and revengeful, and cherishing a ferocious hatred of the subjects who trembled before him—a hatred probably implanted in him in his childhood by the patriotic songs with which the warriors of his tribe kept alive their enmity and contempt for the Roman name. The Roman name had indeed by this time lost all its authority. The army, recruited from all parts of the empire, and including a great number of barbarians in its ranks, was no longer a bulwark against foreign invasion. Maximin, bestowing the chief commands on Pannonians and other mercenaries, treated the empire as a conquered country. He seized on all the wealth he could discover—melted all the golden statues, as valuable from their artistic beauty as for the metal of which they were composed—and was threatening an approach to Rome to exterminate the Senate and sack the devoted town. In this extremity the Senate resumed its long-forgotten power, and named as emperors two men of the name of Gordian —father and son—with instructions "to resist the enemy." But father and son perished in a few weeks, and still the terrible Goth came on. His son, a giant like himself, but beautiful as the colossal statue of a young Apollo, shared in all the feelings of his father. Terrified at its approaching doom, the Senate once more nominated two men to the purple, Maximus and Balbinus: Balbinus, the favourite, perhaps, of the aristocracy, by the descent he claimed from an illustrious ancestry; while Maximus recommended himself to the now perverted taste of the commonalty by having been a carter. Neither was popular with the army; and, to please the soldiers, a son or nephew of the younger Gordian was associated with them on the throne. But nothing could have resisted the infuriated legions of the gigantic Maximin; they were marching with wonderful expedition towards their revenge. At Aquileia they met an opposition; the town shut its gates and manned its walls, for it knew what would be the fate of a city given up to the tender mercies of the Goths. Meanwhile the approach of the destroyer produced great agitation in Rome. The people rose upon the Prætorians, and enlisted the gladiators on their side. Many thousands were slain, and at last a peace was made by the intercession of the youthful Gordian. Glad of the cessation of this civic tumult, the population of Rome betook itself to the theatres and shows. Suddenly, while the games were going on, it was announced that the army before Aquileia had mutinied and that both the Maximins were slain. All at once the amphitheatre was emptied; by an impulse of grateful piety, the emperors and people hurried into the temples of the gods, and offered up thanks for their deliverance. The wretched people were premature in their rejoicing. In less than three months the spoiled Prætorians were offended with the precaution taken by the emperors in surrounding themselves with German guards. They assaulted the palace, and put Maximus and Balbinus to death. Gordian the Third was now sole emperor, and the final struggle with the barbarians drew nearer and nearer.

A.D. 235.

Constantly crossing the frontiers, and willingly received in the Roman ranks, the communities who had been long settled on the Roman confines were not the utterly uncultivated tribes which their name would seem to denote. There was a conterminous civilization which made the two peoples scarcely distinguishable at their point of contact, but which died off as the distance from the Roman line increased. Thus, an original settler on the eastern bank of the Rhine was probably as cultivated and intelligent as a Roman colonist on the other side; but farther up, at the Weser and the Elbe, the old ferocity and roughness remained. Fresh importations from the unknown East were continually taking place; the dwellers in the plains of Pannonia, now habituated to pasturage and trade, found safety from the hordes which pressed upon them from their own original settlements beyond the Caucasus, by crossing the boundary river; and by this means the banks were held by cognate but hostile peoples, who could, however, easily be reconciled by a joint expedition against Rome. New combinations had taken place in the interior of the great expanses not included in the Roman limits. The Germans were no longer the natural enemies of the empire. They furnished many soldiers for its defence, and several chiefs to command its forces. But all round the external circuit of those half-conciliated tribes rose up vast confederacies of warlike nations. There were Cheruski, and Sicambri, and Attuarians, and Bruttuarians, and Catti, all regularly enrolled under the name of "Franks," or the brave. The Sarmatians or Sclaves performed the same part on the northeastern frontier; and we have already seen that the irresistible Goths had found their way, one by one, across the boundary, and cleared the path for their successors. The old enemies of Rome on the extreme east, the Parthians, had fallen under the power of a renovated mountain-race, and of a king, who founded the great dynasty of the Sassanides, and claimed the restoration of Egypt and Armenia as ancient dependencies of the Persian crown. To resist all these, there was, in the year 241, only a gentle-tempered youth, dressed in the purple which had so lost its original grandeur, and relying for his guidance on the wisdom of his tutors, and for his life on the forbearance of the Prætorians. The tutors were wise and just, and victory at

first gave some sort of dignity to the reign of Gordian. The Franks were conquered at Mayence; but Gordian,
A.D. 244. three years after, was murdered in the East; and Philip, an Arabian, whose father had been a robber of the desert, was acknowledged emperor by senate and army. Treachery, ambition, and murder pursued their course. There was no succession to the throne. Sometimes one general, luckier or wiser than the rest, appeared the sole governor of the State. At other times there were numberless rivals all claiming the empire and threatening vengeance on their opponents. Yet amidst this tumult of undistinguishable pretenders, fortune placed at the head of affairs some of the best and greatest men whom the Roman world ever produced. There was Valerian, whom all parties
A.D. 253. agreed in considering the most virtuous and enlightened man of his time. Scarcely any opposition was made to his promotion; and yet, with all his good qualities, he was the man to whom Rome owed the greatest degradation it had yet sustained. He was taken prisoner by Sapor, the Persian king, and condemned, with other captive monarchs, to draw the car of his conqueror. No offers of ransom could deliver the brave and unfortunate prince. He died amid his deriding enemies, who hung up his skin as an offering to their gods. Then, after some years, in which there were twenty emperors at one time, with army drawn up against army, and cities delivered to massacre and rapine by all parties in turn, there arose one of the strong minds which make themselves felt throughout a whole period, and arrest for a while the downward course of
A.D. 276. states. The emperor Probus, son of a man who had originally been a gardener, had distinguished himself under Aurelian, the conqueror of Palmyra, and, having survived all his competitors, had time to devote

himself to the restoration of discipline and the introduction of purer laws. His victories over the encroaching barbarians were decided, but ineffectual. New myriads still pressed forward to take the place of the slain. On one occasion he crossed the Rhine in pursuit of the revolted Germans, overtook them at the Necker, and killed in battle four hundred thousand men. Nir e kings threw themselves at the emperor's feet. Many thousand barbarians enlisted in the Roman army. Sixty great cities were taken, and made offerings of golden crowns. The whole country was laid waste. "There was nothing left," he boasted to the Senate, "but bare fields, as if they had never been cultivated." So much the worse for the Romans. The barbarians looked with keener eyes across the river at the rich lands which had never been ravaged, and sent messages to all the tribes in the distant forests, that, having no occasion for pruning-hooks, they had turned them into swords. But Probus showed a still more doubtful policy in other quarters. When he conquered the Vandals and Burgundians, he sent their warriors to keep the Caledonians in subjection on the Tyne. The Britons he transported to Mœsia or Greece. What intermixtures of race may have arisen from these transplantations it is impossible to say; but the one feeling was common to all the barbarians, that Rome was weak and they were strong. He settled a large detachment of Franks on the shores of the Black Sea; and of these an almost incredible but well-authenticated story is told. They seized or built themselves boats. They swept through the Dardanelles, and ravaged the isles of Greece. They pursued their piratical career down the Mediterranean, passed the pillars of Hercules into the Great Sea, and, rounding Spain and France, rowed up the Elbe into the midst of their astonished countrymen, who had long given them up for dead. A fatal

4

adventure this for the safety of the Roman shores; for there were the wild fishermen of Friesland, and the audacious Angles of Schleswig and Holstein, who heard of this strange exploit, and saw that no coast was too distant to be reached by their oar and sail. But if these forced settlements of barbarians on Roman soil were impolitic, the generous Probus did not feel their bad effect. His warlike qualities awed his foes, and his inflexible justice was appreciated by the hardy warriors of the North, who had not yet sunk under the debasing civilization of Rome. In Asia his arms were attended with equal success. He subdued the Persians, and extended his conquests into Ethiopia and the farthest regions of the East, bringing back some of its conquered natives to swell the triumph at Rome and terrify the citizens with their strange and hideous appearance. But Probus himself must yield to the law which regulated the fate of Roman emperors. He died by treachery and the sword. All that the empire could do was to join in the epitaph pronounced over him by the barbarians, "Here lies the emperor Probus, whose life and actions corresponded to his name."

Three or four more fantastic figures, "which the likeness of a kingly crown have on," pass before our eyes, and at last we observe the powerful and substantial form of Diocletian, and feel once more we have to do with a real man. A Druidess, we are told, had prophesied that he should attain his highest wish if he killed a wild boar. In all his hunting expeditions he was constantly on the look-out, spear in hand, for an encounter with the long-tusked monster. Unluckily for a man who had offended Diocletian before, and who had basely murdered his predecessor, his name was Aper; and unluckily, also, *aper* is Latin for a boar. This fact will perhaps be thought to account for the prophecy. It

A.D. 284.

accounts, at all events, for its fulfilment; for, the wretched Aper being led before the throne, Diocletian descended the steps and plunged a dagger into his chest, exclaiming, "I have killed the wild boar of the prediction." This is a painful example of how unlucky it is to have a name that can be punned upon. Determined to secure the support of what he thought the strongest body in the State, he gratified the priests by the severest of all the many persecutions to which the Christians had been exposed. By way of further showing his adhesion to the old faith, he solemnly assumed the name of Jove, and bestowed on his partner on the throne the inferior title of Hercules. In spite of these truculent and absurd proceedings, Diocletian was not altogether destitute of the softer feelings. The friend he associated with him on the throne—dividing the empire between them as too large a burden for one to sustain—was called Maximian. They had both originally been slaves, and had neither of them received a liberal education. Yet they protected the arts, they encouraged literature, and were the patrons of modest merit wherever it could be found. They each adopted a Cæsar, or lieutenant of the empire, and hoped that, by a legal division of duties among four, the ambition of their generals would be prevented. But the limits of the empire were too extended even for the vigilance of them all. In Britain, Carausius raised the standard of revolt, giving it the noble name of national independence; and, with the instinctive wisdom which has been the safeguard of our island ever since, he rested his whole chance of success upon his fleet. Invasion was rendered impossible by the care with which he guarded the shore, and it is not inconceivable that even at that early time the maritime career of Britain might have been begun and maintained, if treason, as usual, had not cut short the efforts of Carausius, who was soon after murdered by his friend Allectus. The subdivision of the empire was a successful experiment as regarded its external safety, but within, it was the cause of bitter complaining. There were four sumptuous courts to be maintained, and four imperial armies to be paid. Taxes rose, and allegiance waxed cold. The Cæsars were young, and looked probably with an evil eye on the two old men who stood between them and the name of emperor. However it may be, after many victories and much domestic trouble, Diocletian resolved to lay aside the burden of empire and retire into private life. His colleague Maximian felt, or affected to feel, the same distaste for power, and on the same day they quitted the purple; one at Nicomedia, the other at Milan. Diocletian retired to Salona, a town in his native Dalmatia, and occupied himself with rural pursuits. He was asked after a while to reassume his authority, but he said to the persons who made him the request, "I wish you would come to Salona and see the cabbages I have planted with my own hands, and after that you would never wish me to remount the throne."

The characteristic of this century is its utter confusion and want of order. There was no longer the unity even of despotism at Rome to make a common centre round which every thing revolved. There were tyrants and competitors for power in every quarter of the empire—no settled authority, no government or security, left. In the midst of this relaxation of every rule of life, grew surely, but unobserved, the Christian Church, which drew strength from the very helplessness of the civil state, and was forced, in self-defence, to establish a regular organization in order to extend to its members the inestimable benefits of regularity and law. Under many of the emperors Christianity was proscribed; its disciples were put to excruciating deaths, and their property confiscated; but at that very time its inner development increased and strengthened. The community appointed its teachers, its deacons, its office-bearers of every kind; it supported them in their endeavours—it yielded to their directions; and in time a certain amount of authority was considered to be inherent in the office of pastor, which extended beyond the mere expounding of the gospel or administration of the sacraments. The chief pastor became the guide, perhaps the judge, of the whole flock. While it is absurd, therefore, in those disastrous times of weakness and persecution to talk in pompous terms of the succession of the Bishops of Rome, and make out vain catalogues of lordly prelates who sat on the throne of St. Peter, it is incontestable that, from the earliest period, the Christian converts held their meetings—by stealth indeed, and under fear of detection—and obeyed certain canons of their own constitution. These secret associations rapidly spread their ramifications into every great city of the empire. When by the friendship, or the fellowship, of the emperor, as in the case of the Arabian Philip, a pause was given to their fears and sufferings, certain buildings were set apart for their religious exercises; and we read, during this century, of basilicas, or churches, in Rome and other towns. The subtlety of the Greek intellect had already led to endless heresies and the wildest departures from the simplicity of the gospel. The Western mind was more calm, and better adapted to be the lawgiver of a new order of society composed of elements so rough and discordant as the barbarians, whose approach was now inevitably foreseen. With its well-defined hierarchy—its graduated ranks, and the fitness of the offices for the purposes of their creation; with its array of martyrs ready to suffer, and clear-headed leaders fitted to command, the Western Church could look calmly forward to the time when its organization would make it the most powerful, or perhaps the only, body in the State; and so early as the middle of this century the seeds of worldly ambition developed themselves in a schism, not on a point of doctrine, but on the possession of authority. A double nomination had made the anomalous appointment of two chief pastors at the same time. Neither would yield, and each had his supporters. All were under the ban of the civil power. They had recourse to spiritual weapons; and we read, for the first time in ecclesiastical history, of mutual excommunications. Novatian—under his breath, however, for fear of being thrown to the wild beasts for raising a disturbance—thundered his anathemas against Cornelius as an intruder, while Cornelius retorted by proclaiming Novatian an impostor, as he had not the concurrence of the people in his election. This gives us a convincing proof of the popular form of appointing bishops or presbyters in those early days, and prepares us for the energy with which the electors supported the authority of their favourite priests.

But, while this new internal element was spreading life among the decayed institutions of the empire, we have, in this century, the first appearance, in great force, of the future conquerors and renovators of the body politic from without. It is pleasant to think that the centuries cast themselves more and more loose from their connection with Rome after this date, and that the barbarians can vindicate a separate place in history for themselves. In the first century, the bad emperors broke the strength of Rome by their cruelty and extravagance. In the second century, the good emperors carried on the work of weakening the empire by the softening and enervating effects of their gentle and protective policy. The third century unites the evil qualities of the other two, for the people were equally rendered incapable of defending themselves by the unheard-of atrocities of some of the tyrants who oppressed them, and the mistaken measures of the more benevolent rulers, in committing the guardianship of the citizens to the swords of a foreign soldiery, leaving them but the wretched alternative of being ravaged and massacred by an irruption of savage tribes or pillaged and insulted by those in the emperor's pay.

The empire had long been surrounded by its foes. It will suffice to read the long list of captives who were led in triumph behind the car of Aurelian when he re-
A.D. 273. turned from foreign war, to see the fearful array of harsh-sounding names which have afterwards been softened into those of great and civilized nations. It is in following the course of some of these that we shall see how the present distribution of forces in Europe took place, and escape from the polluted atmosphere of Imperial Rome. In that memorable triumph appeared Goths, Alans, Roxolans, Franks, Sarmatians, Vandals, Allemans, Arabs, Indians, Bactrians, Iberians, Saracens, Armenians, Persians, Palmyreans, Egyptians, and ten Gothic women dressed in men's apparel and fully armed. These were, perhaps, the representatives of a large body of female warriors, and are a sign of the recent settlement of the tribe to which they belonged. They had not yet given up the habits of their march, where all were equally engaged in carrying the property and arms of the nation, and where the females encouraged the young men of the expedition by witnessing and sometimes sharing their exploits in battle.

The triumph of Probus, when only seven years had passed, presents us with a list of the same peoples, often conquered but never subdued. Their defeats, indeed, had the double effect of showing to them their own ability to recruit their forces, and of strengthening the degraded people of Rome in the belief of their invincibility. After the loss of a battle, the Gothic or Burgundian chief fell back upon the confederated tribes in his rear; a portion of his army either visited Rome in the character of captives, or enlisted in the ranks of the conquerors. In either case, the wealth of the great city and the undefended state of the empire were permanently fixed in their minds; the populace, on the other hand, had the luxury of a noble show and double rations of bread—the more ambitious of the emperors acting on the professed maxim that the citizen had no duty but to enjoy the goods provided for him by the governing power, and that if he was fed by public doles, and amused with public games, the purpose of his life was attained. The idlest man was the safest subject. A triumph was, therefore, more an instrument of degradation than an encouragement to patriotic exertion. The name of Roman citizen was now extended to all the inhabitants of the empire. The freeman of York was a Roman citizen. Had he any patriotic pride in keeping the soil of Italy undivided? The nation had become too diffuse for the exercise of this local and combining virtue. The love of country, which in the small states of Greece secured the individual's affection to his native city, and yet was powerful enough to extend over the whole of the Hellenic territories, was lost altogether when it was required to expand itself over a region as wide as Europe. It is in this sense that empires fall to pieces by their own weight. The Roman power broke up from within. Its religion was a source of division, not of union—its mixture of nations, and tongues, and usages, lost their cohesion. And nothing was left at the end of this century to preserve it from total dissolution, but the personal qualities of some great rulers and the memory of its former fame.

FOURTH CENTURY.

Emperors.

A.D.
304. Galerius and Constantius.
305. Maximin.
306. Constantine.
337. Constantine II., Constans and Constantius.
361. Julian the Apostate.
363. Jovian.

A.D.	*West.*	A.D.	*East.*
364.	Valentinian.	364.	Valens.
367.	Gratian.		
375.	Valentinian II.	379.	Theodosius.
395.	Honorius.	395.	Arcadius.

Authors.

Donatus, Eutropius, St. Athanasius, Ausonius, Claudian, Arnobius, (303,) Lactantius, (306,) Eusebius, (315,) Arius, (316,) Gregory Nazianzen, (320–389,) Basil the Great, Bishop of Cesarea, (330–379,) Ambrose, (340–397,) Augustine (353–429,) Theodoret, (386–457,) Martin, Bishop of Tours.

THE FOURTH CENTURY.

THE REMOVAL TO CONSTANTINOPLE—ESTABLISHMENT OF CHRISTIANITY—APOSTASY OF JULIAN—SETTLEMENT OF THE GOTHS.

As the memory of the old liberties of Rome died out, a nearer approach was made to the ostentatious despotisms of the East. Aurelian, in 270, was the first emperor who encircled his head with a diadem; and Diocletian, in 284, formed his court on the model of the most gorgeous royalties of Asia. On admission into his presence, the Roman Senator, formerly the equal of the ruler, prostrated himself at his feet. Titles of the most unmanly adulation were lavished on the fortunate slave or herdsman who had risen to supreme power. He was clothed in robes of purple and violet, and loaded with an incalculable wealth of jewels and gold. It was from deep policy that Diocletian introduced this system. Ceremony imposes on the vulgar, and makes intimacy impossible. Etiquette is the refuge of failing power, and compensates by external show for inherent weakness, as stiffness and formality are the refuge of dulness and mediocrity in private life. There was now, therefore, seated on the throne, which was shaken by every commotion, a personage assuming more majestic rank, and affecting far loftier state and dignity, than Augustus had ventured on while the strength of the old Republic gave irresistible force to the new empire, or than the Antonines had dreamt of when the prosperity of Rome was apparently at its height. But there was still some feeling, if not of self-respect, at least of resistance to pretension, in the populace and Senators of the capital. Diocletian visited Rome but once. He was attacked in lampoons, and ridiculed in satirical songs. His colleague established his residence in the military post of Milan. We are not, therefore, to feel surprised that an Orientalized authority sought its natural seat in the land of ancient despotisms, and that many of the emperors had cast longing eyes on the beautiful towns of Asia Minor, and even on the far-off cities of Mesopotamia, as more congenial localities for their barbaric splendours. By a sort of compromise between his European origin and Asiatic tastes, the emperor Constantine, after many struggles with his competitors, having attained the sole authority, transferred the seat of empire from Rome to a city he had built on the extreme limits of Europe, and only divided from Asia by a narrow sea. All succeeding ages have agreed in extolling the situation of this city, called, after its founder, Constantinople, as the finest that could have been chosen. All ages, from the day of its erection till the hour in which we live, have agreed that it is fitted, in the hands of a great and enterprising power, to be the metropolis and arbiter of the world; and Constantinople is, therefore, condemned to the melancholy fate of being the useless and unappreciated capital of a horde of irreclaimable barbarians. To this magnificent city Constantine removed the throne in 329, and for nearly a thousand years after that, while Rome was sacked in innumerable invasions, and all the capitals of Europe were successively occupied by contending armies, Constantinople, safe in her two narrow outlets, and rich in her command of the two continents, continued unconquered, and even unassailed.

Rome was stripped, that Constantinople might be filled. All the wealth of Italy was carried across the

Ægean. The Roman Senator was invited to remove with his establishment. He found, on arriving at his new home, that by a complimentary attention of the emperor, a fac-simile of his Roman palace had been prepared for him on the Propontis. The seven hills of the new capital responded to the seven hills of the old. There were villas for retirement along the smiling shores of the Dardanelles or of the Bosphorus, as fine in climate, and perhaps equal in romantic beauty, to Baiæ or Brundusium. There was a capital, as noble a piece of architecture as the one they had left, but without the sanctity of its thousand years of existence, or the glory of its unnumbered triumphs. One omission was the subject of remark and lamentation. The temples were nowhere to be seen. The images of the gods were left at Rome in the solitude of their deserted shrines, for Constantine had determined that Constantinople should, from its very foundation, be the residence of a Christian people. Churches were built, and a priesthood appointed. Yet, with the policy which characterized the Church at that time, he made as little change as possible in the external forms. There is still extant a transfer of certain properties from the old establishment to the new. There are contributions of wax for the candles, of frankincense and myrrh for the censers, and vestures for the officiating priests as before. Only the object of worship is changed, and the images of the heathen gods and heroes are replaced with statues of the apostles and martyrs.

It is difficult to gather a true idea of this first of the Christian emperors from the historians of after-times. The accounts of him by contemporary writers are equally conflicting. The favourers of the old superstition describe him as a monster of perfidy and cruelty. The Church, raised to supremacy by his favour, sees nothing in him but the greatest of men—the seer of visions, the visible favourite of the Almighty, and the predestined overthrower of the powers of evil. The easy credulity of an emancipated people believed whatever the flattery of the courtiers invented. His mother Helena made a journey to Jerusalem, and was rewarded for the pious pilgrimage by the discovery of the True Cross. Chapels and altars were raised upon all the places famous in Christian story; relics were collected from all quarters, and we are early led to fear that the simplicity of the gospel is endangered by its approach to the throne, and that Constantine's object was rather to raise and strengthen a hierarchy of ecclesiastical supporters than to give full scope to the doctrine of truth. But not the less wonderful, not the less by the divine appointment, was this unhoped-for triumph of Christianity, that its advancement formed part of the ambitious scheme of a worldly and unprincipled conqueror. Rather it may be taken as one among the thousand proofs with which history presents us, that the greatest blessings to mankind are produced irrespective of the character or qualities of the apparent author. A warrior is raised in the desert when required to be let loose upon a worn-out society as the scourge of God; a blood-stained soldier is placed on the throne of the world when the time has come for the earthly predominance of the gospel. But neither is Attila to be blamed nor Constantine to be praised.

It was the spirit of his system of government to form every society on a strictly monarchical model. There was everywhere introduced a clearly-defined subordination of ranks and dignities. Diocletian, we saw, surrounded the throne with a state and ceremony which kept the imperial person sacred from the common gaze. Constantine perfected his work by establishing a titled nobility, who were to stand between the throne and the people, giving dignity to the one, and impressing fresh awe upon the other. In all previous ages it had been the office that gave importance to the man. To be a member of the Senate was a mark of distinction; a long descent from a great historic name was looked on with respect; and the heroic deeds of the thousand years of Roman struggle had founded an aristocracy which owed its high position either to personal actions or hereditary claims. But now that the emperors had so long concentrated in themselves all the great offices of the State —now that the bad rulers of the first century had degraded the Senate by filling it with their creatures, the good rulers of the second century had made it merely the recorder of their decrees, and the anarchy of the third century had changed or obliterated its functions altogether—there was no way left to the ambitious Roman to distinguish himself except by the favour of the emperor. The throne became, as it has since continued in all strictly monarchical countries, the fountain of honour. It was not the people who could name a man to the consulship or appoint him to the command of an army. It was not even in the power of the emperor to find offices of dignity for all whom he wished to advance. So a method was discovered by which vanity or friendship could be gratified, and employment be reserved for the deserving at the same time. Instead of endangering an expedition against the Parthians by intrusting it to a rich and powerful courtier who desired to have the rank of general, the emperor simply named him Nobilissimus, or Patricius, or Illustris, and the gratified favourite, the "most noble," the "patrician," or the "illustrious," took place with the highest officers of the State. A certain title gave him equal rank with the Senator, the judge, or the consul. The diversity of these honorary distinctions became very great. There were the clarissimi—the perfectissimi—and the egregii—bearing the same relative dignity in the court-guide of the fourth century, as the dukes, marquises, earls, and viscounts of the peerage-books of the present day. But so much did all distinction flow from proximity to the throne, that all these high-sounding names owed their value to the fact of their being bestowed on the associates of the sovereign. The word Count, which is still the title borne by foreign nobles, comes from the Latin word which means "companion." There was a Comes, or Companion, of the Sacred Couch, or lord chamberlain—the Companion of the Imperial Service, or lord high steward—a Companion of the Imperial Stables, or lord high constable; through all these dignitaries, step above step, the glorious ascent extended, till it ended in the Companion of Private Affairs, or confidential secretary. At the head of all, sacred and unapproachable, stood the embodied Power of the Roman world, who, as he had given titles to all the magnates of his court, heaped also a great many on himself. His principal appellation, however, was not as in our degenerate days "Majesty," whether "Most Catholic," "Most Christian," or "Most Orthodox," but consisted in the rather ambitious attribute—eternity. "Your Eternity" was the phrase addressed to some miserable individual whose reign was ended in a month. It was proposed by this division of the Roman aristocracy to furnish the empire with a body for show and a body for use; the latter consisting of the real generals of the armies and administrators of the provinces. And with this view the two were kept distinct; but military discipline suffered by this partition. The generals became discontented when they saw wealth and dignities heaped upon the titular nobles of the court; and to prevent the danger arising from ill will among the legions on the frontier, the emperor withdrew the best of his soldiers from the posts where they kept the barbarians in check, and entirely destroyed their military spirit by separating them into small bodies and stationing them in towns. This exposed the empire to the foreign foes who still menaced it from the other side of the boundary, and gave fresh settlements in the heart of the country to the thousands of barbarian youth who had taken service with the eagles. In every legion there was a considerable proportion of this foreign element: in every district of the empire, therefore, there were now settled the advanced guards of the unavoidable invasion. Men with barbaric names, which the Romans could not pronounce, walked about Roman towns dressed in Roman uniforms and clothed with Roman titles. There were consulars and patricians in Ravenna and Naples, whose fathers had danced the war-dance of defiance when beginning their march from the Vistula and the Carpathian range.

All these troops must be supported—all these dignitaries maintained in luxury. How was this done? The ordinary revenue of the empire in the time of Constantine has been computed at forty millions of our money a year. Not a very large amount when you consider the number of the population; but this is the sum which reached the treasury. The gross amount must have been far larger, and an ingenious machinery was invented by which the tax was rigorously collected; and this machinery, by a ludicrous perversion of terms, was made to include one of the most numerous classes of the artificial nobility created by the imperial will. In all the towns of the empire some little remains were still to be found of the ancient municipal government, of which practically they had long been deprived. There were nominal magistrates still; and among these the

Curials held a distinguished rank. They were the men who, in the days of freedom, had filled the civic dignities of their native city—the aldermen, we should perhaps call them, or, more nearly, the justices of the peace. They were now ranked with the peerage, but with certain duties attached to their elevation which few can have regarded in the light of privilege or favour. To qualify them for rank, they were bound to be in possession of a certain amount of land. They were, therefore, a territorial aristocracy, and never was any territorial aristocracy more constantly under the consideration of the government. It was the duty of the curials to distribute the tax-papers in their district; but, in addition to this, it was unfortunately their duty to see that the sum assessed on the town and neighbourhood was paid up to the last penny. When there was any deficiency, was the emperor to suffer? Were the nobilissimi, the patricii, the egregii, to lose their salaries? Oh, no! As long as the now ennobled curial retained an acre of his estate, or could raise a mortgage on his house, the full amount was extracted. The tax went up to Rome, and the curial, if there had been a poor's house in those days, would have gone into it—for he was stripped of all. His farm was seized, his cattle were escheated; and when the defalcation was very great, himself, his wife and children were led into the market and sold as slaves. Nothing so rapidly destroyed what might have been the germ of a middle class as this legalized spoliation of the smaller landholders. Below this rank there was absolutely nothing left of the citizenship of ancient times. Artificers and workmen formed themselves into companies; but the trades were exercised principally by slaves for the benefit of their owners. These slaves formed now by far the greatest part of the Roman population, and though their lot had gradually become softened as their numbers increased, and the domestic bondsman had little to complain of except the greatest of all sorrows, the loss of freedom, the position of the rural labourers was still very bad. There were some of them slaves in every sense of the word—mere chattels, which were not so valuable as horse or dog. But the fate of others was so far mitigated that they could not be sold separate from their family—that they could not be sold except along with the land; and at last glimpses appear of a sort of rent paid for certain portions of the lord's estate in full of all other requirements. But this process had again to be gone through when many centuries had elapsed, and a new state of society had been fully established, and it will be sufficient to remind you that in the fourth century, to which we are now come, the Roman world consisted of a monarchy where all the greatness and magnificence of the empire were concentrated on the emperor and his court; that the monarchical system was rapidly pervading the Church; and that below these two distinct but connected powers there was no people, properly so called—the country was oppressed and ruined, and the ancient dignity of Rome transplanted to new and foreign quarters, at the sacrifice of all its oldest and most elevating associations. The half-depopulated city of Romulus and the Kings—of the Consuls and Augustus, looked with ill-disguised hatred and contempt on the modern rival which denied her the name of Capital, and while fresh from the builder's hand, robbed her of the name of the Eternal City. We shall see great events spring from this jealousy of the two towns. In the mean time, we shall finish our view of Constantine by recording the greatness of his military skill, and merely protest against the enrolment in the list of *saints* of a man who filled his family circle with blood—who murdered his wife, his son, and his nephew,

encouraged the contending factions of the now disputatious Church—gave a fallacious support to the orthodox Athanasius, and died after a superstitious baptism at the hands of the heretical Arius. An unbiassed
A.D. 337.
judgment must pronounce him a great politician, who played with both parties as his tools, a Christian from expediency and not from conviction. It is a pity that the subserviency of the Greek communion has placed him in the number of its holy witnesses, for we are told by a historian that when the emperor, after the dreadful crimes he had perpetrated, applied at the heathen shrines for expiatory rites, the priests of the false gods had truly answered, "there are no purifications for such deeds as these." But nothing could be refused to the benefactor of the Church. The great ecclesiastical council of this age, (325), consisting of three hundred and eighteen bishops, and presided over by Constantine in person, gave the Nicene Creed as the result of their labours—a creed which is still the symbol of Christendom, but which consists more of a condemnation of the heresies which were then in the ascendant, than in the plain enunciation of the Christian faith. A layman, we are told, an auditor of the learned debates in this great assembly, a man of clear and simple common sense, met some of the disputants, and addressed them in these words:—"Arguers! Christ and his apostles delivered to us, not the art of disputation, nor empty eloquence, but a plain and simple rule which is maintained by faith and good works." The disputants, we are further told, were so struck with this undeniable truth that they acknowledged their error at once.

But not yet firm and impregnable were the bulwarks of Christianity. While dreaming anchorites in the deserts of Thebais were repeating the results of fasting and insanity as the manifestation of divine favour, the world

A.D. 360. was startled from its security by the appalling discovery that the emperor himself, the young and vigorous Julian, was a follower of the old philosophers, and a worshipper of the ancient gods. And a dangerous antagonist he was, even independent of his temporal power. His personal character was irreproachable, his learning and talent beyond dispute, and his eloquence and dialectic skill sharpened and improved by an education in Athens itself. Less than forty years had elapsed since Constantine pronounced the sentence of banishment on the heathen deities. It was not possible that the Christian truth was in every instance received where the old falsehood was driven away. We may therefore conclude, without the aid of historic evidence, that there must have been innumerable districts—villages in far-off valleys, hidden places up among the hills—where the name of Christ had not yet penetrated, and all that was known was, that the shrine of the local gods was overthrown, and the priests of the old ceremonial proscribed. When we remember that the heathen worship entered into almost all the changes of the social and family life—that its sanction was necessary at the wedding—that its auguries were indispensable at births—that it crowned the statue of the household god with flowers—that it kept alive the fire upon the altar of the emperor—and that it was the guardian of the tombs of the departed, as it had been the principal consolation during the funeral rites,—we shall perceive that, irrespective of absolute faith in his system of belief, the cessation of the priest's office must have been a serious calamity. The heathen establishment had been enriched by the piety or ostentation of many generations. There must have been still alive many who had been turned out of their comfortable temples, many who viewed the assumption of Christianity into the State as a political engine to strengthen the tyranny under which the nations groaned. We may see that self-interest and patriotism may easily have been combined in the effort made by the old faith to regain the supremacy it had lost. The Emperor Julian endeavoured to lift up the fallen gods. He persecuted the Christians, not with fire and sword, but with contempt. He scorned and tolerated. He preached moderation, self-denial, and purity of life, and practised all these virtues to an extent unknown upon a throne, and even then unusual in a bishop's palace.

How these Christian graces, giving a charm and dignity to the apostate emperor, must have received a still higher authority from the painful contrast they presented to the agitated condition and corrupted morals of the Christian Church! Everywhere there was war and treachery, and ambition and unbelief. Half the great sees were held by Arians, who raved against the orthodox; and the other half were held by Athanasius and his followers, who accused their adversaries of being "more cruel than the Scythians, and more irreconcilable than tigers." At Rome itself there was an orthodox bishop and an Arian rival. It is not surprising that Julian, disgusted with the scenes presented to him by the mutual rage of the Christian sects, thought the surest method of restoring unity to the empire would be to silence all the contending parties and reintroduce the peaceful pageantries of the old Pantheon. If some of the fanciful annotators of the new faith had allegorized the facts of Christianity till they ceased to be facts at all, Julian performed the same office for the heathen gods. Jupiter and the rest were embodiments of the hidden powers of nature. Vulcan was the personification of human skill, and Venus the beautiful representative of connubial affection. But men's minds were now too sharpened with the contact they had had with the real to be satisfied with such fallacies as these. Eloquent teachers arose, who separated the eternal truths of revelation from the accessories with which they were temporarily combined. Ridicule was retorted on the emperor, who had sneered at the Christian services. Who, indeed, who had caught the slightest view of the spirituality of Christ's kingdom, could abstain from laughing at the laborious heathenism of the master of the world? He cut the wood for sacrifice, he slew the goat or bull, and, falling down on his knees, puffed with distended cheeks the sacred fire. He marched to the temple of Venus between two rows of dissolute and drunken worshippers, striving in vain by face and attitude to repress the shouts of riotous exultation and the jeers of the spectators. Then, wherever he went he was surrounded by pythonesses, and augurs, and fortune-tellers, magicians who could work miracles, and necromancers who could raise the dead. When he restored a statue to its ancient niche, he was rewarded by a shake of its head; when he hung up a picture of Thetis or Amphitrite, she winked in sign of satisfaction. Where miracles are not believed, the performance of them is fatal. But his expenditure of money in honouring the gods was more real, and had clearer results. He nearly exhausted the empire by the number of beasts he slew He sent enormous offerings to the shrines of Dodona, and Delos, and Delphi. He rebuilt the temples, which time or Christian hatred had destroyed; and, by way of giving life to his new polity, he condescended to imitate the sect he despised, in its form of worship, in its advocacy of charity, peace, and good will, and in its institutions of celibacy and retirement, which, indeed, had been a portion of heathen virtue before it was admitted into the Christian Church. But his affected con-

tempt soon degenerated into persecution. He would have no soldiers who did not serve his gods. Many resigned their swords. He called the Christians "Galileans," and robbed them of their property and despitefully used them, to try the sincerity of their faith. "Does not your law command you," he said, "to submit to injury, and to renounce your worldly goods? Well, I take possession of your riches that your march to heaven may be unencumbered." All moderation was now thrown off on both sides. Resistance was made by the Christians, and extermination threatened by the emperor. In the midst of these contentions he was called eastward to resist the aggression of Sapor, the Persian king. An arrow stretched Julian on his couch. He called round him his chief philosophers and priests. With them, in imitation of Socrates, he entered into
A.D. 363. deep discussions about the soul. Nothing more heroic than his end, or more eloquent than his parting discourse. But death did not soften the animosity of his foes. The Christians boasted that the arrow was sent by an angel, that visions had foretold the persecutor's fall, and that so would perish all the enemies of God. The adherents of the emperor in return blamed the Galileans as his assassins, and boldly pointed to Athanasius, the leader of the Christians, as the culprit. Athanasius would certainly not have scrupled to rid the world of such an Agag and Holofernes, but it is more probable that the death occurred without either a miracle or a murder. The successors of Julian were enemies of the apostate. They speedily restored their fellow-believers to the supremacy they had lost. A ferocious hymn of exultation by Gregory of Nazianzen was chanted far and wide. Cries of joy and execration resounded in market-places, and churches, and theatres. The market-places had been closed against the Chris-

tians, their churches had been interdicted, and the theatres shut up, by the overstrained asceticism of the deceased. It was perceived that Christianity had taken deeper root than the apostate had believed, and henceforth no effort could be made to revivify the old superstition. After a nominal election of Jovian, the choice of the soldiers fell on two of their favourite leaders, Valentinian and Valens, brothers, and sufferers in the late persecutions for their faith. Named emperors of the Roman world, they came to an amicable division of the empire into East and West. Valens remained in Constantinople to guard the frontiers of the Danube and the Euphrates; while Valentinian, who saw great clouds darkening over Italy and Gaul, fixed his imperial residence in the strong city of Milan. The separation took place in 364, and henceforth the stream of history flows in two distinct and gradually diverging channels. This century has already been marked by the removal of the seat of power to Constantinople; by the attempt at the restoration of Paganism by Julian; and we have now to dwell for a little on the third and greatest incident of all, the invasion of the Goths, and final settlement of hostile warriors on the Roman soil.

Names that have retained their sound and established themselves as household words in Europe now meet us at every turn. Valentinian is engaged in resisting the Saxons. The Britons, the Scots, the Germans, are pushing their claims to independence; and in the farther East, the persecutions and tyranny of the contemptible Valens are suddenly suspended by the news that a people hitherto unheard of had made their appearance within an easy march of the boundary, and that universal terror had taken possession of the soldiers of the empire. Who were those soldiers? We have seen for many years that the policy of the emperors had been to introduce the barbarians into the military service of the State, and to expose the wasted and helpless inhabitants to the rapacity of their tax-gatherers. This system had been carried to such a pitch, that it is probable there were none but mercenaries of the most varying interests in the Roman ranks. Yet such is the effect of discipline, and the pride of military combination, that all other feelings gave way before it. The Gothic chief, now invested with command in the Roman armies, turned his arms against his countrymen. The Albanian, the Saxon, the Briton, elevated to the rank of duke or count, looked back on Marius and Cæsar as their lineal predecessors in opposing and conquering the enemies of Rome. The names of the generals and magistrates, accordingly, which we encounter after this date, have a strangely barbaric sound. There are Ricimer, and Marcomir, and Arbogast—and finally, the name which overtopped and outlived them all, the name of Alaric the Goth. Now, the Goths, we have seen, had been settled for many generations on the northern side of the Danube. Much intercourse must have taken place between the inhabitants of the two banks. There must have been trade, and love, and quarrellings, and rejoicings. At shorter and shorter intervals the bravest of the tribes must have passed over into the Roman territory and joined the Legions. Occasionally a timid or despotic emperor would suddenly order his armies across, and carry fire and sword into the unsuspecting country. But on the whole, the terms on which they lived were not hostile, for the ties which united the two peoples were numerous and strong. Even the languages in the course of time must have come to be mutually intelligible, and we read of Gothic leaders who were excellent judges of Homer and seldom travelled without a few chosen books. This being the case, what was the consternation of the almost civilized Goths in the fertile levels of the present Wallachia and Moldavia to hear that an innumerable horde of dreadful savages, calling themselves Huns and Magyars, had appeared on the western shore of the Black Sea, and spread over the land, destroying, murdering, burning whatever lay in their way! Cooped up for an unknown period, it appeared, on the northeastern side of the Palus Mœotis, now better known to us as the Sea of Azof—living on fish out of the Don, and on the cattle of the long steppes which extend across the Volga, these sons of the Scythian desert had never been heard of either by the Goths or Romans. A hideous people to behold, as the perverted imagination of poet or painter could produce. They were low in stature, but broad-shouldered and strong. Their wide cheek-bones and small eyes gave them a savage and cruel expression, which was increased by their want of nose, for the only visible appearance of that indispensable organ consisted of two holes sunk into the square expanse of their faces. Fear is not a flattering painter, but from these rude descriptions it is easy to recognise the Calmuck countenance; and when we add their small horses, long spears, and prodigious lightness and activity, we shall see a very close resemblance between them and their successors in the same district, the Russian Cossacks of the Don. On, on, came the torrent of these pitiless, fearless, ugly, dirty, irresistible foes. The Goths, terrified at their aspect, and bewildered with the accounts they heard of their numbers and mode of warfare, petitioned the emperor to give them an asylum on the Roman side. Their prayer was granted on condition of depositing their children and arms in Roman hands. They had no time to squabble about terms. Every thing was agreed to. Boats manned by Roman soldiers were busy day and

night in transporting the Gothic exiles to the Roman side. Arms and jewels, and wives and children, the furniture of their tents, and idols of their gods, all got safely across the guarding river. The Huns, the Alans, and the other unsightly hordes who had gathered in the pursuit, came down to the bank, and shouted useless defiance and threats of vengeance. The broad Danube rolled between; and there rested that night on the Roman soil a whole nation, different in interest, in manners and religion, from the population they had joined, numbering upwards of a million souls, bound together by every thing that constitutes the unity of a people. The avarice and injustice of the Roman authorities negatived the clause of the agreement that stipulated for the surrender of the Gothic arms. To redeem their swords and spears, they parted with the silver and gold they had amassed in their predatory incursions on the Roman territory. They knew that once in possession of their weapons they could soon reclaim all they gave—and in no long time the attempt was made. Fritigern, the leader of their name, led them against the armies of Rome. Insulted at their audacity, the Emperor Valens, at the head of three hundred thousand men, met them in the plain of Adrianople. The exist-
A.D. 379. ence of the Gothic people was at stake. They fought with desperation and hatred. The emperor was defeated, leaving two-thirds of his army on the field of battle. Seeking safety in a cottage at the side of the road, he was burned by the inexorable pursuers, who, gathering up their broken lines, marched steadily through the intervening levels and gazed with enraptured eyes on the glittering towers and pinnacles of Constantinople itself. But the walls were high and strongly armed. The barbarians were inveigled into a negotiation, and mastered by the unequal powers of lying,

at all times characteristic of the Greeks. Fritigern consented to withdraw his troops: some were embodied in the levies of the empire, and others dispersed in different provinces. Those settled in Thrace were faithful to their employers, and resisted their ancient enemies the Huns; but the great body of the discontented conquerors were ready for fresh assaults on the Roman land. Theodosius, called to the throne in 379, succeeded in staving off the evil day; but when the final partition of the empire took place between his two sons—Honorius and

A.D. 394. Arcadius—there was nothing to oppose the terrible onset of the Goths. At their head was Alaric, the descendant of their original chiefs, and himself the bravest of his warriors. He broke into Greece, forcing his way through Thermopylæ, and devastated the native seats of poetry and the arts with fire and sword. The ruler at Constantinople heard of his advance with terror, and opposed to him the Vandal Stilicho, the greatest of his generals. But the wily Alaric declined to fight, and out-manœuvred his enemies, escaping to the sure fastnesses of Epirus, and sat down sullen and discontented, meditating further expeditions into richer plains, and already seeing before him the prostrate cities of Italy. The terror of Arcadius tried in vain to soften his rage, or satisfy his ambition with vain titles, among others, that of Count of the Illyrian Border. The spirit of aggression was fairly roused. All the Gothic settlers in the Roman territory were ready to join their countrymen in one great and combined attack; —and with this position of the personages of the drama, the curtain falls on the fourth century, while preparations for the great catastrophe are going on.

FIFTH CENTURY.

Emperors.

A.D.	West.	A.D.	East.
	Honorius—(*cont.*)		Arcadius—(*cont.*)
424.	Valentinian III.	408.	Theodosius II.
455.	Petronius Maximus.	450.	Marcian.
455.	Avitus.	457.	Leo the Great.
457.	Majorianus.	474.	Zeno.
461.	Severus.	491.	Anastasius.
467.	Anthemius.		
472.	Olibius.		
473.	Glycerius.		
474.	Julius Nepos.		
475.	Augustulus Romulus.		

King of the Franks.

481. Clovis.

King of Italy.

489. Theodoric.

Authors.

Chrysostom, Jerome, Augustine, Pelagius, (405,) Sidonius Apollinaris, Patricius, Macrobius, Vicentius of Lerins, (died 450,) Cyril, Bishop of Alexandria, (412–444.)

THE FIFTH CENTURY.

END OF THE ROMAN EMPIRE—FORMATION OF MODERN STATES—GROWTH OF ECCLESIASTICAL AUTHORITY.

We find the same actors on the stage when the curtain rises again, but circumstances have greatly changed. After his escape from Stilicho, Alaric had been "lifted on the shield," the wild and picturesque way in which the warlike Goths nominated their kings, and henceforth was considered the monarch of a separate and independent people, no longer the mere leader of a band of predatory barbarians. In this new character he entered into treaties with the emperors of Constantinople or Rome, and broke them, as if he had already been the sovereign of a civilized state.

In 403 he broke up from his secure retreat on the Adriatic, and burst into Italy, spreading fire and famine wherever he went. Honorius, the Emperor of the West, fled from Milan, and was besieged in Asti by the Goths. Here would have ended the imperial dynasty, some years before its time, if it had not been for the watchful Stilicho. This Vandal chief flew to the rescue of Honorius, repulsed Alaric with great slaughter, and delivered his master from his dangerous position. The grateful emperor entered Rome in triumph, and for the last time the Circus streamed with the blood of beasts and men. He retired after this display to the inaccessible marshes of Ravenna, at the mouths of the Po, and, secure in that fortress, sent an order to have his preserver and

A.D. 408. benefactor murdered; Stilicho, the only hope of Rome, was assassinated, and Alaric once more saw all Italy within his grasp. It was not only the Goths who followed Alaric's command. All the barbarians, of whatever name or race, who had been transplanted either as slaves or soldiers—Alans, Franks, and Germans—rallied round the advancing king, for the impolitic Honorius had issued an order for the extermination of all the tribes. There were Britons, and Saxons, and Suabians. It was an insurrection of all the manly elements of society against the indescribable depravation of the inhabitants of the Peninsula. The wildest barbarian blushed in the midst of his ignorance and rudeness to hear of the manners of the highest and most distinguished families in Rome. Nobody could hold out a hand to avert the judgment that was about to fall on the devoted city. Ambassadors indeed appeared, and bought a short delay at the price of many thousand pounds' weight of gold and silver, and of large quantities of silk; but these were only additional incitements to the cupidity of the invader. Tribe after tribe rose up with fresh fury; warriors of every hue and shape, and with every manner of equipment. The handsome Goth in his iron cuirass; the Alan with his saddle covered with human skin; the German making a hideous sound by shrieking on the sharp edge of his shield; and the countryman of Alaric himself sounding the "horn of battle," which terrified the Romans with its ominous note—all started forward on the march. At the head of each detachment rode a band, singing songs of exultation and defiance; and the Romans, stupefied with fear, saw these innumerable swarms defile towards the Milvian bridge and close up every access to the town. There was no corn from Sicily or Africa; a pest raged in every house, and hunger reduced the inhabitants to despair. The gates were thrown open, and all the pent-up animosity of the desert was poured out upon the mistress and corrupter of the world. For six days the city was given up to remorseless slaughter and universal pillage. The wealth was incalculable. The captives were sold as slaves. The palaces were overthrown, and the river choked with carcasses and the treasures of art which the barbarians could not appreciate. "The new Babylon," cries Bossuet, the great Bishop of Meaux, "rival of the old, swelled out like her with her successes, and, triumphing in her pleasures and riches, encountered as great a fall." And no man lamented her fate.

Alaric, who had thus achieved a victory denied to Hannibal and Pyrrhus, resolved to push his conquests to the end of Italy. But on his march towards the Straits of Sicily, illness overtook him. His life had been unlike that of other men, and his burial was to excite the wonder of the Bruttians, among whom he died. A large river was turned from its course, and in its channel a deep grave was dug and ornamented with monumental stone. To this the body of the barbaric king was carried, clothed in full armour, and accompanied with some of the richest spoils of Rome; and then the stream was turned on again; the prisoners who had executed the works were slaughtered to conceal the secret of the tomb, and nobody has ever found out where the Gothic king reposes. But while the Busentino flowed peaceably on, and guarded the body of the conqueror from the revenge of the Romans, new perils were gathering round the throne of the Western emperor. As if the duration of the empire had been inseparably connected with the capital, the reverence of mankind was never bestowed on Milan or Ravenna, in which the court was now established, as it had been upon Rome. Britain had already thrown off

A.D. 410.

the distant yoke, and submitted to the Saxon invaders. Spain had also peaceably accepted the rule of the three kindred tribes of Sueves and Alans and Vandals. Gaul itself had given its adhesion to the Burgundians (who fixed their seat in the district which still bears their name) and offered a feeble resistance to any fresh invader. Ataulf, the brother of Alaric, came to the rescue of the empire, and of course completed the destruction. He married the sister of Honorius, and retained her as a hostage of the emperor's good faith. He promised to restore the revolted provinces to their former master, and succeeded in overthrowing some competitors who had started up to dispute with Ravenna the wrecks of former power. He then forced his way into Spain, and the hopes of the degenerate Romans were high. But murder, as usual, stopped the career of Ataulf, and all was changed. The emperor ratified the possessions
A.D. 415. which he could not dispute, and in the first twenty years of this century three separate kingdoms were established in Europe. This was soon followed by a Vandal conquest of the shores of Africa, which raised Carthage once more to commercial importance, united Sicily, Corsica, and Sardinia to the new-founded state, and by the creation of a fleet gained the command of the Mediterranean Sea, and threatened Constantinople itself.

With so many provinces not only torn from the empire, but erected into hostile kingdoms, nothing was wanting but some new irruption into the still dependent territories to put a final end to the Roman name. And a new incursion came. In the very involved relations existing between the emperors of the East and West, it is difficult to follow the course of events with any clearness. While the deluded populace of Constantinople were rejoicing in the fall of their Italian rival, they heard with amazement, in 441, that a savage potentate, who had pitched his tents in the plains of Pannonia and Thrace, and kept round him, for defence or conquest, seven hundred thousand of those hideous-featured Huns who had spread devastation and terror all over the populations of Asia, from the borders of China to the Don, had determined on stretching his conquests over the whole world, and merely hesitated with which of the doomed empires to begin his career. His name was Attila, or, according to its native pronunciation, Etzel; and it soon resounded, louder and more terrifying than that of Alaric the Goth. The Emperor of the East sent an embassy to this dreadful neighbour, a minute account of which remains, and from which we learn the barbaric pomp and ceremony of the leader of the Huns, and the perfidy and debasement of the Greeks. An attempt was made to poison the redoubtable chief, and he complained of the guilty ambassador to the very person who had given him his instructions for the deed. Unsatisfied with the result, the Hunnish monarch advanced his camp. Constantinople, anxious to ward off the blow from itself, descanted to the savage king on the exposed condition and ill-defended wealth of the Italian towns. Treachery of another kind came to his aid. An offended sister of the emperor sent to Attila her ring as a mark of espousal, and he now claimed a portion of the empire as the dowry of his bride. When this was refused, he reiterated his old claim of satisfaction for the attempt upon his life, and ravaged the fields of Belgium and Gaul, in the double character of avenger of an insult and claimant of an inheritance. It does not much matter under what plea a barbarous chieftain, with six hundred thousand warriors, makes a demand. It must be answered sword in hand, or on the knees. The newly-established Frankish and Burgundian kings gathered their forces in defence of their Christian faith and their recently-acquired dominions. Attila retired from Orleans, of which he had commenced the siege, and chose for the battle-field, which was to decide the destiny of the world, a vast plain not far from Châlons, on the Marne, where his cavalry would have room to act, and waited the assault of all the forces that France and Italy could collect. The Visigoths prepared for the decisive engagement under their king, Theodoric; the Franks of the Saal under Meroveg; the Ripuarian Franks, the Saxons, and the Burgundians were under leaders of their own. A.D. 451. It was a fight in which were brought face to face the two conquering races of the world, and upon its result it depended whether Europe was to be ruled by a dynasty of Calmucks or left to her free progress under her Gothic and Teutonic kings. Three hundred thousand corpses marked the severity of the struggle, but victory rested with the West. Attila retreated from Gaul, and wreaked his vengeance on the Italian cities. He destroyed Aquileia, whose terrified inhabitants hid themselves in the marshes and lagoons which afterwards bore the palaces of Venice; Vicenza, Padua, and Verona were spoiled and burned. Pavia and Milan submitted without resistance. On approaching Rome, the venerable bishop, Saint Leo, met the devastating Hun, and by the gravity of his appearance, the ransom he offered, and perhaps the mystic dignity which still rested upon the city whose cause he pleaded, prevailed on him to retire. Shortly after, the chief of this brief and terrible visitation died in his tent on the banks of the Danube, and left no lasting memorial of his irruption except the depopulation his cruelty had caused, and the ruin he had spread over some of the fairest regions of the earth.

But Rome, spared by the influence of the bishop from

the ravage of the Huns, could not escape the destroying enmity of Genseric and the Vandals. Dashing across from Africa, these furious conquerors destroyed for destruction's sake, and affixed the name of Vandalism on whatever is harsh and unrefined. For fourteen days the spoilers were at work in Rome, and it is only wonderful that after so many plunderings any thing worth plundering remained. When the sated Vandals crossed to Carthage again, the Gothic and Suevic kings gave the purple to whatever puppet they chose. Afraid still to invest themselves with the insignia of the Imperial power, they bestowed them or took them away, and at last rendered the throne and the crown so contemptible, that when Odoacer was proclaimed King of Italy, the phantom assembly which still called itself the Roman Senate sent back to Constantinople the tiara and purple robe, in sign that the Western Empire had passed away. Zeno, the Eastern ruler, retained the ornaments of the departed sovereignty, and sent to the Herulean Odoacer the title of "Patrician," sole emblem left of the greatness and antiquity of the Roman name. It may be interesting to remember that the last who wore the Imperial crown was a youth who would probably have escaped the recognition of posterity altogether, if he had not, by a sort of cruel mockery of his misfortunes, borne the names of Romulus Augustulus—the former recalling the great founder of the city, and the latter the first of the Imperial line.

Thus, then, in 476, Rome came to her deserved and terrible end; and before we trace the influence of this great event upon the succeeding centuries, it will be worth while to devote a few words to the cause of its overthrow. These were evidently three—the ineradicable barbarity and selfishness of the Roman character, the depravation of manners in the capital, and the want of some combining influence to bind all the parts of the various empire into a whole. From the earliest incidents in the history of Rome, we gather that she was utterly regardless of human life or suffering. Her treatment of her vanquished enemies, and her laws upon parental authority, upon slaves and debtors, show the pitiless disposition of her people. Look at her citizens at any period of her career—her populace or her consuls—in the field of battle or in the forum, you will always find them the true descendants of those blood-stained refugees, who established their den of robbers on the seven hills, and pretended they were led by a man who had been suckled by a wolf. While conquest was their object, this sanguinary disposition enabled them to perform great exploits; but when victory had secured to them the blessings of peace and safety, the same thirst for excitement continued. They cried out for blood in the amphitheatre, and had no pleasure in any display which was not accompanied with pain. The rival chief who had perilled their supremacy in the field was led in ferocious triumph at the wheel of his conqueror, and beheaded or flogged to death at the gate of the Capitol. The wounded gladiator looked round the benches of the arena in hopes of seeing the thumbs of the spectators turned down—the signal for his life being spared; but matrons and maids, the high and the low, looked with unmoved faces upon his agonies, and gave the signal for his death without remorse. They were the same people, even in their amusements, who gave order for the destruction of Numantium and Carthage. But cruelty was not enough. They sank into the wildest vices of sensuality, and lost the dignity of manhood, and the last feelings of self-respect. Never was a nation so easily habituated to slavery. They licked the hand that struck them hardest. They hung garlands for a long time on the tomb of Nero. They insisted on being revenged on the murderers of Commodus, and frequently slew more citizens in broils in the street and quarrels in the theatre, than had fought at Cannæ or Zama. It might have been hoped that the cruelty which characterized the days of their military aggression would be softened down when they had become the acknowledged rulers of the world. Luxury itself, it might be thought, would be inconsistent with the sight of blood. But in this utterly detestable race the two extremes of human society seemed to have the same result. The brutal, half-clothed savage of an early age conveyed his tastes as well as his conquests to the enervated voluptuary of the empire. The virtues, such as they were, of that former period—contempt of danger, unfaltering resolution, and a certain simplicity of life—had departed, and all the bad features were exaggerated. Religion also had disappeared. Even a false religion, if sincerely entertained, is a bond of union among all who profess its faith. But between Rome and its colonies, and between man and man, there was soon no community of belief. The sweltering wretches in the Forum sneered at the existence of Bacchus in the midst of his mysteries, and imitated the actions of their gods, while they laughed at the hypocrisy of priests and augurs, who treated them as divine. A cruel, depraved, godless people—these were the Romans who had enslaved the world with their arms and corrupted it with their civilization. When their capital fell, men felt relieved from a burden and shame. The lessons of Christianity had been thrown away on a population too gross and too truculent to receive them. Some of gentler mould than others had received the Saviour; but to the mass of Romans the language of peace and justice, of forgiveness and brotherhood, was unknown. It was to be the worthier recipients of a pure and elevating faith, that the Goth was called from his wilderness and the German from his forest.

But the faith had to be purified itself before it was fitted for the reception of the new conquerors of the world. The dissensions of the Christian Churches had added only a fresh element of weakness to the empire of Rome. There were heretics everywhere, supporting their opinions with bigotry and violence—Arians, Sabellians, Montanists, and fifty names besides. Torn by these parties, dishonoured by pretended conversions, the result of flattery and ambition, the Christian Church was further weakened by the effect of wealth and luxury upon its chiefs. While contending with rival sects upon some point of discipline or doctrine, they made themselves so notorious for the desire of riches, and the infamous arts they practised to get themselves appointed heirs of the rich members of their congregations, that a law was passed making a conveyance in favour of a priest invalid. And it is not from Pagan enemies or heretical rivals we learn this—it is from the letters still extant of the most honoured Fathers of the Church. One of them tells us that the Prefect Pretextatus, alluding to the luxury of the Pontiffs, and to the magnificence of their apparel, said to Pope Damasus, "Make me Bishop of Rome, and I will turn Christian." "Far, then," says a Roman Catholic historian of our own day, "from strengthening the Roman world with its virtues, the Christian society seemed to have adopted the vices it was its office to overcome." But the fall of Roman power was the resurrection of Christianity. It had a Resurrection, because it had had a Death, and a new world was now prepared for its reception. Its everlasting truths, indeed, had been full of life and vigour all through the sad period of Roman depravation, but the ground was unfitted for their growth; and the great characteristic of this century is not the conquest of Rome by Alaric the Goth, or the dreadful assault on Europe by Attila the Hun, or the final abolition of the old capital of the world by Odoacer the Herulean, but rather the ecclesiastical chaos which spread over the earth. The age of martyrs had passed —the philosophers had begun their pestiferous tamperings with the facts of revelation—and over all rioted and stormed an ambitious and worldly priesthood, who hated their opponents with more bitterness than the heathens had displayed against the Christians, and ran wild in every species of lawlessness and vice. The deserts and caves which used to give retreat to meditative worshippers or timid believers, now teemed with thousands of furious and fanatical monks, who rushed occasionally into the great cities of the empire, and filled their streets with blood and rapine. Guided by no less fanatical bishops, they spread murder and terror over whole provinces. Alexandria stood in more fear of these professed recluses than of an army of hostile soldiers. "There is a race," says Eunapius, "called monks—men indeed in form, but hogs in life, who practise and allow abominable things. Whoever wears a black robe, and is not ashamed of filthy garments, and presents a dirty face to the public view, obtains a tyrannical authority." False miracles, absurd prophecies, and ludicrous visions were the instruments with which these and other impostors established their power. Mad enthusiasts imprisoned themselves in dungeons, or exposed themselves on the tops of pillars, naked, except by the growth of their tangled hair, and the coating of filth upon their persons,—and gained credit among the ignorant for self-denial and abnegation of the world.

All the high offices of the Church were so lucrative and honourable as to be the object of universal desire.

To be established archbishop of a diocese cost more lives than the conquest of a province. When the Christian community needed support from without, they had recourse to some rich or powerful individual, some general of an army, or governor of a district, and begged him to assume the pastoral staff in exchange for his military sword. Sometimes the assembled crowd cried out the name of a favourite who was not even known to be a Christian, and the mitre was conveyed by acclamation to a person who had to undergo the ceremonies of baptism and ordination before he could place it on his head. Sometimes the exigencies of the congregation required a scholar or an orator for its head. It applied to a philosopher to undertake its direction. He objected that his philosophy had been declared inconsistent with the Christian faith, and his mode of life contrary to Christian precept. They forgave him his philosophy, his horses and hounds, his wife and children, and constituted him their chief. Age was of no consequence. A youth of eighteen has been saluted bishop by a cry which seemed to the multitude the direct inspiration of Heaven, and seated in the chair of his dignity almost without his knowledge. Once established on his episcopal seat, he had no superier. The Roman Bishop had not yet asserted his supremacy over the Church. Each prelate was sovereign Pontiff of his own see, and his doctrines for a long time regulated the doctrines of his flock. Under former bishops, Milan had been Arian, under Ambrose it was orthodox, and with a change of master might have been Arian again. The emperors had occasionally interfered with their authoritative decisions, but generally the dispute was left in divided dioceses to be settled by argument, when the rivals' tempers allowed such a mode of warfare, but more frequently by armed bands of the retainers of the respective creeds, and sometimes by an appeal to miracles. But with this century a new spirit of bitterness was let loose upon the Church. Councils were held, at which the doctrines of the minority were declared dangerous to the State, and the civil power was invoked to carry the sentence into effect. In Africa, where the great name of Augustin of Hippo admitted no opposition, the Donatists, though represented by no less than two hundred and seventy-nine prelates, were condemned as heretics, and given over to the persecuting sword. But in other quarters the dissidents looked for support to the civil power, when it happened to be of their opinion in Church affairs. Rome chose Clovis, the politic and energetic Frank, for its guardian and protector, and the Arians threw themselves in the same way on the support of the Visigoths and Burgundians. A difference of faith became a pretext for war. Clovis, who envied his neighbours their territories south of the Loire, led an expedition against them, crying, "It is shameful to see those Arians in possession of such goodly lands!" and everywhere a vast activity was perceptible in the Church, because its interests were now connected with those of kings and peoples. In earlier times, discussions were carried on on a great variety of doctrines which, though widely spread, were not yet authoritatively declared to be articles of faith. St. Jerome himself, and others, had had to defend their opinions against the attacks of various adversaries, who, without ceasing to be considered true members of the Church, wrote powerfully against the worship of martyrs and their relics; against the miracles professedly wrought at their tombs; against fasting, austerities, and celibacy. No appeal was made on those occasions either to the Bishop of Rome as head of the Church, or to the emperor as head of the State. Now, however, the spirit of moderation was banished, and the decrees of councils were considered superior to private or even diocesan judgment. Life and freedom of discussion were at an end under an enforced and rigid uniformity. But the struggle lasted through the century. It was the period of great convulsions in the State, and disputations, wranglings, and struggle in the Church. How these, in a State tortured by perpetual change, and a Church filled with energy and fire, acted upon each other, may easily be supposed. The doubtful and unsteady civil government had subordinated itself to the turbulent ardour of the perplexed but highly-animated Church. After the conquest of Rome, where was the barbaric conqueror to look for any guide to internal unity, or any relic of the vanished empire by which to connect himself with the past? There was only the Church, which was now not only the professed teacher of obedience, peace, and holiness, but the only undestroyed institution of the State. The old population of Rome had been wasted by the sword, and famine, and deportation. The emperors of the West had left the scene; the Roman Senate was no more. There was but one authority which had any influence on the wretched crowd who had returned to their ancient capital, or sought refuge in its ruined palaces or grass-grown streets from the pursuit of their foes; and that was the Bishop of the Christian congregation—whose palace had been given to him by Constantine—who claimed already the inheritance of St. Peter—and who carried to the new government either the support of a willing people, or the enmity of a seditious mob.

A.D. 489. A new hero came upon the scene in the person of Theodoric, the Ostrogoth. Odoacer tried in vain to resist the two hundred thousand warriors of this tribe who poured upon Italy in 490, and, after a long resistance in Ravenna, yielded the kingdom of Italy to his rival. Theodoric, though an Arian, cultivated the good opinion of the orthodox, and gained the favour of the Roman Bishop. He had almost a superstitious veneration for the dignities of ancient Rome. He treated with respect an assembly which called itself the Senate, but did not allow his love of antiquity to blind him to the degeneracy of the present race. He interdicted arms to all men of Roman blood, and tried in vain to prevent his followers from using the appellation "Roman" as their bitterest form of contempt. Lands were distributed to his followers, and they occupied and improved a full third of Italy. Equal laws were provided for both populations, but he forbade the toga and the schools to his countrymen, and left the studies and refinements of life, and offices of civil dignity, to the native race. The hand that holds the pen, he said, becomes unfitted for the sword. But, barbarian as he was called, he restored the prosperity which the fairest region of the earth had lost under the emperors. Bridges, aqueducts, theatres, baths, were repaired; palaces and churches built. Agriculture was encouraged, attempts were made to drain the Pontine Marshes; iron-mines were worked in Dalmatia, and gold-mines in Bruttium. Large fleets protected the coasts of the Mediterranean from pirates and invaders. Population increased, taxes were diminished; and a ruler who could neither read nor write attracted to his court all the learned men of his time. Already the energy of a new and enterprising people was felt to the extremities of his dominions. A new race, also, was established in Gaul. Klodwig, leader of the Franks, received baptism at the hands of St. Remi in 496, and began the great line of French rulers, who, passing his name through the softened sound of Clovis, presented, in the different families who succeeded him, eighteen kings of the name of Louis, as if commemorative of the founder of the monarchy.

In England the petty kingdoms of the Heptarchy were in the course of formation, and though, when viewed closely, we seemed a divided and even hostile collection of individual tribes, the historian combines the separate elements, and tells us that, before the fifth century expired, another branch of the barbarians had settled into form and order, and that the Anglo-Saxon race had taken possession of its place.

With these newly-founded States rising with fresh vigour from among the decayed and festering remains of an older society, we look hopefully forward to what the future years will show us.

SIXTH CENTURY.

Kings of the Franks.

A.D.

CLOVIS.—(*cont.*)

511. CHILDEBERT, THIERRY, CLOTAIRE, CLODOMIR.

559. CLOTAIRE (sole king).

562. CHARIBERT, GONTRAN, SIGEBERT and CHILDERIC.

584. CLOTAIRE II., (of Soissons.)

596. THIERRY II., THEODOBERT, (of Paris and Austrasia.)

Emperors of the East.

A.D.

ANASTASIUS.—(*cont.*)

518. JUSTIN.

527. JUSTINIAN I.

565. JUSTIN II.

578. TIBERIUS II.

582. MAURICE.

Authors.

BÖETHIUS, PROCOPIUS, GILDAS, GREGORY OF TOURS, COLUMBA, (520–597,) PRISCIAN, COLUMBANUS, BENEDICT, EVAGRIUS, (SCHOLASTICUS,) FULGENTIUS, GREGORY THE GREAT.

THE SIXTH CENTURY.

BELISARIUS AND NARSES IN ITALY—SETTLEMENT OF THE LOMBARDS—LAWS OF JUSTINIAN—BIRTH OF MOHAMMED.

THEODORIC, though not laying claim to universal empire in right of his possession of Rome and Italy, exercised a sort of supremacy over his contemporaries by his wisdom and power. He also strengthened his position by family alliances. His wife was sister of Klodwig or Clovis, King of the Franks. He married his own sister to Hunric, King of the Vandals, his niece to the Thuringian king. One of his daughters he gave to Sigismund, King of the Burgundians, and the other to Alaric the Second, King of the Visigoths. Relying on the double influence which his relationship and reputation secured to him, he rebuked or praised the potentates of Europe as if they had been his children, and gave them advice in the various exigencies of their affairs, to which they implicitly submitted. He would fain have kept alive what was left of the old Roman civilization, and heaped honours on the Senator Cassiodorus, one of the last writers of Rome. "We send you this man as ambassador," he said to the King of the Burgundians, "that your people may no longer pretend to be our equals when they perceive what manner of men we have among us." But his rule, though generous, was strict. He imprisoned the Bishop of Rome for disobedience of orders in a commission he had given him, and repressed discontent and the quarrels of the factions with an unsparing hand. But the death of this great and wise sovereign showed on what unstable foundations a barbaric power is built. Frightful tragedies were enacted in his family. His daughter was murdered by her nephew, whom she had associated with her in the guardianship of her son. But vengeance overtook the wrong-doer, and a strange revolution occurred in the history of the world. The emperor reigning at Constantinople was the celebrated Justinian. He saw into what a confused condition the affairs of the new conquerors of Italy had fallen. Rallying round him all the recollections of the past—giving command of his armies to one of the great men who start up unexpectedly in the most hopeless periods of history, whose name, Belisarius, still continues to be familiar to our ears—and rousing the hostile nationalities to come to his aid, he poured into the peninsula an army with Roman discipline and the union which community of interests affords. In a remarkably short space of time, Belisarius achieved the conquest of Italy. The opposing soldiers threw down their arms at sight of the well-remembered eagles. The nations threw off the supremacy of the Ostrogoths. Belisarius had already overthrown the kingdom of the Vandals and restored Africa to the empire of the East. He took Naples, and put the inhabitants to the sword. He advanced upon Rome, which the Goths deserted at his approach. The walls of the great city were restored, and a victory over the fugitives at Perugia seemed to secure the whole land to its ancient masters. But Witig, the Ostrogoth, gathered courage from despair. He besought assistance from the Franks, who had now taken possession of Burgundy; and volunteers from all quarters flocked to his standard, for he had promised them the spoils of Milan. Milan was immensely rich, and had espoused the orthodox faith. The assailants

A.D. 535.

were Arians, and intent on plunder. Such destruction had scarcely been seen since the memorable slaughter of the Huns at Châlons on the Marne. The Ostrogoths and Burgundian Franks broke into the town, and the streets were piled up with the corpses of all the inhabitants. There were three hundred thousand put to death, and multitudes had died of famine and disease. The ferocity was useless, and Belisarius was already on the march; Witig was conquered, in open fight, while he was busy besieging Rome; Ravenna itself, his capital, was taken, and the Ostrogothic king was led in triumph along the streets of Constantinople.

But the conqueror of the Ostrogoths fell into disfavour at court. He was summoned home, and a great man, whom his presence in Italy had kept in check, availed himself of his absence. Totila seemed indeed worthy to succeed to the empire of his countryman Theodoric. He again peopled the utterly exhausted Rome; he restored its buildings, and lived among the new-comers himself, encouraging their efforts to give it once more the appearance of the capital of the world. But these efforts were in vain. There was no possibility of reviving the old fiction of the identity of the freshly-imported inhabitants and the countrymen of Scipio and Cæsar. Only one link was possible between the old state of things and the new. It was strange that it was left for the Christian Bishop to bridge over the chasm that separated the Rome of the Consulship and the Empire from the capital of the Goths. Yet so it was. While the short duration of the reigns of the barbaric kings prevented the most sanguine from looking forward to the stability of any power for the future, the immunity already granted to the clerical order, and the sanctuary afforded, in the midst of the wildest excesses of siege and storm, by their shrines and churches,

A.D. 540.

had affixed a character of inviolability and permanence to the influence of the ecclesiastical chief. At Constantinople, the presence of the sovereign, who affected a grandeur to which the pretensions to divinity of the Roman emperors had been modesty and simplicity, kept the dignity of the Bishop in a very secondary place. But at Rome there was no one left to dispute his rank. His office claimed a duration of upwards of four hundred years; and though at first his predecessors had been fugitives and martyrs, and even now his power had no foundation except in the willing obedience of the members of his flock, the necessity of his position had forced him to extend his claims beyond the mere requirements of his spiritual rule. During the ephemeral occupations of the city by Vandals and Huns and Ostrogoths, and all the tribes who successively took possession of the great capital, he had been recognised as the representative of the most influential portion of the inhabitants. As it naturally followed that the higher the rank of a ruler or intercessor was, the more likely his success would be, the Christians of the orthodox persuasion had the wisdom to raise their Bishop as high as they could. He had stood between the devoted city and the Huns; he had promised obedience or threatened resistance to the Goths, according to the conduct pursued with regard to his flock by the conquerors. He had also lent to Belisarius all the weight of his authority in restoring the power of the emperors, and from this time the Bishop of Rome became a great civil as well as ecclesiastical officer. All parties in turn united in trying to win him over to their cause—the Arian kings, by kindness and forbearance to his adherents; and the orthodox, by increasing the rights and privileges of his see. And already the policy of the Roman Pontiffs began to take the path it has never deserted since. They looked out in all quarters for assistance in their schemes of ambition and conquest. Emissaries were despatched into many nations to convert them, not from heathenism to Christianity, but from independence to an acknowledgment of their subjection to Rome. It was seen already that a great spiritual empire might be founded upon the ruins of the old Roman world, and spread itself over the perplexed and unstable politics of the barbaric tribes. No means, accordingly, were left untried to extend the conquests of the spiritual Cæsar. When Clovis the Frank was converted by the entreaties of his wife from Arianism to the creed of the Roman Church, the orthodox bishops of France considered it a victory over their enemies, though these enemies were their countrymen and neighbours. And from henceforth we find the different confessions of faith to have more influence in the setting up or overthrowing of kingdoms than the strength of armies or the skill of generals. Narses, who was appointed the successor of Belisarius, was a believer in the decrees of the Council of Nice. His orthodoxy won him the support of all the orthodox Huns and Heruleans and Lombards, who formed an army of infuriated missionaries rather than of soldiers, and gained to his cause the majority of the Ostrogoths whom it was his task to fight. Totila in vain tried to bear up against this invasion. The heretical Ostrogoths, expelled from the towns by their orthodox fellow-citizens, and ill supported by the inhabitants of the lands they traversed, were defeated in several battles; and at last, when the resisting forces were reduced to the paltry number of seven thousand men, their spirits broken by defeat, and a continuance in Italy made useless by the hostile feelings of the population, they applied to Narses for some means of saving their lives. He furnished them with vessels, which carried them from the lands which, sixty years before, had been assigned them by the great Theodoric, and they found an obscure termination to so strange and checkered a career, by being lost and mingled in the crowded populations of Constantinople. This was in 553. The Ostrogoths disappear from history. The Visigoths have still a settlement at the southwest of France and in the rich regions of Spain, but they are isolated by their position, and are divided into different branches. The Franks are a great and seemingly well-cemented race between the Rhine and the sea. The Burgundians have a form of government and code of laws which keep them distinct and powerful. There are nations rising into independence in Germany. In England, Christianity has formed a bond which practically gives firmness and unity to the kingdoms of the Heptarchy; and it might be expected that, having seen so many tribes of strange and varying aspect emerge from the unknown regions of the East, we should have little to do but watch the gradual enlightenment of those various races, and see them assuming, by slow degrees, their present respective places; but the undiscovered extremities of the earth were again to pour forth a swarm of invaders, who plunged Italy back into its old state of barbarism and oppression, and established a new people in the midst of its already confused and intermixed populations.

Somewhere up between the Aller and the Oder there had been settled, from some unknown period, a people of wild and uncultivated habits, who had occasionally appeared in small detachments in the various gatherings of barbarians who had forced their way into the South. Following the irresistible impulse which seems to impel all the settlers in the North, they traversed the regions already occupied by the Heruleans and the Gepides, and paused, as all previous invasions had done, on the outer boundary of the Danube. These were the Longobards or Lombards, so called from the spears, *bardi*, with which they were armed; and not long they required to wait till a favourable opportunity occurred for them to cross the stream. In the hurried levies of Narses some of them had offered their services, and had been present at the victory over Totila the Goth. They returned, in all probability, to their companions, and soon the hearts of the whole tribe were set upon the conquest of the beautiful region their countrymen had seen. If they hesitated to undertake so long an expedition, two incidents occurred which made it indispensable. Flying in wild fury and dismay from the face of a pursuing enemy, the Avars, themselves a ferocious Asiatic horde which had terrified the Eastern Empire, came and joined themselves to the Lombards. With united forces, all their tents, and wives and children, their horses and cattle, this dreadful alliance began their progress to Italy. The other incident was, that in revenge for the injustice of his master, and dreading his further malice, Narses himself invited their assistance. Alboin, the Lombard king, was chief of the expedition. He had been refused the hand of Rosamund, the daughter of Cunimond, chief of the Gepides. He poured the combined armies of Lombards and Avars upon the unfortunate tribe, slew the king with his own hand, and, according to the inhuman fashion of his race, formed his drinking-cup of his enemy's skull. He married Rosamund, and pursued his victorious career. He crossed the Julian Alps, made himself master of Milan and the dependent territories, and was lifted on the shield as King of Italy. At a festival in honour of his successes, he forced his favourite wine-goblet into the hands of his wife. She recognised the fearful vessel, and shuddered while she put her lips to the brim. But hatred took possession of her heart. She promised her hand and throne to Kilmich, one of her attendants, if he would take vengeance on the tyrant who had offered her so intolerable a wrong. The attendant was won by the bride, and slew Alboin. But justice pursued the murderers. They were discovered, and fled to Ravenna, where the Exarch held his court. Saved thus from human retribution, Rosamund brought her fate upon herself. Captivated with the prospect of marrying the Exarch, she presented a poisoned cup to Kilmich, now become her husband, as he came from the bath. The effect was immediate, and the agonies he felt told him too surely the author of his death. He just lived long enough to stab the wretched woman with his dagger, and this frightful domestic tragedy was brought to a close.

A.D. 575.

Alboin had divided his dominion into many little states and dukedoms. A kind of anarchy succeeded the strong government of the remorseless and clear-sighted king, and enemies began to arise in different directions. The Franks from the south of France began to cross the Alps. The Greek settlements began to menace the Lombards from the South. Internal disunion was quelled by the public danger, and Antharis, the son of Cleph, was nominated king. To strengthen himself against the orthodox Franks, he professed himself a Christian and joined the Arian communion. With the aid of his co-religionists he repelled the invaders, and had time, in the intervals of their assaults, to extend his conquests to the south of the peninsula. There he overthrew the settlements which owned the Empire of the East; and coming to the extreme end of Italy, the savage ruler pushed his war-horse into the water as deep as it would go, and, standing up in his stirrups, threw forward his javelin with all his strength, saying, "That is the boundary of the Lombard power." Unhappily for the unity of that distracted land, the warrior's boast was unfounded, and it has continued ever since a prey to discord and division. Another kingdom, however, was added to the roll of European states; and this was the last settlement permanently made on the old Roman territory.

A.D. 591.

The Lombards were a less civilized horde than any of their predecessors. The Ostrogoths had rapidly assimilated themselves to the people who surrounded them, but the Lombards looked with haughty disdain on the population they had subdued. By portioning the country among the chiefs of the expedition, they commenced the first experiment on a great scale of what afterwards expanded into the feudal system. There were among them, as among the other northern settlers, an elective king and an hereditary nobility, owing suit and service to their chief, and exacting the same from their dependants; and already we see the working of this similarity of constitution in the diffusion throughout the whole of Europe of the monarchical and aristocratic principle, which is still the characteristic of most of our modern states. From this century some authors date the origin of what are called the "Middle Ages," forming the great and obscure gulf between ancient and modern times. Others, indeed, wish to fix the commencement of the Middle Ages at a much earlier date—even so far back as the reign of Constantine. They found this inclination on the fact that to him we are indebted for the settlement of barbarians within the empire, and the institution of a titled nobility dependent on the crown. But many things were needed besides these to constitute the state of manners and polity which we recognise as those of the Middle Ages, and above them all the establishment of the monarchical principle in ecclesiastical government, and the recognition of a sovereign priest. This was now close at hand, and its approach was heralded by many appearances.

How, indeed, could the Church deprive itself of the organization which it saw so powerful and so successful in civil affairs? A machinery was all ready to produce an exact copy of the forms of temporal administration. There were bishops to be analogous to the great feudataries of the crown; priests and rectors to represent the smaller freeholders dependent on the greater barons; but where was the monarch by whom the whole system was to be combined and all the links of the great chain held together by a point of central union? The want of this had been so felt, that we might naturally have expected a claim to universal superiority to have long ere this been made by a Pope of Rome, the ancient seat of the temporal power. But with his residence perpetually a prey to fresh inroads, a heretical king merely granting him toleration and protection, the pretension would have been too absurd during the troubles of Italy, and it was not advanced for several years. The necessity of the case, however, was such, that a voice was heard from another quarter calling for universal obedience, and this was uttered by the Patriarch of Constantinople. Rome, we must remember, had by this time lost a great portion of her ancient fame. It was reserved for this wonderful city to rise again into all her former grandeur, by the restoration of learning and the knowledge of what she had been. At this period all that was known of her by the ignorant barbarians was, that she was a fresh-repaired and half-peopled town, which had been sacked and ruined five times within a century, that her inhabitants were collected from all parts of the world, and that she was liable to a repetition of her former misfortunes. They knew nothing of the great men who had raised her to such pre-eminence.

She had sunk even from being the capital of Italy, and could therefore make no intelligible claim to be considered the capital of the world. Constantinople, on the other hand, which, by our system of education, we are taught to look upon as a very modern creation compared with the Rome of the old heroic ages of the kings and consuls, was at that period a magnificent metropolis, which had been the seat of government for three hundred years. The majesty of the Roman name had transferred itself to that new locality, and nothing was more natural than that the Patriarch of the city of Constantine, which had been imperial from its origin, and had never been defiled by the presence of a Pagan temple, should claim for himself and his see a preeminence both in power and holiness. Accordingly, a demand was made in 588 for the recognition throughout the Christian world of the universal headship of the bishopric of Constantinople. But at that time there was a bishop of Rome, whom his successors have gratefully dignified with the epithet of Great, who stood up in defence, not of his own see only, but of all the bishoprics in Europe. Gregory published, in answer to the audacious claim of the Eastern patriarch, a vigorous protest, in which these remarkable words occur:—"This I declare with confidence, that whoso designates himself Universal Priest, or, in the pride of his heart, consents to be so named—he is the forerunner of Antichrist." It was therefore to Rome, on the broad ground of the Christian equality of all the chief pastors of the Church, that we owe this solemn declaration against the pretensions of the ambitious John of Constantinople.

But Constantinople itself was about to fade from the minds of men. Dissatisfied with the opposition to its supremacy, the Eastern Church became separated in interest and discipline and doctrine from its Western branch. The intercourse between the two was hostile, and in a short time nearly ceased. The empire also was so deeply engaged in defending its boundaries against the Persians and other enemies in Asia, that it took small heed of the proceedings of its late dependencies, the newly-founded kingdoms in Europe. It is probable that the refined and ostentatious court of Justinian, divided as it was into fanatical parties about some of the deepest and some of the most unimportant mysteries of the faith, and contending with equal bitterness about the charioteers of the amphitheatre according as their colours were green or blue, looked with profound contempt on the struggles after better government and greater enlightenment of the rabble of Franks, and Lombards, and Burgundians, who had settled themselves in the distant lands of the West. The interior regulations of Justinian formed a strange contrast with the grandeur and success of his foreign policy. By his lieutenants Belisarius and Narses, he had reconquered the lost inheritance of his predecessors, and held in full sovereignty for a while the fertile shores of Africa, rescued from the debasing hold of the Vandals; he had cleared Italy of Ostrogoths, Spain even had yielded an unwilling obedience, and his name was reverenced in the great confederacy of the Germanic peoples who held the lands from the Atlantic eastward to Hungary, and from Marseilles to the mouth of the Elbe. But his home was the scene of every weakness and wickedness that can disgrace the name of man. Kept in slavish submission to his wife, he did not see, what all the rest of the world saw, that she was the basest of her sex, and a disgrace to the place he gave her. Beginning as a dancer at the theatre, she passed through every grade of infamy and vice, till the name of Theodora became a synonym for every thing vile and shameless. Yet this man, successful in war and politic in action, though contemptible in private life, had the genius of a legislator, and left a memorial of his abilities which extended its influence through all the nations which succeeded to any portion of the Roman dominion, and has shaped and modified the jurisprudence of all succeeding times. He was not so much a maker of new laws, as a restorer and simplifier of the old; and as the efforts of Justinian in this direction were one of the great features by which the sixth century is distinguished, it will be useful to devote a page or two to explain in what his work consisted.

The Roman laws had become so numerous and so contradictory that the administration of justice was impossible, even where the judges were upright and intelligent. The mere word of an emperor had been considered a decree, and legally binding for all future time. No lapse of years seems to have brought a law once promulgated into desuetude. The people, therefore, groaned under the uncertainty of the statutes, which was further increased by the innumerable glosses or interpretations put upon them by the lawyers. All the decisions which had ever been given by the fifty-four emperors, from Adrian to Justinian, were in full force. All the commentaries made upon them by advocates and judges, and all the sentences delivered in accordance with them, were contained in thousands of volumes; and the result was, when Justinian came to the throne in 526, that there was no point of law on which any man could be sure. He employed the greatest jurisconsults of that time, Trebonian and others, to bring some order into the chaos; and such was the diligence of the commissioners, that in fourteen months they produced the Justinian Code in twelve books, containing a
A.D. 527. condensation of all previous constitutions. In

the course of seven years, two hundred laws and fifty judgments were added by the emperor himself, and a new edition of the Code was published in 534. Under the name of Institutes appeared a new manual for the legal students in the great schools of Constantinople, Berytus, and Rome, where the principles of Roman law are succinctly laid down. The third of his great works was one for the completion of which he gave Trebonian and his assessors ten years. It is called the Digest or Pandects of Justinian, because in it were digested, or put in order in a general collection, the best decisions of the courts, and the opinions and treatises of the ablest lawyers. All previous codes were ransacked, and two thousand volumes of legal argument condensed; and in three years the indefatigable law-reformers published their work, wherein three million leading judgments were reduced to a hundred and fifty thousand. Future confusion was guarded against by a commandment of the emperor abolishing all previous laws and making it penal to add note or comment to the collection now completed. The sentences delivered by the emperor, after the appearance of the Pandects, were published under the name of the Novellæ; and with this great clearing-out of the Augean stable of ancient law, the salutary labours of Trebonian came to a close. In those laws are to be seen both the virtues and the vices of their origin. They sprang from the wise liberality of a despot, and handle the rights of subjects, in their relation to each other, with the equanimity and justice of a power immeasurably raised above them all. But the unlimited supremacy of the ruler is maintained as the sole foundation for the laws themselves. So we see in these collections, and in the spirit which they have spread over all the codes which have taken them for their model, a combination of humanity

A.D. 533.

and probity in the civil law, with a tendency to exalt to a ridiculous excess the authority of the governing power.

This has been a century of wonderful revolutions. We have seen the kingdom of the Ostrogoths take the lead in Europe under the wise government of Theodoric the Great. We have seen it overthrown by an army of very small size, consisting of the very forces they had so recently triumphed over in every battle; and finally, after the victories over them of Belisarius and Narses, we have seen the last small remnant of their name removed from Italy altogether and eradicated from history for all future time. But, strange as this reassertion of the Greek supremacy was, the rapidity of its overthrow was stranger still. A new people came upon the stage, and established the Lombard power. The empire contracted itself within its former narrow bounds, and kept up the phantom of its superiority merely by the residence of an Exarch, or provincial governor, at Ravenna. The fiction of its power was further maintained by the Emperor's official recognition of certain rulers, and his ratification of the election of the Roman bishops. But in all essentials the influence had departed from Constantinople, and the Western monarchies were separated from the East.

In the Northwest, the confederacy of the Franks, which had consolidated into one immense and powerful kingdom under Clovis, became separated, weakened, and converted into open enemies under his degenerate successors.

But as the century drew to a close, a circumstance occurred, far away from the scene of all these proceedings, which had a greater influence on human affairs than the reconquest of Italy or the establishment of France. This was the marriage of a young man in a town of Arabia with the widow of his former master. In 564 this young man was born in Mecca, where his family had long held the high office of custodiers and guardians of the famous Caaba, which was popularly believed to be the stone that covered the grave of Abraham. But when he was still a child his father died, and he was left to the care of his uncle. The simplicity of the Arab character is shown in the way in which the young noble was brought up. Abu Taleb initiated him in the science of war and the mysteries of commerce. He managed his horse and sword like an accomplished cavalier, and followed the caravan as a merchant through the desert. Gifted with a high poetical temperament, and soaring above the grovelling superstitions of the people surrounding him, he used to retire to meditate on the great questions of man's relation to his Maker, which the inquiring mind can never avoid. Meditation led to excitement. He saw visions and dreamed dreams. He saw great things before him, if he could become the leader and lawgiver of his race. But he was poor and unknown. His mistress Cadijah saw the aspirations of her noble servant, and offered him her hand. He was now at leisure to mature the schemes of national regeneration and religious improvement which had occupied him so long, and devoted himself more than ever to study and contemplation. This was Mohammed, the Prophet of Islam, who retired in 594 to perfect his scheme, and whose empire, before many years elapsed, extended from India to Spain, and menaced Christianity and Europe at the same time from the Pyrenees and the Danube.

SEVENTH CENTURY.

Kings of the Franks.		Emperors of the East.	
A.D.		A.D.	
	THIERRY II. and THEODOBERT II.—(*cont.*)		MAURICE—(*cont.*)
614.	CLOTAIRE III. (sole king.)	602.	PHOCAS.
628.	DAGOBERT and CHARIBERT.	611.	HERACLIUS.
638.	SIGEBERT and CLOVIS II.	641.	CONSTANTINE, (and others.)
654.	CHILDERIC II.	642.	CONSTANS.
679.	THIERRY IV.	668.	CONSTANTIUS V.
692.	CLOVIS III. (PEPIN, Mayor.)	685.	JUSTINIAN II.
695.	CHILDEBERT III. (do.)	695.	LEONTIUS.
		697.	TIBERIUS.

Authors.

NENNIUS, (620,) BEDE, (674–735,) ALDHELM, ADAMNANUS.

THE SEVENTH CENTURY.

POWER OF ROME SUPPORTED BY THE MONKS—CONQUESTS OF THE MOHAMMEDANS.

THIS, then, is the century during which Mohammedanism and Christianity were marshalling their forces —unknown, indeed, to each other, but preparing, according to their respective powers, for the period when they were to be brought face to face. We shall go eastward, and follow the triumphant march of the warriors of the Crescent from Arabia to the shores of Africa; but first we shall cast a desponding eye on the condition and prospects of the kingdoms of the West. Conquest, spoliation, and insecurity had done their work. Wave after wave had passed over the surface of the old Roman State, and obliterated almost all the landmarks of the ancient time. The towns, to be sure, still remained, but stripped of their old magnificence, and thinly peopled by the dispossessed inhabitants of the soil, who congregated together for mutual support. Trade was carried on, but subject to the exactions, and sometimes the open robberies, of the avaricious chieftains who had reared their fortresses on the neighbouring heights. Large tracts of country lay waste and desolate, or were left to the happy fertility of nature in the growth of spontaneous woods. Marshes were formed over whole districts, and the cattle picked up an uncertain existence by browsing over great expanses of poor and unenclosed land. These flocks and herds were guarded by hordes of armed serfs, who camped beside them on the fields, and led a life not unlike that of their remote ancestors on the steppes of Tartary. A man's wealth was counted by his retainers, and there was no supreme authority to keep the dignitaries, even of the same tribe, from warring on each other and wasting their rival's country with fire and sword. Agriculture, therefore, was in the lowest state, and famines, plagues, and other concomitants of want were common in all parts of Europe. One beautiful exception must be made to this universal neglect of agriculture, in favour of the Benedictine monks, established in various parts of Italy and Gaul in the course of the preceding century. Religious reverence was a surer safeguard to those lowly men than castles or armour could have been. No marauder dared to trespass on lands which were under the protection of priest and bishop. And these Western recluses, far from imitating the slothful uselessness of the Eastern monks, turned their whole attention to the cultivation of the soil. In this they bestowed a double benefit on their fellow-men, for, in addition to the positive improvement of the land, they rescued labour from the opprobrium into which it had fallen, and raised it to the dignity of a religious duty. Slavery, we have seen, was universally practised in all the conquered territories, and as only the slaves were compelled to the drudgeries of the field, the work itself borrowed a large portion of the degradation of the unhappy beings condemned to it; and robbery, pillage, murder, and every crime, were considered far less derogatory to the dignity of free Frank or Burgundian than the slightest touch of the mattock or spade. How surprised, then, were the haughty countrymen and descendants of Clovis or Alboin to see the revered hands from which they believed the highest blessings of Heaven to flow, employed in the daily labour of digging, planting, sowing, reaping, thrashing, grinding, and baking! At first they looked incredulously on. Even the monks were disposed to consider it no part of their conventual duties. But the founder of their institution wrote to them, "to beware of idleness, as the greatest enemy of the soul," and not to be uneasy if at any time the cares of the harvest hindered them from their formal readings and regulated prayers. "No person is ever more usefully employed than when working with his hands or following the plough, providing food for the use of man." And the effects of these exhortations were rapidly seen. Wherever a monastery was placed, there were soon fertile fields all round it, and innumerable stacks of corn. Generally chosen with a view to agricultural pursuits, we find sites of abbeys at the present day which are the perfect ideal of a working farm; for long after the outburst of agricultural energy had expired among the monks of St. Benedict, the choice of situation and knowledge of different soils descended to the other ecclesiastical establishments, and skill in agriculture continued at all times a characteristic of the religious orders. What could be more enchanting than the position of their monastic homes? Placed on the bank of some beautiful river, surrounded on all sides by the low flat lands enriched by the neighbouring waters, and protected by swelling hills where cattle are easily fed, we are too much in the habit of attributing the selection of so admirable a situation to the selfishness of the portly abbot. When the traveller has admired the graces of Melrose or of Tintern—the description applies equally to almost all the foundations of an early date—and has paid due attention to the chasteness of the architecture, and beauty of "the long-resounding aisle and fretted vault," he sometimes contemplates with a sneer the matchless charm of the scenery, and exceeding richness of the haugh or strath in which the building stands. "Ah," he says, "they were knowing old gentlemen, those monks and priors. They had fish in the river, fat beeves upon the meadow, red-deer on the hill, ripe corn on the water-side, a full grange at Christmas, and snowy sheep at midsummer." And so they had, and deserved them all. The head of that great establishment was not wallowing in the fat of the land to the exclusion of envious baron or starving churl. He was, in fact, setting them an example which it would have been wise in them to follow. He merely chose the situation most fitted for his purpose, and bestowed his care on the lands which most readily yielded him his reward. It was not necessary for the monks in those days to seek out some neglected corner, and to restore it to cultivation, as an exercise of their ingenuity and strength. They were free to choose from one end of Europe to the other, for the whole of it lay useless and comparatively barren. But when these able-bodied recluses, if such they may be called, had shown the results of patient industry and skill, the peasants, who had seen their labours, or occasionally been employed to assist them, were able to convey to their lay proprietors or masters the lessons they had received. And at last something venerable was thought to reside in the act of farming itself. It was so uniformly found an accompaniment of the priestly character, that it acquired a portion of its sanctity, and the rude Lombard or half-civilized Frank looked with a kind of awe upon waving corn and rich clover, as if they were the result of a higher intelligence and purer life than he possessed. Even the highest officers in the Church were expected to attend to these agricultural conquests. In this century we find, that when kings summoned bishops to a council, or an archbishop called his brethren to a conference, care was taken to fix the time of meeting at a season which did not interfere with the labours of the farm. Privileges naturally followed these beneficial labours. The kings, in their wondering gratitude, surrounded the monasteries with fresh defences against the envy or enmity of the neighbouring chiefs. Their lands became places of sanctuary, as the altar of the Church had been. Freedmen—that is, persons manumitted from slavery, but not yet endowed with property—were everywhere put under the protection of the clergy. Immunities were heaped upon them, and methods found out of making them a separate and superior race. At the Council of Paris, in 613, it was decreed that the priest who offended against the common law should be tried by a mixed court of priests and laymen. But soon this law, apparently so just, was not considered enough, and the trial of ecclesiastics was given over to the ecclesiastical tribunals, without the admixture of the civil element. Other advantages followed from time to time. The Church was found in all the kingdoms to be so useful as the introducer of agriculture, and the preserver of what learning had survived the Roman overthrow, that the ambitious hierarchy profited by the royal and popular favour. They were the most influential, or perhaps it would be more just to say they were the only, order in the State. There was a nobility, but it was jarring and disunited; there were citizens, but they were powerless and depressed; there was a king, but he was but the first of the peers, and stood in dignified isolation where he was not subordinate to a combination of the others. The clergy, therefore, had no enemy or rival to dread, for they had all the constituents of power which the other portions of the population wanted. Their property was more secure; their lands were better cultivated; they were exempt from many of the dangers and burdens to which the lay barons were exposed; they were not liable to the risks and losses of private war; they had more intelligence than their neighbours, and could summon assistance, either in advice, or support, or money, from the farthest extremity of Europe. Nothing, indeed, added more, at the commencement of this century, to the authority of those great ecclesiastical chieftains, than the circumstance that their interests were supported, not only by their neighbouring brethren, but by mitred abbot and lordly bishop in distant lands. If a prior or his monks found themselves ill used on the banks of the Seine, their cause was taken up by all other monks and priors wherever they were placed. And the rapidity of their intercommunication was extraordinary. Each monastery seems to have had a number of active young brethren who traversed the wildest regions with letters or messages, and brought back replies, almost with the speed and regularity of an established post. A convent on Lebanon was informed in a very short time of what had happened in Provence—the letter from the Western abbot was read and deliberated on, and an answer intrusted to the messenger, who again travelled over the immense tract lying between, receiving hospitality at the different religious establishments that occurred upon his way, and everywhere treated with the kindness of a brother. Monasteries in this way became the centres of news as well as of learning, and for many hundred years the only people who knew any thing of the state of feeling in foreign nations, or had a glimpse of the mutual interests of distant kingdoms, were the cowled and gowned individuals who were supposed to have given up the world and to be totally immersed in penances and prayers. What could Hereweg of the strong hand do against a bishop or abbot, who could tell at any hour what were the political designs of conquerors or kings in countries which the astonished warrior did not know even by name; who retained by traditionary transmission the politeness of manner and elegance of accomplishment which had characterized the best period of the Roman power, when Christianized noblemen, on being promoted to an episcopal see, had retained the delicacies of their former life, and wrote love-songs as graceful as those of Catullus, and epigrams neither so witty nor so coarse as those of Martial? Intelligence asserted its superiority over brute force, and in this century the supremacy of the Church received its accomplishment in spite of the depravation of its principles. It gained in power and sank in morals. A hundred years of its beneficial action had made it so popular and so powerful that it fell into temptations, from which poverty or unpopularity would have kept it free. The sixth century was the period of its silent services, its lower officers endearing themselves by useful labour, and its dignitaries distinguishing themselves by learning and zeal. In the seventh century the fruit of all those virtues was to be gathered by very different hands. Ambitious contests began between the different orders composing the gradually rising hierarchy, from the monk in his cell to the Bishop of Rome or Constantinople on their pontifical thrones. It is very sad, after the view we have taken of the early benefits bestowed on many nations by the labours and example of the priests and monks, to see in the period we have reached the total cessation of life and energy in the Church;—of life and energy, we ought to say, in the fulfilment of its duties; for there was no want of those qualities in the gratification of its ambition. Forgetful of what Gregory had pronounced the chief sign of Antichrist, when he opposed the pretension of his rival metropolitan to call himself Universal Bishop, the Bishops of Rome were deterred by no considerations of humility or religion from establishing their temporal power. Up to this time they had humbly received the ratification of their election from the Emperors of the East, whose subjects they still remained. But the seat of their empire was far off, their power was a tradition of the past, and great thoughts came into the hearts of the spiritual chiefs, of inroads on the territory of the temporal rulers. In this design they looked round for supporters and allies, and with a still more watchful eye on the quarters from which opposition was to be feared. The bishops as a body had fallen not only into contempt but hatred. One century had sufficed to extinguish the elegant scholarship I have mentioned, at one time characteristic of the Christian prelates. Ignorance had become the badge of all the governors of the Church—ignorance and debauchery, and a tyrannical oppression of their inferiors. The wise old man in Rome saw what advantage he might derive from this, and took the monks under his peculiar protection, relieved them from the supervision of the local bishop, and made them immediately dependent on himself. By this one stroke he gained the unflinching support of the most influential body in Europe. Wherever they went they held forth the Pope as the first of earthly powers, and began already, in the enthusiasm of their gratitude, to speak of him as something more than mortal. To this the illiterate preachers and prelates had nothing to reply. They were sunk either in the grossest darkness, or involved in the wildest schemes of ambition, bishoprics being even held by laymen, and by both priest and laymen used as instruments of advancement and wealth. From these the Pontiff on the Tiber, whose weaknesses and vices were unknown, and who was held up for invidious contrast with the bishops of their acquaintance by the libellous and grateful monks, had nothing to fear. He looked to another quarter in the political sky, and perceived with satisfaction that the kingly office also had fallen into contempt. Having lost the first impulse which carried it triumphantly over the dismembered Roman world, and made it a tower of strength in the hands of warriors like Theodoric the Goth and Clovis the Frank, it had forfeited its influence altogether in the pitiful keeping of the bloodthirsty or do-nothing kings who had submitted to the tutelage of the Mayors of the Palace.

One of the great supports of the royal influence was the fiction of the law by which all lands were supposed to hold of the Crown. As in ancient days, in the German or Scythian deserts, the ambitious chieftain had presented his favourite with spear or war-horse in token of approval, so in the early days of the conquest of Gaul, the leader had presented his followers with tracts of land. The war-horse, under the old arrangement, died, and the spear became rotten; but the land was subject neither to death nor decay. What, then, was to become of the warrior's holding when he died? On this question, apparently so personal to the barbaric chiefs of the time of Dagobert of Gaul, depended the whole course of European history. The kings claimed the power of re-entering on the lands in case of the demise of the proprietor, or even in case of his rebellion or disobedience. The Leud, as he was called—or feudatory, as he would have been named at a later time—disputed this, and contended for the perpetuity and inalienability of the gift. It is easy to perceive who were the winners in this momentous struggle. From the success of the leuds arose the feudal system, with limited monarchies and national nobilities. The success of the kings would have resulted in despotic thrones and enslaved populations. Foremost in the struggle for the royal supremacy had been the famous and unprincipled Brunehild, a woman more resembling the unnatural creation of a romance than a real character. She had succeeded at one time in subordinating the leuds, by exterminating the recusants with remorseless cruelty; and her triumph might have been final and irrevocable if she had not had the bad luck or impolitic hardihood to offend the Church. The Abbot Columba, a holy man from the far-distant island of Iona in the Hebrides of Scotland, had ventured to upbraid her with her crimes. She banished him from the Abbey of Luxeuil with circumstances of peculiar harshness, and there was no hope for her more. The leuds she might have overcome singly, for they were disunited and scattered; but now there was not a monastery in Europe which did not side with her foes. Clotaire, her grandson, marched against her at the instigation of priests and leuds combined. She was conquered and taken. She was tortured for three days with all the ingenuity of hatred, and on the fourth was tied to the tails of four wild horses and torn to pieces, though the mother, sister, daughter, of kings, and now more than eighty years of age. And this brings us to the institution and use of the strange officers we have already named Mayors of the Palace.

To aid them in their efforts against the royal assumptions, the leuds long ago had elected one of themselves to be domestic adviser of the king, and also to command the armies in war. This soon became the recognised right of the Mayor of the Palace; and as in that state of society the wars were nearly perpetual, and bearers of arms the only wielders of power, the person invested with the command was in reality the supreme authority in the State. When the king happened to be feeble either in body or mind, the mayor supplied his place, without even the appearance of inferiority; and when Dagobert, the last active member of the Merovingian family, died in 638, his successors were merely the nominal holders of the Crown. A new race rose into importance, and it will not be very long before we meet the hereditary Mayors of the Palace as hereditary Kings of the Franks. Here, then, was the whole of Europe heaving with some inevitable change. It will be interesting to look at the position of its different parts before they settled into their new relations. The constitutions of the various kingdoms were very nearly alike at this time. There were popular assemblies in every nation. In France they were called the "Fields of May" or of "March," in England the "Wittenagemot," in Spain the "Council of Toledo." These meetings consisted of the freemen and landholders and bishops. But it was soon found inconvenient for the freemen and smaller proprietors to attend, in consequence of the length of the journey and the miserable condition of the roads; and the nobles and bishops were the sole persons who represented the State. The nobles held a parallel rank to each other in all countries, though called by different names. In France, a person in possession of any office connected with the court, or of lands presented by the Crown, was called a leud or entrustion, a count or companion, or vassal. In England he was called a royal thane. The lower order of freemen were called herimans, or inferior thanes; in Latin *liberi*, or more simply, *boni homines*, good men. Below these were the Romans, or old inhabitants of the country; below these, the serfs or bondmen attached to the soil; and far down, below them all, out of all hope or consideration, the slaves, who were the mere chattels of their lords. This, then, was the constitution of European society when the Arabian conquests began—at the head of the nation the King, at the head of the people the Church; the nobles followed according to their birth or power; the freemen, whether citizens engaged in the first infant struggles of trade, or occupying a farm, came next; and the wretched catalogue was ended by the despoiled serf, from whom every thing, even his property in himself, had been taken away. There were laws for the protection or restraint of each of these orders, and we may gather an idea of the ranks they held in public estimation by the following table of the price of blood:—

	Sols.
For the murder of a freeman, companion, or leud of the king, killed in his palace by an armed band	1800
A duke—among the Bavarians, a bishop	960
A relation of a duke	640
The king's leud, a count, a priest, a judge	600
A deacon	500
A freeman, of the Salians or Ripuarians	200
A freeman, of the other tribes	160
The slave—a good workman in gold	100
The man of middle station, a colon, or good workman in silver	100
The freedman	80
The slave, if a barbarian—that is, of the conquering tribe	55
The slave, a workman in iron	50
The serf of the Church or the king	45
The swineherd	30
The slave, among the Bavarians	20

Distinctions of dress pointed out still more clearly the difference of rank and station. The principal variety, however, was the method of wearing the hair. The chieftain among the Franks considered the length and profusion of his locks as the mark of his superiority. His broad flowing tresses were divided up the middle of his head, and floated over his shoulders. They were curled and oiled—not with common butter, like some other nations, says an author quoted by Chateaubriand; not twisted in little plaits, like those of the Goths, but carefully combed out to their full luxuriance. The common soldier, on the other hand, wore his hair long in front, but trimmed close behind. They swore by their hair as the most sacred of their oaths, and offered a tress to the Church on returning from a successful war. From this peculiar consideration given to the hair arose the custom, still prevalent, of shaving the heads of ecclesiastics. They were the serfs of God, and sacrificed their locks in token that they were no longer free. When a chief was dishonoured, when a king was degraded, when a rival was to be rendered incapable of opposition, he was not, as in barbarous countries, put to death: he was merely made bald. No amount of popularity, no degree of right, could rouse the people in support of a person whose head was bare. When his hair grew again, he might again become formidable; but the scissors were always at hand. A tyrannical king clipped his enemies' hair, instead of taking off their heads. They were condemned to the barber instead of the executioner, and sometimes thought the punishment more severe. The sons of Clothilde sent an emissary to her, bearing in his hand a sword and a pair of scissors. "O queen," he said, "your sons, our masters, wish to know whether you will have your grandchildren slain or clipped." The queen paused for a moment, and then said, "If my grandchildren are doomed not to mount the throne, I would rather have them dead than hairless."

Distinguished thus from the lower orders, the nobility soon found that their interests differed from those of the Church. The Church placed itself at the head of the democracy in opposition to the overweening pretensions of the chiefs. It opened its ranks to the conquered races, and invested even the converted serf with dignities which placed him above the level of Thane or

Count. The head of the Western Church, now by general consent recognised in the Bishop of Rome, was not slow to see the advantage of his position as leader of a combination in favour of the million. The doctrine of the equality of all men in the sight of Heaven was easily commuted into a demand of universal submission to the Holy See; and so wide was the range given to this claim to obedience that it embraced the proudest of the nobles and haughtiest of kings. It was a satisfaction to the slave in his dungeon to hear that the great man in his castle had been forced to do homage to the Church. There was one earthly power to which the oppressed could look up with the certainty of support. It was this intimate persuasion in the minds of the people which gave such undying vigour to the counsels and pretensions of the ecclesiastical power. It was a power sprung from the people, and exercised for the benefit of the people. The Popes themselves were generally selected from the lowest rank. But what did it matter to the man who led the masses of the trampled nations, and stood as a shield between them and their tyrants, whether he claimed relationship with emperors or slaves? What did it matter, on the other hand, to those hoping and trusting multitudes, whether the object of their confidence was personally a miracle of goodness and virtue, or a monster of sin and cruelty? It was his office to trample on the necks of kings and nobles, and bid the captive go free. While he continued true to the people, the people were true to him. Monarchs who governed mighty nations, and dukes who ruled in provinces the size of kingdoms, looked on with surprise at the growth of a power supported apparently by no worldly arms, but which penetrated to them through their courts and armies. There was no great mind to guide the opposition to its claims. The bishops were sunk in ignorance and sloth, and had lost the respect of their countrymen. The populations everywhere were divided. The succession to the throne was uncertain. The Franks, the leading nation, were never for any length of time under one head. Neustria, or the Western State, comprising all the land between the Meuse, the Loire, and the Mediterranean, Austrasia, or the Eastern State, comprising the land between the Rhine, the Meuse, and the Moselle, and Burgundy, extending from the Loire to the Alps, were at one time united under a common head, and at another held by hostile kings. The Visigoths were obscurely quarrelling about points of divinity within their barrier of the Pyrenees. England was the battle-field of half a dozen little chieftains who called themselves kings; Germany was only civilized on its western border. Italy was cut up into many States, Lombards looking with suspicion on the Exarchate, which was still nominally attached to the Eastern Empire, and Greeks established in the South, sighing for the restoration of their power. Over all this chaos of contending powers appeared the mitre and crozier of the Pope; always at the head of the disaffected people, supported by the monks, who felt the tyranny of the bishops as keenly as the commonalty felt the injustice of their lords; always threatening vengeance on overweening baron or refractory monarch —enhancing his influence with the glory of new miracles wrought in his support, and witnessed unblushingly by preaching friars, who were the missionaries of papal power; concentrating all authority in his hands, and gradually laying the foundation for a trampling and domination over mind and body such as the world had never seen. From this almost universal prostration before the claims of Rome, it is curious to see that the native Irish were totally free. With contemptuous independence, they for a long time rejected the arrogant assumptions of the successor of St. Peter, and were firm in their maintenance of the equality of all the Sees. It was from the newly-converted Anglo-Saxons that the chief recruits in the campaign against the liberties of the national churches were collected. Almost all the names of missionaries on behalf of the Roman pontiff in this century have the home-sound in our ears of "Wighert," "Willibald," "Wernefried," or "Adalbert." But there are no Gaelic patronymics from the Churches of Ireland or Wales. They were sisters, they haughtily said, not daughters of the Roman See, as the Anglo-Saxon Church had been; and dwelt with pride on the antiquity of their conversion before the pretensions of the Roman Bishops had been heard of; and thus was added one more to the elements of dissension which wasted the strength of Europe at the very time when unanimity was most required.

But towards the end of this period the rumours of a new power in the East drew men's attention to the defenceless state in which their internal disagreements had left them. The monasteries were filled with exaggerated reports of the progress of this vast invasion, which not only threatened the national existences of Europe, but the Christian faith. It was a hostile creed and a destroying enemy. What had the Huns been, compared with this new swarm—not of savage warriors turned aside with a bribe or won by a prayer, but enthusiasts in what they considered a holy cause, flushed with victory, armed and disciplined in a style superior to any thing the West could show? We should try to enter into the feelings of that distant time, when day by day myriads of strange and hitherto unconquerable enemies were reported to be on their march.

In the year 621 of the Christian era, Mohammed

made his triumphant entry into Medina, a great city of Arabia, having been expelled from Mecca by the enmity of the Jews and the tribe of Koreish. This entry is called the Hegira or Flight, and forms the commencement of the Moslem chronology. All their records are dated from this event. The persons who accompanied him were few in number—his father-in-law, some of his wives, and some of his warriors; but the procession was increased by the numerous believers in his prophetship who resided in the town. At this place began the public worship inculcated by the leader. The worshippers were summoned by a voice sounding from the highest pinnacle of the mosque or church, and pronouncing the words which to this hour are heard from every minaret in the East:—"God is great! God is great! There is no God but God. Mohammed is the apostle of God. Come to prayers, come to prayers!" and when the invitation is given at early dawn, the declaration is added, "Prayer is better than sleep! prayer is better than sleep." These exhortations were not without their intended effect. Prayer was uttered by many lips, and sleep was banished from many eyes; but the prayers were never thought so effectual as when accompanied by sword and lance. Courage and devotedness were now the great supports of the faith. Ali, the husband of Fatima the favourite daughter of the chief, fought and prayed with the same irresistible force. He conquered the unbelieving Jews and Koreishites, cleaving armed men from the crown to the chin with one blow, and wielding a city gate which eight men could not lift, as a shield. Abou Beker, whose daughter was one of the wives of Mohammed, was little inferior to Ali; and Mohammed himself saw visions which comforted and inspired his followers in the midst of battle, and shouted, "On, on! Fight and fear not! The gates of Paradise are under the shade of swords. He will assuredly find instant admission who falls fighting for the faith!" It was impossible to play the hypocrite in a religion where such strength of arm and sharpness of blade were required. Prayers might indeed be mechanical, or said for show, but the fighting was a real thing, and, as such, prevailed over all the shams which were opposed to it. Looking forth already beyond the narrow precincts of his power, Mohammed saw in the distance, across the desert, the proud empires of Persia and Constantinople. To both he wrote letters demanding their allegiance as God's Prophet, and threatening vengeance if they disobeyed. Chosroes, the Persian, tore the letter to pieces. "Even so," said Mohammed, "shall his kingdom be torn." Heraclius the Greek was more respectful. He placed the missive on his pillow, and very naturally fell asleep, and thought of it no more. But his descendants were not long of having their pillows quite so provocative of repose. The city of Medina grew too small to hold the Prophet's followers, and they went forth conquering and to conquer. There were Abou Beker the wise, and Omar the faithful, and Khaled the brave, and Ali the sword of God. Mecca fell before them, and city after city sent in its adhesion to the claims of a Prophet who had such dreadful interpreters as these. The religion he preached was comparatively true. He destroyed the idols of the land, inculcated soberness, chastity, charity, and, by some faint transmission of the precepts of the Bible, inculcated brotherly love and forgiveness of wrong. But the sword was the true gospel. Its light was spread in Syria and all the adjoining territories. People in apparently sheltered positions could never be sure for an hour that the missionaries of the new faith would not be climbing over their walls with shouts of conquest, and giving them the option of conversion or death. Power spread in gradually-widening circles, but at the centre sad things were going on. Mohammed was getting old. He lost his only son. He laid him in the grave with tears and sighs, and made his farewell pilgrimage to Mecca. Had he no relentings at the visible approach of the end? Was he to go to the grave untouched by all the calamities he had brought upon mankind? the blood he had shed, the multitudes he had beguiled? He had no touch of remorse for any of these things; rather he continued firmer in his course than ever—seemed more persuaded of the genuineness of his mission, and uttered prophecies of the universal extension of his faith. "When the angels ask thee who thou art," he said, as the body of his son was lowered into the tomb, "say, God is my Lord, the Prophet of God was my father, and my faith was Islam!" Islam continued his own faith till the last. He tottered to the mosque where Abou Beker was engaged in leading the prayers of the congregation, and addressed the people for the last time. "Every thing happens," he said, "according to the will of God, and has its appointed time, which is not to be hastened or avoided. My last command to you is that you remain united; that you love, honour, and uphold each other; that you exhort each other to faith and constancy in belief, and to the performance of pious deeds: by these alone men prosper; all else leads to destruction." A few days after this there was grief and lamentation all over the faithful lands. He died on his sixty-third birthday, in the eleventh year of the Hegira, which answers to our year 632.

Great contentions arose among the chief disciples for the succession to the leadership of the faithful. Abou Beker was father-in-law of the Prophet, and his daughter supported his cause. Omar was also father-in-law of the

Prophet, and his daughter supported his cause. Othman had married two of the daughters of the Prophet, but both were dead, and they had left no living child. Ali, the hero of the conquest, was cousin-german of the Prophet, and husband of his only surviving daughter. Already the practices of a court were perceptible in the Emir's tent. The courtiers caballed and quarrelled; but Ayesha, the daughter of Abou Beker, had been Mohammed's favourite wife, and her influence was the most effectual. How this influence was exercised amid the Oriental habits of the time, and the seclusion to which the women were subjected, it is difficult to decide; but, after a struggle between her and Hafya, the daughter of Omar, the widowed Othman was found to have no chance; and only Ali remained, still young and ardent, and fittest, to all ordinary judgments, to be the leader of the armies of Allah. While consulting with some friends in the tent of Fatima, his rivals came to an agreement. In a distant part of the town a meeting had been called, and the claims of the different pretenders debated. Suddenly Omar walked across to where Abou Beker stood, bent lowly before him, and kissed his hand in token of submission, saying, "Thou art the oldest companion and most secret friend of the Prophet, and art therefore worthy to rule us in his place." The example was contagious, and Abou Beker was installed as commander and chief of the believers. A resolution was come to at the same time, that any attempt at seizing the supremacy against the popular will should be punished with death. Ali was constrained to yield, but lived in haughty submission till Fatima died. He then rose up in his place, and taking his two sons with him, Hassan and Hossein, retired into the inner district of Arabia, carrying thus from the camp of the usurping caliph the only blood of the Prophet.

chief which flowed in human veins. Yet the spirit of the Prophet animated the whole mass. Energy equal to Ali's was exhibited in Khaled. Omar was earnest in the collection of all the separated portions of the Koran. Othman was burning to spread the new empire over the whole earth; and in this combination of courage, ambition, and fanaticism all Arabia found its interest to join, and ere a year had elapsed from the death of the Prophet, the whole of that peninsula, and all the swart warriors who travelled its sandy steppes, had accepted the great watchword of his religion—"There is no God but God, and Mohammed is the Prophet of God." Ere another year had elapsed the desert had sent forth its swarms. The plains of Asia were overflowed. The battle-cry of Zeyd, the general of the army, was heard in the great commercial cities of the East, and in the lands where the gospel of peace had first been uttered, Emasa and Damascus, and on the banks of Jordan. It was natural that the first effort of the false should be directed against the true. But not indiscriminate was the wrath of Abou Beker against the professors of Christianity. The claims of that dispensation were ever treated with respect, but the depraved priesthood were held up to contempt. "Destroy not fruit-tree nor fertile field on your path," these were the instructions of the Caliph to the leaders of the host. "Be just, and spare the feelings of the vanquished. Respect all religious persons who live in hermitages or convents, and spare their edifices. But should you meet with a class of unbelievers of a different kind, who go about with shaven crowns, and belong to the synagogue of Satan, be sure you cleave their skulls, unless they embrace the true faith or render tribute."

Gentle and merciful, therefore, to the peaceful inhabitants, respectful to the gloomy anchorite and industrious monk, but breathing death and disgrace against the proud bishop and ambitious presbyter, the mighty horde moved on. Syria fell; the Persian monarchy was menaced, and its western provinces seized; a Christian kingdom called Hira, situated on the confines of Babylonia, was made tributary to Medina; and Khaled stood triumphant on the banks of the Euphrates, and sent a message to the Great King, commanding him either to receive the faith, or atone for his incredulity with half his wealth. The despot's ears were unaccustomed to such words, and the fiery deluge went on. At the end of the third year, Abou Beker died, and Omar was the successor appointed by his will. This was already a departure from the law of popular election, but Islam was busy with its conquests far from its central home, and accepted the nomination. Khaled's course continued westward and eastward, forcing his resistless wedge between the exhausted but still majestic empires of the Greeks and Persians. Blow after blow resounded as the great march went on. Constantinople, and Madayn upon the Tigris, the capitals of Christianity and Mithrism, were equally alarmed and equally powerless. Omar, the Caliph—the word means the *Successor* of the Apostle—determined to join the army which was encamped against the walls of Jerusalem, and added fresh vigour to the assailants by the knowledge that they fought under his eye.

Heraclius, the degenerate inheritor of the throne of Constantine, and Yezdegird, the successor of Darius and Xerxes, if they had moved towards the seat of war, would have been surrounded by all the pomp of their exalted stations. Battalions of guards would have encompassed their persons, and countless officers of their courts attended their progress.

Omar, who saw already the world at his feet, journeyed

by slow stages on a wretched camel, carrying his provisions hanging from his saddle-bow, and slept at night under the shelter of some tree, or on the margin of some well. He had but one suit, and that of worsted material, and yet his word was law to all those breathless listeners, and wherever he placed his foot from that moment became holy ground. Jerusalem and Aleppo yielded; Antioch, the chief seat of Grecian government, fell into his hands; Tyre and Tripoli submitted to his power; and the Saracenic hosts only paused when they reached the border of the sea, which they knew washed the fairest shores of Africa and Europe. It did not much matter who was in nominal command. Khaled died; Amru took his place; and yet the tide went on. The great city of Alexandria, which disputed with Constantinople the title of Capital of the World, with its almost fabulous wealth, its four thousand palaces, and five thousand baths, and four hundred theatres, was twice taken, and brought on the submission and conversion of the whole of Egypt. Amru in his hours of leisure was devoted to the cultivation of taste and genius. In John the Grammarian, a Christian student, he found a congenial spirit. Poetry, philosophy, and rhetoric were treated of in the conversations of the Arabic conqueror and the monkish scholar. At last, in reliance on his literary taste, the priest confided to the Moslem that in a certain building in the town there was a library so vast that it had no equal on earth either for number or value of the manuscripts it contained. This was too important a treasure to be dealt with without the express sanction of the Caliph. So the Christian legend is, that Omar replied to the announcement of his general, "Either what those books contain is in the Koran, or it is not. If it is, these volumes are useless; if it is not, they are wicked. Burn them." The skins and parchments heated the baths of Alexandria for many months, irrecoverable monuments of the past, and an everlasting disgrace to the Saracen name. Yet the story has been doubted; at least, the extent of the destruction. Rather, it has been supposed, the ignorant fanaticism of the illiterate monks, in covering with the legends of saints the obliterated lines of the classic authors, has been more destructive to the literary treasures of those ancient times than the furious zeal of Amru or the bigotry of Omar.

If this great overflow from the desert of Arabia had consisted of nothing but armed warriors or destructive fanatics, its course would have been as transient as it was terrible. The Gothic invaders who had desolated Europe fortunately possessed the flexibility and adaptiveness of mind which fitted them for the reception of the purer faith and more refined manners of the vanquished races. They mixed with the people who submitted to their power, and in a short time adopted their habits and religion. Whatever faith they professed in their original seats, seems to have worn out in the long course of their immigration. The powers they had worshipped in their native wilds were local, and dependent on clime and soil. An easy opening, therefore, was left for Christianity into hearts where no hostile deity guarded the portal of approach. But with the Saracens the case was reversed. Incapable of assimilation with any rival belief—jealously exclusive of the commonest intercourse with the nations they subdued—unbending, contemptuous to others, and carried on by burning enthusiasm in their own cause, and confidence in the Prophet they served, there was no possibility of softening or elevating them from without. The pomps of religious worship, which so awed the wondering tribes of Franks and Lombards, were lost on a people who considered all pomp offensive both to God and man. They saw the sublimity of simple plainness both in word and life. Their caliph lived on rice, and saddled his camel with his own hands. He ordered a palace to be burned, which Seyd, who had conquered for him the capital of Persia, had built for his occupation. Unsocial, bigoted, austere, drinking no wine, accumulating no personal wealth, how was the mind of this warrior of the wilderness to be trained to the habits of civilized society, or turned aside from the rude instincts of destructiveness and domination? But the Arab intellect was subtle and active. Mohammedanism, indeed, armed the multitude in an exciting cause, and sent them forth like a destroying fire; but there was wisdom, policy, refinement, among the chiefs. While they devasted the worn-out territories of the Persian, and laid waste his ostentatious cities, which had been purposely built in useless places to show the power of the king, they founded great towns on sites so adapted for the purposes of trade and protection that they continue to the present time the emporiums and fortresses of their lands. Balsorah, at the top of the Persian Gulf, at the junction of the Tigris and the Euphrates, was as wisely selected for the commercial wants of that period as Constantinople itself. Bagdad was encouraged, Cufa built and peopled in exchange for the gorgeous but unwholesome Madayn, from which Yezdegird was driven. Many other towns rose under the protection of the Crescent; and by the same impulse which made the Saracens anxious to raise new centres of wealth and enterprise in the East, they were excited to the most amazing efforts to make themselves masters of the greatest city in the world, the seat of arts, of literature, and religion; and they pushed forward from river to river, from plain to plain, till, in the year 672, they raised their victorious standard in front of the walls of Constantinople. Here, however, a new enemy came to the encounter, and for the first time scattered dismay among the Moslem ranks. From the towers and turrets came down a shower of fire, burning, scorching, destroying, wherever it touched. Projected to great distances, and wrapping in a moment ship after ship in unextinguishable flames, these discharges appeared to the warriors of the Crescent a supernatural interference against them. This was the famous Greek fire, of which the components are not now known, but it was destructive beyond gunpowder itself. Water could not quench it, nor length of time weaken its power. For five successive years the assault was renewed by fresh battalions of the Saracens, but always with the same result. So, giving up at last their attempts against a place guarded by lightning and by the unmoved courage of the Greek population, they poured their thousands along the northern shores of Africa. Cyrene, the once glorious capital of the Pentapolis, in which Carthage saw her rival and Athens her superior, yielded to their power. Everywhere high-peaked mosques, rising where a short time before the shore had been unoccupied or in cities where the Basilicas of Christian worship had been thrown down, marked the course of conquest. Carthage received its new lords. Hippo, the bishopric of the best of ancient saints, the holy Augustine, saw its church supplanted by the temples of the Arabian impostor. A check was sustained at Tchuda, where their course was interrupted by a combined assault of Christian Greeks and the indigenous Berbers. Internal troubles also arrested their career, for there were disputes for the succession, and court intrigues and open murders, and all the usual accompaniments of a contest for an elective throne. One after another, the Caliphs had been murdered, or had died of broken hearts. The old race—the "Companions," as they were called, because they had been the contemporaries and friends of Mohammed—had died out. Ali, after three disappointments, had at last been chosen. His sons Hassan and Hossein had been put to death; and it was only in the time of the eighth successor, when Abdelmalek had overcome all competition, that the unity of the Moslem Empire was restored, and the word given for conquest as before. This was in the 77th year of the Hegira, (698 of our era,) and an army was let loose upon the great city of Carthage, at the same time that movements were again ordered across the limits of the Grecian Empire, in Asia, and advances made towards Constantinople. Carthage fell—Tripoli was occupied—and now, with their territories stretching in unbroken line from Syria along the two thousand miles of the southern shore of the great Mediterranean Sea, the conquerors rested from their labours for a while, and prepared themselves for a dash across the narrow channel, from which the hills of Atlas and the summits of Gibraltar are seen at the same time. What has Europe, with its divided peoples, its worn-out kings, its indolent Church, and exhausted fields, to oppose to this compact phalanx of united blood, burning with fanatical faith, submissive to one rule, and supported by all the wealth of Asia and Africa; whose fleets sweep the sea, and whose myriads are every day increased by the accession of fresh nations of Berbers, Mauritanians, and the nameless children of the desert?

This is the hopeless century. Manhood, patriotism,

Christianity itself, are all at the lowest ebb. But let us turn to the next, and see how good is worked out of evil, and acknowledge, as in so many instances the historian is obliged to do, that man can form no estimate of the future from the plainest present appearances, but that all things are in the hands of a higher intelligence than ours.

EIGHTH CENTURY.

Kings of the Franks.

A.D.		
	CHILDEBERT III.—(*cont.*)	
711.	DAGOBERT III.	CHARLES MARTEL Mayor.
716.	CHILDERIC.	
720.	THIERRY.	
742.	CHILDERIC III.	

Carlovingian Line.

751. PEPIN THE SHORT.

768. CHARLEMAGNE.

Emperors of the East.

A.D.

TIBERIUS.—(*cont.*)

711. PHILIPPICUS BARDANES.

713. ANASTASIUS II.

714. THEODOSIUS III.

716. LEO THE ISAURIAN.

741. CONSTANTINE COPRONYMUS.

775. LEO IV.

781. CONSTANTINE PORPHYROGENITUS.

802. NICEPHORUS.

Authors.

ALCUIN, (735–804,) BEDE, (674–735,) EGBERT, CLEMENS, DUNGAL, ACCA, JOHN DAMASCANUS.

THE EIGHTH CENTURY.

TEMPORAL POWER OF THE POPES—THE EMPIRE OF CHARLEMAGNE.

This is indeed a great century, which has Pepin of Heristhal at its commencement and Charlemagne at its end. In this period we shall see the course of the dissolution of manners and government arrested throughout the greater part of Europe, and a new form given to its ruling powers. We must remember that up to this time the progress of what we now call civilization was very slow; or we may perhaps almost say that the extent of civilized territory was smaller than it had been at the final breaking up of the Roman Empire four hundred years before. England had lost the elevating influences which the residence of Roman generals and the presence of disciplined forces had spread from the seats of their government. Every occupied position had been a centre of life and learning; and we see still, from the discoveries which the antiquaries of the present day are continually making, that the dwellings of the Prætors and military commanders were constructed in a style of luxury and refinement which argues a high state of culture and art. All round the circumference of the Romanized portion of Britain these head-quarters of order and improvement were fixed; outside of it lay the obscure and tumultuous populations of Wales and Scotland; and if we trace the situations of the towns with terminations derived from *castra*, (a camp,) we shall see, by stretching a line from Winchester in the south to Ilchester, thence up to Gloucester, Worcester, Wroxeter, and Chester, how carefully the Western Gael were prevented from ravaging the peaceful and orderly inhabitants; and, as the same precautions were taken to the North against the Picts and Scots, we shall easily be able to estimate the effect of those numerous schools of life and manners on the country-districts in which they were placed. All these establishments had been removed. Barbarism had reasserted her ancient reign; and at the century we have now reached, the institution which alone could compete in its elevating effect with the old imperial subordination, the Christian Church, had not yet established its authority except for the benefit of ambitious bishops; and the same anarchy reigned in the ecclesiastical body as in the civil orders. The eight or nine kingdoms spread over the land were sufficiently powerful in their separate nationalities to prevent any unity of feeling among the subjects of the different crowns. A prelate of the court of Deiria had no point of union with a prelate protected by the kings of Wessex. And it was this very incapacity of combination at home, from the multiplicity of kings, which led to the astonishing spectacle in this century of the efforts of the Anglo-Saxon clergy in behalf of the Bishop of Rome in distant countries. In this great struggle to extend the power of the Popes, the regular orders particularly distinguished themselves. The fact of submitting to convent-rules, of giving up the stormy pleasures of independence for the safe placidity of unreasoning obedience, is a proof of the desire in many human minds of having something to which they can look up, something to obey, in obeying which their self-respect may be preserved, even in the act of offering up their self-will—a desire which, in civil actions and the atmosphere of a court, leads to slavery and every vice, but in a monastery conducts to the noblest sacrifices, and fills the pages of history with saints and martyrs. The Anglo-Saxon, looking out of his convent, saw nothing round him which could give him hope or comfort. Laws were unsettled, the various little principalities were either hostile or unconnected, there was no great combining authority from which orders could be issued with the certainty of being obeyed; and even the clergy, thinly scattered, and dependent on the capricious favour or exposed to the ignorant animosity of their respective sovereigns, were torn into factions, and practically without a chief. But theoretically there was the noblest chiefship that ever was dreamed of by ambition. The lowly heritage of Peter had expanded into the universal government of the Church. In France this claim had not yet been urged; in the East it had been contemptuously rejected; in Italy the Lombard kings were hostile; in Spain the Visigoths were heretic, and at war among themselves; in Germany the gospel had not yet been heard; in Ireland the Church was a rival bitterly defensive of its independence; but in England, among the earnest, thoughtful Anglo-Saxons, the majestic idea of a great family of all the Christian Churches, wherever placed, presided over by the Vicar of Christ and receiving laws from his hallowed lips, had impressed itself beyond the possibility of being effaced. Rome was to them the residence of God's vicegerent upon earth; obedience to him was worship, and resistance to his slightest wish presumption and impiety. So at the beginning of this century holy men left their monasteries in Essex, and Warwickshire, and Devon, and knelt at the footstool of the Pope, and swore fealty and submission to the Holy See.

It has often been observed that the Papacy differs from other powers in the continued vitality of its mem bers long after the life has left it at the heart. Rome was weak at the centre, but strong at the extremity of its domain. The Emperor of Constantinople looked on the Pope as his representative in Church-affairs, ratified his election, and exacted tribute on his appointment. The Exarch of Ravenna, representing as he did the civil majesty of the successor of the Cæsars, looked down on him as his subordinate. There was also a duke in Rome whose office it was to superintend the proceedings of the bishop, and another officer resident in the Grecian court to whom the bishop was responsible for the management of his delegated powers. But outside of all this depression and subordination, among tribes of half-barbaric blood, among dreamy enthusiasts contemplating what seemed to them the simple and natural scheme of an earthly judge infallible in wisdom and divinely inspired; among bewildered and trampled ecclesiastics, looking forth into the night, and seeing, far above all the storms and darkness that surrounded them in their own distracted land, a star by which they might steer their course, undimmed and unalterable—the Pope of Rome was the highest and holiest of created men. No thought is worth any thing that continues in barren speculation. Honour, then, to the brave monks of England who went forth the missionaries of the Papal kings! Better the struggles and dangers of a plunge among the untamed savages of Friesland, and the blood-stained forests of the farthest Germany, in fulfilment of the office to which they felt themselves called, than the lazy, slumbering way of life which had already begun to be considered the fulfilment of conventual vows. Soldiers of the Cross were they, though fighting for the advancement of an ambitious commander more than the success of the larger cause; and we may well exult in the virtues which their undoubting faith in the supremacy of the pontiff called forth, since it contrasts so nobly with the apathy and indifference to all high and self-denying co-operation which characterized the rest of the world. We shall see the monk Winifried penetrate, as the Pope's minister, into the darkness beyond the Rhine, and emerge, with crozier and mitre, as Boniface the Archbishop of Mayence, and converter to the Christian faith of great and populous nations which were long the most earnest supporters of the rights and pre-eminence of Rome. This is one strong characteristic of this century, the increased vigour of the Papacy by the efforts of the Anglo-Saxons on its behalf; and now we are going to another still stronger characteristic, the further increase of its influence by the part it played in the change of dynasty in France.

A strange fortune, which in the old Greek mythologies would have been looked on as a fate, overshadowing the blood-stained house of Clovis, had befallen his descendants through all their generations for more than a hundred years. Feeble in mind, and even degenerated in body, the kings of that royal line had been a sight of grief and humiliation to their nominal subjects. Married at fifteen, they had all sunk into premature old age, or died before they were thirty. Too listless for work, and too ignorant for council, they had accepted the restricted sphere within which their duties were confined, and showed themselves, on solemn occasions, at the festivals of the Church, and other great anniversaries, bearing, like their ancestors, the long flowing locks which were the natural sign of their crowned supremacy, seated in a wagon drawn by oxen, and driven by a wagoner with a goad—a primitive relic of vanished times, and as much out of place in Paris in the eighth century as the state carriage of the Queen or the Lord-Mayor's coach of the present day among ourselves.

Strange thoughts must have passed through the minds of the spectators as they saw the successors of the rough leader of the Franks degraded to this condition; but the change had been gradual; the public sentiment had become reconciled to the apparent uselessness of the highest offices of the State; for under another title, and with much inferior rank, there was a man who held the reins of government with a hand of iron, and whose power was perhaps strengthened by the fiction which called him the servant and minister of the *fainéant* or do-nothing king. A succession of men arose in the family of the mayors of the palace, as remarkable for policy and talent as the representatives of the royal line were for the want of these qualities. The origin of their office was conveniently forgotten, or converted by the flattery of their dependants into an equality with the monarchs. Chosen, they said, by the same elective body which nominated the king, they were as much entitled to the command of the army and the administration of the law as their nominal masters to the possession of the palace and royal name. And when for a long period this claim was allowed, who was there to stand up in opposition, either legal or forcible, to a man who appointed all the judges and commanded all the troops? The office at last became hereditary. The successive mayors left their dignity to their sons by will; and time might have been slow in bringing power and title into harmony with each by giving the name of king to the man who already exercised all the kingly power and fulfilled all the kingly duties, if Charles Martel, the mayor, had not, in 732, established such claims to the gratitude of Europe by his defeat of the Saracens, who were about to overrun the whole of Christendom, that it was impossible to refuse either to himself or his successor the highest dignity which Europe had to bestow. When other rulers and princes were willing to acknowledge his superiority, not only in power, but in rank and dignity, it was necessary that their submission should be offered, not to a mere Major-domo, or chief domestic of a court, but to a free sovereign and anointed king. The two most amazing fictions, therefore, which ever flourished on the contemptuous forbearance of mankind, were both about to expire beneath the breath of reality at this time—the kingship of the descendants of Clovis, and the pretensions of the successors of Constantine. The Saracens appeared upon the scene, and those gibbering and unsubstantial ghosts, as if they scented the morning air, immediately disappeared. The Emperors of the East, by a self-deluding process, which preserved their dignity and flattered their pride, professed still to consider themselves the lords of the Roman Empire, and took particular pains to acknowledge the kings and potentates, who established themselves in the various portions of it, as their representatives and lieutenants. They lost no time in sending the title of Patrician and the ensigns of royal rank to the successful founders of a new dynasty, and had gained their object if they received the new ruler's thanks in return. At Rome, as we have said, they protected the bishop, and gave him the investiture of his office. They retained also the territories called the Exarchate of Ravenna, but with no power of vindicating their authority if it was disputed, or of exacting revenue, except what the gratitude of the bishop or the Exarch might induce them to present to their patron on their nomination or instalment. A long-haired, sad-countenanced, decrepit young man in a wagon drawn by oxen, and a vain voluptuary, wrapped in Oriental splendour, without influence or wealth, were the representatives at this time of the irresistible power of the Frankish warriors, and the glories of Julius and Augustus. But the present had its representatives as well as the past. Charles Martel had still the Frankish sword at his command; the Roman Pontiff had thousands ready to believe and support his claims to be the spiritual ruler of the world. Something was required to unite them in one vast effort at unity and independence, and this opportunity was afforded them by the common danger to which the Saracenic invasion exposed equally the civil and ecclesiastical power. Africa, we have seen, was fringed along the whole of the Mediterranean border with the followers of the Prophet. In one generation the blood of the Arabian and Mauritanian deserts became so blended, that no distinction whatever existed between the men of Mecca and Medina and the native tribes. Where Carthaginian and Roman civilization had never penetrated, the faith of Mohammed was accepted as an indigenous growth. Fanaticism and ambition sailed across the Channel; and early in this century the hot breath of Mohammedanism had dried up the promise of Spain; countless warriors crossed to Gibraltar; their losses were supplied by the inexhaustible populations from the interior, (the ancestors of the Abd-el Kaders and Ben Muzas of modern times,) and, elate with hopes of universal conquest, the crowded tents of the Moslem army were seen on the northern slopes of the Pyrenees, and presently all the plains of Languedoc, and the central fields of France as far up as the Loire, were inundated by horse and man. Incredible accounts are given of the number and activity of the desert steeds bestrode by these turbaned apostles. A march of a hundred miles—a village set on fire, and all the males extirpated—strange-looking visages, and wild arrays of galloping battalions seen by terrified watchers from the walls of Paris itself; then, in the twinkling of an eye, nothing visible but the distant dust raised up in their almost unperceived retreat,—these were the peculiarities of this new and unheard-of warfare. And while these dashes were made from the centre of the invasion, alarming the inhabitants at the extremities of the kingdom, the host steadily moved on, secured the ground behind it before any fresh advance, and united in this way the steadiness of European settlement with the wild fury of the original mode of attack. Already the provinces abutting on the Pyrenees had owned their power. Gascony up to the Garonne, and the Narbonnais nearly to the Rhine, had submitted to the conquerors; but when the dispossessed proprietors of Novempopulania and Septimania, as those districts were then called, and the powerful Duke of Aquitaine, also fled before the advancing armies; when all the churches were filled with prayer, and all the towns were in momentary expectation of seeing the irresistible horsemen before their walls, patriotism and religion combined to call upon all the Franks and all the Christians to expel the infidel invader. So Charles, the son of Pepin, whose exploits against the Frisons and other barbaric peoples in the North had already acquired for him the complimentary name of Martel, or the Hammer, put himself at the head of the military forces of the land, and encountered the Saracenic myriads on the great plain round Tours. The East and West were brought front to front—Christianity and Mohammedanism stood face to face for the first time; and it is startling to consider for a moment what the result of an Asiatic victory might have been. If ever there was a case in which the intervention of Divine Providence may be claimed without presumption on the conquering side, it must be here, where the truths of revelation and the progress of society were dependent on the issue. The two faiths, according to all human calculation, had rested their supremacy on their respective champions. If Charles and his Franks and Germans were defeated, there was nothing to resist the march of the perpetually-increasing numbers of the Saracens till they had planted their standards on the pinnacles of Rome. The first glow of Christian belief had been exchanged, we have seen, for ambitious disputes, or died off in many of the practices of superstition. The very man in whom the Christian hope was placed was suspected of leaning to the Wodenism of his Northern ancestors, and was scarcely bought over to the defence of the Church's faith by a permission to pillage the Church's wealth. Mohammedanism, on the other hand, was fresh and young. Its promises were clear and tempting—its course triumphant, and its doctrines satisfactory equally to the pride and the indolence of the human heart. But in the former, though unperceived by the warriors at Tours and the prelates at Rome, lay the germ of countless blessings—elevating the mind by the discovery of its strength at the same moment in which it is abased by the feeling of its weakness, and gifted above all with the power of expansion and universality; themselves proofs of its divine original, to which no false religion can lay the slightest claim. Cultivate the Christian mind to the highest—fill it with all knowledge—place round it the miracles of science and art—station it in the snows of Iceland or the heats of India—Christianity, like the all-girding horizon of the sky, widens its circle so as to include the loftiest, and contain within its embrace the utmost diversities of human life and speculation. But with the Mohammedan, as with other impostures, the range is limited. When intellect expands, it bursts the cerement in which it has been involved; and with Buddhism, and Mithrism, and Hindooism, it will be as it was with Druidism, and the more elegant heathendom of Greece and Rome: there will be no safety for them but in the ignorance and barbarism of their disciples. On the result of that great day at Tours in the year 732, therefore, depended the intellectual improvement and civil freedom of the human race. Few particulars are preserved of this momentous battle; but the result showed that the light cavalry, in which the Saracens excelled, were no match for the firm line of the Franks. When confusion once began among the swarthy cavaliers of Abderachman, there was no restoration possible. In wild confusion the *mêlée* was continued; and all that can be said is, that the slaughter of upwards of three hundred thousand of these impulsive pilgrims of the desert so weakened the Saracenic power in Europe, that in no long time their hosts were withdrawn from the soil of Gaul, and guarded with difficulty the conquest they had made behind the barrier of the Pyrenees. Could the gratitude of Church or State be too generous to the man who preserved both from the sword of the destroyer? If Charles pillaged a monastery or seized the revenues of a bishopric, nobody found any fault. It was almost just that he should have the wealth of the cathedral from which he had driven away the mufti and muezzin. But monasteries and bishops were still powerful, and did not look on the proceedings of Charles the Hammer with the equanimity of the unconcerned spectators. They perhaps thought the battle of Tours had only given them a choice of spoilers, instead of protection from spoliation. In a short time, however, the policy of the sagacious leader led him to see the necessity of gaining over the only united body in the State. He became a benefactor of the Church, and a staunch ally of the Roman bishop. Both had an object to obtain. What the phantom king was to

Charles, the phantom emperor was to the Pope. If there was unison between the two dependants, it would be easy to get rid of the two superiors. Presents and compliments were interchanged, and moral support trafficked for material aid. Wherever the one sent missionaries with the Cross, the other sent warriors to their support. The Pontiff bestowed on the Mayor the keys of the sepulchre of St. Peter, and the title of Consul and Patrician, and begged him to come to his assistance against Luitprand, the Lombard king. But this was far too great an exploit to be expected by a simple Bishop, and performed by a simple Mayor of the Palace. So the next great thing we meet with in this century is the investiture of the Mayor with the title of king, and of the Bishop with the sovereignty of Rome and Ravenna. This happened in 752. Pepin the Short, as he was unflatteringly called by his subjects, succeeded Charles in the government of the Franks. The king was Childeric the Third, who lived in complete seclusion and cherished his long hair as the only evidence of monarchy left to the sons of Clovis. Wars in various regions established the reputation of Pepin as the worthy successor of Charles; and by a refinement of policy, the crown, the consummation of all his hopes, was reached in a manner which deprived it of the appearance of injustice, for it was given to him by the hands of saints and popes, and ratified by the council of the nation. He had already asked Pope Zachariah, "who had the best right to the name of king?—he who had merely the title, or he who had the power?" And in answer to this, which was rather a puzzling question, our countryman Winifried, in his new character of Boniface and archbishop, placed upon his head the golden round, and Might and Right were restored to their original combination. But St. Boniface was not enough. In two years the Pope himself clambered over the Alps and anointed the new monarch with holy oil; and by the same act stripped the long hair from the head of the Merovingian puppet, and condemned him and his descendants to the privacy of a cloister.

Now then that Pepin is king, let Luitprand, or any other potentate, beware how he does injury to the Pope of Rome. Twice the Frank armies are moved into Italy in defence of the Holy See; and at last the Exarchate is torn from the hands of its Lombard oppressor, and handed over in sovereignty to the Spiritual Power. Rome itself is declared at the same time the property of the Bishop, and free forever from the suzerainty of the Emperors of the East. No wonder the gratitude of the Popes has made them call the kings of France the eldest sons of the Church. Their donations raised the bishopric to the rank of a royal state; yet it has been remarked that the generosity of the French monarchs has always been limited to the gift of other people's lands. They were extremely liberal in bestowing large tracts of country belonging to the Lombard kings or the Byzantine Cæsars; but they kept a very watchful eye on the possessions of pope and bishop within their own domain. They reserved to themselves the usufruct of vacant benefices, and the presentations to church and abbey. At almost all periods, indeed, of their history, they have seemed to retain a very clear remembrance of the position which they held towards the Papacy from the beginning, and, while encouraging its arrogance against other principalities and powers, have held a very contemptuous language towards it themselves.

This, then, is the great characteristic of the present century, the restoration of the monarchical principle in the State, and its establishment in the Church. During all these wretched centuries, from the fall of the Roman

Empire, the progress has been towards diffusion and separation. Kings rose up here and there, but their kingships were local, and, moreover, so recent, that they were little more than the first officer or representative of the warriors whose leaders they had been. A longing for some higher and remoter influence than this had taken possession of the chiefs of all the early invasions, and we have seen them (even while engaged in wresting whole districts from the sway of the old Roman Empire) accepting with gratitude the ensigns of Roman authority. We have seen Gothic kings glorying in the name of Senator, and Hunnish savages pacified and contented by the title of Prætor or Consul. The world had been accustomed to the oneness of Consular no less than Imperial Rome for more than a thousand years; for, however the parties might be divided at home, the great name of the Eternal City was the sole sound heard in foreign lands. The magic letters, the initials of the Senate and People, had been the ornament of their banners from the earliest times, and a division of power was an idea to which the minds of mankind found it difficult to become accustomed. It was better, therefore, to have only a fragment of this immemorial unity than the freshness of a new authority, however extensive or unquestionable. Vague traditions must have come down—magnified by distance and softened by regret—of the great days before the purple was torn in two by the transference of the seat of power to Constantinople. There were nearly five hundred years lying between the periods; and all the poetic spirits of the new populations had cast longing, lingering looks behind at the image of earthly supremacy presented to them by the existence of an acknowledged master of the world. A pedantic sophist, speaking Greek—the language of slaves and scholars—wearing the loftiest titles, and yet hemmed in within the narrow limits of a single district, assumed to be the representative of the universal "Lord of human kind," and called himself Emperor of the East and West. The common sense of Goth and Saxon, of Frank and Lombard, rebelled against this claim, when they saw it urged by a person unable to support it by fleets and armies. When, in addition to this want of power, they perceived in this century a want of orthodox belief, or even what they considered an impious profanity, in the successor of Augustus and Constantine, they were still more disinclined to grant even a titular supremacy to the Byzantine ruler. Leo, at that time wearing the purple, and zealous for the purity of the faith, issued an order for the destruction of the marble representations of saints and martyrs which had been used in worship; and within the limits of his personal authority his mandate was obeyed. But when it reached the West, a furious opposition was made to his command. The Pope stood forward as champion of the religious veneration of "storied urn and animated bust." The emperor was branded with the name of Iconoclast, or the Image-breaker, and the eloquence of all the monks in Europe was let loose upon the sacrilegious Cæsar. Interest, it is to be feared, added fresh energy to their conscientious denunciations, for the monks had attracted to themselves a complete monopoly of the manufacture of these aids to devotion—and obedience to Leo's order would have impoverished the monasteries all over the land. A Western emperor, it was at once perceived, would not have been so blind to the uses of those holy sculptures, and soon an intense desire was manifested throughout the Western nations for an emperor of their own. Already they were in possession of a spiritual chief, who claimed the inheritance of the Prince of the Apostles, and looked down on the Patriarchs of Constantinople as bishops subordinate to his throne. Why should not they also have a temporal ruler who should renew the old glories of the vanished Empire, and exercise supremacy over all the governors of the earth? Why, indeed, should not the first of those authorities exert his more than human powers in the production of the other? He had converted a Mayor of the Palace into a King of the Franks. Could he not go a step further, and convert a King of the Franks into an Emperor of the West? With this hope, not yet perhaps expressed, but alive in the minds of Pepin and the prelates of France, no attempt was made to check the Roman pontiffs in the extravagance of their pretensions. Lords of wide domains, rich already in the possession of large tracts of country and wealthy establishments in other lands, they were raised above all competition in rank and influence with any other ecclesiastic; and relying on spiritual privileges, and their exemption from active enmity, they were more powerful than many of the greatest princes of the time. Everywhere the mystic dignity of their office was dwelt upon by their supporters. For a long time, as we have seen, their omnipotence was acknowledged by the two classes who saw in the use of that spiritual dominion a counterpoise to the worldly sceptres by which they were crushed. But now the worldly sceptres came to the support of the spiritual dominion. Its limit was enlarged, and made to include the regulation of all human affairs. It was its office to subdue kings and bind nobles in links of iron; and when the son of Pepin, Charles, justly called the Great, though travestied by French vanity into the name of Charlemagne, sat on the throne of the Franks, and carried his arms and influence into the remotest States, it was felt that the hour and the man

A.D. 768.

were come; and the Western Empire was formally renewed.

The curious thing is, that this longing for a restoration of the Roman Empire, and dwelling on its usefulness and grandeur, were dominant, and productive of great events, in populations which had no drop of Roman blood in their veins. The last emperor resident in Rome had never heard the names of the hordes of savages whose descendants had now seized the plains of France and Italy. Yet it seemed as if, with the territory of the Roman Empire, they had inherited its traditions and hopes. They might be Saxons, or Franks, or Burgundians, or Lombards, by national descent, but by residence they were Romans as compared with the Greeks in the East,—and by religion they were Romans as compared with the Sclaves and Saracens, who pressed on them on the North and South. It would not be difficult in this country to find the grandchildren of French refugees boasting with patriotic pride of the English triumphs at Cressy and Agincourt—or the sons of Scottish parents rejoicing in their ancestors' victory under Cromwell at Dunbar; and here, in the eighth century, the descendants of Alaric and Clovis were patriotically loyal to the memory of the old Empire, and were reminded by the victories of Charlemagne of the trophies of Scipio and Marius. These victories, indeed, were not, as is so often found to be the case, the mere efforts of genius and ambition, with no higher object than to augment the conqueror's power or reputation. They were systematically pursued with a view to an end. In one advancing tide, all things tended to the Imperial throne. Whatever nation felt the force of Charlemagne's sword felt also a portion of its humiliation lightened when its submission was perceived to be only an advancement towards the restoration of the old dominion. It might have been degrading to acknow ledge the superiority of the son of Pepin—but who could offer resistance to the successor of Augustus? So, after thirty years of uninterrupted war, with campaigns succeeding each in the most distant regions, and all crowned with conquest; after subduing the Saxons beyond the Weser, the Lombards as far as Treviso, the Arabs under the walls of Saragossa, the Bavarians in the neighbourhood of Augsburg, the Sclaves on the Elbe and Oder, the Huns and Avars on the Raab and Danube, and the Greeks themselves on the coast of Dalmatia; when he looked around and saw no rebellion against his authority, but throughout the greater part of his domains a willing submission to the centralizing power which rallied all Christian states for the defence of Christianity, and all civilized nations for the defence of civilization,—nothing more was required than the mere expression in definite words of the great thing that had already taken place, and Charlemagne, at the extreme end of this century, bent before the successor of St. Peter at Rome, and stood up crowned Emperor of the West, and champion and chief of Christendom.

The period of Charlemagne is a great date in history; for it is the legal and formal termination of an antiquated state of society. It was also the introduction to another, totally distinct from itself and from its predecessor. It was not barbarism; it was not feudalism; but it was the bridge which united the two. By barbarism is meant the uneasy state of governments and peoples, where the tribe still predominated over the nation; where the Frank or Lombard continued an encamped warrior, without reference to the soil; and where his patriotism consisted in fidelity to the traditions of his descent, and not to the greatness or independence of the land he occupied. In the reign of

A.D. 786–814.

Charlemagne, the land of the Frank became practically, and even territorially, France; the district occupied by the Lombards became Lombardy. The feeling of property in the soil was added to the ties of race and kindred; and at the very time that all the nations of the Invasion yielded to the supremacy of one man as emperor, the different populations asserted their separate independence of each other, as distinct and self-sufficing kingdoms—kingdoms, that is to say, without the kings, but in all respects prepared for those individualized expressions of their national life. For though Charlemagne, seated in his great hall at Aix-la-Chapelle, gave laws to the whole of his vast domains, in each country he had assumed to himself nothing more than the monarchic power. To the whole empire he was emperor, but to each separate people, such as Franks and Lombards, he was simply king. Under him there were dukes, counts, viscounts, and other dignitaries, but each limited, in function and influence, to the territory to which he belonged. A French duke had no preeminence in Lombardy, and a Bavarian graf had no rank in Italy. Other machinery was at times employed by the central power, in the shape of temporary messengers, or even of emissaries with a longer tenure of office; but these persons were sent for some special purpose, and were more like commissioners appointed by the Crown, than possessors of authority inherent in themselves. The term of their ambassadorship expired, their salary, or the lands they had provisionally held in lieu of salary, reverted to the monarch, and they returned to court with no further pretension to power or influence than an ambassador in our days when he returns from the country to which he is accredited. But when the great local nobility found their authority indissolubly connected with their possessions, and that ducal or princely privileges were hereditary accompaniments of their lands, the foundations of modern feudalism were already laid, and the path to national kingship made easy and unavoidable. When Charlemagne's empire broke into pieces at his death, we still find, in the next century, that each piece was a kingdom. Modern Europe took its rise from these fragmentary though complete portions; and whereas the breaking-up of the first empire left the world a prey to barbaric hordes, and desolation and misery spread over the fairest lands, the disruption of the latter empire of Charlemagne left Europe united as one whole against Saracen and savage, but separated in itself into many well-defined states, regulated in their intercourse by international law, and listening with the docility of children to the promises or threatenings of the Father of the Universal Church. For with the empire of Charlemagne the empire of the Papacy had grown. The temporal power was a collection of forces dependent on the life of one man; the spiritual power is a principle which is independent of individual aid. So over the fragments, as we have said, of the broken empire, rose higher than ever the unshaken majesty of Rome. Civil authority had shrunk up within local bounds; but the Papacy had expanded beyond the limits of time and space, and shook the dreadful keys and clenched the two-edged sword which typified its dominion over both earth and heaven.

NINTH CENTURY.

Emperors.

A.D.	*West.*	A.D.	*East.*
800.	Charlemagne, (crowned by the Pope.)		Nicephorus—(*cont.*)
814.	Louis the Debonnaire.	811.	Michael.
840.	Charles the Bald.	813.	Leo the Armenian.
877.	Louis the Stammerer.	821.	Michael the Stammerer.
879.	Louis III. and Carloman.	829.	Theophilus.
884.	Charles the Fat.	842.	Michael III.
887.	Arnold.	886.	Leo the Philosopher.
899.	Louis IV.		

Kings of France.

887. Eudes, (Count of Paris.) 898. Charles the Simple.

Kings of England.

827. Egbert.
837. Ethelwolf.
857. Ethelbald.
860. Ethelbert.
866. Ethelred.
872. Alfred the Great.

Authors.

John Scotus, (Erigena,) Hincmar, Heric, (preceded Des Cartes in philosophical investigation,) Macarius.

THE NINTH CENTURY.

DISMEMBERMENT OF CHARLEMAGNE'S EMPIRE—DANISH INVASION OF ENGLAND—WEAKNESS OF FRANCE—REIGN OF ALFRED.

THE first year of this century found Charlemagne with the crown of the old Empire upon his head, and the most distant parts of the world filled with his reputation. As in the case of the first Napoleon, we find his antechambers crowded with the fallen rulers of the conquered territories, and even with sovereigns of neighbouring countries. Among others, two of our Anglo-Saxon princes found their way to the great man's court at Aix-la-Chapelle. Eardulf of Northumberland pleaded his cause so well with Charlemagne and the Pope, that by their good offices he was restored to his states. But a greater man than Eardulf was also a visitor and careful student of the vanquisher and lawgiver of the Western world. Originally a Prince of Kent, he had been expelled by the superior power or arts of Beortrick, King of the West Saxons, and had betaken himself for protection, if not for restoration, to the most powerful ruler of the time. Whether Egbert joined in his expeditions or shared his councils, we do not know, but the history of the Anglo-Saxon monarchies at this date (800 to 830) shows us the exact counterpart, on our own island, of the actions of Charlemagne on the wider stage of continental Europe. Egbert, on the death of Beortrick, obtained possession of Wessex, and one by one the separate states of the British Heptarchy were subdued;

some reduced to entire subjection, others only to subordinate rank and the payment of tribute, till, when all things were prepared for the change, Egbert proclaimed the unity of Southern Britain by assuming the title of Bretwalda, in the same way as his prototype had restored the unity of the empire by taking the dignity of Emperor. It is pleasant to pause over the period of Charlemagne's reign, for it is an isthmus connecting two dark and unsatisfactory states of society,—a past of disunion, barbarity, and violence, and a future of ignorance, selfishness, and crime. The present was not, indeed, exempt from some or all of these characteristics. There must have been quarrellings and brutal animosities on the outskirts of his domain, where half-converted Franks carried fire and sword, in the name of religion, among the still heathen Saxons; there must have been insolence and cruelty among the bishops and priests, whose education, in the majority of instances, was limited to learning the services of the Church by heart. Many laymen, indeed, had seized on the temporalities of the sees; and, in return, many bishops had arrogated to themselves the warlike privileges and authority of the counts and viscounts. But within the radius of Charlemagne's own influence, in his family apartments, or in the great Hall of Audience at Aix-la-Chapelle, the astonishing sight was presented of a man refreshing himself, after the fatigues of policy and war, by converting his house into a college for the advancement of learning and science. From all quarters came the scholars, and grammarians, and philosophers of the time. Chief of these was our countryman, the Anglo-Saxon monk Alcuin, and from what remains of his writings we can only regret that, in the infancy of that new civilization, his genius, which was undoubtedly great, was devoted to trifles of no real importance. Others came to fill up that noble company; and it is surely a great relief from the bloody records with which we have so long been familiar, to see Charlemagne at home, surrounded by sons and daughters, listening to readings and translations from Roman authors; entering himself into disquisitions on philosophy and antiquities, and acting as president of a select society of earnest searchers after information. To put his companions more at their ease, he hid the terrors of his crown under an assumed name, and only accepted so much of his royal state as his friends assigned to him by giving him the name of King David. The best versifier was known as Virgil. Alcuin himself was Horace; and Angelbert, who cultivated Greek, assumed the proud name of Homer. These literary discussions, however, would have had no better effect than refining the court, and making the days pass pleasantly; but Charlemagne's object was higher and more liberal than this. Whatever monastery he founded or endowed was forced to maintain a school as part of its establishment. Alcuin was presented with the great Abbey of St. Martin of Tours, which possessed on its domain twenty thousand serfs, and therefore made him one of the richest land-owners in France. There, at full leisure from worldly cares, he composed a vast number of books, of very poor philosophy and very incorrect astronomy, and perhaps looked down from his lofty eminence of wealth and fame on the humble labours of young Eginhart, the secretary of Charlemagne, who has left us a Life of his master, infinitely more interesting and useful than all the dissertations of the sage. From this great Life we learn many delightful characteristics of the great man, his good-heartedness, his love of justice, and blind affection for his children. But it is with his public works, as acting on this century, that we have now to do. Throughout the whole extent of his empire he founded Academies, both for learning and for useful occupations. He encouraged the study and practice of agriculture and trade. The fine arts found him a munificent patron; and though the objects on which the artist's skill was exercised were not more exalted than the carving of wooden tables, the moulding of metal cups, and the casting of bells, the circumstances of the time are to be taken into consideration, and these efforts may be found as advanced, for the ninth century, as the works of the sculptors and metallurgists of our own day. It is painful to observe that the practice of what is now called adulteration was not unknown at that early period. There was a monk of the name of Tancho, in the monastery of St. Gall, who produced the first bell. Its sound was so sweet and solemn, that it was at once adopted as an indispensable portion of the ornament of church and chapel, and soon after that, of the religious services themselves. Charlemagne, hearing it, and perhaps believing that an increased value in the metal would produce a richer tone, sent him a sufficient quantity of silver to form a second bell. The monk, tempted by the facility of turning the treasure to his own use, brought forward another specimen of his skill, but of a mixed and very inferior material. What the just and severe emperor might have done, on the discovery of the fraud, is not known; but the story ended tragically without the intervention of the legal sword. At the first swing of the clapper it broke the skull of the dishonest founder, who had apparently gone too near to witness the action of the tongue; and the bell was thenceforth looked on with veneration, as the discoverer and punisher of the unjust manufacturer.

The monks, indeed, seem to have been the most refractory of subjects, perhaps because they were already exempted from the ordinary punishments. In order to produce uniformity in the services and chants of the Church, the emperor sent to Rome for twelve monkish musicians, and distributed them in the twelve principal bishoprics of his dominions. The twelve musicians would not consent to be musical according to order, and made the confusion greater than ever, for each of them taught different tunes and a different method. The disappointed emperor could only complain to the Pope, and the Pope put the recusant psalmodists in prison. But it appears the fate of Charlemagne, as of all persons in advance of their age, to be worthy of congratulation only for his attempts. The success of many of his undertakings was not adequate to the pains bestowed upon them. He held many assemblages, both lay and ecclesiastical, during his lengthened reign; he published many excellent laws, which soon fell into disuse; he tried many reforms of churches and monasteries, which shared the same fortune; he held the Popes of Rome and the dignitaries of his empire in perfect submission, but professed so much respect for the office of Pontiff and Bishop, that, when his own overwhelming superiority was withdrawn, the Church rebelled against the State, and claimed dominion over it. His sense of justice, as well as the custom of the time, led him to divide his states among his sons, which not only insured enmity between them, but enfeebled the whole of Christendom. Clouds, indeed, began to gather over him some time before his reign was ended. One day he was at a city of Narbonese Gaul, looking out upon the Mediterranean Sea. He saw some vessels appear before the port "These," said the courtiers, "must be ships from the coast of Africa, Jewish merchantmen, or British traders." But Charlemagne, who had leaned a long time against the wall of the room in a passion of tears, said, "No! these are not the ships of commerce; I know by their lightness of movement. They are the galleys of the Norsemen; and, though I know such miserable pirates can do me no harm, I cannot help weeping when I think of the miseries they will inflict on my descendants and the lands they shall rule." A true speech, and just occasion for grief, for the descents of these Scandinavian rovers are the great characteristic of this century, by which a new power was introduced into Europe, and great changes took place in the career of France and England.

It would perhaps be more correct to say that, by this new mixture of race and language, France and England were called into existence. England, up to this date, had been a collection of contending states; France, a tributary portion of a great Germanic empire. Slowly stretching northward, the Roman language, modified, of course, by local pronunciation, had pushed its way among the original Franks. Latin had been for many years the language of Divine Service, and of history, and of law. All westward of the Rhine had yielded to these influences, and the old Teutonic tongue which Clovis had brought with him from Germany had long disappeared, from the Alps up to the Channel. When the death of Charlemagne, in 814, had relaxed

A.D. 814.

the hold which held all his subordinate states together, the diversity of the language of Frenchman and German pointed out, almost as clearly as geographical boundaries could have done, the limits of the respective nations. From henceforward, identity of speech was to be considered a more enduring bond of union than the mere inhabiting of the same soil. But other circumstances occurred to favour the idea of a separation into well-defined communities; and among these the principal was a very long experience of the disadvantages of an encumbered and too extensive empire.

Even while the sword was held by the strong hand of Charlemagne, each portion of his dominions saw with dissatisfaction that it depended for its peace and prosperity on the peace and prosperity of all the rest, and yet in this peace and prosperity it had neither voice nor influence. The inhabitants of the banks of the Loire were, therefore, naturally discontented when they found their provisions enhanced in price, and their sons called to arms, on account of disturbances on the Elbe, or hostilities in the south of Italy. These evils of their position were further increased when, towards the end of Charlemagne's reign, the outer circuit of enemies became more combined and powerful. In proportion as he had extended his dominion, he had come into contact with tribes and states with whom it was impossible to be on friendly terms. To the East, he touched upon the irreclaimable Sclaves and Avars—in the South, he came on the settlements of the Italian Greeks—in Spain, he rested upon the Saracens of Cordova. It was hard for the secure centre of the empire to be destroyed and ruined by the struggles of the frontier populations, with which it had no more sympathy in blood and language than with the people with whom they fought. Already, also, we have seen how local their government had become. They had their own dukes and counts, their own bishops and priests to refer to. The empire was, in fact, a name, and the land they inhabited the only reality with which they were concerned. We shall not be surprised, therefore, when we find that universal rebellion took place when Louis the Debonnaire, the just and saint-like successor of Charlemagne, endeavoured to carry on his father's system. Even his reforms served only to show his own unselfishness, and to irritate the grasping and avaricious offenders whom it was his object to amend. Bishops were stripped of their lay lordships

—prevented from wearing sword and arms, and even deprived of the military ornament of glittering spurs to their heels. The monks and nuns, who had almost universally fallen into evil courses, were forcibly reformed by the laws of a second St. Benedict, whose regulations were harsh towards the regular orders, but useless to the community at large—a sad contrast to the agricultural and manly exhortations of the first conventual legislator of that name. Nothing turned out well with this simplest and most generous of the Carlovingian kings. His virtues, inextricably interlaced as they were with the weaknesses of his character, were more injurious to himself and his kingdom than less amiable qualities would have been. Priest and noble were equally ignorant of the real characteristics of a Christian life. When he refunded the exactions of his father, and restored the conquests which he considered illegally acquired, the universal feeling of astonishment was only lost in the stronger sentiment of disdain. An excellent monk in a cell, or judge in a court of law, Louis the Debonnaire was the most unfit man of his time to keep discordant nationalities in awe. His children were as unnatural as those of Lear, whom he resembled in some other respects: for he found what little reverence waits upon a discrowned king; and personal indignities of the most degrading kind were heaped upon him by those whose duty it was to maintain and honour him. Superstition was set to work on his enfeebled mind, and twice he did public penance for crimes of which he was not guilty; and on the last occasion, stripped of his military baldric—the lowest indignity to which a Frankish monarch could be subjected—clothed in a hair shirt by the hands of an ungrateful bishop, he was led by his triumphant son, Lothaire, through the streets of
A.D. 833. Aix-la-Chapelle. But natural feeling was not

extinguished in the hearts of the staring populace. They saw in the meek emperor's lowly behaviour, and patient endurance of pain and insult, an image of that other and holier King who carried his cross up the steeps of Jerusalem. They saw him denuded of the symbols of earthly power and of military rank, oppressed and wronged—and recognised in that downtrodden man a representation of themselves. This sentiment spread with the magic force of sympathy and remorse. All the world, we are told, left the unnatural son solitary and friendless in the very hour of his success; and Louis, too pure-minded himself to perceive that it was the virtue of his character which made him hated, persisted in pushing on his amendments as if he had the power to carry them into effect. He ordered all lands and other goods which the nobles had seized from the Church to be restored—a tenderness of conscience utterly inexplicable to the marauding baron, who had succeeded by open force, and in a fair field, in despoiling the marauding bishop of land and tower. It was arming his rival, he thought, with a two-edged sword, this silence as to the inroads of the churchman on the property of the nobles, and prevention of their just reprisals on the property of the prelate, by placing it under the safeguard of religion. The rugged warrior kept firm hold of the bishopric or abbey he had secured, and the belted bishop reimbursed himself by appropriating the wealth of his weaker neighbours.

But Louis was as unfortunate in his testamentary arrangement as in all the other regulations of his life. Lothaire was to retain the eastern portion of the empire; Charles, his favourite, had France as far as the Rhine; while Louis was limited to the distant region of Bavaria.

A.D. 840. And having made this disposition of his power, the meek and useless Louis descended into the tomb—a striking example, the French historians tell us, of the great historic truth renewed at such distant dates, that the villanies and cruelties of a race of kings bring misery on the most virtuous of their descendants. All the crimes of the three preceding reigns—the violence and disregard of life exhibited by Charlemagne himself—found their victim and expiation in his meek and gentle-minded son. The harshness of Henry VIII. of England, they add, and the despotic claims of James, were visited on the personally just and amiable Charles; and they point to the parallel case of their own Louis XVI., and see in the sad fortune of that mild and guileless sovereign the final doom of the murderous Charles IX., and the voluptuous and hypocritical Louis XIV. But these kings are still far off in the darkness of the coming centuries. It is a strange sight, in the middle of the ninth century, to see the successor of the great Emperor stealing through the confused and chaotic events of that wretched period, stripped as it were of sword and crown, but everywhere displaying the beauty of pure and simple goodness. He refused to condemn his enemies to death. He was only inexorable towards his own offences, and sometimes humbled himself for imaginary sins. A protector of the Church, a zealous supporter of Rome, it would give additional dignity to the act of canonization if the name of Louis the Debonnaire were added to the list of Saints.

But we have left the empire which it had taken so long to consolidate, now legally divided into three. There is a Charles in possession of the western division; a Louis in the farther Germany; and Lothaire, the unfilial triumpher at Aix-la-Chapelle, invested with the remainder of the Roman world. But Lothaire was not to be satisfied with remainders. Once in power, he was determined to recover the empire in its undivided state.

He was King of Italy; master of Rome and of the Pope; he was eldest grandson of Charlemagne, and A.D. 842. defied the opposition of his brothers. A battle was fought at Fontenay in 842, in which these pretensions were overthrown; and the final severance took place in the following year between the French and German populations. The treaty between the brothers still remains. It is written in duplicate—one in a tongue still intelligible to German ears, and the other in a Romanized speech, which is nearer the French of the present day than the English of Alfred, or even of Edward the Confessor, is to ours.

France, which had hitherto attained that title in right A.D. 843. of its predominant race, held it henceforth on the double ground of language and territory. But there is a curious circumstance connected with the partition of the empire, which it may be interesting to remember. France, in gaining its name and language, lost its natural boundary of the Rhine. Up to this time, the limit of ancient Gaul had continued to define the territory of the Western Franks. In rude times, indeed, there can be no other divisions than those supplied by nature; but now that a tongue was considered a bond of nationality, the French were contented to surrender to Lothaire the Emperor a long strip of territory, running the whole way up from Italy to the North Sea, including both banks of the Rhine, and acting as a wall of partition between them and the German-speaking people on the other side,—a great price to pay, even for the easiest and most widely-spread language in Europe. Yet the most ambitious of Frenchmen would pause before he undid the bargain and reacquired the "exulting and abounding river" at the sacrifice of his inimitable tongue.

Very confused and uncertain are all the events for a

long time after this date. We see perpetual attempts made to restore the reality as well as the name of the Empire. These battles and competitions of the line of Charlemagne are the subject of chronicles and treaties, and might impose upon us by the grandeur of their appearance, if we did not see, from the incidental facts which come to the surface, how unavailing all efforts must be to arrest the dissociation of state from state. The principle of dissolution was at work everywhere. Kingship itself had fallen into contempt, for the great proprietors had been encouraged to exert a kind of personal power in the reign of Charlemagne, which contributed to the strength of his well-consolidated crown; but when the same individual influence was exercised under the nominal supremacy of Louis the Debonnaire or Charles the Bald, it proved a humiliating and dangerous contrast to the weakness of the throne. A combination of provincial dignitaries could at any time outweigh the authority of the king, and sometimes, even singly, the owners of extensive estates threw off the very name of subject. They claimed their lands as not only hereditary possessions, but endowed with all the rights and privileges which their personal offices had bestowed. If their commission from the emperor had given them authority to judge causes, to raise taxes, or to collect troops, they maintained from henceforth that those high powers were inherent in their lands. The dukes, therefore, invested their estates with ducal rights, independent of the Crown, and left to the holder of the kingly name no real authority except in his own domains. Brittany, and Aquitaine, and Septimania, withdrew their allegiance from the poor King of France. He could not compel the ambitious owners of those duchies to recognise his power, and condescended even to treat them as rival and acknowledged kings. Then there were other magnates who were not to be left mere subjects when dukes had risen to such rank. So the Marquises of Toulouse and Gothia, a district of Languedoc, and Auvergne, were treated more as equals than as appointed deputies recallable at pleasure. But worse enemies of kingly dignity than duke or marquis were the ambitious bishops, who looked with uneasy eyes on the rapid rise of their rivals the lay nobility. Already the hereditary title of those territorial potentates was an accomplished fact; the son of the count inherited his father's county. But the general celibacy of the clergy fortunately prevented the hereditary transmission of bishopric and abbey. To make up for the want of this advantage, they boldly determined to assert far higher claims as inherent in their rank than marquis or count could aim at. Starting from the universally-conceded ground of their right to reprimand and punish any Christian who committed sin, they logically carried their pretension to the right of deposing kings if they offended the Church. More than fifty years had passed since Charlemagne had received the imperial crown from the hands of the Pope of Rome. Dates are liable to fall into confusion in ignorant times and places, and it was easy to spread a belief that the popes had always exercised the power of bestowing the diadem upon kings. To support these astounding claims with some certain guarantee, and give them the advantage of prescriptive right by a long and legitimate possession, certain documents were spread abroad at this time, purporting to be a collection by Isidore, a saint of the sixth century, of the decretals or judicial sentences of the popes from a very early period, asserting the unquestioned spiritual supremacy of the Roman See at a date when it was in reality but one of many feeble seats of Christian authority; and to equalize its earthly grandeur with its religious pretension, the new edition of Isidore contained a donation by Constantine himself, in the beginning of the fourth century, of the city of Rome and enormous territories in Italy, to be held in sovereignty by the successors of St. Peter. These are now universally acknowledged to be forgeries and impostures of the grossest kind, but at the time they appeared they served the purpose for which they were intended, and gave a sanction to the Papal assumptions far superior to the rights of any existing crown.

Charles the Bald was a true son of Louis the Debonnaire in his devotion to the Church. When the A.D. 859. bishops of his own kingdom, with Wenilon of Sens as their leader, offended with some remissness he had temporarily shown in advancing their worldly interests, determined to depose him from the throne, and called Louis the German to take his place, Charles fled and threw himself on the protection of the Pope. And when by submission and promises he had been permitted to re-enter France, he complained of the conduct of the prelates in language which ratified all their claims. "Elected by Wenilon and the other bishops, as well as by the lieges of our kingdom, who expressed their consent by their acclamations, Wenilon consecrated me king according to ecclesiastic tradition, in his own diocese, in the Church of the Holy Cross at Orleans. He anointed me with the holy oil; he gave me the diadem and royal sceptre, and seated me on the throne. After that consecration I could not be removed from the throne, or supplanted by any one, at least without being heard and judged by the bishops, by whose ministry I was consecrated king. It is they who are as the thrones of the Divinity. God reposes upon them, and by them he gives forth his judgments. At all times I have been ready to submit to their fatherly corrections, to their just castigations, and am ready to do so still." What more could the Church require? Its wealth was the least of its advantages, though the abbacies and bishoprics were richer than dukedoms all over the land. Their temporal power was supported by the terrors of their spiritual authority; and kings, princes, and people appeared so prone to the grossest excesses of credulity and superstition, that it needed little to throw Europe itself at the feet of the priesthood, and place sword and sceptre permanently in subordination to the crozier. Blindly secure of their position, rioting in the riches of the subject land, the bishops probably disregarded, as below their notice, the two antagonistic principles which were at work at this time in the midst of their own body—the principle of absolute submission to authority in articles of faith, and the principle of free inquiry into all religious doctrine. The first gave birth to the great mystery of transubstantiation, which now first made its appearance as an indispensable belief, and was hailed by the laity and inferior clergy as a crowning proof of the miraculous powers inherent in the Church. The second was equally busy, but was not productive of such permanent effects. At the court of Charles the Bald there was a society of learned and ingenious men, presided over by the celebrated John Scot Erigena, (or native of Ireland,) who had studied the early Fathers and the Platonic philosophy, and were inclined to admit human reason to some participation in the reception of Christian truths. There were therefore discussions on the real presence, and free-will, and predestination, which had the usual unsatisfactory termination of all questions transcending man's understanding, and only embittered their respective adherents without advancing the settlement on either side. While these exercitations of talent and dialectic quickness were carried on, filling the different dioceses with wonder and perplexity, the great body of the people in various countries of Europe were recalled to the practical business of life by disputes of a far more serious character than the wordy wars of Scotus and his foes. Michelet, the most picturesque of the recent historians of France, has given us an amazing view of the state of affairs at this time. It is the darkest period of the human mind; it is also the most unsettled period of human society. Outside of the narrowing limits of peopled Christendom, enemies are pressing upon every side. Saxons on the East are laying their hands in reverence on the manes of horses, and swearing in the name of Odin; Saracens, in the South and West, are gathering once more for the triumph of the Prophet; and suddenly France, Germany, Italy, and England, are awakened to the presence and possible supremacy of a more dreaded invader than either, for the Vikinger, or Norsemen, were abroad upon the sea, and all Christendom was exposed to their ravages. Wherever a river poured its waters into the ocean, on the coast of Narbonne, or Yorkshire, or Calabria, or Friesland, boats, small in size, but countless in number, penetrated into the inland towns, and disembarked wild and fearless warriors, who seemed inspired by the mad fanaticism of some inhuman faith, which made charity and mercy a sin. Starting from the islands and rugged mainland of the present Denmark and Norway, they swept across the stormy North Sea, shouting their hideous songs of glory and defiance, and springing to land when they reached their destination with the agility and bloodthirstiness of famished wolves. Their business was to carry slaughter and destruction wherever they went. They looked with contempt on the lazy occupations of the inhabitants of town or farm, and, above all, were filled with hatred and disdain of the monks and priests.

Their leaders were warriors and poets. Gliding up noiseless streams, they intoned their battle-cry and shouted the great deeds of their ancestors when they reached the walls of some secluded monastery, and rejoiced in wrapping all its terrified inmates in flames. Bards, soldiers, pirates, buccaneers, and heathens, destitute of fear, or pity, or remorse, amorous of danger, and skilful in management of ship and weapon, these were the most ferocious visitants which Southern Europe had ever seen. No storm was sufficient to be a protection against their approach. On the crest of the highest waves those frail barks were seen by the affrighted dwellers on the shore, careering with all sail set, and steering right into their port. All the people on the coast, from the Rhine to Bayonne, and from Toulouse to the Grecian Isles, fled for protection to the great proprietors of the lands. But the great proprietors of the lands were the peaceful priors of stately abbeys, and bishops of wealthy sees. Their pretensions had been submitted to by kings and nobles; they were the real rulers of France; and even in England their authority was very great. Excommunications had been their arms against recusant baron and refractory count; but the Danish Northmen did not care for bell, book, and candle. The courtly circle of scholars and divines could give no aid to the dishoused villagers and trembling cities, however ingenious the logic might be which reconciled Plato to St. Paul; and Charles the Bald, surprised, no doubt, at the inefficacy of prayers and processions, was forced to replace the influence in the hands, not which carried the crozier and cross, but which curbed the horse and couched the spear. The invasion of the Danes was, in fact, the resuscitation of the courage and manliness of the nationalities they attacked. Dreadful as the suffering was at the time, it was not given to any man then alive to see the future benefits contained in the present woe. We, with a calmer view, look back upon the whole series of those events, and in the inter mixture of the new race perceive the elements of greatness and power. Priest-ridden, down-trodden populations received a fresh impulse from those untamed children of the North; and in the forcible relegation of ecclesiastics to the more peaceable offices of their calling, we see the first beginning of the gradation of ranks, and separation of employments, which gave honourable occupation to the respective leaders in Church and State; which limited the clergyman to the unostentatious discharge of his professional duties, and left the baron to command his warriors and give armed protection to all the dwellers in the land. For feudalism, as understood in the Middle Ages, was the inevitable result of the relative positions of priest and noble at the time of the Norsemen's forays. It was found that the possession of great domains had its duties as well as its rights, and the duty of defence was the most imperative of all. Men held their grounds, therefore, on the obligation of keeping their vassals uninjured by the pirates; the bishops were found unable to perform this work, and the territory passed away from their keeping. Vast estates, no doubt, still remained in their possession, but they were placed in the guardianship of the neighbouring chateaux; and though at intervals, in the succeeding centuries, we shall see the prelate dressing himself in a coat of mail, and rendering in person the military service entailed upon his lands, the public feeling rapidly revolted against the incongruity of the deed. The steel-clad bishop was looked on with slender respect, and was soon found to do more damage to his order, by the contrast between his conduct and his profession, than he could possibly gain for it by his prowess or skill in war.

Feudalism, indeed, or the reciprocal obligation of protection and submission, reached its full development by the formal deposition of a descendant of Charlemagne, on the express ground of his inability to defend his
A.D. 879. people from the enemies by which they were surrounded. A congress of six archbishops, and seventeen bishops, was held in the town of Mantela, near Vienne; and after consultation with the nobility, they came to the following resolution:—"That whereas the great qualities of the old mayors of the palace were their only rights to the throne, and Charlemagne, whom all willingly obeyed, did not transmit his talents, along with his crown, to his posterity, it was right to leave that house." They therefore sent an offer of the throne of Burgundy to Boso, Count of the Ardennes, with the conditions "that he should be a true patron and defender of high and low, accessible and friendly to all, humble before God, liberal to the Church, and true to his word."

By this abnegation of temporal weapons, and dependence on the armed warrior for their defence, the prelates put themselves at the head of the unarmed peoples at the same moment that they exercised their spiritual authority over all classes alike. It was useless for them to draw the sword themselves, when they regulated every motion of the hand by which the sword was held.

While this is the state of affairs on the Continent—while the great Empire of Charlemagne is falling to pieces, and the kingly office is practically reduced to a mere equality with the other dignities of the land—while this disunion in nations and weakness in sovereigns is exposing the fairest lands in Europe to the aggressions of enemies on every side—let us cast our eyes for a moment on England, and see in what condition our ancestors are placed at the middle of this century. A most dreadful and alarming condition as ever Old England was in. For many years before this, a pirate's boat or two from the North would run upon the sand, and send the crews to burn and rob a village on the coast of Berwick or Northumberland. Pirates we superciliously call them, but that is from a misconception of their point of honour, and of the very different estimate they themselves formed of their pursuits and character. They were gentleman, perhaps, "of small estate" in some outlying district of Denmark or Norway, but endowed with stout arms and a great wish to distinguish themselves—if the distinction could be accompanied with an increase of their worldly goods. They considered the sea their own domain, and whatever was found on it as theirs by right of possession. They were, therefore, lords of the manor, looking after their rights, their waifs and strays, their flotsams and jetsams. They were also persons of a strong religious turn, and united the spirit of the missionary to the courage of the warrior and the avidity of the conqueror. Odin was still their god, the doors of the Walhalla were still open to them after death, and the skulls of their enemies were foaming with intoxicating mead. The English were renegades from the true faith, a set of drivelling wretches who believed in a heaven where there was no beer, and worshipped a god who bade them pray for their enemies and bless the very people who used them ill. The remaining similarity in the language of the two peoples must have added a bitterness to the contemptuous feelings of the unreclaimed rovers of the deep; and probably, on their return, these enterprising warriors were as proud of the number of priests they had slain, as of the more valuable trophies they carried home. Denmark itself, up to this time, had been distracted with internal wars. It was only the more active spirits who

had rushed across from the Sound, and solaced themselves, in the intervals of their own campaigns, with an onslaught upon an English town. But now the scene was to change. The inroads of separate crews were to be exchanged for national invasions. Harold of
A.D. 838.
the Fair Hair was seated on an undisputed throne, and repressed the outrages of these adventurous warriors by a strong and determined will. He stretched his sceptre over all the Scandinavian world, and neither the North Sea nor the Baltic were safe places for piracy and spoil. One of his countrymen had founded the royal line of Russia, and from his capital of Kieff or Novgorod was civilizing, with whip and battle-axe, the original hordes which now form the Empire of the Czars. Already, from their lurking-places on the shores of the Black Sea, the Norwegian predecessors of the men of Odessa and Sebastopol were threatening a dash upon Constantinople; while sea-kings and jarls, compelled to be quiet and peaceable at home, but backed by all the wild populations of the North, anxious for glory, and greedy of gold and corn, resolved to reduce England to their obedience, and collected an enormous fleet in the quiet recesses of the Baltic, withdrawn from the observation of Harold. It seems fated that France is always, in some sort or other, to set the fashion to her neighbours. We have seen, at the beginning of this century, how England followed the example of the Frankish peoples in consolidating itself into one dominion. Charlemagne was recognised chief potentate of many states, and Egbert was sovereign of all the Saxon lands, from Cornwall to the gates of Edinburgh. But the model was copied no less closely in the splitting-up of the central authority than in its consolidation. While Louis the Debonnaire and Charles the Bald were weakening the throne of Charlemagne, the states of Egbert became

parcelled out in the same way between the descendants of the English king. Ethelwolf was the counterpart of Louis, and carried the sceptre in too gentle a hand. He still further diminished his authority by yielding to the dissensions of his court. Like the Frankish ruler, also, he left portions of his territory to his four sons; of whom it will be sufficient for us to remember that the youngest was the great Alfred—the foremost name in all mediæval history; and by an injudicious marriage with the daughter of Charles the Bald, and his unjust divorce of the mother of all his sons, he offended the feelings of the nation, and raised the animosity of his children. Ethelbald his son completed the popular discontent by marrying his father's widow, the French princess, who had been the cause of so much disagreement; and while the people were thus alienated, and the guiding hand of a true ruler of men was withdrawn,
A.D. 839. the terrible invasion of Danes and Jutlanders went on. They sailed up the Thames and pillaged London. Winchester was given to the flames. The whole isle of Thanet was seized and permanently occupied. The magic standard, a raven, embroidered by the daughters of the famous Regner Lodbrog, (who had been stung to death by serpents in a dungeon into which he was thrown by Ella, King of Northumberland,) was carried from point to point, and was thought to be the symbol of victory and revenge. The offending Northumbrian now felt the wrath of the sons of Lodbrog. They landed with a great army, and after a battle, in which the chiefs of the English were slain, took the Northumbrian kingdom. Nottingham was soon after captured and destroyed. It was no longer a mere incursion. The nobles and great families of Denmark came over to their new conquest, and stationed themselves in strong fortresses, commanding large cir-

cles of country, and lived under their Danish regulations. The land, to be sure, was not populous at that time, and probably the Danish settlements were accomplished without the removal of any original occupiers. But the castles they built, and the towns which rapidly grew around them, acted as outposts against the remaining British kingdoms; and at last, when fleet after fleet disembarked their thousands of warlike colonists

A.D. 860.

—when Leicester, Lincoln, Stamford, York, and Chester, were all in Danish hands, and stretched a line of intrenchments round the lands they considered their own—the divided Anglo-Saxons were glad to purchase a cessation of hostilities by guaranteeing to them forever the places and territories they had secured. And there was now a Danish kingdom enclosed by the fragments of the English empire; there were Danish laws and customs, a Danish mode of pronunciation, and for a good while a still broader gulf of demarcation established between the peoples by their diversity in religious

A.D. 872.

faith. But when Alfred attained the supreme power—and although respecting the treaties between the Danes and English, yet evidently able to defend his countrymen from the aggressions of their foreign neighbour—the pacified pirate, tired of the sea, and softened by the richer soil and milder climate of his new home, began to perceive the very unsatisfactory nature of his ancient belief, and rapidly gave his adhesion to the lessons of the gospel. Guthrum, the Danish chieftain, became a zealous Christian according to his lights, and was baptized with all his subjects. Alfred acted as godfather to the neophyte, and restrained the wildest of his followers within due bounds. Perhaps, even, he was assisted by his Christianized allies in the great and final struggle against Hastings and a new swarm of Scandinavian rovers, whose defeat is the concluding act of this tumultuous century. Alfred drew up near London, and met the advancing hosts on the banks of the river Lea, about twenty miles from town. The patient angler in that suburban river seldom thinks what great events occurred upon its shore. Great ships—all things are comparative—were floating upon its waters, filled with armed Danes. Alfred cut certain openings in the banks and lowered the stream, so that the hostile navy stranded. Out sprang the Danes, astonished at the interruption to their course, and retreated across the country, nor stopped till they had placed themselves in inaccessible positions on the Severn. But the century came to a close. Opening with the great days of Charlemagne, it is right that it should close with the far more glorious reign of Alfred the patriot and sage;—a century illuminated at its two extremes, but in its middle period dark with disunion and ignorance, and not unlikely, unless controlled to higher uses, to give birth to a state of more hopeless barbarism than that from which the nations of Europe had so recently emerged.

TENTH CENTURY.

Emperors of Germany.

A.D.

Louis IV.—(*cont.*)
911. Conrad.
920. Henry the Fowler.
936. Otho the Great.
973. Otho II.
983. Otho III.

Emperors of the East.

A.D.

Leo.—(*cont.*)
911. Constantine IX.
915. Constantine and Romanus.
959. Romanus II.
963. Nicephorus Phocas.
969. John Zimisces.
975. Basilius and Constantine X.

Kings of France.

Charles the Simple.—(*cont.*)
923. Rodolph.
936. Louis IV., (d'Outremer.)
954. Lothaire.
986. Louis V., (le Fainéant.)
987. Hugh Capet, (new dynasty.)
996. Robert the Wise.

Kings of England.

Alfred.—(*cont.*)
901. Edward the Elder.
925. Athelstane.
941. Edmund I.
948. Eldred.
955. Edwy.
959. Edgar.
976. Edward II.
978. Ethelred II.

Authors.

Suidas, (Lexicographer), Gerbert, Odo, Dunstan.

THE TENTH CENTURY.

DARKNESS AND DESPAIR.

The tenth century is always to be remembered as the darkest and most debased of all the periods of modern history. It was the midnight of the human mind, far out of reach of the faint evening twilight left by Roman culture, and further still from the morning brightness of the new and higher civilization. If we try to catch any hope of the future, we must turn from the oppressed and enervated populations of France and Italy to the wild wanderers from the North. By following the latter detachment of Norsemen who made their settlements on the Seine, we shall see that what seemed the wedge by which the compactness of an organized kingdom was to be split up turned out to be the strengthening beam by which the whole machinery of legal government had been kept together. Romanized Gauls, effeminated Franks, Goths, and Burgundians, were found unfitted for the duties either of subjects or rulers. They were too ambitious to obey, and too ignorant to command. Religion itself had lost its efficacy, for the populations had been so fed with false legends, that they had no relish for the truths of the gospel, which, indeed, as an instrument of instruction, had fallen into complete disuse. Ship-loads of false relics, and army-rolls of imaginary saints, were poured out for the general veneration. The higher dignitaries of the Church were looked on with very different feelings, according to the point of view taken of them. When regarded merely as possessors of lands and houses, they were loved or hated according to the use they made of their power; but at the very time when cruelties and vices made them personally the objects of detestation or contempt, the sacredness of their official characters remained. Petitions were sent to the kings against the prelates being allowed to lead their retainers into battle, not entirely from a scruple as to the unlawfulness of such a proceeding, but from the more serious consideration that their death or capture would be taken as a sign of the vengeance of Heaven, and damp the ardour of the party they supported. Churches and cathedrals were filled with processionary spectacles, and their altars covered with the offerings of the faithful; and yet so brutal were the manners of the times, and so small the respect entertained for the individual priest, that laymen of the highest rank thought nothing of knocking down the dignitaries of the Church with a blow on the head, even while solemnly engaged in the offices of devotion. The Roman pontiffs, we have seen, did not scruple to avail themselves of the forgeries of their enthusiastic supporters to establish their authority on the basis of antiquity, and at the middle of this century we should find, if we inquired into it, that the sacred city and chair of St. Peter were a prey to the most violent passions. Many devout Roman Catholics have been, at various periods, so horrified with the condition of their chiefs, and of the perverted religion which had arisen from tradition and imposture, that they have claimed the mere continued existence of the Papacy as a proof of its Divine institution, and a fulfilment of the prophecy that "the gates of hell should not prevail against it." Yet even in the midst of this corruption and ignorance, there were not wanting some redeeming qualities, which soften our feelings towards the ecclesiastic power. It was at all times, in its theory, a protest against the excesses of mere strength and violence. The doctrines it professed to teach were those of kindness and charity; and in the great idea of the throned fisherman at Rome, the poorest saw a kingdom which was not of this world, and yet to which all the kingdoms of this world must bow. Temporal ranks were obliterated when the descendants of kings and emperors were seen paying homage to the sons of serfs and workmen. The immunity, also, from spoil and slaughter, which to a certain extent still adhered to episcopal and abbatial lands, reflected a portion of their sanctity on the person of the bishop and abbot. Mysterious reverence still hung round the convents, within which such ceaseless prayers were said and so many relics exposed, and whither it was also known that all the learning and scholarship of the land had fled for refuge. The doles at monastery-doors, however objected to by political economists, as encouragements of mendicancy and idleness, were viewed in a very different light by the starving crowds, who, besides being qualified by destitution and hunger for the reception of charitable food, had an incontestable right, under the founder's will, to be supported by the establishment on whose lands they lived. The abbot who neglected tofeed the poor was not only an unchristian contemner of the precepts of the faith, but ran counter to the legal obligations of his place. He was administrator of certain properties left for the benefit of persons about whose claims there was no doubt; and when the rapacious methods of maintaining their adherents, which were adopted by the count and baron, were compared with the baskets of broken victuals, and the jugs of foaming beer, which were distributed at the buttery of the abbey, the decision was greatly in favour of the spiritual chief. His ambling mule, and swift hound, and hooded hawks, were not grudged, nor his less defensible occupations seriously inquired into, as long as the beef and mutton were not stinted, and the liquor flowed in reasonable streams. As to his theological tenets, or knowledge of history, either sacred or profane, the highest ecclesiastic was on the same level of utter ignorance and indifference with the lowest of his serfs. There were no books of controversial divinity in all this century. There were no studies exacted from priest or prelate. All that was required was an inordinate zeal in the discovery of holy relics, and an acquaintance with the unnumbered ceremonies performed in the celebration of the service. Morals were in as low a state as learning. Debauchery, drunkenness, and uncleanness were the universal characteristics both of monk and secular. So it is a satisfaction to turn from the wretched spectacle of the decaying and corrupt condition of an old society, to the hardier vices of a new and undegenerated people. Better the unreasoning vigour of the Normans, and their wild trust in Thor and Odin—their spirit of personal independence and pride in the manly exercises—than the creeping submission of an uneducated population, trampled on by their brutal lay superiors, and cheated out of money and labour by the artifices of their priests.

Rollo, the Norman chief, had pushed his unresisted galleys up the Seine, and strongly intrenched himself in Rouen, in the first year of this century. From this citadel, so admirably selected for his purposes, whether of defence or conquest, he spread his expeditions on every side. The boats were so light that no shallowness of water hindered their progress even to the great valleys where the river was still a brook. When impediments were encountered on the way, in the form of waterfall, or, more rarely, of bridge or weir, the adventurers sprang to shore and carried their vessels along the land. When greater booty tempted them, they even crossed long tracts of country, hauling their boats along with them, and launching them in some peaceful vale far away from the sea. Every islet in the rivers was seized and fortified; so that, dotted about over all the beautiful lands between the Seine and the borders of Flanders, were stout Norman colonies, with all the pillage they had obtained securely guarded in those unassailable retreats, and ready to carry their maritime depredations wherever a canoe could swim. Their rapidity of locomotion was equal to that of the Saracenic hordes who had poured down from the Pyrenees in the days of Charles the Hammer. But the Norsemen were of sterner stuff than the light chivalry of Abderachman. Where they stopped they took root. They found it impossible to carry off all the treasure they had seized, and therefore determined to stay beside it. Rouen was at first about to be laid waste, but the policy of the bishop preserved it from destruction, while the wisdom of the rovers converted it into a fortress of the greatest strength. Strong walls were reared all round. The beautiful river was guarded night and day by their innumerable fleet, and in a short time it was recognised equally by friend and foe as the capital and headquarters of a new race. Nor were the Normans left entirely to Scandinavia for recruits. The glowing reports of their success, which successively arrived at their ancient homes, of course inspired the ambitious listeners with an irresistible desire to launch forth and share their fortune; but there were not wanting thousands of volunteers near at hand. King and duke, bishop and baron, were all unable to give protection to the cultivator of the soil and shepherd of the flock. These humble sufferers saw their cabins fired, and all their victuals destroyed. Rollo was too politic to make it a war of extermination against the unresisting inhabitants, and easily opened his ranks for their reception. The result was that, in those disastrous excursions, shouting the war-cry of Norway, and brandishing the pirate's axe, were many of the original Franks and Gauls, allured by the double inducement of escaping further injury themselves and taking vengeance on their former oppressors. Religious scruples did not stand in their way. They gave in their adhesion to the gods of the North, and proved themselves true converts to Thor and Odin, by eating the flesh of a horse that had been slain in sacrifice. It is perhaps this heathen association with horse-flesh as an article of food, which has banished it from Christian consumption for so long a time. But an effort is now made in France to rescue the fattened and roasted steed from the obloquy of its first introduction; and the success of the movement would be complete if there were no other difficulty to contend against than the stigma of its idolatrous origin. Yet the recruits were not all on one side, for we read of certain sea-kings who have grown tired of their wandering life, and taken service under the kings of France. Of these the most famous was Hastings, whom we saw defeated at the end of the last century, on the banks of the river Lea. He is old now, and so far forgetful of his Scandinavian origin that some French annalists claim him as a countryman of their own, and maintain that he was the son of a husbandman near Troyes. He is now a great landed lord, Count of Chartres, and in high favour with the French king. When Rollo had established his forces on the banks of the Eure, one of the tributaries of the Seine, the ancient pirate went at the head of an embassy to see what the new-comer required. Standing on the farther bank of the little river, he raised his voice, and in good Norwegian demanded who they were, and who was their lord. "We have no lord!" they said: "we are all equal." "And why do you come into this land, and what are you going to do?" "We are going to chase away the inhabitants, and make the country our home. But who are you, who speak our language so well?" The count replied, "Did you never hear of Hastings the famous pirate, who had so many ships upon the sea, and did such evil to this realm?" "Of course," replied the Norsemen: "Hastings began well, but has ended poorly." "Have you no wish, then," said Hastings, "to submit yourselves to King Charles, who offers you land and honours on condition of fealty and service?" "Off! off!—we will submit ourselves to no man; and all we can take we shall keep, without dependence on any one. Go and tell the king so, if you like." Hastings returned from his unsuccessful embassy, and the attempt at compromise was soon after followed by a victory of Rollo, which decided the fate of the kingdom. The conquerors mounted the Seine, and laid siege to Paris; but failing in this, they retraced their course to Rouen, and made themselves masters of Bayeux, and of other places. Rollo was now raised to supreme command by the voices of his followers, and took rank as an independent chief. But he was too sagacious a leader to rely entirely on the favour or success of his countrymen. He protected the native population, and reconciled them to the absence of their ancient masters, by the increased security in life and property which his firmness produced. He is said to have hung a bracelet of gold in an exposed situation, with no defence but the terror of his justice, and no one tried to remove it. He saw, also, that however much his power might be dreaded, and his family feared, by the great nobility of France with whom he was brought into contact, his position as a heathen and isolated settler placed him in an inferior situation. The Archbishop of Rouen, who had been his ally in the peaceable occupation of the city, was beside him, with many arguments in favour of the Christian faith. The time during which the populations had been intermixed had smoothed many difficulties on either side. The worship of Thor and Odin was felt to be out of place in the midst of great cathedrals and wealthy monasteries, and it created no surprise when, in a few years, the ambitious Rollo descended from his proud independence, A.D. 911. did suit and service to his feeble adversary Charles the Simple, and retained all his conquests in full property as Duke of Normandy and Peer of France.

Already the divinity that hedged a king placed the crown, even when destitute of real authority, at an immeasurable height above the loftiest of the nobles; and it will be well to preserve this in our memory; for to the belief in this mystical dignity of the sovereign, the monarchical principle was indebted for its triumph in all the states of Europe. No matter how powerless the anointed ruler might be—no matter how greatly a combination of vassals, or a single vassal, might excel him in men and money—the ineffable supremacy of the sacred head was never denied. This strange and ennobling sentiment had not yet penetrated the mind of Rollo and his followers, at the great ceremonial of his reception as a feudatory of the Crown. He declined to bend the knee before his suzerain, but gave him his oath of obedience and faith, standing at his full height. When a stickler for court etiquette insisted on the final ceremony of kissing the foot of the feudal superior, the duke made a sign to one of his piratical attendants to go through the form instead of him. Forth stalked the Norseman towards the overjoyed Charles, and without stooping his body laid hold of the royal boot, and, lifting it with all his strength up to his mouth, upset the unfortunate and short-legged monarch on his back, to the great consternation of his courtiers, and the hilarious enjoyment of his new subjects. But there was henceforth a new element in French society. The wanderers were unanimously converted to Christianity, and the shores of the whole kingdom perpetually guarded from piratical invaders by the contented and warlike countrymen of Hastings and Rollo. Normandy and Brittany were the appanage of the new duke, and perhaps they were more useful to the French monarch, as the well-governed territories of a powerful vassal, than if he had held them in full sovereignty in their former disorganized and helpless state. Language soon began to exert its combining influence on the peoples thus brought into contact, and in a few years the rough Norse gave place to the Romanized idiom of the rest of the kingdom, and the descendants of Rollo in the next generation required an interpreter if any of their relatives came to visit them from Denmark.

But the true characteristic event of this century was the first establishment of real feudalism. The hereditary nature of lands and tenements had long been recognised; the original granter had long surrendered his right to reclaim the property on the death of the first possessor. Gradually also, and by sufferance, the offices to which, in the stronger periods of royalty, the favoured subjects had been promoted for life or a definite time were considered to belong to the descendant of the holder. But it was only now, in the weak administration of a series of nominal kings, that the rights and privileges of a titular nobility were legally recognised, and large portions of the monarchy forever conveyed away from the control of the Crown. There is a sort of natural feudalism which must always exist where there are degrees of power and influence, and which is as potent at this moment as in the time we are describing. A man who expects a favour owes and performs suit and service to the man who has the power of bestowing it. A man with land to let, with money to lend, with patronage to exert, is in a sort of way the "superior" of him who wants to take the farm, or borrow the money, or get the advancement. The obligations of these positions are mutual; and only very advanced philosophers in the theory of disunion and ingratitude would object to the reciprocal feelings of kindness and attachment they naturally produce. In a less settled state of society, such as that now existing, or which lately existed, at the Cape of Good Hope and in New Zealand, the feudal principle is fresh and vigorous, though not recognised under that name, for the peaceful or weak are glad to pay deference and respect to the wielder of the protective sword. In the tenth century there were customs, but no laws, for laws presuppose some external power able to enforce them, and the decay of the kingly authority had left the only practical government in the hands of the great and powerful. They gave protection in return for obedience. But when more closely inquired into, this assumption of authority by a nobility or upper class is found to have been purely defensive on the part of the lay proprietors, against the advancing tide of a spiritual Democracy, which threatened to submerge the whole of Europe. Already the bishops and abbots had got possession of nearly half the realm of France, and in other countries they were equally well provided. Those great officers were the leaders of innumerable priests and monks, and owed their dignities to the popular will. The Pope himself—a sovereign prince when once placed in the chair of St. Peter—was indebted for his exaltation to a plurality of votes of the clergy and people of Rome. Election was, in fact, the universal form of constituting the rule under which men were to live. But who were the electors? The appointment was still nominally in the people, but the people were almost entirely under the influence of the clerical orders. Mechanics and labourers were the serfs or dependants of the rich monasteries, and tillers of the episcopal lands. The citizens had not yet risen into wealth or intelligence, and, though subject in their persons to the baron whose castle commanded their walls, they were still under the guidance of their priests. No middle class existed to hold the balance even between the nobility and the Church; and the masses of the population were naturally disposed to throw power into the hands of persons who sprang, in most instances, from families no better than their own, and recommended themselves to popular favour by opposition (often just, but always domineering) to the proceedings of the lay aristocracy. The labouring serfs, who gave the vote, were not much inferior in education or refinement to the ordained serfs who canvassed for their favour. Abbacies, priories, bishoprics, parochial incumbencies, and all cathedral dignities, were held by a body distinct from the feudal gentry, and elevated, mediately or immediately, by universal suffrage. If some stop had not been put to the aggressions of the priesthood, all the lands in Christendom would have been absorbed by its insatiable greed—all the offices of the State would have been conveyed to sacerdotal holders; all kings would have been nominated by the clerical voice alone, and freedom and progress would never have had their birth. The monarchs—though it is almost mockery to call them so in England—were waging an unsuccessful war with the pretensions of St.

Dunstan, who was an embodiment of the pitiless harshness and blind ambition of a zealot for ecclesiastic supremacy. In France a succession of imbecile rulers, whose characters are clearly enough to be guessed from the descriptive epithets which the old chroniclers have attached to their names, had left the Crown a prey to all its enemies. What was to be expected from a series of governors whose mark in history is made by such nicknames as "The Bald," "The Stammerer," "The Fat," and finally, without circumlocution, "The Fool"? Everybody tried to get as much out of the royal plunder as he could. Bishops got lands and churches. Foreign pirates, we have seen, got whole counties at a time, and in self-defence the nobility were forced to join in the universal spoil. Counties as large as Normandy were retained as rightful inheritances, independent of all but nominal adhesion to the throne. Smaller properties were kept fast hold of, on the same pretence. And by this one step the noble was placed in a position of advantage over his rival the encroaching bishop. His power was not the mere creation of a vote or the possession of a lifetime. His family had foundations on which to build through a long succession of generations. Marriage, conquest, gift, and purchase, all tended to the consolidation of his influence; and the result was, that, instead of one feeble and decaying potentate in the person of the king, to resist the aggressions of an absorbing and levelling Church, there were hundreds all over the land, democratic enough in regard to their dislike of the supremacy of the sovereign, but burning with a deep-seated aristocratic hatred of the territorial aggrandizement of the dissolute and low-born clergy. Europe was either in this century to be ruled by mailed barons or surpliced priests. Sometimes they played into each other's hands. Sometimes the warrior

overwhelmed an adversary by enlisting on his side the sympathies of the Church. Sometimes the Church, in its controversies with the Crown, cast itself on the protection of the warrior, but more frequently it threw its weight into the scale of the vacillating monarch, who could reward it with such munificent donations. But those munificent donations were equivalent to aggressions on the nobles. There was no use in their trying to check the aggrandizement of the clerical power, if the Crown continued its gifts of territory and offices to the priests and churches. And at last, when the strong-handed barons of France were tired out with the fatuity of their effete kings, they gave the last proof of the supremacy they had attained, by departing from the line of Charlemagne and placing one of themselves upon the throne. Hugh Capet, the chief of the feudal nobles, was chosen to wear the crown as delegate and representative of the rest. The old Mayors of the Palace had been revived in his family for some generations; and when Louis the son of Lothaire died, after a twelvemonth's permissive reign, in 987, the warriors and land owners turned instinctively to the strongest and most distinguished member of their body to be the guardian of the privileges they had already secured. This was an aristocratic movement against the lineal supremacy of the Crown, and in reply to the democratic policy of the Church. But the Pope was too clear-sighted to lose the chance of attaching another champion to the papal chair. He
A.D. 987. made haste to ratify the new nomination to the throne, and pronounced Hugh Capet "King of France in right of his great deeds."

Hugh Capet had been first of the feudal nobility; but from thenceforth he laboured to be "every inch a king." He tried to please both parties, and to humble them at the same time. He did not lavish crown-lands or lofty employments on the clergy; he took a new and very economical way of attaching them to his cause. He procured his election, it is not related by what means, to the highest dignities in the Church, and, although not in holy orders, was invested with the abbacies of St. Denis and St. Martin's and St. Germain's. The clergy were delighted with the increase to the respectability of their order, which had thus a king among its office-bearers. The Pope, we have seen, was first to declare his legitimacy; the bishops gave him their support, as they felt sure that, as a threefold abbot, he must have interests identical with their own. He was fortunate, also, in gaining still more venerated supporters; for while he was building a splendid tomb at St. Valery, the saint of that name appeared to him and said, with larger promise than the witches to Banquo, "Thou and thy descendants shall be kings to the remotest generations."

With the nobles he proceeded in a different manner. His task, you will remember, was to regain the universal submission of the nation; and success at first seemed almost hopeless, for his real power, like that of the weakest of his immediate predecessors, extended no further than his personal holdings. In his fiefs of France proper (the small district including Paris) and Burgundy he was all-powerful; but in the other principalities and dukedoms he was looked on merely as a neighbouring potentate with some shadowy claims of suzerainty, with no right of interference in their internal administration. The other feudatories under the old monarchy, but who were in reality independent sovereigns under the new, were the Dukes of Normandy and Flanders, and Aquitaine and Toulouse. These made the six lay peerages of the kingdom, and, with the six ecclesiastical chief rulers, made the Twelve Peers of France.

Of the lay peerages it will be seen that Hugh was in possession of two—the best situated and most populous of all. The extent of his possessions and the influence of his name were excellent starting-points in his efforts to restore the power of the Crown; but other things were required, and the first thing he aimed at was to place his newly-acquired dignity on the same vantage-ground of hereditary succession as his dukedoms had long been. With great pomp and solemnity he himself was anointed with the holy oil by the hands of the Pope; and he took advantage of the self-satisfied security of the other nobles to have the ceremony of
A.D. 989. a coronation performed on his son during his lifetime, and by this arrangement the appearance of election was avoided at his death. Its due weight must be given to the universal superstition of the time, when we attribute such importance to the formal consecration of a king. Externals, in that age, were all in all. Something mystic and divine, as we have said before, was supposed to reside in the very fact of having the crown placed on the head with the sanction and prayers of the Church. Opposition to the wearer became not only treason, but impiety; and when the same policy was pursued by many generations of Hugh's successors, in always procuring the coronation of their heirs before their demise, and thus obliterating the remembrance of the elective process to which they owed their position, the royal power had the vast advantage of hereditary descent added to its unsubstantial but never-abandoned claim of paramount authority. The effects of this momentous change in the dynasty of one of the great European nations were felt in all succeeding centuries. The family connection between the house of France and the Empire was dissolved; and the struggle between the old condition of society and the rising intelligence

of the peoples—which is the great characteristic of the Middle Ages—took a more defined form than before: aristocracy assumed its perfected shape of king and nobility combined for mutual defence on one side, and on the other the towns and great masses of the nations striving for freedom and privilege under the leadership of the sympathizing and democratic Church; for the Church was essentially democratic, in spite of the arrogance and grasping spirit of some of its principal leaders. From hereditary aristocracy and hereditary royalty it was equally excluded; and the celibacy of the clergy has had this good effect, if no other: Its members were recruited from the people, and derived all their influence from popular support. In Germany the same process was going on, though without the crowning consummation of making the empire non-elective. Otho, however —worthier of the name of Great than many who have borne that ambitious title—succeeded in limiting that highest of European dignities to the possessors of the
A.D. 962. German crown, and commenced the connection between Upper Italy and the Emperors which still subsists (so uneasily for both parties) under the house of Austria.

In England the misery of the population had reached its maximum. The immigration of the Norsemen had been succeeded by numberless invasions, accompanied with all the horrors of barbarism and religious hatred; for the Danes who devastated the shores in this age were as remorselessly savage, and as bitterly heathen, as their predecessors a hundred years before. No place was safe for the unhappy Christianized Saxons. Their sufferings were of the same kind as those of the inhabitants of Normandy when Rollo began his ravages. Their priest-ridden kings and impoverished nobles could give them no protection. Bribes were paid to the assailants, and only brought over increasing and hungrier hordes. The land was a prey to wretchedness of every kind, and it was slender consolation to the starving and trampled multitudes that all the world was suffering to almost the same extent. Saracens were devastating the coasts of Italy, and a wild tribe of Sclaves trying to burst through the Hungarian frontier. At Rome itself, the capital of intellect and religion, such iniquities were perpetrated on every side that Protestant authors themselves consent to draw a veil over them for the sake of human nature; and in these sketches we require to do nothing more than allude to the crimes and wickedness of the papal court as one of the features by which the century was marked. Women of high rank and infamous character placed the companions of their vices in the highest offices of the Church, and seated their sons or paramours on the papal throne. Spiritual pretensions rose almost in proportion to personal immorality, and the curious spectacle was presented of a power losing all respect at home by conduct which the heathen emperors of the first century scarcely equalled; of popes alternately dethroning and imprisoning each other—sometimes of two popes at a time—always dependent for life or influence on the will of the emperor, or whoever else might be dominant in Italy—and yet successfully claiming the submission and reverence of distant nations as "Bishop of all the world" and lineal "successors of the Prince of the Apostles." This claim had never been expressly made before, and is perhaps the most conclusive proof of the darkness and ignorance of this period. Men were too besotted to observe the incongruity between the life and profession of those blemishes of the Church, even when by travelling to the seat of government they had the opportunity of seeing the Roman pontiff and his satellites and patrons. The rest of the world had no means of learning the real state of affairs. Education had almost died out among the clergy themselves. Nobody else could write or read. Travelling monks gave perverted versions, we may believe, of every thing likely to be injurious to the interests of the Church; and the result was, that everywhere beyond the city-walls the thunder of a Boniface the Seventh, or a John the Twelfth, was considered as good thunder as if it had issued from the virtuous indignation of St. Paul.

But just as this century drew to a close, various circumstances concurred to produce a change in men's minds. It was a universally-diffused belief that the world would come to an end when a thousand years from the Saviour's birth were expired. The year 999 was therefore looked upon as the last which any one would see. And if ever signs of approaching dissolution were shown in heaven and earth, the people of this century might be pardoned for believing that they were made visible to them. Even the breaking up of morals and law, and the wide deluge of sin which overspread all lands, might be taken as a token that mankind were deemed unfit to occupy the earth any more. In addition to these appalling symptoms, famines were renewed from year to year in still increasing intensity and brought plague and pestilence in their train. The land was left untilled, the house unrepaired, the right unvindicated; for who could take the useless trouble of ploughing or building, or quarrelling about a property, when so few months were to put an end to all terrestrial interests? Yet even for the few remaining days the multitudes must be fed. Robbers frequented every road, entered even into walled towns; and there was no authority left to protect the weak, or bring the wrong-doer to punishment. Corn and cattle were at length exhausted; and in a great part of the Continent the most frightful extremities were endured; and when endurance could go no further, the last desperate expedient was resorted to, and human flesh was commonly consumed. One man went so far as to expose it for sale in a populous market-town. The horror of this open confession of their needs was so great, that the man was burned, but more for the publicity of his conduct than for its inherent guilt. Despair gave a loose to all the passions. Nothing was sacred—nothing safe. Even when food might have been had, the vitiated taste made bravado of its depravation, and women and children were killed and roasted in the madness of the universal fear. Meantime the gentler natures were driven to the wildest excesses of fanaticism to find a retreat from the impending judgment. Kings and emperors begged at monastery-doors to be admitted brethren of the Order. Henry of Germany and Robert of France were saints according to the notions of the time, and even now deserve the respect of mankind for the simplicity and benevolence of their characters. Henry the Emperor succeeded in being admitted as a monk, and swore obedience on the hands of the gentle abbot who had failed in turning him from his purpose. "Sire," he said at last, "since you are under my orders, and have sworn to obey me, I command you to go forth and fulfil the duties of the state to which God has called you. Go forth, a monk of the Abbey of St. Vanne, but Emperor of the West." Robert of France, the son of Hugh Capet, placed himself, robed and crowned, among the choristers of St. Denis, and led the musicians in singing hymns and psalms of his own composition. Lower men were satisfied with sacrificing the marks of their knightly and seignorial rank, and placed baldrics and swords on the altars and before the images of saints. Some manumitted their serfs, and bestowed large sums upon charitable trusts, commencing their disposition with words implying the approaching end of all Crowds of the common people would sleep nowhere but in the porches, or at any rate within the shadow, of the churches and other holy buildings; and as the day of doom drew nearer and nearer, greater efforts were made to appease the wrath of Heaven. Peace was proclaimed between all classes of men. From Wednesday night till Monday evening of each week there was to be no violence or enmity or war in all the land. It was to be a Truce of God; and at last, all their strivings after a better state, acknowledgments of a depraved condition, and heartfelt longings for something better, purer, nobler, received their consummation, when, in the place of the unprincipled men who had disgraced Christianity by carrying vice and incredulity into the papal chair, there was appointed to the highest of ecclesiastical dignities a man worthy of his exaltation; and the good and holy Gerbert, the tutor, guide, and friend of Robert of France, was appointed Pope in 998, and took the name of Sylvester the Second.

ELEVENTH CENTURY.

Emperors of Germany.

A.D.

Otho III.—(*cont.*)

1002. Henry of Bavaria.

1024. Conrad II.

1039. Henry III.

1056. Henry IV.

Kings of England.

Ethelred II.—(*cont.*)

1013. Sweyn.
1015. Canute the Great.
1017. Edmund II.
1039. Harold and Hardicanute.

Danes.

1042. Edward the Confessor.

1066. Harold, (son of Godwin.)

1066. William the Conqueror.

1087. William Rufus.

Emperors of the East.

A.D.

Basilius.—(*cont.*)

1028. Romanus III.

1042. Empress Zoe and Theodora.

1056. Michael VI.

1057. Isaac Comnenus.

1059. Constantine X., (Ducas.)

1067. Eudoxia and Constantine XI.

1068. Romanus IV., (Diogenes.)

1071. Michael.

1078. 1081. Two Princes of the House of the Comneni.

1081. Alexis I.

Kings of France.

Robert the Wise.—(*cont.*)

1031. Henry I.

1060. Philip I.

1096. The First Crusade.

Authors.

Anselm, (1003–1079,) Abelard, (1079–1142,) Berengarius, Roscelin, Lanfranc, Theophylact, (1077.)

THE ELEVENTH CENTURY.

THE COMMENCEMENT OF IMPROVEMENT—GREGORY THE SEVENTH—FIRST CRUSADE.

AND now came the dreaded or hoped-for year. The awful Thousand had at last commenced, and men held their breath to watch what would be the result of its arrival. "And he laid hold of the dragon, that old serpent, which is the Devil, and Satan, and bound him for a thousand years, and cast him into the bottomless pit, and shut him up, and set a seal upon him, that he should deceive the nations no more, till the thousand years should be fulfilled: and after that he must be loosed a little season." (Revelation xx. 2, 3.) With this text all the pulpits in Christendom had been ringing for a whole generation. And not the pulpits only, but the refection-halls of convents, and the cottages of the starving peasantry. Into the castle also of the noble, we have seen, it had penetrated; and the most abject terror pervaded the superstitious, while despair, as in shipwrecked vessels, displayed itself amid the masses of the population in rioting and insubordination. The spirit of evil for a little season was to be let loose upon a sinful world; and when the observer looked round at the real condition of the people in all parts of Europe—at the ignorance and degradation of the multitude, the cruelty of the lords, and the unchristian ambition and unrestrained passions of the clergy—it must have puzzled him how to imagine a worse state of things even when the chain was loosened from "that old serpent," and the world placed unresistingly in his folds. Yet, as if men's minds had now reached their lowest point, there was a perpetual rise from the beginning of this date. When the first day of the thousand-and-first year shone upon the world, it seemed that in all nations the torpor of the past was to be thrown off. There were strivings everywhere after a new order of things. Coming events cast their shadows a long way before; for in the very beginning of this century, when it was reported that Jerusalem had been taken by the Saracens, Sylvester uttered the memorable words, "Soldiers of Christ, arise and fight for Zion." By a combination of all Christian powers for one object, he no doubt hoped to put an end to the party quarrels by which Europe was torn in pieces. And this great thought must have been germinating in the popular heart ever since the speech was spoken; for we shall see at the end of the period we are describing how instantaneously the cry for a crusade was responded to in all lands. In the mean time, the first joy of their deliverance from the expected destruction impelled all classes of society in a more honourable and useful path than they had ever hitherto trod. As if by universal consent, the first attention was paid to the maintenance of the churches, those holy buildings by whose virtues the wrath of Heaven had been turned away. In France, and Italy, and Germany, the fabrics had in many places been allowed to fall into ruin. They were now renovated and ornamented with the costliest materials, and with an architectural skill which, if it previously existed, had had no room for its display. Stately cathedrals took the place of the humble buildings in which the services had been conducted before. Every thing was projected on a gigantic scale, with the idea of permanence prominently brought forward, now that the threatened end of all things was seen to be postponed. The foundations were broad and deep, the walls of immense thickness, roofs steep and high to keep off the rain and snow, and square buttressed towers to sustain the church and furnish it at the same time with military defence. It was a holy occupation, and the clergy took a prominent part in the new movement. Bishops and monks were the principal members of a confraternity who devoted themselves to the science of architecture and founded all their works on the exact rules of symmetry and fitness. Artists from Italy, where Roman models were everywhere seen, and enthusiastic students from the south of France, where the great works of the Empire must have exercised an ennobling influence on their taste and fancy, brought their tribute of memory or invention to the design. Tall pillars supported the elevated vault, instead of the flat roof of former days; and gradually an approach was made to what, in after-periods, was recognised as the pure Gothic. Here, then, was at last a real science, the offspring of the highest aspirations of the human mind. Churches rising in rich profusion in all parts of the country were the centres of architectural taste. The castle of the noble was no longer to be a mere mass of stones huddled on each other, to protect its inmates from outward attack. The skill of the learned builder was called in, and on picturesque heights, safe from hostile assault by the difficulty of approach, rose turret and bartizan, arched gateway and square-flanked towers, to add new features to the landscape, and help the march of civilization, by showing to that allegorizing age the result, both for strength and beauty, of regularity and proportion. For at this time allegory, which gave an inner meaning to outward things, was in full force. There was no portion of the parish church which had not its mystical significance; and no doubt, at the end

of this century, the architectural meaning of the external alteration of the structure was perceived, when the great square tower, which typified resistance to worldly aggression, was exchanged for the tall and graceful spire which pointed encouragingly to heaven. Occasions were eagerly sought for to give employment to the ruling passion. Building went on in all quarters. The beginning of this century found eleven hundred and eight monasteries in France alone. In the course of a few years she was put in possession of three hundred and twenty-six more. The magnificent Abbey of
A.D. 1035. Fontenelle was restored in 1035 by William of Normandy; and this same William, whom we shall afterwards see in the somewhat different character of Conqueror and devastator of England, was the founder and patron of more abbeys and monasteries than any other man. Many of them are still erect, to attest the solidity of his work; the ruins of the others raise our surprise that they are not yet entire—so vast in their extent and gigantic in their materials. But the same character of permanence extended to all the works of this great builder's* hands—the systems of government no less than the fabrics of churches. The remains of his feudalism in our country, no less than the fragments of his masonry at Bayeux, Fecamp, and St. Michael's, attest the cyclopean scale on which his superstructures were reared. Nor were these great architectural efforts which characterize this period made only on behalf of the clergy. It gives a very narrow notion, as Michelet has observed, of the uses and purposes of those enormous buildings, to view them merely as places for public worship and the other offices of religion. The church in a district was, in those days, what a hundred other

---

* He was called Le Grand Bâtisseur.

buildings are required to make up in the present. It was the town-hall, the market-place, the concert-room, the theatre, the school, the news-room, and the vestry, all in one. We are to remember that poverty was almost universal. The cottages in which the serfs and even the freemen resided were wretched hovels. They had no windows, they were damp and airless, and were merely considered the human kennels into which the peasantry retired to sleep. In contrast to this miserable den there arose a building vast and beautiful, consecrated by religion, ornamented with carving and colour, large enough to enable the whole population to wander in its aisles, with darker recesses under the shade of pillars, to give opportunity for familiar conversation or the enjoyment of the family meal. The church was the poor man's palace, where he felt that all the building belonged to him and was erected for his use. It was also his castle, where no enemy could reach him, and the love and pride which filled his heart in contemplating the massive proportions and splendid elevation of the glorious fane overflowed towards the officers of the church. The priest became glorified in his eyes as the officiating servant in that greatest of earthly buildings, and the bishop far outshone the dignity of kings when it was known that he had plenary authority over many such majestic fabrics. Ascending from the known to the unknown, the Pope of Rome, the Bishop of Bishops, shone upon the bewildered mind of the peasant with a light reflected from the object round which all his veneration had gathered from his earliest days—the scene of all the incidents of his life—the hallowed sanctuary into which he had been admitted as an infant, and whose vaults should echo to the funeral service when he should have died.

But this century was distinguished for an upheaving

of the human mind, which found its development in other things besides the bursting forth of architectural skill. It seemed that the chance of continued endurance, vouchsafed to mankind by the rising of the sun on the first morning of the eleventh century, gave an impulse to long-pent-up thoughts in all the directions of inquiry. The dulness of unquestioning undiscriminating belief was disturbed by the freshening breezes of dissidence and discussion. The Pope himself, the venerable Sylvester the Second, had acquired all the wisdom of the Arabians by attending the Mohammedan schools in the royal city of Cordova. There he had learned the mysteries of the secret sciences, and the more useful knowledge—which he imported into the Christian world—of the Arabic numerals. The Saracenic barbarism had long yielded to the blandishments of the climate and soil of Spain; and emirs and sultans, in their splendid gardens on the Guadalquivir, had been discussing the most abstruse or subtle points of philosophy while the professed teachers of Christendom were sunk in the depths of ignorance and credulity. Sylvester had made such progress in the unlawful learning accessible at the head-quarters of the unbelievers, that his simple contemporaries could only account for it by supposing he had sold himself to the enemy of mankind in exchange for such prodigious information. He was accused of the unholy arts of magic and necromancy; and all that orthodoxy could do to assert her superiority over such acquirements was to spread the report, which was very generally credited, that when the years of the compact were expired, the paltering fiend appeared in person and carried off his debtor from the midst of the affrighted congregation, after a severe logical discussion, in which the father of lies had the best of the argument. This was a conclusive proof of the danger of all logical acquirements. But as time passed on, and the darkness of the tenth century was more and more left behind, there arose a race of men who were not terrified by the fate of the philosophic Sylvester from cultivating their understandings to the highest pitch. Among those there were two who particularly left their marks on the genius of the time, and who had the strange fortune also of succeeding each other as Archbishops of Canterbury. These were Lanfranc and Anselm. When Lanfranc was still a monk at Caen, he had attracted to his prelections more than four thousand scholars; and Anselm, while in the same humble rank, raised the schools of Bec in Normandy to a great reputation. From these two men, both Italians by birth, the Scholastic Philosophy took its rise. The old unreasoning assent to the doctrines of Christianity had now new life breathed into it by the permitted application of intellect and reason to the support of truth. In the darkness and misery of the previous century, the deep and mysterious dogma of Transubstantiation had made its first authoritative appearance in the Church. Acquiesced in by the docile multitude, and accepted by the enthusiastic and imaginative as an inexpressible gift of fresh grace to mankind, and a fitting crown and consummation of the daily-recurring miracles with which the Mother and Witness of the truth proved and maintained her mission, it had been attacked by Berenger of Tours, who used all the resources of reason and ingenuity to demonstrate its unsoundness. But Lanfranc came to the rescue, and by the exercise of a more vigorous dialectic, and the support of the great majority of the clergy, confuted all that Berenger advanced, had him stripped of his archdeaconry of Angers and other preferments, and left him in such destitution and disfavour that the discomfited opponent of the Real Presence was

A.D. 1042.

A.D. 1059. forced to read his retractation at Rome, and only expiated the enormity of his fault by the rigorous seclusion of the remainder of his life. The hopeful feature in this discussion was, that though the influence of ecclesiastic power was not left dormant, in the shape of temporal ruin and spiritual threats, the exercise of those usual weapons of authority was accompanied with attempts at argument and conviction. Lanfranc, indeed, in the very writings in which he used his talents to confute the heretic, made such use of his reasoning and inductive faculties that he nearly fell under the ban of heresy himself. He had the boldness to imagine a man left to the exercise of his natural powers alone, and bringing observation, argument, and ratiocination to the discovery of the Christian dogmas; but he was glad to purchase his complete rehabilitation, as champion of the Church, by a work in which he admits reason to the subordinate position of a supporter or commentator, but by no means a foundation or inseparable constituent of an article of the faith. Any thing was better than the blindness and ignorance of the previous age; and questions of the purest metaphysics were debated with a fire and animosity which could scarcely have been excited by the greatest worldly interests. The Nominalists and Realists began their wordy and unprofitable war, which after occasional truces may at any moment break out, as it has often done before, though it would now be confined to the professorial chairs in our universities, and not exercise a preponderating influence on the course of human affairs. The dispute (as the names of the disputants import) arose upon the question as to whether universal ideas were things or only the names of things, and on this the internecine contest went on. All the subtlety of the old Greek philosophies was introduced into the scholasticisms and word-splittings of those useless arguers; and vast reputations, which have not yet decayed, were built on this very unsubstantial foundation.

It shows how immeasurably the efforts of the intellect, even when misapplied, transcend the greatest triumphs of military skill, when we perceive that in this age, which was illustrated by the Conquest of England, first by the Danes, and then by William, by the marvellous rise and triumphant progress of the sons of Tancred of Hauteville, and by the startling incidents of the First Crusade,—the central figure is a meagre, hard-featured monk, who rises from rank to rank, till he governs and tramples on the world under the name of Gregory the Seventh. It may seem to some people, who look at the present condition of the Romish Church, that too prominent a place is assigned in these early centuries to the growth and aggrandizement of the ecclesiastical power; but as the object of these pages is to point out what seems the main distinguishing feature of each of the periods selected for separate notice, it would be unpardonable to pass over the Papacy, varying in extent of power and pretension at every period when it comes into view, and always impressing a distinct and individualizing character on the affairs with which it is concerned. It is the most stable, and at the same time the most flexible, of powers. Kingdoms and dynasties flourish and decay, and make no permanent mark on the succeeding age. The authority of a ruler like Charlemagne or Otho rises in a full tide, and, having reached its limits, yields to the irresistible ebb. But Roman influence knows no retrocession. Even when its pretensions are defeated and its assaults repulsed, it claims as *de jure* what it has lost *de facto*, and, though it were reduced to the possession of a single church, would continue to issue its orders to the habitable globe.

Like the last descendant of the Great Mogul, who professed to rule over Hindostan while his power was limited to the walls of his palace at Delhi, the bearer of the Tiara abates no jot of his state and dignity when every vestige of his influence has disappeared. While ridiculed as a puppet or pitied as a sufferer at home, he arrogates more than royal power in regions which have long thrown off his authority, and announces his will by the voice of blustering and brazen heralds to a deaf and rebellious generation, which looks on him with no more respect than the grotesquely-dressed conjurers before a tent-door at a fair. But the herald's voice would have been listened to with respect and obedience if it had been heard at the Pope's gate in 1073. There had never been such a pope before, and never has been such a pope since. Others have been arrogant and ambitious, but no one has ever equalled Hildebrand in arrogance and ambition. Strength of will, also, has been the ruling character of many of the pontiffs, but no one has ever equalled Hildebrand in the undying tenacity with which he pursued his object. He was like Roland, the hero of Roncesvalles, who even in defeat knew how to keep his enemies at a distance by blowing upon his horn. When Durandal foiled the vanquished Gregory, he spent his last breath in defiant blasts upon his Olifant.

But there were many circumstances which not only rendered the rise of such a person possible, but made his progress easy and almost unavoidable. First of all, the crusading spirit which commenced with this century had introduced a great change in the principles and practice of the higher clergy. It is a mistake to suppose that the expedition to Jerusalem, under the preaching of Peter the Hermit, which took place in 1094, was the earliest manifestation of the aggressive spirit of the Christian, as such, against the unbeliever. A holy war was proclaimed against the Saracens of Italy at an early date. An armed assault upon the Jews, as descendants of the murderers of Christ, had taken place in 1080. Even the Norman descent on England was considered by the more devout of the Papist followers in the light of a crusade against the enemies of the Cross, as the Anglo-Saxons were not sufficiently submissive to the commands of Rome. Bishops, we saw, were held in a former century to derogate from the sanctity of their characters when they fought in person like the other occupants of fiefs. But the sacred character which expeditions like those against Sicily and Salerno gave to the struggle made a great difference in the popular estimate of a prelate's sphere of action. He was now held to be strictly in the exercise of his duty when he was slaying an infidel with the edge of the sword. He was not considered to be more in his place at the head of a procession in honour of a saint than at the head of an army of cavaliers destroying the enemies of the faith. Warlike skill and personal courage became indispensable in a bishop of the Church; and in Germany these qualities were so highly prized, that the inhabitants of a diocese in the empire, presided over by a man of peace and holiness, succeeded in getting him deposed by the Pope on the express ground of his being "placable and far from valiant." The epitaph of a popular bishop was, that he was "good priest and brave chevalier." The manners and feelings of the camp soon became disseminated among the reverend divines, who inculcated Christianity with a battle-axe in their hands. They quarrelled with neighbouring barons for portions of land. They seized the incomes of churches and abbeys. Bishop and baron strove with each other who could get most for himself out of the property of the Church. The layman forced his serfs to elect his infant son to an abbacy or bishopric, and then pillaged the estate and stripped the lower clergy in the minor's name. Other abuses followed; and though the strictness of the rule against the open marriage of priests had long ceased, and in some places the superiority of wedded incumbents had been so recognised that the appointment of a pastor was objected to unless he was accompanied by a wife—still, the letter of the Church-law, enjoining celibacy on all orders of the clergy, had never been so generally neglected as at the present time. No attempt was made to conceal the almost universal infraction of the rule. Bishops themselves brought forward their wives on occasions of state and ceremony, who disputed the place of honour with the wives of counts and barons. When strictly inquired into, however, these alliances were not allowed to have the effect of regular matrimony. They were looked upon merely as a sort of licensed and not dishonourable concubinage, and the children resulting from them were deprived of the rights of legitimacy. Yet the wealth and influence of their parents made their exclusion from the succession to land of little consequence. They were enriched sufficiently with the spoil of the diocese to be independent of the rights of heirship. This must have led, however, to many cases of hardship, when the feudal baron, tempted by the riches of the neighbouring see, had laid violent hands on the property, and by bribery or force procured his own nomination as bishop. The children of any marriage contracted after that time lost their inheritance of the barony by the episcopal incapacity of their father, and must have added to the general feeling of discontent caused by the junction of the two characters. For when the tyrannical lord became a prelate, it only added the weapons of ecclesiastic domination to the baronial armory of cruelty and extortion. He could now withhold all the blessings of the Church, as bishop, unless the last farthing were yielded up to his demands as landlord. An appalling state of things, when the refractory vassal, who had escaped the sword, could be knocked into submission by the crozier, both wielded by the same man. The Church, therefore, in its highest offices, had become as mundane and ambitious as the nobility. And it must have been evident to a far dimmer sight than Hildebrand's, that, as the power and independence of the barons had been gained at the expense of the Crown, the wealth and possessions of the bishops would weaken their allegiance to the Pope. Sprung from the lowest ranks of the people, the grim-hearted monk never for a moment was false to his order. He looked on lords and kings as tyrants and oppressors, on bishops themselves as lording it over God's heritage and requiring to be held down beneath the foot of some levelling and irresistible power, which would show them the nothingness of rank and station; and for this end he dreamed of a popedom, universal in its claims, domineering equally over all conditions of men—an incarnation of the fiercest democracy, trampling on the people, and of the bitterest republicanism, aiming at more than monarchical power. He had the wrath of generations of serfdom rankling in his heart, and took a satisfaction, sweetened by revenge, in bringing low the haughty looks of the proud. And in these strainings after the elevation of the Papacy he was assisted by several powers on which he could securely rely.

The Normans, who by a wonderful fortune had made themselves masters of England under the guidance of William, were grateful to the Pope for the assistance he had given them by prohibiting all opposition to their conquest on the part of the English Church. Another branch of Normans were still more useful in their support of the papal chair. A body of pilgrims to Jeru salem, amounting to only forty men, had started from Scandinavia in 1006, and, having landed at Salerno, were turned aside from completing their journey by the equally meritorious occupation of resisting the Saracens who were besieging the town. They defeated them with great slaughter, and were amply rewarded for their prowess with goods and gear. News of their gallantry and of their reward reached their friends and relations at home. In a few years they were followed by swarms of their countrymen, who disposed of their acquisitions in Upper Italy to the highest bidder, and were remunerated by grants of land in Naples for their exertion on behalf of Sergius the king. But in 1037 a fresh body of adventurers proceeded from the neighbourhood of Coutances in Normandy, under the command of three brothers of the family of Hauteville, to the assistance of the same monarch, and, with the usual prudence of the Norman race, when they had chased the enemy from the endangered territory, made no scruple of keeping it for themselves. Robert, called Guiscard, or the Wise, was the third brother, and succeeded to the newly-acquired sovereignty in 1057. In a short time he alarmed the Pope with the prospect of so unscrupulous and so powerful a neighbour. His Holiness, therefore, demanded the assistance of the German Emperor, and boldly took the field. The Normans were no whit daunted with the opposition of the Father of Christendom, and dashed through all obstacles till they succeeded in taking him prisoner. Instead of treating him with harshness, and exacting exorbitant ransom, as would have been the action of a less sagacious politician, the Norman threw himself on his knees before the captive pontiff, bewailed his hard case in being forced to appear so contumacious to his spiritual lord and master, and humbly besought him to pardon his transgression, and accept the suzerainty of all the lands he possessed and of all he should hereafter subdue. It was a delightful surprise to the Pope, who immediately ratified all the proceedings of his repentant son, and in a short time was rewarded by seeing Apulia and the great island of Sicily held in homage as fiefs of St. Peter's chair. From thenceforth the Italian Normans were the bulwarks of the papal throne. But, more powerful than the Normans of England, and more devoted personally to the popes than the greedy adventurers of Apulia, the Countess Matilda was the greatest support of all the pretensions of the Holy See. Young and beautiful, the holder of the greatest territories in Italy, this lady was the most zealous of all the followers of the Pope. Though twice married, she on both occasions separated from her husband to throw herself with more undivided energy into the interests of the Church. With men and money, and all the influence that her position as a princess and her charms as a woman could give, the sovereign pontiff had no enemy to fear as long as he retained the friendship of his enthusiastic daughter.

A.D. 1059.

Hildebrand was the ruling spirit of the papal court, and was laying his plans for future action, while the world was still scarcely aware of his existence. He began, while only Archdeacon of Rome, by a forcible reformation of some of the irregularities which had crept into the practice of the clergy, as a preparatory step to making the clergy dominant over all the other orders in the State. He gave orders, in the name of Stephen the Tenth, for every married priest to be displaced and to be separated from his wife. For this end he stirred up the ignorant fanaticism of the people, and encouraged them in outrages upon the

A.D. 1060.

offending clergy, which frequently ended in death. The virtues of the cloister had still a great hold on the popular veneration, in spite of the notorious vices of the monastic establishments, both male and female; and Hildebrand's invectives on the wickedness of marriage, and his praises of the sanctity of a single life, were listened to with equal admiration. The secular clergy were forced to adopt the unsocial and demoralizing principles of their monkish rivals; and when all family affections were made sinful, and the feelings of the pastor concentrated on the interests of his profession, the popes had secured, in the whole body of the Church, the unlimited obedience and blind support which had hitherto been the characteristic of the monastic orders. With the assistance of the warlike Normans, the wealth and influence of the Countess Matilda, the adhesion of the Church to his schemes of aggrandizement, he felt it time to assume in public the power he had exercised so long in the subordinate position of counsellor of the popes; and the monk seated himself on what he considered the highest of earthly thrones, and immediately the contest between the temporal and spiritual powers began. The King of France (Philip the First) and the Emperor of Germany (Henry the Fourth) were both of disreputable life, and offered an easy mark for the assaults of the fiery pontiff. He threatened and reprimanded them for simony and disobedience, proclaimed his authority over kings and princes as a fact which no man could dispute without impiety, and had the inward pleasure of seeing the proudest of the nobles, and finally the most powerful of the sovereigns, of Europe, forced to obey his mandates. The pent-up hatred of his race and profession was gratified by the abasement of birth and power.

A.D. 1073.

The struggle with the Empire was on the subject of

investiture. The successors of Charlemagne had always retained a voice in the appointment of the bishops and Church dignitaries in their states; they had even frequently nominated to the See of Rome, as to the other bishoprics in their dominions. The present wearer of the iron crown had displaced three contending popes, who were disturbing the peace of the city by their ferocious quarrels, and had appointed others in their room. There was no murmur of opposition to their appointment. They were pious and venerable men; and of each of them the inscrutable Hildebrand had managed to make himself the confidential adviser, and in reality the guide and master. Even in his own case he waited patiently till he had secured the emperor's legal ratification of his election, and then, armed with legitimacy, and burning with smothered indignation, he kicked down the ladder by which he had risen, and wrote an insulting letter to the emperor, commanding him to abstain from simony, and to renounce the right of investiture by the ring and cross. These, he maintained, were the signs of spiritual dignity, and their bestowal was inherent in the Pope. The time for the message was admirably chosen; for Henry was engaged in a hard struggle for life and crown with the Saxons and Thuringians, who were in open revolt. Henry promised obedience to the pontiff's wish, but when his enemies were defeated he withdrew his concession. The Pope thundered a sentence of excommunication against him, released his subjects from their oath of fealty, and pronounced him deprived of the throne. The emperor was not to be left behind in the race of objurgation. He summoned his nobles and prelates to a council at Worms, and pronounced sentence of deprivation on the Pope. Then arose such a storm against the unfortunate Henry as only religious

A.D. 1076.

differences can create. His subjects had been oppressed, his nobility insulted, his clergy impoverished, and all classes of his people were glad of the opportunity of hiding their hatred of his oppressions under the cloak of regard for the interests of religion. He was forced to yield; and, crossing the Alps in the middle of winter, he presented himself at the castle of Canossa. Here the Pope displayed the humbleness and generosity of his Christian character, by leaving the wretched man three days and nights in the outer court, shivering with cold and barefoot, while His Holiness and the Countess Matilda were comfortably closeted within. And after this unheard-of degradation, all that could be wrung from the hatred of the inexorable monk was a promise that the suppliant should be tried with justice, and that, if he succeeded in proving his innocence, he should be reinstated on his throne; but if he were found guilty, he should be punished with the utmost rigour of ecclesiastical law.

Common sense and good feeling were revolted by this unexampled insolence. Friends gathered round Henry when the terms of his sentence were heard. The Romans themselves, who had hitherto been blindly submissive, were indignant at the presumption of their bishop. None continued faithful except the imperturbable Countess Matilda. He was still to her the representative of divine goodness and superhuman power. But her troops were beaten and her money was exhausted in the holy quarrel. Robert Guiscard, indeed, came to the rescue, and rewarded himself for delivering the Pope by sacking the city of Rome. Half the houses were burned, and half the population killed or sold as slaves. It was from amidst the desolation his ambition had caused that the still-unsubdued Hildebrand was guarded by the Normans to the citadel of

Salerno, and there he died, issuing his orders and curses to his latest hour, and boasting with his last breath that "he had loved righteousness and hated iniquity, and that therefore he expired in exile." After this A.D. 1085. man's throwing off the mask of moderation under which his predecessors had veiled their claims, the world was no longer left in doubt of the aims and objects of the spiritual power. There seems almost a taint of insanity in the extravagance of his demands. In the published collection of his maxims we see the full extent of the theological tyranny he had in view. "There is but one name in the world," we read; "and that is the Pope's. He only can use the ornaments of empire. All princes ought to kiss his feet. He alone can nominate or displace bishops and assemble or dissolve councils. Nobody can judge him. His mere election constitutes him a saint. He has never erred, and never shall err in time to come. He can depose princes and release subjects from their oaths of fidelity." Yet, in spite of the wildness of this language, the ignorance of the period was so great, and the relations of European nations so hostile, that the most daring of these assumptions found supporters either in the superstitious veneration of the peoples or the enmity and interests of the princes. The propounder of those amazing propositions was apparently defeated, and died disgraced and hated; but his successors were careful not to withdraw the most untenable of his claims, even while they did not bring them into exercise. They lay in an armory, carefully stored and guarded, to be brought out according to the exigencies either of the papal chair itself, or of the king or emperor who for the moment was in possession of the person of the Pope. None of the great potentates of Europe, therefore, was anxious to diminish a power which might be employed for his own advantage, and all of them by turns encouraged the aggressions of the Papacy, with a short-sighted wisdom, to be an instrument of offence against their enemies. Little encouragement, indeed, was offered at this time to opposition to the spiritual despot. Though Hildebrand had died a refugee, it was remarked with pious awe that Henry the Fourth, his rival and opponent, was punished in a manner which showed the highest displeasure of Heaven. His children, at the instigation of the Pope, rebelled against him. He was conquered in battle and taken prisoner by his youngest son. He was stripped of all his possessions, and at last so destitute and forsaken that he begged for a sub-chanter's place in a village church for the sake of its wretched salary, and died in such extremity of want and desolation that hunger shortened his days. For five years his body was left without the decencies of interment in a cellar in the town of Spires.

A.D. 1106.

But an immense movement was now to take place in the European mind, which had the greatest influence on the authority of Rome. A crusade against the enemies of the faith was proclaimed in the year 1095, and from all parts of Europe a great cry of approval was uttered in all tongues, for it hit the right chord in the ferocious and superstitious heart of the world; and it was felt that the great battle of the Cross and the Crescent was most fitly to be decided forever on the soil of the Holy Land.

A.D. 1095.

From the very beginning of this century the thought of armed intervention in the affairs of Palestine had been present in the general mind. Religious difference had long been ready to take the form of open war. As the Church strengthened and settled into more dogmatic unity, the desire to convert by force and retain within the fold by penalty and proscription had increased. As yet some reluctance was felt to put a professing Christian to death on merely a difference of doctrine, but with the open gainsayers of the faith no parley could be held. Thousands, in addition to their religious animosities, had personal injuries to avenge; for pilgrimage to Jerusalem was already in full favour, and the weary wayfarers had to complain of the hostility of the turbaned possessors of the Holy Sepulchre, and the indignities and peril to which they were exposed the moment they came within the infidel's domain. Why should the unbelievers be allowed any longer to retain the custody of such inherently Christian territories as the Mount of Olives and the Garden of Gethsemane? Why should the unbaptized followers of Mohammed, those children of perdition, pollute with hostile feet the sacred ground which had been the witness of so many miracles and still furnished so many relics which manifested superhuman power? Besides, what was the wealth of other cities—their gold and precious jewels—to the store of incalculable riches contained in the very stones and woodwork of the metropolis and cradle of the faith? Bones of martyrs—garments of saints—nails of the cross—thorns of the crown—were all lying ready to be gathered up by the faithful priesthood who would lead the expedition. And who could be held responsible, in this world or the next, for any sins, however grievous, who had washed them out by purifying the floors of Zion with the blood of slaughtered Saracens and saying prayers and kneeling in contemplation within sight of the Sepulchre itself? So Peter the Hermit, an enthusiast who preached a holy war, was listened to as if he spake with the tongues of angels. The ravings of his lunacy had a prodigious effect on all classes and in all lands; and suddenly there was gathered together a confused rabble of pilgrims, armed in every variety of fashion—princes and beggars, robbers and adventurers—the scum of great cities and the simple-hearted peasantry from distant farms—upwards of three hundred thousand in number, all pouring down towards the seaports and anxious to cross over to the land where so many high hopes were placed. Vast numbers of this multitude found their way from France through Italy; and luckily for Urban the Second—the fifth in succession from Gregory—they took the opportunity of paying a visit to the city of Rome, scarcely less venerable in their eyes than Jerusalem itself. They were the soldiers of the Cross, and in that character felt bound to pay a more immediate submission to the Chief of Christianity than to their native kings. They found the city divided between two rivals for the tiara, and, having decided in favour of Urban, chased away the anti-pope who was appointed by the Imperial choice. Terrified at the accession of such powerful supporters, the Germans were withdrawn from Italy, and Urban felt that the claims of Hildebrand were not incapable of realization if he could get quit of unruly barons and obstinate monarchs by engaging them in a distant and ruinous expedition. It needed little to spread the flame of fanaticism over the whole of Christendom. The accounts given of this first Crusade transcend the wildest imaginings of romance. An indiscriminate multitude of all nations and tongues seemed impelled by some irresistible impulse towards the East. Ostensibly engaged in a religious service, enriched with promises and absolutions from the Pope, giving up all their earthly possessions, and filled with the one idea of liberating the Holy Land, it might have been expected that the sobriety and order of their march would have been characteristic of such elevating aspirations. But the infamy of their behaviour, their debauchery, irregularity, and dishonesty, have never been equalled by the basest and most degraded of mankind. Like a flood they poured through the lands of Italy, Bohemia, and Germany, polluting the cities with their riotous lives, and poisoning the air with the festering corruption of their innumerable dead. They at last found shipping from the ports, and presented themselves, drunk with fanatical pride, and maddened with the sufferings they had undergone, before the astonished people of Constantinople. That enervated and over-civilized population looked with disgust on the unruly mass. Of the vast multitudes who had started under the guidance of Peter the Hermit, not more than 20,000 survived; and of these none found their way to the object of their search. The Turks, who had by this time obtained the mastery of Asia, cut them in pieces when they had left the shelter of Constantinople, and Alexis Comnenus, the Grecian emperor, had little hope of aid against the Mohammedan invaders from the unruly levies of Europe.

But in the following year a new detachment made their appearance in his states. This was the second ban, or crusade of the knights and barons. Better regulated in its military organization than the other, it presented the same astonishing scenes of debauchery and vice; and dividing, for the sake of sustenance, into four armies, and taking four different routes, they at length, in greatly-diminished numbers, but with unabated hope and energy, presented themselves before the walls of Constantinople. This was no mob like their famished and fainting predecessors. All the gallant lords of Europe were here, inspired by knightly courage and national rivalries to distinguish themselves in fight and council. Of these the best-known were Godfrey of Bouillon, Baldwyn of Flanders, Robert of Normandy, (William the Conqueror's eldest son,) Hugh the Great, Count of Vermandois, and Raymond of St. Gilles. Six hundred thousand men had left their homes, with innumerable attendants—women, and jugglers, and servants, and workmen of all kinds. Tens of thousands perished by the way; others established themselves in the cities on their route to keep up the communication; and at last the Genoese and Pisan vessels conveyed to the Golden Horn the strength of all Europe, the hardy survivors of all the perils of that unexampled march—few indeed in number, but burning with zeal and bravery. Alexis lost no time in diverting their dangerous strength from his own realms. He let them loose upon Nicea, and when it yielded to their valour he had the cleverness to outwit the Christian warriors, and claimed the city as his possession. On pursuing their course, they found themselves, after a victory over the Turks at Dorylæum, in the great Plain of Phrygia. Hunger, thirst, the extremity of heat, and the difficulty of the march, brought confusion and dismay into their ranks. All the horses died. Knights and chevaliers were seen mounted on asses, and even upon oxen; and the baggage was packed upon goats, and not unfrequently on swine and dogs. Thirst was fatal to five hundred in a single day. Quarrels between the nationalities added to these calamities. Lorrains and Italians, the men of Normandy and of Provence, were at open feud. And yet, in spite of these drawbacks, the great procession advanced. Baldwyn and Tancred succeeded in getting possession of the town of Edessa, on the Euphrates, and opened a communication with the Christians of Armenia.

A.D. 1098.

The siege of Antioch was their next operation, and the luxuries of the soil and climate were more fatal to the Crusaders than want and pain had been. On the rich banks of the Orontes, and in the groves of Daphne, they lost the remains of discipline and self-command and gave themselves up to the wildest excesses. But with the winter their enjoyment came to an end. Their camp was flooded; they suffered the extremities of famine; and when there were no more horses and impure animals to eat, they satiated their hunger on the bodies of their slaughtered enemies. Help, however, was at hand, or they must have perished to the last man. Bohemund corrupted the fidelity of a renegade officer in Antioch, and, availing themselves of a dark and stormy night, they scaled the walls with ladders, and rushed into the devoted city, shouting the Crusaders' war-cry:—"It is the will of God!" and Antioch became a Christian princedom. But not without difficulty was this new possession retained. The Turks, under the orders of Kerboga, surrounded it with two hundred thousand men. There was neither entrance nor exit possible, and the worst of their previous sufferings began to be renewed. But Heaven came to the rescue. A monk of the name of Peter Bartholomew dreamt that under the great altar of the church would be found the spear which pierced the Saviour on the cross. The precious weapon rewarded their toil in digging, and armed with this the Christian charge was irresistible, and the Turks were cut in pieces or dispersed. Instead of making straight for Jerusalem, they lingered six months longer in Antioch, suffering from plague and the fatigues they had undergone. When at last the forward order was given, a remnant, consisting of fifty thousand men out of all the original force, began the march. As they got nearer the object of their search, and recognised the places commemorated in Holy Writ, their enthusiasm knew no bounds. The last elevation was at length surmounted, and Jerusalem lay in full view. "O blessed Jesus," cries a monk who was present, "when thy Holy City was seen, what tears fell from our eyes!" Loud shouts were raised of "Jerusalem! Jerusalem! God wills it! God wills it!" They stretched out their hands, fell upon their knees, and embraced the consecrated ground. But Jerusalem was yet in the hands of the Saracens, and the sword must open their way into its sacred bounds. The governor had offered to admit the pilgrims within the walls, but in their peaceful dress and merely as visitors. This they refused, and determined to wrest it from its unbelieving lords. On the 15th of July, 1099, they found that their situation was no longer tenable, and that they must conquer or give up the siege. The brook Kedron was dried up, the sun poured upon them with unendurable heat, their provisions were exhausted, and in agonies of despair as well as of military ardour they gave the final assault. The struggle was long and doubtful. At length the Crusaders triumphed. Tancred and Godfrey were the first to leap into the devoted town. Their soldiers followed, and filled every street with slaughter. The Mosque of Omar was vigorously defended, and an indiscriminate massacre of Mussulmans and Jews filled the whole place with blood. In the mosque itself the stream of gore was up to the saddle-girths of a horse. The onslaught was occasionally suspended for a while, to allow the pious conquerors to go barefoot and unarmed to kneel at the Holy Sepulchre; and, this act of worship done, they returned to their ruthless occupation, and continued the work of extermination for a whole week. The depopulated and reeking town was added to the domains of Christendom, and the kingdom of Jerusalem was offered to Godfrey of Bouillon. With a modesty befitting the most Christian and noble-hearted of the Crusaders, Godfrey contented himself with the humbler name of Baron of the Holy Sepulchre; and with three hundred knights—which were all that remained to him when that crowning victory had set the other survivors at liberty to revisit their native lands—he established a standing garrison in the captured city, and anxiously awaited reinforcements from the warlike spirits they had left at home.

TWELFTH CENTURY.

Emperors of Germany.

A.D.

HENRY IV.—(*cont.*)

1106. HENRY V.

House of Suabia.

1138. CONRAD III.

1152. FREDERICK BARBAROSSA.

1190. HENRY VI.

1198. PHILIP and OTHO IV., (of Brunswick.)

Kings of England.

1100. HENRY I.

1135. STEPHEN.

1154. HENRY II.

1189. RICHARD I.

1199. JOHN.

Emperors of the East.

A.D.

ALEXIS I.—(*cont.*)

1118. JOHN.

1143. MANUEL.

1183. ANDRONICUS I.

1185. ISAAC II., (the Angel.)

1195. ALEXIS III.

Kings of France.

PHILIP I.—(*cont.*)

1108. LOUIS VI.

1137. LOUIS VII.

1180. PHILIP AUGUSTUS.

King of Scotland.

1165. WILLIAM.

1147. SECOND CRUSADE, led by Louis VII. of France.

1189. THIRD CRUSADE, led by Frederick Barbarossa, Philip Augustus, and Richard of England.

Authors.

BERNARD, (1091–1153,) BECKET, (1119–1170,) EUSTATHIUS, THEODORUS, BALSAMON, PETER LOMBARD, WILLIAM OF MALMESBURY, (1096–1143.)

THE TWELFTH CENTURY.

ELEVATION OF LEARNING—POWER OF THE CHURCH—THOMAS À-BECKETT.

THE effect of the first Crusade had been so prodigious that Europe was forced to pause to recover from its exhaustion. More than half a million had left their homes in 1095; ten thousand are supposed to have returned; three hundred were left with Godfrey in the Christian city of Jerusalem; and what had become of all the rest? Their bones were whitening all the roads that led to the Holy Land; small parties of them must have settled in despair or weariness in towns and villages on their way; many were sold into slavery by the rapacity of the feudal lords whose lands they traversed; and when the madness of the time had originated a Crusade of Children, and ninety thousand boys of ten or twelve years of age had commenced their journey, singing hymns and anthems, and hoping to conquer the infidels with the spiritual arms of innocence and prayer, the whole band melted away before they reached the coast. Barons, and counts, and bishops, and dukes, all swooped down upon the devoted march, and before many weeks' journeying was achieved the Crusade was brought to a close. Most of the children had died of fatigue or starvation, and the survivors had been seized as legitimate prey and sold as slaves.

Meantime the brave and heroic Godfrey—the true hero of the expedition, for he elevated the ordinary virtues of knighthood and feudalism into the nobler feelings of generosity and romance—gained the object of his earthly ambition. Having prayed at the sepulchre, and cleansed the temple from the pollution of the unbelievers' presence, wearied with all his labours, and

A.D. 1100. feeling that his task was done, he sank into deep despondency and died. Volunteers in small numbers had occasionally gone eastward to support the Cross. Ambition, thoughtlessness, guilt, and fanaticism sent their representatives to aid the conqueror of Judea; and his successors found themselves strong enough to bid defiance to the Turkish power. They carried all their Western ideas along with them. They had their feudal holdings and knightly quarrels. The most venerated names in Holy Writ were desecrated by unseemly disputes or the most frivolous associations. The combination, indeed, of their native habits and their new acquisitions might have moved them to laughter, if the men of the twelfth century had been awake to the ridiculous. There was a Prince of Galilee, a Marquis of Joppa, a Baron of Sidon, a Marquis of Tyre. Our own generation has renewed the strange juxtaposition of the East and West by the language employed in steamboats and railways. Trains will soon cross the Desert with warning whistles and loud jets of steam and all the phraseology of an English line. For many years the waters of the mysterious Red Sea have been dashed into foam by paddles made in Liverpool or Glasgow. But these are visitors of a very different kind from Bohemund and Baldwyn. Baldwyn, indeed, seemed less inclined than his companions to carry his European training to its full extent. He Orientalized himself in a small way, perhaps in imitation of Alexander the Great; and, dressed in the long flowing robes of the country, he made his attendants serve him with prostrations, and almost with worship. He married a daughter of the land, and in other respects endeavoured to ingratiate himself with the Saracens by treating them with kindness and consideration. The bravery of those warriors of the Desert endeared them to the rough-handed barons of the West. It was impossible to believe that men with that one pre-eminent virtue could be so utterly hateful as they had been represented; and when the intercourse between the races became more unrestrained, even the religious asperities of the Crusaders became mitigated, they found so many points of resemblance between their faiths. There was not an honour which the Christian paid to the Virgin which was not yielded by the Mohammedan to Fatima. All the doctrines of the Christian creed found their counterparts in the professions of the followers of the Law. Allah was an incarnation of the Deity; and even the mystery of the Trinity was not indistinctly seen in the legend of the three rays which darted from the idea of Mohammed in the mind of the Creator. While this community of sentiment softened the animosity of the crusading leaders towards their enemies, a still greater community of suffering and danger softened their feelings towards their followers and retainers. In that scarcity of knights and barons, the value of a serf's arm or a mechanic's skill was gratefully acknowledged. There had been many mutual kindnesses between the two classes all through those tedious and blood-stained journeys and desperate fights. A peasant had brought water to a wounded lord when he lay fainting on the burning soil; a workman had had the revelation of the true crown: they were no longer the property and slaves of the noble, who considered them beings of a different blood, but fellow-soldiers, fellow-sufferers, fellow-Christians. They were not spoken of in the insulting language of the West, and called "our thralls," "our slaves," "our bondsmen;" at the worst they were called "our poor," and lifted by that word into the quality of brothers and men. The precepts of the gospel in favour of the humble and suffering were felt for the first time to have an application to the men who had toiled on their lands and laboured in their workshops, but who were now their support in the shock of battle, and companions when the victory was won. Only they were poor; they had no lands; they had no arms upon their shields. So Baldwyn gave them large tracts of country; and they became vassals and feudatories for fertile fields near Jericho and rich farms on the Jordan. They were gentlemen by the strength of their own right hands, as the fathers of their lords and suzerains had been.

But the amalgamation of race and condition was not carried on in the East more surely or more extensively than in the West. The expenses of preparing for the pilgrimage had impoverished the richest of the lords of the soil. They had been forced to borrow money and to mortgage their estates to the burghers of the great commercial towns, which, quietly and unobserved, had spread themselves in many parts of France and Italy. Genoa had already attained such a height of prosperity that she could furnish vessels for the conveyance of half the army of the Crusade. In return for her cargoes of knights and fighting-men, she brought back the wealth of the East,—silks, and precious stones, and spices, and vessels of gold and silver. The necessities of the time made the money-holder powerful, and the men who swung the hammer, and shaped the sword, and embroidered the banner, and wove the tapestry, indispensable. And what hold, except kindness, and privilege, and grants of land, had the baron on the skilful smith or the ingenious weaver who could carry his skill and energy wherever he chose? Besides, the multitudes who had been carried away from the pursuits of industry to fall at the siege of Antioch or perish by thirst in the Desert had given a greatly-increased value to their fellow-labourers left at home. While the castle became deserted, and all the pomp of feudalism retreated from its crumbling walls, the village which had grown in safety under its protection flourished as much as ever—flourished, indeed, so much that it rapidly became a town, and boasted of rich citizens who could help to pay off their suzerain's encumbrances and present him with an offering on his return. The impoverished and grateful noble could do no less, in gratitude for gift and contribution, than secure them in the enjoyment of greater franchises and privileges than they had possessed before. The Church also gained by the diminished number and power of the lords, who had seized upon tithe and offering and had looked with disdain and hostility on the aggressions of the lower clergy. True to its origin, the Church still continued the leader of the people, in opposition to the pretensions of the feudal chiefs. It was still a democratic organization for the protection of the weak against the powerful; and though we have seen that the bishops and other dignitaries frequently assumed the state and practised the cruelties of the grasping and illiterate baron, public opinion, especially in the North of Europe, was not revolted against these instances of priestly domination, for whatever was gained by the crozier was lost to the sword. It was even a consolation to the injured serf to see the truculent landlord who had oppressed him oppressed in his turn by a still more truculent bishop, especially when that bishop had sprung from the dregs of the people, and—crown and consummation of all—when the Pope, God's vicegerent upon earth, who dethroned emperors and made kings hold his stirrup as he mounted his mule, was descended from no more distinguished a family than himself. It was the effort of the Church, therefore, in all this century, to lower the noble and to elevate the poor. To gain popularity, all arts were resorted to. The clergy were the showmen and play-actors of the time. The only amusement the labourer could aim at was found for him, in rich processions and gorgeous ceremony, by the priest. How could any fault of the abbot or prelate turn away the affection of the peasant from the Church, which was in a peculiar manner his own establishment? Never had the drunkenness, the debauchery and personal indulgences of the upper ecclesiastics reached such a pitch before. The gluttony of friars and monks became proverbial. The community of certain monasteries complained of the austerity of their abbots in reducing their ordinary dinners from sixteen dishes to thirteen. The great St. Bernard describes many of the rulers of the Church as keeping sixty horses in their stables, and having so many wines upon their board that it was impossible to taste one-half of them. Yet nothing shook the attachment of the uneducated commons. Their priest got up dances and concerts and miracles for their edification, and had a right to enjoy all the luxuries of life. Once freed, therefore, from the watchful enmity of lord and king, the Church was well aware that its power would be irresistible. The people were devoted to it as their earthly defender against their earthly oppressors, the caterer of all their amusements, and as their guide in the path to heaven. Gratitude and credulity, therefore, were equally engaged in its behalf. And new influences came to its support. Romance and wonder gathered round the champions of the Faith fighting in the distant regions of the East. Every thing became magnified when seen through the medium of ignorance and fanaticism. The tales, therefore, strange enough in themselves, which were related by pilgrims returning from the Holy Land, and amplified a hundredfold by the natural exaggeration of the vulgar, raised higher than ever the glory of the Church. The fastings and self-inflicted scourgings of holy men, it was believed, effected more than the courage of Godfrey or Bohemund; and even of Godfrey it was said that his ascetic life and painful penances caused more losses to the enemy than his matchless strength and military skill.

It would be delightful if we could place ourselves in the position of the breathless crowds at that time listening for the news from Palestine. No telegraphic despatch from the Crimea or Hindostan was ever waited for with such impatience or received with such emotion. The baron summoned the palmer into his hall, and heard the strange history of the march to Jerusalem, and the crowning of a Christian king, and the creation of a feudal court, with a pang, perhaps, of regret that he had not joined the pilgrimage, which might have made him Duke of Bethlehem or monarch of Tiberias. But the peasants in their workshops, or the whole village assembled in the long aisles of their church, lent far more attentive ears to the wayfaring monk who had escaped from the prison of the Saracen, and told them of the marvels accomplished by the bones of martyrs and apostles which had been revealed to holy pilgrims in their dream on the Mount of Olives. Footprints on the heights of Calvary, and portions of the manger in Bethlehem, were described in awe-struck voice; and when it was announced that in the belt of the narrator, enwrapped in a silken scarf,—itself a fabric of incalculable worth,—was a hair of an apostle's head, (which their lord had purchased for a large sum,) to be deposited upon their altar, they must have thought the sacrifices and losses of the Crusade amply repaid. And no amount of these sacred articles seemed in the least to diminish their importance. The demand was always greatly in advance of the supply, however vast it might be. And as the mines of California and Australia have hitherto deceived the prophets of evil, by having no perceptible effect on the price of the precious metals, the incalculable importation of saints' teeth, and holy personages' clothes, and fragments of the true Cross, and prickles of the real Crown of Thorns, had no depressing effect on the market-value of similar commodities with which all Christian Europe was inundated. Faith seemed to expand in proportion as relics became plentiful, as credit expands on the security of a supply of gold. And as many of those articles were actually of as clearly-recognised a pecuniary value as houses or lands, and represented in any market or banking-house a definite and very considerable sum, it is not too much to say that the capital of the West was greatly increased by these acquisitions from the East. The cup of onyx, carved in one stone, which was believed to have been that in which the wine of the Last Supper was held when our Saviour instituted the Communion, was pledged by its owner for an enormous sum, and—what is perhaps more strange—was redeemed when the term of the loan expired by the repayment of principal and interest. The intercourse, therefore, between power and money showed that each was indispensable to the other. The baron relaxed his severity, and the citizen opened his purse-strings; the Church inculcated the equality of all men in presence of the altar; and when the kings perceived what merchandise might be made of privileges and exemptions accorded to their subjects, and how at one great blow the townsman's squeezable riches would be increased and the baron's local influence diminished, there was a struggle between all the crowned heads as to which should be most favourable to the commons. It was in this century, owing to the Crusades, which made the commonalty indispensable and the nobility weak, which strengthened the Crown and the Church and made it their joint interest to restrain the exactions of the feudal proprietors, that the liberties of Europe took their rise in the establishment of the third estate. In the county of Flanders, the great towns had already made themselves so wealthy and independent that it scarcely needed a legal ratification of their franchise to make them free cities. But in Italy a step further had been made, and the great word Republic, which had been silent for so many years, had again been heard, and had taken possession of the general mind. In spite of the opposition and the military successes of Roger, the Norman king of Sicily, the spirit which animated those great trading communities was never subdued. In Venice itself—the greatest and most illustrious of those republics, the first founded and last overthrown—the original municipal form of government had never been abolished. At all times its liberties had been preserved and its laws administered by officers of its own choice, and from it proceeded at this time a feeling of social equality and an example of commercial prosperity which had a strong effect on the nascent freedom of the lower and industrious classes over all the world. Genoa was not inferior either in liberty or enterprise to any of its rivals. Its fleets traversed the Mediterranean, and, being equally ready to fight or to trade, brought wealth and glory home from the coasts of Greece and Asia. It is to be observed that the first reappearance of self-government was presented in the towns upon the coast, whose situation enabled them to compensate for smallness of territory by the command of the sea. The shores of Italy and the south of France, and the indented sea-line of Flanders, followed in this respect the example set in former ages by Greece, and Tyre, and Pentapolis, and Carthage. There can be no doubt that the sight of these powerful communities, governed by their consuls and legislated for by their parliamentary assemblies, must have put new thoughts into the heads of the serfs and labourers returning, in vessels furnished by citizens like themselves, from the conquest of Cyprus and Jerusalem, where the whole harvest of wealth and glory had been reaped by their lords. Encouraged by these examples, and by the protection of the King of France and Emperor of Germany, the towns in Central and Western Europe exerted themselves to emulate the republican cities of the South. The nearest approach they could hope to the independence they had seen in Pisa or Venice was the possession of the right of electing their own magistrates and making their own laws. These privileges, we have seen, were insured to them by the helplessness and impoverishment of the feudal aristocracy and the countenance of the Church.

But the Church towards the middle of this century found that the countenance she had given to liberty in other places was used as an argument against herself in the central seat of her power. Rome, the city of consuls and tribunes, was carried away by the great idea; and under the guidance of Arnold of Brescia, a monk who believed himself a Brutus, the standard was again hoisted on the Capitol, displaying the magic letters S. P. Q. R., (Senatus Populus que Romanus.) The Pope was expelled by the population, the freedom of the city proclaimed, the separation of the spiritual and temporal powers pronounced by the unanimous voice, the government of priests abolished, and measures taken to maintain the authority the citizens had assumed. The banished Pope had died while these things were going on, and his successor was hunted down the steps of the Capitol, and the revolution was accomplished. "Throughout the peninsula," says a German historian, "except in the kingdom of Naples, from Rome to the smallest city, the republican form prevailed." Every thing had concurred to this result,—the force of arms, the rise of commerce, and the glorious remembrance of the past. St. Bernard himself acquiesced in the position now occupied by the Pope, and he wrote to his scholar Eugenius the Third, to "leave the Romans alone, and to exchange the city against the world," ("urbem pro orbe mutatam.") But the effervescence of the popular will was soon at an end. The fear of republicanism made common cause between the Pope and Emperor. Frederick Barbarossa revenged the indignities cast on the chair of St. Peter by burning the rebellious Arnold and re-establishing the ancient form of government by force. Yet the spirit of equality which was thus repressed by violence fermented in secret; nor was equality all that was aimed at amid some of the swarming seats of population and commerce. We find indeed, from this time, that in a great number of instances the original relations between the town and baron were reversed: the noble put himself under the protection of the municipality, and received its guarantee against the assaults or injuries of the prouder and less politic members of his class. It was a strange thing to see a feudal lord receive his orders from the municipal officers of a country town, and still stranger to perceive the low opinion which the courageous and high-fed burghers entertained of the pomp and circumstance of the mailed knights of whom they had been accustomed to stand in awe. Their ramparts were strong, their granaries well filled, their companions stoutly armed; and they used to lean over the wall, when a hostile champion summoned them to submit to the exactions of a great proprietor, and watch the clumsy charger staggering under his heavy armour, with shouts of derision. Men, who had thus thrown off their hereditary veneration for the lords of the soil, and contentedly saw the deposition of the Roman Pope by a Roman Senate and People, were not likely to pay a blind submission to the spiritual dictation of their priests. In the towns, accordingly, a spirit of free inquiry into the mysteries of the faith began; and, while country districts still heard with awe the impossible wonders of the monkish legends, there were rash and daring scholars in several countries, who threw doubt upon the plainest statements of Revelation. Of these the best-known is the still famous Abelard, whose exertions as a religious inquirer have been thrown into the shade by his more interesting character of the hero of a love-story. The letters of Eloisa, and the unfortunate issue of their affection, have kept their names from the oblivion which has fallen upon their metaphysical triumphs. And yet during their lives the glory of Abelard did not depend on the passionate eloquence of his pupil, but arose from the unequalled sharpness of his intellect and his skill in argumentation. Of noble family, the handsomest man of his time, wonderfully gifted with talent and accomplishment, he was the first instance of a man professing the science of theology without being a priest. Wherever he went, thousands of enthusiastic scholars surrounded his chair. His eloquence was so fascinating that the listener found himself irresistibly carried away by the stream; and if an opponent was hardy enough to stand up against him, the acuteness of his logic was as infallible as the torrent of his oratory had been, and in every combat he carried away the prize. He doubted about original sin, and by implication about the atonement, and many other articles of the Christian belief. The power and constitution of the Church were endangered by the same weapons which assailed the groundworks of the faith; and yet in all Europe no sufficient champion for truth and orthodoxy could be found. Abelard was triumphant over all his gainsayers, till at length Bernard of Clairvaux, who even in his lifetime was looked on with the veneration due to a saint, who refused an archbishopric, and the popedom itself, took up the gauntlet thrown down by the lover of Eloisa, and reduced him to silence by the superiority of his reasonings and the threats of a general council. It is sufficient to remark the appearance of Abelard in this century, as the commencement of a reaction against the dogmatic authority of the Church. It was henceforth possible to reason and to inquire; and there can be no doubt that Protestantism even in this modified and isolated form had a beneficial effect on the establishment it assailed. A new armory was required to meet the assaults of dialectic and scholarship. Dialecticians and scholars were therefore, henceforth, as much valued in the Church as self-flagellating friars and miracle-performing saints. The faith was now guarded by a noble array of highly-polished intellects, and the very dogma of the total abnegation of the understanding at the bidding of the priest was supported by a show of reasoning which few other questions had called forth. With the enlargement of the clerical sphere of knowledge, refinement in taste and sentiment took place. And at this time, as philosophic discussion took its rise with Abelard, the ennobling and idealization of woman took its birth contemporaneously with the sufferings of Eloisa. Up to this period the Church had avowedly looked with disdain on woman, as inheriting in a peculiar degree the curse of our first parents, because she had been the first to break the law.

Knightly gallantry, indeed, had thought proper to elevate the feminine ideal and clothe with imaginary virtues the heroines of its fictitious idolatry. It made her the aim and arbiter of all its achievements. The principal seat in hall and festival was reserved for the softer sex, which hitherto had been considered scarcely worthy of reverence or companionship. Perhaps this courtesy to the ladies on the part of knights and nobles began in an opposition to the wife-secluding habits of the Orientals against whom they fought, as at an earlier date the worship of images was certainly maintained by Rome as a protest against the unadorned worship of the Saracens. Perhaps it arose from the gradual expansion of wealth and the security of life and property, which left time and opportunity for the cultivation of the female character. Ladies were constituted chiefs of societies of nuns, and were obeyed with implicit submission. Large communities of young maidens were presided over by widows who were still in the bloom of youth; and so holy and pure were these sisterhoods considered, that brotherhoods and monks were allowed to occupy the same house, and the sexes were only separated from each other, even at night, by an aged abbot sleeping on the floor between them. Though this experiment failed, the fact of its being tried proved the confidence inspired by the spotlessness of the female character. Other things conspired to give a greater dignity to what had been called the inferior sex. The death of whole families in the Crusade had left the daughters heiresses of immense possessions. In every country but France the Crown itself was open to female succession, and it was henceforth impossible to affect a superiority over a person merely because she was corporeally weak and beautiful, who was lady of strong castles and could summon a thousand retainers beneath the banners of her house. The very elevation of the women with whom they were surrounded—the peeresses, and princesses, and even the ladies of lower rank, to whom the voice of the troubadours attributed all the virtues under heaven—necessitated in the mind of the clergy a corresponding elevation in the character of the queen and representative of the female sex, whom they had already worshipped as personally without sin and endowed with superhuman power. At this time the immaculate conception of the Holy Virgin was first broached as an article of belief,—a doctrine which, after being dormant at intervals and occasionally blossoming into declaration, has finally received its full ratification by the authority of the present Pope,—Pius the Ninth. In the twelfth century it was acknowledged and propagated as a fresh increase to the glory of the mother of God; but it is now fixed forever as indispensable to the salvation of every Christian.

Such, then, are the great features by which to mark this century,—the combination of rank with rank caused by the mutual danger of lord and serf in the Crusade, the rise of freedom by the commercial activity imparted by the same cause to the towns, the elevation of the idea of woman, without which no true civilization can take place. These are the leading and general characteristics: add to them what we have slightly alluded to, —the first specimens of the joyous lays and love-sonnets of the young knights returning from Palestine and pouring forth their admiration of birth and beauty in the soft language of Italy or Languedoc,—the intercourse between distant nations, which was indispensable in the combined expeditions against the common foe, so that the rough German cavalier gathered lessons in manner or accomplishment from the more polished princes of Anjou or Aquitaine,—and it will be seen that

this was the century of awakening mind and softening influences. There were scholars like Abelard, introducing the hitherto unknown treasures of the Greek and Hebrew tongues, and yet presenting the finest specimens of gay and accomplished gentlemen, unmatched in sweetness of voice and mastery of the harp; and there were at the other side of the picture saints like Bernard of Clairvaux, not relying any longer on visions and the traditionary marvels of the past, but displaying the power of an acute diplomatist and wide-minded politician in the midst of the most extraordinary self-denial and the exercises of a rigorous asceticism, which in former ages had been limited to the fanatical and insane. To this man's influence was owing the
A.D. 1147. Second Crusade, which occurred in 1147. Different from the first, which had been the result of popular enthusiasm and dependent for its success on undisciplined numbers and religious fury, this was a great European and Christian movement, concerted between the sovereigns and ratified by the peoples. Kings took the command, and whole nations bestowed their wealth and influence on the holy cause. Louis the Seventh of France led all the paladins of his land; and Conrad, the German Emperor, collected all the forces of the West to give the finishing-blow to the power of the Mohammedans and restore the struggling kingdom of Jerusalem. Seventy thousand horsemen and two hundred and fifty thousand foot-soldiers were the smallest part of the array. Whole districts were depopulated by the multitudes of artificers, shopmen, women, children, buffoons, mimics, priests, and conjurers who accompanied the march. It looked like one of the great movements which convulsed the Roman Empire when Goths or Burgundians poured into the land. But the results were nearly the same as in the days of God-

frey and Bohemund. Valour and discipline, national emulation and knightly skill, were of no avail against climate and disease. Again the West astonished the Turks with the impetuosity of its courage and the display of its hosts, but lay weakened and exhausted when the convulsive effort was past. A million perished in the useless struggle. Forty years scarcely sufficed to restore the nobility to sufficient power to undertake
A.D. 1191. another suicidal attempt. But in 1191 the Third Crusade departed under the conduct of Richard of England, and earned the same glory and unsuccess. The century was weakened by those wretched but not fruitless expeditions, which, in round numbers, cost two millions of lives, and produced such memorable effects on the general state of Europe; yet it will be better remembered by us if we direct our attention to some of the incidents which have a more direct bearing on our own country. Of these the most remarkable is the commencement of the long-continued enmity between France and England, of the wars which lasted so many years, which made our most eminent politicians at one time believe that the countries were natural enemies, incapable of permanent union or even of mutual respect; and these took their rise, as most great wars have done, from the paltriest causes, and were continued on the most unfounded pretences.

Henry the First was the son of William the Conqueror. On the death of his brother William Rufus he seized the English crown, though the eldest of the family, Robert, was still alive. Robert was fond of fighting without the responsibility of command, and delighted to be religious without the troubles of a religious life. He therefore joined the First Crusade to gratify this double desire, and mortgaged his dukedom of Normandy to Henry to supply him with horses and arms and enable him to support his dignity as a Christian prince at Jerusalem. His dukedom he never could recover, for his extravagances prevented him from repayment of the loan. He tried to reconquer it by force, but was defeated at the battle of Tinchebray, and was guarded by the zealous affection of his brother all the rest of his life in the Tower of London. He left a son, who was used as an instrument of assault against Henry by the Suzerain of Normandy, Louis the Sixth, King of France. Orders were issued to the usurping feudatory to resign his possessions into the hands of the rightful heir; but, however obedient the Duke of Normandy might profess to be to his liege lord the King of France, the King of England held a very different language, and took a different estimate of his position.

A.D. 1153.

And in the time of the second Henry a change took place in their respective situations which seemed to justify the assumptions of the English king. That grandson of Henry the First had opposed his liege lord of France by arms and arts, and at last by one great master-stroke turned his own arms upon his rival and strengthened himself on his spoils. In the Second Crusade the scrupulous delicacy of Louis the Seventh of France had been revolted by the indiscreet or guilty conduct of Eleanor his wife. He repudiated her as unworthy of his throne; and Henry, who had no delicacies of conscience when they interfered with his interest, offered the rejected Eleanor his hand; for she continued the undoubted mistress of Poitou and Guienne. No stain derived from her principles or conduct was reflected in the eyes of the ambitious Henry on those noble provinces, and from henceforth his Continental possessions far exceeded those of his suzerain. The other feudatories, encouraged by this example, owned a very modified submission to their nominal head; and the inheritors of the throne of the Capets were again reduced to the comparative weakness of their predecessors of the Carlovingian line. Yet there was one element of vitality of which the feudal barons had not deprived the king. A fief, when it lapsed for want of heirs, was reattached to the Crown; and in the turmoil and adventure of those unsettled times the extinction of a line of warriors and pilgrims was not an uncommon event. Even while a family was numerous and healthy the uncertain nature of their possession deprived it of half its value, for at the end of that gallant line of knights and cavaliers, slain as they might be in battle, carried off by the pestilences which were usual at that period, or wasted away in journeys to the Holy Land and sieges in the heats of Palestine, stood the feudal king, ready to enter into undisputed possession of the dukedoms or counties which it had cost them so much time and danger to make independent and strong. In the case of Normandy or Guienne themselves, Louis might have looked without much uneasiness on the building of castles and draining of marshes, when he reflected that but a life or two lay between him and the enriched and strengthened fief; and when those lives were such desperadoes as Richard and such cowards as John, the prospect did not seem hopeless of an immediate succession. But the French kings were still more fortunate in being opposed to such unamiable rivals as the coarse and worldly descendants of the Conqueror. The personal characters of those men, however their energy and courage might benefit them in actual war, made them feared and hated wherever they were known. They were sensual, cruel, and unprincipled to a degree unusual even in those ages of rude manners and undeveloped conscience. Their personal appearance itself was an index of the ungovernable passions within.

Fat, broad-shouldered, low-statured, red-haired, loud voiced, they were frightful to look upon even in their calmest moods; but when the Conqueror stormed, no feeling of ruth or reverence stood in his way. When he was refused the daughter of the Count of Boulogne, he forced his way into the chamber of the countess, seized her by the hair of her head, dragged her round the room, and stamped on her with his feet. Robert his son was of the same uninviting exterior. William Rufus was little and very stout. Henry the Second was gluttonous and debauched. Richard the Lion-Heart was cruel as the animal that gave him name; and John was the most debased and contemptible of mankind. A race of gentle and truthful men, on the other hand, ennobled the crown of France. The kings, from Louis the Debonnaire to Louis the Seventh, or Young, were favourites of the Church and champions of the people. The harsh and violent nobility despised them, but they were venerated in the huts where poor men lie. The very scruple which induced Louis to divorce his wife, whose conduct had stained the purity of the Crusade, almost repaid the loss of her great estates by the increased love and respect of his subjects. And when the line of pure and honourable rulers was for a while interrupted by the appearance, upon a throne so long established in equity, of an armed warrior in the person of Philip Augustus, it was felt that the sword was at last in the hands of an avenger, who was to execute the decrees of Heaven upon the enemies whom the moderation, justice, and mercy of his predecessors had failed to move.

A.D. 1180.

But before we come to the personal relations of the French and English kings we must take a rapid view of one of the great incidents by which this century is marked,—an incident which for a long time attracted

the notice of all Europe, and was productive of very important consequences within our own country. Hitherto England had played the part of a satellite to the Court of Rome. Previous to the quarrels with France, indeed, one great tie between her and the Continental nations was the community of their submission to the Pope. Foreigners have at all times found wealth and kind treatment here. Germans, Italians, Frenchmen, any one who could make interest with the patrons of large livings, held rank and honours in the English Church. Little enough, it was felt, was all that could be done in
A.D. 1154 behalf of foreign ecclesiastics to repay them for
–1159. the condescension they showed in elevating Nicholas Breakspear, an Anglo-Saxon of St. Alban's, to the papal chair. But Nicholas, in taking another name, lost his English heart. As Adrian the Fourth, he preferred Rome to England, and maintained his authority with as high a hand as any of his predecessors. Knights and nobles, and even the higher orders of the clergy, were at length discontented with the continual exactions of the Holy See; and in 1162 the same battle which had agitated the world between Henry the Fourth of Germany and Gregory the Seventh was fought out in a still bitterer spirit between Henry the Second of England and Thomas à-Beckett. All the story-books of English history have told us the romantic incidents of the birth of the ambitious priest. It is possible the obscurity of his origin was concealed by his contemporaries under the interesting legend, which must have been a very early subject for the fancy of the poet and troubadour, of a love between a Red-Cross pilgrim and a Saracen emir's daughter. It shows a remarkable softening of the ancient hatred to the infidels, that the votaress of Mohammed should have been chosen as the mother of a saint. But whatever doubt there may arise about the

reality of the deserted maiden's journey in search of her admirer, and her discovery of his abode by the mere reiteration of his name, which is beautifully said to be the only word of English she remembered, there is no doubt of the early favour which the young Anglo-Saracen attained with the king, or of the desire the sagacious Henry entertained to avail himself of the great talents which made his favourite delightful as a companion and indispensable as a chancellor, in the higher position still of Archbishop of Canterbury and Comptroller of the English Church. For high pretensions were put forward by the clergy: they insisted upon the introduction of the canon laws; they claimed exemption from trial by civil process; they were to be placed beyond the reach of the ordinary tribunals, and were to be under their own separate rulers, and directly subject in life and property to the decrees of Rome.

Henry knew but one man in his dominions able to contend in talent and acuteness with the advocates of the Church, and that was his chancellor and friend, the gay and generous and affectionate à-Beckett. So one day, without giving him much time for preparation, he persuaded him to be made a priest, and at the same moment named him Archbishop of Canterbury and Primate of all England. Now, he thought, we have a champion who will do battle in our cause and stand up for the liberties of his native land. But à-Beckett had dressed himself in a hair shirt and flogged himself with an iron scourge. He had invited the holiest of the priests to favour him with their advice, and had thrown himself on his knees on the approach of the most ascetic of the monks and friars. All his fine establishments were broken up; his horses were sent away; his silver table-services sold; and the new archbishop fasted on bread and water and lay on the hard floor. Henry was astonished and uneasy; and he had soon very good cause for his uneasiness, for his favourite orator, his boon-companion, his gallant chancellor, from whom he had expected support and victory, turned against him with the most ruthless animosity, and pushed the pretensions of Rome to a pitch they had never reached before. Nobody, however he may blame the double-dealing or the ambition of à-Beckett, can deny him the praise of personal courage in making opposition to the king. The Norman blood was as hot in him as in any of his predecessors. When he got into a passion, we are told by a contemporary chronicler, his blue eyes became filled with blood. In a fit of rage he bit a page's shoulder. A favourite servant having contradicted him, he rushed after the man on the stair, and, not being able to catch him, gnawed the straw upon the boards. We may therefore guess with what feelings the injured Plantagenet received the behaviour of his newly-created primate. He stormed and raged, terrified the other prelates to join him in his measures for curbing the power of the Church, chafed himself for several years against the unconquerable firmness of the arrogant archbishop, and finally failed in every object he had aimed at. The violence of the king was met with the affected resignation of the sufferer; and at last, when the impatience of Henry gave encouragement to his followers to put the refractory priest to death, the quarrel was lifted out of the ordinary category of a dispute between the crown and the crozier: it became a combat between a wilful and irreligious tyrant and a martyred saint. It requires us to enter into the feelings of the twelfth century to be able to understand the issue of this great conflict. In our own day the assumptions of à-Beckett, and his claims of exemption from the ordinary laws, have no sympathizers among the lovers of progress or freedom. But in the time of the second Henry the only chance of either, in England, was found under the shelter of the Church. That great establishment was still the only protection against the lawless violence of the king and nobles. The Norman possessors of the land were still an army encamped on hostile soil and levying contributions by the law of the strong hand. Disunion had not yet arisen between the sovereign and his lords, except as to the division of the spoil. The Crusades had not depopulated England to the same extent as some of the other countries in Europe; and the wars of the troubled days of Stephen and Matilda, though fatal to the prosperity of the land, and destructive of many of the nobles on either side, had attracted an immense number of high-born and strong-handed adventurers, who amply supplied their place. The clergy had been forced to retain their original position as leaders of the popular mind, superintendents of the interests of their flocks, and teachers and comforters of the oppressed: à-Beckett, therefore, was not in their eyes an ambitious priest, sacrificing every thing for the elevation of his order. He was a champion fighting the battles of the poor against the rich,—a ransomer of at least one powerful body in the State from the capricious cruelty of Henry and the grasping avarice of the Norman spoliation. The down-trodden Saxons received with the transports of gratified revenge any humiliation inflicted on the proud aristocracy which had thriven on the ruin of their ancestors. The date of the Conquest was not yet so distant as to hinder the feeling of personal wrong from mingling in the conflict between the races. A man of sixty remembered the story told him by his father of his dispossession of holt and field, on which the old manor-house had stood since Alfred's days, and which now had been converted into a crenelated tower by the foreign conqueror. Nor are we to forget, in the midst of the idea of antiquity conveyed at the present time by the fact of a person's ancestor having "come in with William," that the bitterness of dispossession was increased in the eyes of the long-descended Saxon franklin by the lowness of his dispossessor's birth. Half the roll-call of the Norman army was made up of the humblest names,—barbers and smiths, and tailors and valets, and handicraftsmen of all descriptions. And yet, seated in his fortified keep, supported by the sixty thousand companions of his success, enriched by the fertile harvests of his new domain, this upstart adventurer filled the wretched cottages of the land with a distressed and starving peasantry; and where were those friendless and helpless outcasts to look for succour and consolation? They found them in the Church. Their countrymen generally filled the lower offices, speaking in good Saxon, and feeling as good Saxons should; while the lordly abbot or luxurious bishop kept high state in his monastery or palace, and gave orders in Norman French with feelings as foreign as his tongue. But à-Beckett was an Englishman; à-Beckett was Archbishop of Canterbury, and chief of all the churchmen in the land. To honour à-Beckett was to protest against the Conquest; and when the crowning glory came, and the crimes of Henry against themselves attained their full consummation in the murder of the prelate at the altar,—the patriot in his resistance to oppression,—the enthusiasm of the country knew no bounds. The penitential pilgrimage which the proudest of the Plantagenets made to the tomb of his victim was but small compensation for so enormous a wickedness, and for ages the name of à-Beckett was a household word at the hearths of the English peasantry, as their great representative and deliverer,—only completing the care he took of their temporal interests while on earth by the superintendence he bestowed on their spiritual benefit now that he was a saint in heaven. Curses fell upon the head and heart of the royal murderer, as if by a visible retribution. His children rebelled and died; the survivors were false and hostile. Richard, who had the one sole virtue of animal courage, was incited by his mother to resist his father, and was joined in his unnatural rebellion by his brother John, who had no virtue at all. His mind, before he died, had lost the energy which kept the sceptre steady; and the century went down upon the glory of England, which lay like a wreck upon the water, and was stripped gradually, and one by one, of all the possessions which had made it great, and even the traditions of military power which had made it feared. John was on the throne, and the nation in discontent.

THIRTEENTH CENTURY.

Emperors of Germany.

A.D.

OTHO, (of Brunswick.)—(*cont.*)
1212. FREDERICK II.
1247. WILLIAM, (of Holland.)
1257. RICHARD, (of Cornwall.)
1257. ALPHONSO, (of Castile.)
1273. RODOLPH, (of Hapsburg.)
1291. ADOLPH, (of Nassau.)
1298. ALBERT I., (of Austria.)

Kings of France.

PHILIP AUGUSTUS.—(*cont.*)
1223. LOUIS VIII.
1226. LOUIS IX., (the Fat.)
1270. PHILIP III., (the Hardy.)
1285. PHILIP IV., (the Handsome.)

Kings of Scotland.

WILLIAM.—(*cont.*)
1214. ALEXANDER II.
1249. ALEXANDER III.
1286. MARGARET.
1291. JOHN BALIOL, deposed 1296.

Emperors of Constantinople.

A.D.

1203. ISAAC.
1204. ALEXIS IV.
1204. DUCAS, (Usurper,) dethroned by warriors of Fourth Crusade.

Latin Empire.

1204. BALDWYN, (of Flanders.)
1206. HENRY, (his brother.)
1216. PETER, (of Courtney.)
1219. ROBERT, (his son.)
1228. JOHN, (of Brienne.)
1231. BALDWYN.

Greek Empire of Nicæa.

1222. JOHN DUCAS.
1255. THEODORUS II.
1261. JOHN LASCARIS—retakes Constantinople.
1261. MICHAEL.
1282. ANDRONICUS II.

Kings of England.

JOHN.—(*cont.*)
1216. HENRY III.
1276. EDWARD I.

1201. FOURTH CRUSADE.
1217. FIFTH CRUSADE.
1228. SIXTH CRUSADE.
1248. SEVENTH CRUSADE.
1270. EIGHTH AND LAST CRUSADE, by St. Louis against Tunis.

Authors.

ROGER BACON, MATTHEW PARIS, ALEXANDER HALES, (Irrefragable Doctor,) THOMAS AQUINAS, (the Angelic Doctor.)

THE THIRTEENTH CENTURY.

FIRST CRUSADE AGAINST HERETICS—THE ALBIGENSES—MAGNA CHARTA—EDWARD I.

THE progress and enlightenment of Europe proceed from this period at a constantly-increasing rate. The rise of commercial cities, the weakening of the feudal aristocracy, the introduction of the learning of the Saracenic schools, and the growth of universities for the cultivation of science and language, contributed greatly to the result. Another cause used to be assigned for this satisfactory advance, in the discovery which had been made in the last century at Amalfi, of a copy of the long-forgotten Pandects of Justinian, and the reintroduction of the Roman laws, in displacement of the conflicting customs and barbarous enactments of the various states; but the fact of the continued existence of the Roman Institutes is not now denied, though it is probable that the discovery of the Amalfi manuscript may have given a fresh impulse to the improvement of the local codes. But an increase of mental activity had at first its usual regretable accompaniment in the contemporaneous rise of dangerous and unfounded opinions. Philosophy, which began with an admiration of the skill and learning of Aristotle, ended by enthroning him as the uncontrolled master of human reason. Wherever he was studied, all previous standards of faith and argument were overthrown. The cleverest intellects of the time could find themselves no higher task than to reconcile the Christian Scriptures with the decrees of the

Stagyrite, for it was felt that in the case of an irreconcilable divergence between the teaching of Christ and of Aristotle the scholars of Christendom would have pronounced in favour of the Greek. A formulary, indeed, was found out for the joint reception of both; many statements were declared to be "true in philosophy though false in religion," so that the most orthodox of Churchmen could receive the doctrines of the Church by an act of belief, while he gave his whole affection to Aristotle by an act of the understanding. When teachers and preachers tamper with the human conscience, the common feelings of honour and fair play revolt at the degrading attempt. Men of simple minds, who did not profess to understand Aristotle and could not be blinded by the subtleties of logic, endeavoured to discover "the more excellent way" for themselves, but were bewildered by the novelty of their search for Truth. There were mystic dreamers who saw God everywhere and in every thing, and counted human nature itself a portion of the Deity, or maintained that it was possible for man to attain a share of the divine by the practice of virtue. This Pantheism gave rise to numerous displays of popular ignorance and impressibility. Messiahs appeared in many parts of Europe, and were followed by great multitudes. Some enthusiasts taught that a new dispensation was opening upon man; that God was the Governor of the world during the Old Testament period; that Christ had reigned till now, but that the reign of the Holy Spirit was about to commence, and all things would be renewed. Others, more hardy, declared their adhesion to the Persian principle of a duality of persons in heaven, and revived the old Manichean heresy that the spirit of Hatred was represented in the Jewish Scriptures and the spirit of Love in the Christian; that the Good god had created the soul, and the Evil god the body,—on which were justified the sufferings they voluntarily inflicted on the workmanship of Satan, and the starvings and flagellations required to bring it into subjection. This belief found few followers, and would have died out as rapidly as it had arisen; but the malignity of the enemies of any change found it convenient to identify those wild enthusiasts with a very different class of persons who at this time rose into prominent notice. The rich counties of the South of France were always distinguished from the rest of the nation by the possession of greater elegance and freedom. The old Roman civilization had never entirely deserted the shores of the Mediterranean or the valleys of Languedoc and Provence. In Languedoc a sect of strange thinkers had given voice to some startling doctrines, which at once obtained the general consent. Toulouse was the chief encourager of these new beliefs, and in its hostility to Rome was supported by its reigning sovereign, Count Raymond VI. This potentate, from the position of his States,—abutting upon Barcelona, where the Spaniards, who remembered their recent emancipation from the Mohammedan yoke, were famous for their tolerance of religious dissent,—and deriving the greater portion of his wealth from the trade and industry of the Jews and Arabs established in his seaport towns, saw no great evil in the principles professed by his people. Those principles, indeed, when stripped of the malicious additions of his enemies, were not different from the creed of Protestantism at the present time. They consisted merely of a complete denial of the sovereignty of the Pope, the power of the priesthood, the efficacy of prayers for the dead, and the existence of purgatory.

The other princes of the South looked on religion as a mere instrument for the advancement of their own interests, and would have imitated the greater sovereigns of Europe, several of whom for a very slender consideration would have gone openly over to the standard of Mohammed. The inhabitants, therefore, of those opulent regions, by the favour of Raymond and the indifference of the rest, were left for a long time to their own devices, and gave intimation of a strong desire to break off their connection with the hierarchy of Rome. And no wonder they were tired of their dependence on so grasping and unprincipled a power as the Church had proved to them. More depraved and more exacting in this district than in any other part of Europe, the clergy had contrived to alienate the hearts of the common people without gaining the friendship of the nobility. Equally hated by both,—despised for their sensuality, and no longer feared for their spiritual power,—the priests could offer no resistance to the progress of the new opinions. Those opinions were in fact as much due to the vices of the clergy as to the convictions of the congregations. Any thing hostile to Rome was welcomed by the people. A musical and graceful language had grown up in Languedoc, which was universally recognised as the fittest vehicle for descriptions of beauty and declarations of love, and had been found equally adapted for the declamations of political hatred and denunciations of injustice. But now the whole guild of troubadours, ceasing to dedicate their muses to ladies' charms or the quarrels of princes, poured forth their indignation in innumerable songs on their clerical oppressors. The infamies of the whole order—the monks black and white, the deacons, the abbots, the bishops, the ordinary priests—were now married to immortal verse. Their spoiling of orphans, their swindling of widows and wards, their gluttony and drunkenness, were chronicled in every township, and were incapable of denial. Their dishonesty became proverbial. The simplest peasant, on hearing of a scandalous action, was in the habit of saying, "I would rather be a priest than be guilty of such a deed." But there were two men then alive exactly adapted to meet the exigencies of the time. One was a noble Castilian of the name of Dominic Guzman, who had become disgusted with the world, and had taken refuge from temptations and strife among the brethren of a reformed cathedral in Spain. But temptations and strife forced their way into the cells of Asma, and the eloquent friar was torn away from his prayers and penances and brought prominently forward by the backslidings of the men of Languedoc. The saturnine and self-sacrificing Spaniard had no sympathy with the joyous proceedings of the princes and merchants of the South. He saw sin in their enjoyment even of the gifts of nature,—their gracious air and beautiful scenery. How much more when the gayety of their meetings was enlivened by interludes throwing ridicule on the pretensions of the bishops, by hootings at any ecclesiastic who presented himself in the street, and by sneers and loud laughter at the predictions and miracles with which the Church resisted their attack! The unbelieving populace did not spare the personal dignity of the missionary himself. They pelted him with mud, and fixed long tails of straw at the back of his robe; they outraged all the feelings of his heart, his Castilian pride, his Christian belief, his clerical obedience. There is no denying the energy with which he exerted himself to recall those wandering sheep to the true fold. His biographer tells us of the successes of his eloquence, and of the irresistible effect of the inexhaustible fountain of tears with which he inundated his face till they formed a river down to his robes. His writings, we are assured, being found unanswerable by the heretics, were submitted to the ordeal of fire. Twice they resisted the hottest flames which could be raised by wood and brimstone, and still without converting the incredulous subjects of Count Raymond. His miracles, which were numerous and undeniable, also had no effect. Even his prayers, which seem to have moved houses and walls, had no efficacy in moving the obdurate hearts of the unbelievers; and at last, tired out with their recalcitrancy, the dreadful word was spoken. He cursed the men of Languedoc, the inhabitants of its towns, the knights and gentlemen who received his oratory with insult, and in addition to his own anathemas called in the spiritual thunder of the Pope.

This was the other man peculiarly fitted for the work he had to do. His cruelty would have done no dishonour to the blood-stained scutcheon of Nero, and his ambition transcended that of Gregory the Seventh. His name was Innocent the Third. For one-half of the crimes alleged against those heretics, who, from their principal seat in the diocese of Albi, were known as Albigenses, he would have turned the whole of France into a desert; and when, with greedy ear, he heard the denunciations of Dominic, he declared war on the devoted peasants,—war on the consenting princes; a holy war—more meritorious than a Crusade against the Turks and infidels —where no life was to be spared, and where houses and lands were to be the reward of the assailants. All the wild spirits of the age were wakened by the call. It was a pilgrimage where all expenses were paid, without the danger of the voyage to the East or the sword of the Saracen. Foremost among those who hurried to this mingled harvest of money and blood, of religious absolution and military fame, was the notorious Simon de Montfort, a man fitted for the commission of any wickedness requiring a powerful arm and unrelenting heart. Forward from all quarters of Europe rushed the exterminating emissaries

A.D. 1207.

of the Pope and soldiers of Dominic. "You shall ravage every field; you shall slay every human being: strike, and spare not. The measure of their iniquity is full, and the blessing of the Church is on your heads." These words, sung in sweet chorus by the Pope and the Monk, were the instructions on which De Montfort was prepared to act; and what could the sunny Languedoc, the land of song and dance, of olive-yard and vineyard, do to repel this hostile inroad? Suddenly all the music of the troubadours was hushed in dreadful expectation. Raymond was alarmed, and tried to temporize. Promises were made and explanations given, but without any offer of submission to the yoke of Rome: so the
A.D. 1208. infuriated warriors came on, burning, slaying, ravaging, in terms of their commission, till Dominic himself grew ashamed of such blood-stained missionaries; and when their slaughters went on, when they had murdered half the population in cold blood, and ridden down the peasantry whom despair had summoned to the defence of their houses and properties, the saintly-minded Spaniard could no longer honour their hideous butcheries with his presence. He contented himself with retiring to a church and praying for the good cause with such zeal and animation that De Montfort and eleven hundred of his ruffians put to flight a hundred thousand of the armed soldiers of the South, who felt themselves overthrown and scattered by an invisible power. Yet not even the prayers of Dominic could keep the outraged people in unresisting acquiescence. Simon de Montfort was expelled from the territories he had usurped, and found a mysterious death under the walls of Toulouse in 1218.

The old family was restored in the person of Ray-
A.D. 1223. mond the Seventh, and preparations made for defence. But Louis the Eighth of France came

to the aid of the infuriated Pope. Two hundred thousand men followed in the holy campaign. All the atrocities of the former time were renewed and surpassed. Town after town yielded, for all the defenders had died. Pestilence broke out in the invading force, and Louis himself was carried off by fever. Champions, however, were ready in all quarters to carry on the glorious cause. Louis the Ninth was now King of France, and under the government of his mother, Blanche of Castile, the work commenced by her countryman was completed. The final victory of the crusaders and punishment of the rebellious were celebrated by the introduction of the Inquisition, of which the ferocious Dominic was the presiding spirit. The fire of persecution under his holy stirrings burnt up what the sword of the destroyer had left, and from that time the voice of rejoicing was heard no more in Languedoc: her freedom of thought and elegance of sentiment were equally crushed into silence by the heel of persecution. The "gay science" perished utterly; the very language in which the sonnets of knight and troubadour had been composed died away from the literatures of the earth; and Rome rejoiced in the destruction of poetry and the restoration of obedience. This is a very mark-worthy incident in the thirteenth century, as it is the first experiment, on a great scale, which the Church made to retain her supremacy by force of arms. The pagan and infidel, the denier of Christ and the enemies of his teaching, had hitherto been the objects of the wrath of Christendom. This is the first instance in which a difference of opinion between Christians themselves had been the ground for wholesale extermination; for those unfortunate Albigenses acknowledged the divinity of the Saviour and professed to be his disciples. It is the crowning proof of the totally-secularized nature of the established faith. Its weapons were no longer argument and proof, or even persuasion and promise. The horse up to his fetlocks in blood, the sword waved in the air, the trampling of marshalled thousands, were henceforth the supports of the religion of love and charity; and fires glowing in every market-place and dungeons gaping in every episcopal castle were henceforth the true expositors of the truth as it is in Jesus. Fires, indeed, and dungeons, were required to compensate for the incompleteness, as it appeared to the truly orthodox, of the vengeance inflicted on the rebels. The Abbot of Citeaux, who gave his spiritual and corporeal aid to the assault on Beziers, was for a moment made uneasy by the difficulty his men experienced in distinguishing between the heretics and believers at the storm of the town. At last he got out of the difficulty by saying, "Slay them all! The Lord will know his own." The same benevolent dignitary, when he wrote an account of his achievement to the Pope, lamented that he had only been able to cut the throats of twenty thousand. And Gregory the Ninth would have been better pleased if it had been twice the number. "His vast revenge had stomach for them all," and already a quarter of a million of the population were the victims of his anger. Every thing had prospered to his hand. Raymond was despoiled of the greater portion of his estates, the voice of opposition was hushed, the castles of the nobles confiscated to the Church; and yet, when the treaty of Meaux, in 1229, by which the war was concluded, came to be considered, it was perceived that the pacification of Languedoc turned not so much to the profit of Rome as of the rapidly-coalescing monarchy of France.

Long before this, in 1204, Philip Augustus had found little difficulty in tearing the continental possessions of the English crown, except Guienne, from the trembling hands of John. The possession of Normandy had already made France a maritime power; and now, by the acquisition of the Narbonnais and Maguelonne from Raymond the Seventh, she not only extended her limits to the Mediterranean, but, by the extinction of two such vassals as the Count of Toulouse and the Duke of Normandy, incalculably strengthened the royal crown. Extinguished, indeed, was the power of Toulouse; for by the same treaty the unfortunate Raymond bought his peace with Rome by bestowing the county of Venaissin and half of Avignon on the Holy See. These sacrifices relieved him from the sentence of excommunication, and made him the best-loved son of the Church, and the poorest prince in Christendom.

While monarchy was making such strides in France, a counterbalancing power was formed in England by the combination of the nobility and the rise of the House of Commons. The story of Magna Charta is so well known that it will be sufficient to recall some of its principal incidents, which could not with propriety be omitted in an account of the important events of the thirteenth century. No event, indeed, of equal importance occurred in any other country of Europe. However more startling a crusade or a victory might be at the time, the results of no single incident have ever been so enduring or so wide-spread as those of the meeting of the barons at Runnymede and the summoning of the burgesses to Parliament.

The whole reign of John (1199–1216) is a tale of wickedness and degradation. Richard of the Lion-Heart had been cruel and unprincipled; but the sharpness of his sword threw a sort of respectability over the worst portions of his character. His practical talents, also, and the romantic incidents of his life, his confinement, and even of his death, lifted him out of the ordinary category of brutal and selfish kings and converted a very ferocious warrior into a popular hero. But John was hateful and contemptible in an equal degree. He deserted his father, he deceived his brother, he murdered his nephew, he oppressed his people. He had the pride that made enemies, and wanted the courage to fight them. A knight without truth, a king without justice, a Christian without faith,—all classes rebelled against him. Innocent the Third scented from afar the advantage he might obtain from a monarch whose nobility despised him and who was hated by his people. And when John got up a quarrel about the nomination of an archbishop to Canterbury, the Pope soon saw that though Langton was no à-Beckett, still less was John a Henry the Second. A sentence of excommunication was launched at the coward's head, and the crown of England offered to Philip Augustus of France. Philip Augustus had the modesty to refuse the splendid bribe, and contented himself with aiding to weaken a throne he did not feel inclined to fill. It is characteristic of John, that in the agonies of his fear, and of his desire to gain support against his people, he hesitated between invoking the assistance of the Miramolin of Morocco and the Pope of Rome. As good Mussulman with the one as Christian with the other, he finally decided on Innocent, and signed a solemn declaration of submission, making public resignation of the crowns of England and Ireland "to the Apostles Peter and Paul, to Innocent and his legitimate successors;" and, aided by the blessings of these new masters, and by the enforced neutrality of France, he was enabled to defeat his indignant nobles, and force them for two years to wear the same chains of submission to Rome which weighed upon himself. But in 1215 the patience of noble and peasant, of bishop and priest, was utterly exhausted.

John fled on the first outburst of the collected storm, and thought himself fortunate in stopping its
A.D. 1215.
violence by signing the Great Charter, the written ratification of the liberties which had been conferred by some of his predecessors, but whose chief authority was in the traditions and customs of the land. This was not an overthrow of an old constitution and the substitution of a new and different code, but merely a formal recognition of the great and fundamental principles on which only government can be carried on,—security of person and property, and the just administration of equitable laws. All orders in the State were comprehended in this national agreement. The Church was delivered from the exactions of the king, and left to an undisturbed intercourse on spiritual matters with her spiritual head. She was to have perfect freedom of election to vacant benefices, and the king's rapacity was guarded against by a clause reducing any fine he might impose on an ecclesiastic to an accordance with his professional income, and not with the extent of his lay possessions. The barons, of course, took equal care of their own interests as they had shown for those of the Church. They corrected many abuses from which they suffered, in respect to their feudal obligations. They regulated the fines and quit-rents on succession to their fiefs, the management of crown wards, and the marriage of heiresses and widows. They insisted also on the assemblage of a council of the great and lesser barons, to consult for the general weal, and put some check on the disposal of their lands by their tenants, in order to keep their vassals from impoverishment and their military organization unimpaired. But when church and aristocracy were thus protected from the tyranny of the king, were the interests of the great mass of the people neglected? This has sometimes

been urged against the legislators of Runnymede, but very unjustly; for as much attention was paid to the liberties and immunities of the municipal corporations and of ordinary subjects as to those of the prelates and lords. Every person had the right to dispose of his property by will. No arbitrary tolls could be exacted of merchants. All men might enter or leave the kingdom without restraint. The courts of law were no longer to be stationary at Westminster, to which complainants from Northumberland or Cornwall never could make their way, but were to travel about, bringing justice to every man's door. They were to be open to every one, and justice was to be neither "sold, refused, nor delayed." Circuits were to be held every year. No man was to be put on his trial from mere rumour, but on the evidence of lawful witnesses. No sentence could be passed on a freeman except by his peers in jury assembled. No fine could be imposed so exorbitant as to ruin the culprit. But the bishops and clergy, the nobility and their vassals, the corporations and freemen, were not the main bodies of the State; and the framers of Magna Charta have been blamed for neglecting the great majority of the population, which consisted of serfs or villeins. This accusation is, however, not true, even with respect to the words of the Charter; for it is expressly provided that the carts and working-implements of that class of the people shall not be seizable in satisfaction of a fine; and in its intention the accusation is more untenable still; for although the reformers of 1215 had no design of granting new privileges to any hitherto-unprivileged order and their work was limited to the legal re-establishment of privileges which John had attempted to overthrow, the large and liberal spirit of their declarations is shown by the notice they take of the hitherto-unconsidered classes. For the protection accorded to their ploughs and carts, which are specifically named in the Charter, ratified at once their right to hold property,—the first condition of personal freedom and independence,—and, by an analogy of reasoning, restrained their more immediate masters from tyranny and injustice. It could not be long before a man secured by the national voice in the possession of one species of property extended his rights over every thing else. If the law guaranteed him the plough he held, the cart he drove, the spade he plied, why not the house he occupied, the little field he cultivated? And if the poorest freeman walked abroad in the pride of independence, because the baron could no longer insult him, or the priest oppress him, or the king himself strip him of land and gear, how could he deny the same blessings to his neighbour, the rustic labourer, who was already master of cart and plough and was probably richer and better fed than himself?

But a firmer barrier against the encroachments of kings and nobles than the written words of Magna Charta was still required, and people were not long in seeing how little to be trusted are legal forms when the contracting parties are disposed to evade their obligations. John indeed attempted, in the very year that saw his signature to the Charter, to expunge his name from the obligatory deed by the plenary power of the Pope. Innocent had no scruple in giving permission to his English vassal to break the oath and swerve from his engagement. But the English spirit was not so broken as the king's, and the barons took the management of the country into their own hands. When the experience of a few years of Henry the Third had shown them that there was no improvement on the personal character of his predecessor, they took effectual measures for the protection of all classes of the people.

Henry began his inglorious reign in 1216, and ended it in 1272. In those fifty-six years great changes took place, but all in an upward direction, out of the darkness and unimpressionable stolidity of previous ages. The dawn of a more intellectual period seemed at hand, and already the ghosts of ignorance and oppression began to scent the morning air. In 1264 an example was set by England which it would have been well if all the other Western lands had followed, for by the institution of a true House of Commons it laid the foundation for the only possible liberal and improvable government,—the only government which can derive its strength from the consent of the governed legitimately expressed, and vary in its action and spirit with the changes in the general mind. In cases of error or temporary delusion, there is always left the most admirable machinery for retracing its steps and rectifying what is wrong. In cases of universal approval and unanimous exertion, there is no power, however skilfully wielded by autocrats or despots, which can compare with the combined energy of a whole and undivided people.

The contemporary of this Henry on the throne of
A.D. 1226 France was the gentle and honest Louis the
–1270. Ninth. If those epithets do not sound so high as the usual phraseology applied to kings, we are to consider how rare are the examples either of honesty or gentleness among the rulers of that time, and how difficult it was to possess or exercise those virtues. But this gentle and honest king, who was scarcely raised in rank when the Church had canonized him as a saint, achieved as great successes by the mere strength of his character as other monarchs had done by fire and sword. His love of justice enabled him to extend the royal power over his contending vassals, who chose him as umpire of their quarrels and continued to submit to him

as their chief. He heard the complaints of the lower orders of his people in person, sitting, like the kings of the East, under the shade of a tree, and delivering judgment solely on the merits of the case. His undoubted zeal on behalf of his religion permitted him, without the accusation of heresy, to put boundaries to the aggressions of the Church. He resisted its more violent claims, and gave liberty to ecclesiastics as well as laymen, who were equally interested in the curtailment of the Papal power. He granted a great number of municipal charters, and published certain Establishments, as they were called, which were improvements on the old customs of the realm and were in a great measure founded on the Roman law. The spirit of the time was popular progress; and both in France and England great advances were made; deliberative national assemblies took their rise,—in France, under the conscientious monarch, with the full aid and influence of the royal authority, in England, under the feeble and selfish Henry, by the necessity of gaining the aid of the Commons against the Crown to the outraged and insulted nobility. In both nations these assemblies bore for a long time very distinguishable marks of their origin. The Parliaments of France, sprung from the royal will, were little else than the recorders of the decrees of the monarch; while the Parliaments of England, remembering their popular origin, have always had a feeling of independence, and a tendency to make rather hard bargains with our kings. Even before this time the Great Council had occasionally opposed the exactions of the Crown; but when the falsehood and avarice of Henry III. had excited the popular odium, the barons of 1263, in noble emulation of their predecessors of 1215, had risen in defence of the nation's liberties, and the last hand was put to the building up of our present constitution, by the summoning, "to consult on public affairs," of certain burgesses from the towns, in addition to the prelates, knights, and freeholders who had hitherto constituted the parliamentary body. But those barons and tenants-in-chief attended in their own right, and were altogether independent of the principle of election and representation. The summons issued by Simon de Montfort (son of the truculent hero of the Albigensian crusade, and brother-in-law of Henry) invested with new privileges the already-enfranchised boroughs. From this time the representatives of the Commons are always mentioned in the history of parliaments; and although this proceeding of De Montfort was only intended to strengthen his hands against his enemies, and, after his temporary object was gained, was not designed to have any further effect on the constitutional progress of our country, still, the principle had been adopted, the example was set, and the right to be represented in Parliament became one of the most valued privileges of the enfranchised commons.

A.D. 1265.

It is observable that this increase of civil freedom in the various countries of Europe was almost in exact proportion to the diminution of ecclesiastical power. It is equally observable that the weakening of the priestly influence rapidly followed the infamous excesses into which its intolerance and pride had hurried the princes and other supporters of its claims. Never, indeed, had it appeared in so palmy and flourishing a state as in the course of this century; and yet the downward journey was begun. The devastation it carried into Languedoc, and the depopulation of all those sunny regions near the Mediterranean Sea—the crusades against the Saracens in Asia, to which it sent the strength of Europe, and against the Moors in Africa, to which it impelled the most obedient, and also, when his religious passions were roused, the most relentless, of the Church's sons, no other than St. Louis—and the submission of the Patriarchates of Jerusalem and Alexandria to the Romish See—these and other victories of the Church were succeeded, before the century closed, by a manifest though silent insurrection against its spiritual domination. There were many reasons for this. The inferior though still dignified clergy in the different nations were alienated by the excessive exactions of their foreign head. In France the submissive St. Louis was forced to become the guardian of the privileges and income of the Gallican Church. In England the number of Italian incumbents exceeded that of the English-born; and in a few years the Pope managed to draw from the Church and State an amount equal to fifteen millions of our present coin. In Scotland, poorer and more proud, the king united himself to his clergy and nobles, and would not permit the Romish exactors to enter his dominions. The avarice and venality of Rome were repulsive equally to priest and layman. The strong support, also, which hitherto had arisen to the Holy See from the innumerable monks and friars, could no longer be furnished by the depressed and vitiated communities whom the coarsest of the common people despised for their sensuality and vice. In earlier times the worldly pretensions of the secular clergy were put to shame by the poverty and self-denial of the regular orders. Their ascetic retirement, and fastings, and scourgings, had recommended them to the peasantry round their monasteries, by the contrast their peaceful lives presented to the pomp and self-indulgence of bishops and priests. But now the character of the two classes was greatly changed. The parson of the parish, when he was not an Italian absentee, was an English clergyman, whose interests and feelings were all in unison with those of his flock; the

monks were an army of mercenary marauders in the service of a foreign prince, advocating his most unpopular demands and living in the ostentatious disregard of all their vows. Even the lowest class of all, the thralls and villeins, were not so much as before in favour of their tonsured brothers, who had escaped the labours of the field by taking refuge in the abbey; for Magna Charta had given the same protection against oppression to themselves, and the enfranchisement of the boroughs had put power into the hands of citizens and freemen, who would not be so apt to abuse it as the martial baron or mitred prelate had been. The same principles were at work in France; and when the newly-established Franciscans and Dominicans were pointed to as restoring the purity and abnegation of the monks of old, the time for belief in those virtues being inherent, or even possible, in a cloister, was past, and little effect was produced in favour of Rome by the bloodthirsty brotherhood of the ferocious St. Dominic or the more amiable professions of the half-witted St. Francis of Assisi. The tide, indeed, had so completely turned after
A.D. 1272. the commencement of the reign of Edward the First, that the Churchmen, both in England and France, preferred being taxed by their own Sovereign to being subjected to the arbitrary exactions of the Pope. Edward gave them no exemption from the obligation to support the expenses of the State in common with all the other holders of property, and pressed, indeed, rather more heavily upon the prelates and rich clergy than on the rest of the contributors, as if to drive to a decision the question, to which of the potentates—the Pope or the sovereign—tribute was lawfully due. When this object was gained, a bull was let loose upon the sacrilegious monarch by Boniface the Eighth, which positively forbids any member of the priesthood to con-

tribute to the national exchequer on any occasion or emergency whatever. But the king made very light of the papal authority when it stood between him and the revenues of his crown, and the national clergy submitted to be taxed like other men. In France the same discussion led to the same result. The Gallican and English Churches asserted their liberties in a way which must have been peculiarly gratifying to the kings,—namely, by subsidies to the Crown, and disobedience to the fulminations of the Pope.

But no surer proof of the increased wisdom of mankind can be given than the termination of the Crusades. Perhaps, indeed, it was found that religious excitement could be combined with warlike distinction by assaults on the unbelieving or disobedient at home. There seemed little use in traversing the sea and toiling through the deserts of Syria, when the same heavenly rewards were held out for a campaign against the inhabitants of Languedoc and the valleys of the Alps. Clearer views also of the political effect of those distant expeditions in strengthening the hands of the Pope, who, as spiritual head of Christendom, was *ex officio* commander of the crusading armies, must no doubt have occurred to the various potentates who found themselves compelled to aid the very authority from whose arrogance they suffered so much. The exhaustion of riches and decrease of population were equally strong reasons for repose. But none of all these considerations had the least effect on the simple and credulous mind of Louis the Ninth. Resisting as he did the interference of the Pope in his character of King of France, no one could yield more devoted submission to the commands of the Holy Father when uttered to him in his character of Christian knight. At an early age he vowed himself to the sacred cause, and in the year

1248 the seventh and last crusade to the Holy Land took its way from Aigues-Mortes and Marseilles, under the guidance of the youthful King and the Princes of France. Disastrous to a more pitiful degree than any of its predecessors, this expedition began its course in Egypt by the conquest of Damietta, and from thenceforth sank from misery to misery, till the army, surprised by the inundations of the Nile, and hemmed in by the triumphant Mussulmans, surrendered its arms, and the nobility of France, with its king at its head, found itself the prisoner of Almohadam. An insurrection in a short time deprived their conqueror of life and crown, and a treaty for the payment of a great ransom set the captives free. Ashamed, perhaps, to return to his own country, sighing for the crown of martyrdom, zealous at all events for the privileges of a pilgrim, Louis betook himself to Palestine, and, as he was bound by the convention not to attack Jerusalem, he wasted four years in uselessly rebuilding the fortifications of Ptolemais, and Sidon, and Jaffa, and only embarked on his homeward voyage when the death of his mother and the discontent of his subjects necessitated his return. After an absence of six years, the enfeebled and exhausted king

A.D. 1254. sat once more in the chair of judgment, and gained all hearts by his generosity and truth. Yet the old fire was not extinct. His oath was binding still, and in 1270, girt with many a baron bold, and accompanied by his brother, Charles of Anjou, and the gay Prince Edward of England, he fixed the red cross upon his shoulder and led his army to the sea-shore. The ships were all ready, but the destination of the war was changed. A new power had established itself at Tunis, more hostile to Christianity than the Moslem of Egypt, and nearer at hand. In an evil hour the King was persuaded to attack the Tunisian Caliph. He landed at Carthage, and besieged the capital of the new dominion. But Tunis witnessed the death of its besieger, for Louis, worn out with fatigue and broken with disappointment, was stricken by a contagious malady, and expired with the courage of a hero and the pious resignation of a Christian. With him the crusading spirit vanished from every heart. All the Christian armies were withdrawn. The Knights-Hospitallers, the Templars, the Teutonic Order, passed over to Cyprus, and left the hallowed spots of sacred story to be profaned by the footsteps of the Infidel. Asia and Europe henceforth pursued their separate courses; and it was left to the present day to startle the nations of both quarters of the world with the spectacle of a war about the possession of the Holy Places.

The century which has the slaughter of the Albigenses, the Magna Charta, the rise of the Commons, the termination of the Crusades, to distinguish it, will not need other features to be pointed out in order to abide in our memories. Yet the reign of Edward the First, the greatest of our early kings, must be dwelt on a little longer, as it would not be fair to omit the personal merits of a man who united the virtues of a legislator to those of a warrior. Whether it was the prompting of ambition, or a far-sighted policy, which led him to attempt the conquest of Scotland, we need not stop to inquire. It might have satisfied the longings both of policy and ambition if he had succeeded in creating a compact and irresistible Great Britain out of England harassed and Scotland insecure. And if, contented with his undivided kingdom, he had devoted himself uninterruptedly to the introduction and consolidation of excellent laws, and had extended the ameliorations he introduced in England to the northern portion of his dominions, he would have earned a wider fame than the sword has given him, and would have been received with blessings as the Justinian of the whole island, instead of establishing a rankling hatred in the bosoms of one of the cognate peoples which it took many centuries to allay, if, indeed, it is altogether obliterated at the present time; for there are not wanting enthusiastic Scotchmen who show considerable wrath when treating of his assumptions of superiority over their country and his interference with their national affairs.

Edward's sister had been the wife of Alexander the Third of Scotland. Two sons of that marriage had died, and the only other child, a daughter, had married Eric the Norwegian. In Margaret, the daughter of this king, the Scottish succession lay, and when her grandfather died in 1290, the Scottish states sent a squadron to bring the young queen home, and great preparations were made for the reception of the "Maid of Norway." But the Maid of Norway was weak in health; the voyage was tempestuous and long; and weary and exhausted she landed on one of the Orkney Islands, and in a short time a rumour went round the land that the hope of Scotland was dead. Edward was among the first to learn the melancholy news. He determined to assert his rights, and began by trying to extend the feudal homage which several of the Scottish kings had rendered for lands held in England, over the Scottish crown itself. When the various competitors for the vacant throne submitted their pretensions to his decision he made their acknowledgment of his supremacy an indispensable condition. Out of the three chief candidates he fixed on John Baliol, who, in addition to the most legal title, had perhaps the equal recommendation of being the feeblest personal character. Robert Bruce and Hastings, the other candidates, submitted to their disappointment, and Baliol became the mere vice-

roy of the English king. He obeyed a summons to Westminster as a vassal of Edward, to answer for his conduct, and was treated with disdain. But the Scottish
A.D. 1293.
barons had more spirit than their king. They forced him to resist the pretensions of his overbearing patron, and for the first time, in 1295, began the long connection between Franch and Scotland by a treaty concluded between the French monarch and the twelve Guardians of Scotland, to whom Baliol had delegated his authority before retiring forever to more peaceful scenes. From this time we find that, whenever war was declared by France on England, Scotland was let loose on it to distract its attention, in the same way as, whenever war was declared upon France, the hostility of Flanders was roused against its neighbour. But the benefits bestowed by England on her Low Country ally were far greater than any advantage which France could offer to Scotland. Facilities of trade and favourable tariffs bound the men of Ghent and Bruges to the interests of Edward. But the friendship of France was limited to a few bribes and the loan of a few soldiers. Scotland, therefore, became impoverished by her alliance, while Flanders grew fat on the liberality of her powerful friend. England itself derived no small benefit both from the hostility of Scotland and the alliance of the Flemings. When the Northern army was strong, and the King was hard pressed by the great Wallace, the sagacious Parliament exacted concessions and immunities from its imperious lord before it came liberally to his aid; and whenever we read in one page of a check to the arms of Edward, we read in the next of an enlargement of the popular rights. When the first glow of the apparent conquest of Scotland was past, and the nation was seen rising under the Knight of Elderslie after it had been deserted by its natural leaders, the

lords and barons,—and, later, when in 1297 he gained a great victory over the English at Stirling,—the English Parliament lost no time in availing themselves of the defeat, and sent over to the king, who was at the moment in Flanders menacing the flanks of France, a parchment for his signature, containing the most ample ratification of their power of granting or withholding the supplies. It was on the 10th of October, 1297, that this important document was signed; and, satisfied with this assurance of their privileges, the "nobles, knights of the shire, and burgesses of England in parliament assembled" voted the necessary funds to enable their sovereign lord to punish his rebels in Scotland. Perhaps these contests between the sister countries deepened the patriotic feeling of each, and prepared them, at a later day, to throw their separate and even hostile triumphs into the united stock, so that, as Charles Knight says in his admirable "Popular History," "the Englishman who now reads of the deeds of Wallace and Bruce, or hears the stirring words of one of the noblest lyrics of any tongue, feels that the call to 'lay the proud usurper low' is one which stirs his blood as much as that of the born Scotsman; for the small distinctions of locality have vanished, and the great universal sympathies for the brave and the oppressed stay not to ask whether the battle for freedom was fought on the banks of the Thames or of the Forth. The mightiest schemes of despotism speedily perish. The union of nations is accomplished only by a slow but secure establishment of mutual interests and equal rights."

FOURTEENTH CENTURY.

Emperors of Germany.

A.D.

ALBERT.—(*cont.*)

1308. HENRY VII., (of Luxemburg.)

1314. LOUIS IV., (of Bavaria.) } Rival Emperors.

1314. FREDERICK III., (of Austria,) died 1330. } Rival Emperors.

1347. CHARLES IV., (of Luxemburg.)

1378. WENCESLAS, (of Bohemia.)

Kings of France.

PHILIP IV.—(*cont.*)

1314. LOUIS X., (Hutin.)

1316. PHILIP V., (the Long.)

1322. CHARLES IV., (the Handsome.)

1328. PHILIP VI.

1350. JOHN II., (the Good.)

1364. CHARLES V., (the Wise.)

1380. CHARLES VI., (the Beloved.)

Emperors of the East.

A.D.

ANDRONICUS II.—(*cont.*)

1332. ANDRONICUS III.

1341. JOHN PALÆOLOGUS.

1347. JOHN CANTACUZENUS.

1355. JOHN PALÆOLOGUS, (restored.)

1391. MANUEL PALÆOLOGUS.

Kings of England.

EDWARD I.—(*cont.*)

1307. EDWARD II.

1327. EDWARD III.

1377. RICHARD II.

1399. HENRY IV.

Kings of Scotland.

1306. ROBERT BRUCE.

1329. DAVID II.

1371. ROBERT II.

1390. ROBERT III.

1311. Suppression of the Knights Templars.

1343. Cannon first used.

1370. John Huss born.

1383. Bible first translated into a vulgar tongue, (Wickliff's.)

Authors.

DANTE, PETRARCH, BOCCACCIO, CHAUCER, FROISSART, JOHN DUNS SCOTUS, BRADWARDINE, WILLIAM OCCAM, WICKLIFF.

THE FOURTEENTH CENTURY.

ABOLITION OF THE ORDER OF THE TEMPLARS—RISE OF MODERN LITERATURES—SCHISM OF THE CHURCH.

In the year 1300 a jubilee was celebrated at Rome, when remission of sins and other spiritual indulgences were offered to all visitors by the liberal hand of Pope Boniface the Eighth. And for the thirty days of the solemn ceremonial, the crowds who poured in from all parts of Europe, and pursued their way from church to church and kissed with reverential lips the relics of the saints and martyrs, gave an appearance of strength and universality to the Roman Church which had long departed from it. Yet the downward course had been so slow, and each defection or defeat had been so covered from observation in a cloud of magnificent boasts, that the real weakness of the Papacy was only known to the wise and politic. Even in the splendours and apparent triumph of the jubilee processions it was perceived by the eyes of hostile statesmen that the day of faith was past.

Dante, the great poet of Italy, was there, piercing with his Ithuriel spear the false forms under which the spiritual tyranny concealed itself. Countless multitudes deployed before him without blinding him for a moment to the unreality of all he saw. Others were there, not deriving their conclusions, like Dante, from the intuitive insight into truth with which the highest imaginations are gifted, but from the calmer premises of reason and observation. Even while the pæans were loudest and the triumph at its height, thoughts were entering into many hearts which had never been harboured before, but which in no long space bore their fruits, not only in opposition to the actual proceedings of Rome, but in undisguised contempt and ridicule of all its claims. Boniface himself, however, was ignorant of all these secret feelings. He was now past eighty years of age, and burning with a wilder personal ambition and more presumptuous ostentation than would have been pardonable at twenty. He appeared in the processions of the jubilee, dressed in the robes of the Empire, with two swords, and the globe of sovereignty carried before him. A herald cried, at the same time, "Peter, behold thy successor! Christ, behold thy vicar upon earth!" But the high looks of the proud were soon to be brought low. The King of France at that time was Philip the Handsome, the most unprincipled and obstinate of men, who stuck at no baseness or atrocity to gain his ends,—who debased the Crown, pillaged the Church, oppressed the people, tortured the Jews, and impoverished the nobility,—a self-willed, strong-handed, evil-hearted despot, and glowing with an intense desire to humble and spoil the Holy Father himself. If he could get the Pope to be his tax-gatherer, and, instead of emptying the land of all its wealth for the benefit of the Roman exchequer, pour Roman, German, English, European contributions into his private treasury, the object of his life would be gained. His coffers would be overflowing, and his principal opponent disgraced. A wonderful and apparently impossible scheme, but which nevertheless succeeded. The combatants at first seemed very equally matched. When Boniface made an extravagant demand, Philip sent him a contemptuous reply. When Boniface turned for alliances to the Emperor or to England, Philip threw himself on the sympathy of his lords and the inhabitants of the towns; for the parts formerly played by Pope and King were now reversed. The Papacy, instead of recurring to the people and strengthening itself by contact with the masses who had looked to the Church as their natural guard from the aggressions of their lords, now had recourse to the more dangerous expedient of exciting one sovereign against another, and weakened its power as much by concessions to its friends as by the hostility of its foes. The king, on the other hand, flung himself on the support of his subjects, including both the Church and Parliament, and thus raised a feeling of national independence which was more fatal to Roman preponderance than the most active personal enmity could have been. Accordingly, we find Boniface offending the population of France by his intemperate attacks on the worst of kings, and that worst of kings attracting the admiration of his people by standing up for the dignity of the Crown against the presumption of the Pope. The fact of this national spirit is shown by the very curious circumstance that while Philip and his advisers, in their quarrels with Boniface, kept within the bounds of respectful language in the letters they actually sent to Rome, other answers were disseminated among the people as having been forwarded to the Pope, outraging all the feelings of courtesy and respect. It was like the conduct of the Chinese mandarins, who publish vainglorious and triumphant bulletins among their people, while they write in very different language to the enemy at their gates. Thus, in reply to a very insulting brief of Boniface, beginning, "Ausculta, fili," (Listen, son,) and containing a catalogue of all his complaints against the French king, Philip published a version of it, omitting all the verbiage in which the insolent meaning was involved, and accompanied it in the same way with a copy of the unadorned eloquence which constituted his reply. In this he descended to very plain speaking. "Philip," he says, "by the grace of God, King of the French, to Boniface, calling himself Pope, little or no salutation. Be it known to your Fatuity that we are subject in temporals to no man alive; that the collation of churches and vacant prebends is inherent in our Crown; that their 'fruits' belong to us; that all presentations made or to be made by us are valid; that we will maintain our presentees in possession of them with all our power; and that we hold for fools and idiots whosoever believes otherwise." This strange address received the support of the great majority of the nation, and was meant as a translation into the vulgar tongue of the real intentions of the irritated monarch, which were concealed in the letter really despatched in a mist of polite circumlocutions. Boniface perceived the animus of his foe, but bore himself as loftily as ever. When a meeting of the barons, held in the Louvre, had appealed to a General Council and had passed a vote of condemnation against the Pope as guilty of many crimes, not exclusive of heresy itself, he answered, haughtily, that the summoning of a council was a prerogative of the Pope, and that already the King had incurred the danger of excommunication for the steps he had taken against the Holy Chair. To prevent the publication of the sentence, which might have been made a powerful weapon against France in the hands of Albert of Germany or Edward of England, it was necessary to give notice of an appeal to a General Council into the hands of the Pope in person. He had retired to Anagni, his native town, where he found himself more secure among his friends and relations than in the capital of his See. Colonna, a discontented Roman and sworn enemy of Boniface, and Supino, a military adventurer, whom Philip bought over with a bribe of ten thousand florins, introduced Nogaret, the French chancellor and chief adviser of the king, into Anagni, with cries from their armed attendants of "Death to the Pope!" "Long live the King of France!" The cardinals fled in dismay. The inhabitants, not being able to prevent their visitors from pillaging the shops, joined them in that occupation, and every thing was in confusion. The Pope was in despair. His own nephew had abandoned his cause and made terms for himself. Accounts vary as to his behaviour in these extremities. Perhaps they are all true at different periods of the scene. At first, overwhelmed with the treachery of his friends, he is said to have burst into tears. Then he gathered his ancient courage, and, when commanded to abdicate, offered his neck to the assailants; and at last, to strike them with awe, or at least to die with dignity, he bore on his shoulders the mantle of St. Peter, placed the crown of Constantine on his head, and grasped the keys and cross in his hands. Colonna, they say, struck him on the cheek with his iron gauntlet till the blood came. Let us hope that this is an invention of the enemy; for the Pope was eighty-six years old, and Colonna was a Roman soldier. There is always a tendency to elevate the sufferer in the cause we favour, by the introduction of ennobling circumstances. In this and other instances of the same kind there is the further temptation in orthodox historians to make the most they can of the martyrdom of one of their chiefs, and in a peculiar manner to glorify the wrongs of their hero by their resemblance to the sufferings of Christ. But the rest of the story is melancholy enough without the aggravation of personal pain. The pontiff abstained from food for three whole days. He consumed his grief in secret, and was only relieved at last from fears of the dagger or poison by an insurrection of the people. They fell upon the French escort when they perceived how weak it was, and carried the Pope into the market-place. He said, "Good people, you have seen how our enemies have spoiled me of my goods. Behold me as poor as Job. I tell you truly, I have nothing to eat or drink. If there is any good woman who will charitably bestow on me a little bread and wine, or even a little water, I will give her God's blessing and mine. Whoever will bring me the smallest thing in this my necessity, I will give him remission of all his sins." All the people cried, "Long live the Holy Father!" They ran and brought him bread and wine, and any thing they had. Everybody would enter and speak to him, just as to any other of the poor. In a short time after this he proceeded to Rome, and felt once more in safety. But his heart was tortured by anger and a thirst for vengeance. He became insane; and when he tried to escape from the restraints his state demanded, and found his way barred by the Orsini, his insanity became madness. He foamed at the mouth and ground his teeth when he was spoken to. He repelled the offers of his friends with curses and violence, and died without the sacraments or consolations of the Church. The people remembered the prophecy made of him by his predecessor Celestin:—"You mounted like a fox; you will reign like a lion; you will die like a dog."

A.D. 1303.

But the degradation of the papal chair was not yet complete, and Philip was far from satisfied. Merely to have harassed to death an old man of eighty-six was not sufficient for a monarch who wanted a servant in the Pope more than a victim. To try his power over Benedict the Eleventh, the successor of Boniface, he began a process in the Roman court against the memory of his late antagonist. Benedict replied by an anathema in general terms on the murderers of Boniface, and all Philip's crimes and schemings seemed of no avail. But one day the sister of a religious order presented His Holiness with a basket of figs, and in a short time the pontifical throne was vacant.

Now was the time for the triumph of the king. He had devoted much time and money to win over a number of cardinals to his cause, and obtained a promise under their hands and seals that they would vote for whatever candidate he chose to name. He was not long in fixing on a certain Bernard de Goth, Archbishop of Bordeaux, the most greedy and unprincipled of the prelates of France, and appointed a meeting with him to settle the terms of a bargain. They met in a forest they heard mass together, and took mutual oaths of secrecy, and then the business began. "See, archbishop," said the king: "I have it in my power to make you Pope if I choose; and if you promise me six favours which I will ask of you, I will assure you that dignity, and give you evidence of the truth of what I say." So saying, he showed the letters and delegation of both the electoral colleges. The archbishop, filled with covetousness, and seeing at once how entirely the popedom depended on the king, threw himself trembling with joy at Philip's feet. "My lord," he said, "I now perceive you love me more than any man alive, and that you render me good for evil. It is for you to command,—for me to obey; and I shall always be ready to do so." The king lifted him up, kissed him on the mouth, and said to him, "The six special favours I have to ask of you are these. First, that you will reconcile me entirely with the Church, and get me pardoned for my misdeed in arresting Pope Boniface. Second, that you will give the communion to me and all my supporters. Third, that you will give me tithes of the clergy of my realm for five years, to supply the expenses of the war in Flanders. Fourth, that you will destroy and annul the memory of Boniface the Eighth. Fifth, that you will give the dignity of Cardinal to Messer Jacopo, and Messer Piero de la Colonna, along with certain others of my friends. As for the sixth favour and promise, I reserve it for the proper time and place, for it is a great and secret thing." The archbishop promised all by oath on the Corpus Domini, and gave his brother and two nephews as hostages. The king, on the other hand, made oath to have him elected Pope.

His Holiness Clement the Fifth was therefore the thrall and servant of Philip le Bel. No office was too lowly, or sacrifice too large, for the grateful pontiff. He carried his subserviency so far as to cross the Alps and receive the wages of his obedience, the papal tiara, at Lyons. He became in fact a citizen of France, and subject of the crown. He delivered over the clergy to the relentless hands of the king. He gave him tithes of all their livings; and as the Count of Flanders owed money to Philip which he had no means of paying, the generosity of the Pope came to the rescue, and he gave the tithes of the Flemish clergy to the bankrupt count in order to enable him to pay his debt to the exacting monarch. But the gift of these taxes was not a transfer from the Pope to the king or count: His Holiness did not reduce his own demands in consideration of the subsidies given to those powers. He completed, indeed, the ruin the royal tax-gatherers began; for he travelled in more than imperial state from end to end of France, and ate bishop and abbot, and prior and prebendary, out of house and home. Wherever he rested for a night or two, the land became impoverished; and all this wealth was poured into the lap of a certain Brunissende de Périgord, who cost the

A.D. 1305.

Church, it was popularly said, more than the Holy Land. But the capacity of Christian contribution was soon exhausted; and yet the interminable avarice of Pope and King went on. The honourable pair hit upon an excellent expedient, and the Jews were offered as a fresh pasture for the unimpaired appetite of the Father of Christendom and the eldest son of the Church. Philip hated their religion, but seems to have had a great respect for the accuracy of their proceedings in trade. So, to gratify the first, he stripped them of all they had, and, to prove the second, confiscated the money he found entered in their books as lent on interest to Christians. He was found to be a far more difficult creditor to deal with than the original lenders had been, and many a baron and needy knight had to refund to Philip the sums, with interest at twenty per cent., which they might have held indefinitely from the sons of Abraham and repudiated in an access of religious fervour at last.

But worse calamities were hanging over the heads of knights and barons than the avarice of Philip and the dishonesty of Clement. Knighthood itself, and feudalism, were about to die,—knighthood, which had offered at all events an ideal of nobleness and virtue, and feudalism, which had replaced the expiring civilization of Rome founded on the centralization of power in one man's hands, and the degradation of all the rest, with a new form of society which derived its vitality from independent action and individual self-respect. It was by a still wider expansion of power and influence that feudalism was to be superseded. Other elements besides the possession of land were to come into the constitution of the new state of human affairs. The man henceforth was not to be the mere representative of so many acres of ground. His individuality was to be still further defined, and learning, wealth, knowledge, arts, and sciences were from this time forth to have as much weight in the commonwealth as the hoisted pennon and strong-armed followers of the steel-clad warrior.

> "The old order changeth, giving place to new,
> Lest one good custom should corrupt the world."

We have already seen the prosperity of the towns, and have even heard the contemptuous laughter with which the high-fed burghers of Ghent or Bruges received the caracollings of their ponderous suzerain as, armed *cap-á-pied,* he rode up to their impregnable walls. Not less barricaded than the contemptuous city behind the steel fortifications with which he protected his person, the knight had nothing to fear so long as he bestrode his war-horse and managed to get breath enough through the openings of his cross-barred visor. He was as safe in his iron coating as a turtle in its shell; but he was nearly as unwieldy as he was safe. When galloping forward against a line of infantry, nothing could resist his weight. With heavy mace or sweeping sword he cleared his ground on either side, and the unarmoured adversary had no means of repelling his assault. A hundred knights, therefore, we may readily believe, very often have put their thousands or tens of thousands to flight. We read, indeed, of immense slaughters of the common people, accompanied with the loss of one single knight; and this must be attributed to the perfection which the armourer's art had attained, by which no opening for arrow or spear-point was left in the whole suit. But military instruments had for some time been invented, which, by projecting large stones with enormous force, flattened the solid cuirass or crushed the glittering helm. Once get the stunned or wounded warrior on the ground, there was no further danger to be apprehended. He lay in his iron prison unable to get up, unable to breathe, and with the additional misfortune of being so admirably protected that his enemies had difficulty in putting him out of his pain. This, however, was counterbalanced by the ample time he possessed, during their futile efforts to reach a vital part, to bargain for his life; and this was another element in the safety of knightly war. A ransom could at all times preserve his throat, whereas the disabled foot-soldier was pierced with relentless point or trodden down by the infuriated horse. The knight's position, therefore, was more like that of a fighter behind walls, only that he carried his wall with him wherever he went, and even when a breach was made could stop up the gap with a sum of money. Nobody had ever believed it possible for footmen to stand up against a charge of cavalry. No manœuvres were learned like the hollow squares of modern times, which, at Waterloo and elsewhere, have stood unmoved against the best swordsmen of the world. But once, at the beginning of this century, in 1302, a dreadful event happened, which gave a different view of the capabilities of determined infantry in making head against their assailants, and commenced the lesson of the resistibility of mounted warriors which was completed by Bannockburn in Scotland, and Crecy and Poictiers.

The dreadful event was the entire overthrow of the knights and gentlemen of France by the citizens of a Flemish manufacturing town at the battle of Courtrai. Impetuous valour, and contempt for smiths and weavers, blinded the fiery nobles. They rushed forward with loose bridles, and, as they had disdained to reconnoitre the scene of the display, they fell headlong, one after another, horse and plume, sword and spur, into one enormous ditch which lay between them and their enemies. On they came, an avalanche of steel and horseflesh, and floundered into the muddy hole. Hundreds, thousands, unable to check their steeds, or afraid to appear irresolute, or goggling in vain through the deep holes left for their eyes, fell, struggled, writhed, and choked, till the ditch was filled with trampled knights and tumbling horses, and the burghers on the opposite bank beat in the helmets of those who tried to climb up, with jagged clubs, and hacked their naked heads. And when the whole army was annihilated, and the spoils were gathered, it was found there were princes and lords in almost incredible numbers, and four thousand golden spurs to mark the extent of the knightly slaughter and give name to the engagement. It is called the Battle of the Spurs,—for a nobler cause than another engagement of the same name, which we shall meet with in a future century, and which derived its appellation from the fact that spurs were more in requisition than swords.

Philip was at this moment in the middle of his quarrel with Boniface. He determined to compensate himself for the loss he had sustained in military fame at Courtrai by fiercer exactions on his clergy and bitterer enmity to the Pope. We have seen how he pursued the wretched Boniface to the grave, and persisted in trying to force the obsequious Clement to blacken his memory after he was dead. Clement was unwilling to expose the vices and crimes of his predecessor, and yet he had given a promise in that strange meeting in the forest to work his master's will; he was also resident in France, and knew how unscrupulous his protector was. Philip availed himself of the discredit brought on knighthood by the loss of all those golden spurs, and compounded for leaving the deceased pontiff alone, by exacting the consent of Clement to his assault on the order of the Templars, the wealthiest institution in the world, who held thousands of the best manors in France, and whose spoils would make him the richest king in Christendom. Yet the Templars were no contemptible foes. In number they were but fourteen thousand, but their castles were over all the land; they were every one of them of noble blood, and strong in the relationship of all the great houses in Europe. If they had united with their brethren, the Knights Hospitallers, no sovereign could have resisted their demands; but, fortunately for Philip, they were rivals to the death, and gave no assistance to each other when oppressed. Both, in fact, had outlived the causes of their institution, and had forfeited the respect of the masses of the people by their ostentatious abnegation of all the rules by which they professed to be bound. Poverty, chastity, and brotherly kindness were the sworn duties of the most rich, sensual, and unpitying society which ever lived. When Richard of England was dying, he made an imaginary will, and said, "I leave my avarice to the Citeaux, my luxury to the Grey Friars, and my pride to the Templars." And the Templars took possession of the bequest. When driven from the Holy Land, they settled in all the Christian kingdoms from Denmark to the south of Italy, and everywhere presented the same spectacle of selfishness and debauchery. In Paris they had got possession of a tract of ground equal to one-third of the whole city, and had covered it with towers and battlements, and within the unapproachable fortress lived a life of the most luxurious self-indulgence. Strange rumours got abroad of the unholy rites with which their initiations were accompanied. Their receptions into the order were so mysterious and sacred that an interloper (if it had been the King of France) would have been put to death for his intrusion. Frightful stories were told of their blasphemies and hideous ceremonials. Reports came even from over the sea, that while in Jerusalem they had conformed to the Mohammedan faith and had exchanged visits and friendly offices with the chiefs of the unbelievers. Against so dark and haughty an association it was easy to stir up the popular dislike. Nobody could take their part, they lived so entirely to themselves and shunned sympathy and society with so cold a disdain. They were men of religious vows without the humility of that condition, so they were hated by the nobles, who looked on priests as their natural inferiors; they were nobles without the individual riches of the barons and counts, and they were hated by the priests, who were at all times the foes of the aristocracy. Hated, therefore, by priest and noble, their policy would have been to make friends of the lower orders, rising citizens, and the great masses of the people. But they saw no necessity for altering their lofty course. They bore right onward in their haughty disregard of all the rest of the world, and were condemned by the universal feeling before any definite accusation was raised against them.

Clement yielded a faint consent to the proceedings of Philip, and that honourable champion of the faith gave full loose to his covetousness and hatred. First of all he prayed meekly for admission as a brother of the order. He would wear the red cross upon his shoulder and obey their godly laws. If he had obtained his object, he would have procured the grand-mastership for himself and disposed of their wealth at his own discretion. The order might have survived, but their possessions would have been Philip's. They perhaps perceived his aim, and declined to admit him into their ranks. A rejected candidate soon changes his opinion of the former object of his ambition. He now reversed his plan, and declared they were unworthy, not only to wallow in the wealth and splendour of their commanderies, but to live in a Christian land. He said they were guilty of all the crimes and enormities by which human nature was ever disgraced. James de Molay, the grand-master, and all the knights of the order throughout France, were seized and thrown into prison. Letters were written to all other kings and princes, inciting them to similar conduct, and denouncing the doomed fraternity in the harshest terms. The promise of the spoil was tempting to the European sovereigns, but all of them resisted the inducement, or at least took gentler methods of attaining the same end. But Philip was as much pleased with the pursuit as with the catching of the game. He summoned a council of the realm, and obtained at the same time a commission of inquiry from the Pope. With these two courts to back him, it was impossible to fail. The knights were kept in noisome dungeons. They were scantily fed, and tormented with alternate promises and threats. When physically weak and mentally depressed, they were tortured in their secret cells, and under the pressure of fear and desperation confessed to whatever was laid to their charge. Relieved from their torments for a moment, they retracted their confessions; but the written words remained. And in one day, before

A.D. 1312. the public had been prepared for such extremity of wrong, fifty-four of these Christian soldiers—now old, and fallen from their high estate—were publicly burned in the place of execution, and no further limit was placed to the rapacity of the king. Still the odious process crept on with the appearance of law, for already the forms of perverted justice were found safer and more certain than either sword or fagot; and at last, in 1314, the ruined brotherhood were allowed to join themselves to other fraternities. The name of Templar was blotted out from the knightly roll-call of all Europe; and in every nation, in England and Scotland particularly, the order was despoiled of all its possessions. Clement, however, was furious at seeing the moderation of rulers like Edward II., who merely stripped the Templars of their houses and lands, and did not dabble, as his patron Philip had done, in their blood, and rebuked them in angry missives for their coldness in the cause of religion.

Now, early in this century, a Pope had been personally ill used, and his successor had become the pensioner and prisoner of one of the basest of kings; a glorious brotherhood of Christian knights had been shamelessly and bloodily destroyed. Was there no outcry from outraged piety?—no burst of indignation against the perpetrator of so foul a wrong? Pity was at last excited by the sufferings and humiliations of the brothers of the Temple; but pity is not a feeling on which knighthood can depend for vitality or strength. Perhaps, indeed, the sympathy raised for the sad ending of that once-dreaded institution was more fatal to its revival, and more injurious to the credit of all surviving chivalry, than the greatest amount of odium would have been. Speculative discussions were held about the guilt or innocence of the Templars, but the worst of their crimes was the crime of being weak. If they had continued united and strong, nobody would have heard of the excesses laid to their charge. Passing over the impossible accusations brought against them by ignorance and hatred, the offence they were charged with which raised the greatest indignation, and was least capable of disproof, was that in their reception into the order they spat upon the crucifix and trampled on the sign of our salvation. Nothing can be plainer than that this, at the first formation of the order, had been a symbol, which in the course of years had lost its significance.

At first introduced as an emblem of Peter's denial and of worldly disbelief, to be exchanged, when once they were clothed with the Crusader's mantle, for unflinching service and undoubting Faith,—a passage from death unto life,—it had been retained long after its intention had been forgotten; and nothing is so striking as the confession of some of the younger knights, of the reluctance, the shame and trembling, with which, at the request of their superior, they had gone through the repulsive ceremony. This is one of the dangers of a symbolic service. The symbol supersedes the fact. The imitation of Peter becomes a falling away from Christ. But a century before this time, who can doubt that all Christendom would have rushed to the rescue of the Pope if he had been seized in his own city and maltreated as Boniface had been, and that every gentleman in Europe would have drawn sword in behalf of the noble Templars?

But papacy, feudalism, and knighthood, as they had risen and flourished together, were enveloped in the same fall. The society of the Dark Ages had been perfect in its symmetry and compactness. Kings were but feudal leaders and chiefs in their own domains. Knighthood was but the countenance which feudalism turned to its enemies, while hospitality, protection, and alliance were its offerings to its friends. Over all, representative of the heavenly power which cared for the helpless multitudes, the serfs and villeins, those who had no other friend,—the Church extended its sheltering arms to the lowest of the low. Feudalism could take care of itself; knighthood made itself feared; but the multitudes could only listen and be obedient. All, therefore, who had no sword, and no broad acres, were natural subjects of the Pope. But with the rise of the masses the relations between them and the Church became changed. It was found that during the last two hundred years, since the awakening of mercantile enterprise by the Crusades and the commingling of the population in those wild and yet elevating expeditions, by the progress of the arts, by the privileges wrung from king and noble by flourishing towns or purchased from them with sterling coin, by the deterioration in the morals of priest and baron, and the rise in personal importance of burghers, who could fight like those of Courtrai or raise armies like those of Pisa and Genoa,—that the state of society had gradually been changed; that the commons were well able to defend their own interest; that the feudal proprietor had lost his relative rank; that the knight was no longer irresistible as a warrior; and that the Pope had become one of the most worldly and least scrupulous of rulers. Far from being the friend of the unprotected, the Church was the subject of all the ballads of every nation, wherein its exactions and debaucheries were sung at village fairs and conned over in chimney-corners. Cannon were first used in this century at the siege of Algesiras in 1343; and with the first discharge knighthood fell forever from the saddle. The Bible was first translated into a national tongue,* and Popery fell forever from its unopposed dominion. How, indeed, even without this incident, could the Papacy have retained its power? From 1305 till 1376 the wearers of the tiara were the mere puppets of the Kings of France. They lived in a nominal freedom at Avignon, but the college of electors was in the pay of the French sovereign, and the Pope was the creature of his hands. This was fatal to the notion of his independence. But a heavier blow was struck at the unity of the papal power when a double election, in 1378, established two

* Wickliff's English Bible, 1383.

supreme chiefs, one exacting the obedience of the faithful from his palace on the banks of the Rhone, and the other advancing the same claim from the banks of the Tiber. From this time the choice of the chief pontiff became a political struggle between the principal kings. There were French and German, and even English, parties in the conclave, and bribes were as freely administered as at a contested election or on a dubious question in the time of Sir Robert Walpole. Family interest also, from this time, had more effect on the policy of the Popes than the ambition to extend their spiritual authority. They sacrificed some portion of their claims to insure the elevation of their relations. Alliances were made, not for the benefit of the Roman chair, but for some kinsman's establishment in a principality. Dukedoms became appanages of the papal name, and every new Pope left the mark of his beneficence in the riches and influence of the favourite nephew whom he had invested with sovereign rank. Italy became filled with new dynasties created by these means, and the politics of the papal court became complicated by this diversity of motive and influence. Yet feudalism struggled on in spite of cannon and the rise of the middle orders; and Popery struggled on in spite of the spread of information and the diffusion of wealth and freedom. For some time, indeed, the decline of both those institutions was hidden by a factitious brilliancy reflected on them by other causes. The increase of refinement gave rise to feelings of romance, which were unknown in the days of darkness and suffering through which Europe had passed. A reverence for antiquity softened the harsher features by which they had been actually distinguished, and knighthood became subtilized into chivalry. As the hard and uninviting reality retreated into the past, the imagination clothed

it in enchanting hues; and at the very time when the bowmen and yeomanry of England had shown at Crecy how unfounded were the "boast of heraldry, the pomp of power," Edward III. had instituted the Order of the
A.D. 1350. Garter,—a transmutation as it were of the rude shocks of knighthood into carpet pacings in the gilded halls of a palace; as in a former age the returned Crusaders had supplied the want of the pride and circumstance of the real charge against the Saracen by introducing the bloodless imitation of it afforded by the tournament. In the same way the personal disqualification of the Pope was supplied by an elevation of the ideal of his place and office. Religion became poetry and sentiment; and though henceforth the reigning pontiff was treated with the harshness and sometimes the contempt his personal character deserved, his throne was still acknowledged as the loftiest of earthly thrones. The plaything of the present was nevertheless an idol and representative of the past; and kings who drove him from his home, or locked him up in their prisons, pretended to tremble at his anger, and received his letters on their knees.

It must have been evident to any far-seeing observer that some great change was in progress during the whole of this century, not so much from the results of Courtrai, or Crecy, or Poictiers, or the migration of the Pope to Avignon, or the increasing riches of the trading and manufacturing towns, as from the great uprising of the human mind which was shown by the almost simultaneous appearance of such stars of literature as Dante, and Petrarch, and Boccaccio, and our English Chaucer. I suppose no single century since has been in possession of four such men. Great geniuses, indeed, and great discoveries, seem to come in crops, as if a certain period had been fixed for their bursting into flower; and we find the same grand ideas engaging the intellects of men widely dispersed, so that a novelty in art or science is generally disputed between contending nations. But this synchronous development of power is symptomatic of some wide-spread tendency, which alters the ordinary course of affairs; and we see in the Canterbury Tales the dawning of the Reformation; in Shakspeare and Bacon the inauguration of a new order of government and manners; in Locke and Milton a still further liberation from the chains of a worn-out philosophy; in Watt, and Fulton, and Cartwright, we see the spread of civilization and power. In Walter Scott and Wordsworth, and the wonderful galaxy of literary stars who illuminated the beginning of this century, we see Waterloo and Peace, a widening of national sympathies, and the opening of a great future career to all the nations of the world. For nothing is so true an index of the state and prospects of a people as the healthfulness and honest taste of its literature. It was in this sense that Fletcher of Saltoun said, (or quoted,) "Give me the making of the ballads of a people, and I don't care who makes the laws." While we have such pure and wholesome literature as is furnished us by Hallam, and Macaulay, and Alison, by Tennyson, Dickens, Thackeray, and the rest, philosophy like Hamilton's, and science like Herschel's and Faraday's, we have no cause to look forward with doubt or apprehension.

"Naught shall make us rue
If England to herself do rest but true."

But those pioneers of the Fourteenth Century had dangers and difficulties to encounter from which their successors have been free. It is a very different thing for authors to write for the applause of an appreciating public, and for them to create an appreciating public for themselves. Their audience must at first have been hostile. First, the critical and scholarly part of the world was offended with the bad taste of writing in the modern languages at all. Secondly, the pitch at which they struck the national note was too high for the ears of the vulgar. A correct and dignified use of the spoken tongue, the conveyance, in ordinary and familiar words, of lofty or poetical thoughts, filled both those classes with surprise. To the scholar it seemed good materials enveloped in a very unworthy covering. To "the general" it seemed an attempt to deprive them of their vernacular phrases and bring bad grammar and coarse expressions into disrepute. Petrarch was so conscious of this that he speaks apologetically of his sonnets in Italian, and founds his hope of future fame on his Latin verses. But more important than the poems of Dante and Chaucer, or the prose of Boccaccio, was the introduction of the new literature represented by Froissart. Hitherto chronicles had for the most part consisted of the record of such wandering rumours as reached a monastery or were gathered in the religious pilgrimages of holy men. Mingled, even the best of them, with the credulity of inexperienced and simple minds, their effect was lost on the contemporary generation by the isolation of the writers. Nobody beyond the convent-walls knew what the learned historians of the establishment had been doing. Their writings were not brought out into the light of universal day, and a knowledge of European society gathered point by point, by comparing, analyzing, and contrasting the various statements contained in those dispersed repositories. But at this time there came into notice the most inquiring, enterprising, picturesque, and entertaining chronicler that had ever appeared since Herodotus read the result of his personal travels and sagacious inquiries to the assembled multitudes of Greece.

John Froissart, called by the courtesy of the time Sir John, in honour of his being priest and chaplain, devoted a long life to the collection of the fullest and most trustworthy accounts of all the events and personages characteristic of his time. From 1326, when his labours commenced, to 1400, when his active pen stood still, nothing happened in any part of Europe that the Paul Pry of the period did not rush off to verify on the spot. If he heard of an assemblage of knights going on at the extremities of France or in the centre of Germany, of a tournament at Bordeaux, a court gala in Scotland, or a marriage festival at Milan, his travels began,—whether in the humble guise of a solitary horseman with his portmanteau behind his saddle and a single greyhound at his heels, as he jogged wearily across the Border, till he finally arrived in Edinburgh, or in his grander style of equipment, gallant steed, with hackney led beside him, and four dogs of high race gambolling round his horse, as he made his dignified journey from Ferrara to Rome. Wherever life was to be seen and painted, the indefatigable Froissart was to be found. Whatever he had gathered up on former expeditions, whatever he learned on his present tour, down it went in his own exquisite language, with his own poetical impression of the pomps and pageantries he beheld; and when at the end of his journey he reached the court of prince or potentate, no higher treat could be offered to the "noble lords and ladies bright" than to form a glittering circle round the enchanting chronicler and listen to what he had written. From palace to palace, from castle to castle, the unwearied "picker-up of unconsidered trifles" (which, however, were neither trifles nor unconsidered, when their true value became known, as giving life and reality to the annals of a whole period) pursued his happy way, certain of a friendly reception when he arrived, and certain of not losing his time by negligence or blindness on the road. If he overtakes a stately cavalier, attended by squires and men-at-arms, he enters into conversation, drawing out the experiences of the venerable warrior by relating to him all he knew of things and persons in which he took an interest. And when they put up at some hostelry on the road, and while the gallant knight was sound asleep on his straw-stuffed couch, and his followers were wallowing amid the rushes on the parlour floor, Froissart was busy with pen and note-book, scoring down all the old gentleman had told him, all the fights he had been present at, and the secret history (if any) of the councils of priests and kings. In this way knights in distant parts of the world became known to each other. The same voice which described to Douglas at Dalkeith the exploits of the Prince of Wales sounded the praises of Douglas in the ears of the Black Prince at Bordeaux. A community of sentiment was produced between the upper ranks of all nations by this common register of their acts and feelings; and knighthood received its most ennobling consummation in these imperishable descriptions, at the very time when its political and military influence came to a close. Froissart's Chronicles are the epitaph of feudalism, written indeed while it was yet alive, but while its strength was only the convulsive energy of approaching death. The standard of knightly virtue became raised in proportion as knightly power decayed. In the same way as the increased civilization and elevating influences of the time clothed the Church in colours borrowed from the past, while its real influence was seriously impaired, the expiring embers of knighthood occasionally flashed up into something higher; and in this century we read of Du Guesclin of France, Walter Manny and Edward the Third of England, and many others, who illustrated the order with qualifications it had never possessed in its palmiest state.

Courtrai was fought and Amadis de Gaul written almost at the same time. Let us therefore mark, as a characteristic of the period we have reached, the decay of knighthood, or feudalism in its armour of proof, and the growth at the same time of a sense of honour and generosity, which contrasted strangely in its softened and sentimentalized refinement with the harshness and cruelty which still clung to the ordinary affairs of life. Thus the young conqueror of Poictiers led his captive John into London with the respectful attention of a grateful subject to a crowned king. He waited on him at table, and made him forget the humiliation of defeat and the griefs of imprisonment in the sympathy and reverence with which he was everywhere surrounded. This same prince was regardless of human life or suffering where the theatrical show of magnanimity was not within his reach, bloodthirsty and tyrannical, and is declared by the chronicler himself to be of "a high, overbearing spirit, and cruel in his hatred." It shows, however, what an advance had already been made in the influence of public opinion, when we read how generally the treatment of the noble captive, John of France, was appreciated. In former ages, and even at present in nations of a lower state of feelings, the kind treatment of a fallen enemy, or the sparing of a helpless population, would be attributed to weakness or fear. Chivalry, which was an attempt to amalgamate the Christian virtues with the rougher requirements of the feudal code, taught the duty of being pitiful as well as brave. And though at this period that feeling only existed between knight and knight, and was not yet extended to their treatment of the common herd, the principle was asserted that war could be carried on without personal animosity, and that courage, endurance, and the other knightly qualities were to be admired as much in an enemy as a friend.

There was, however, another reason for this besides the natural admiration which great deeds are sure to call forth in natures capable of performing them; and that was, that Europe was divided into petty sovereignties, too weak to maintain their independence without foreign aid, too proud to submit to another government, and trusting to the support their money or influence could procure. In all countries, therefore, there existed bodies of mercenary soldiers—or Free Lances, as they were called—claiming the dignity and rank of knights and noblemen, who never knew whether the men they were fighting to-day might not be their comrades and followers to-morrow. In Italy, always a country of divisions and enmities, there were armed combatants secured on either side. Unconnected with the country they defended by any ties of kindred or allegiance, they found themselves opposed to a body, perhaps of their countrymen, certainly of their former companions; and, except so much as was required to earn their pay and preserve their reputation, they did nothing that might be injurious to their temporary foes. Battles accordingly were fought where feats of horsemanship and dexterity at their weapons were shown; where rushes were made into the vacant space between the armies by contending warriors, and horse and man acquitted themselves with the acclamations, and almost with the safety, of a charge in the amphitheatre at Astley's. But no blood was spilt, no life was taken; and a long summer day has seen a confused mêlée going on between the hired combatants of two cities or principalities, without a single casualty more serious than a cavalier thrown from his horse and unable to rise from the weight and tightness of his armour. Fights of this kind could scarcely be considered in earnest, and we are not surprised to find that the burden and heat of an engagement was thrown upon the light-armed foot: we gather, indeed, towards the end of Froissart's Chronicles, that while the cavaliers persisted in endeavouring to distinguish their individual prowess, as at the battle of Navareta in Spain, and got into confusion in their eagerness of assault, "the sharpness of the English arrows began to be felt," and the fate of the battle depended on the unflinching line and impregnable solidity of the archers and foot-soldiers. These latter took a deeper interest in the result than the more showy performers, and were not carried away by the vanities of personal display.

Look at the year 1300, with the jubilee of Boniface going on. Look at 1400, with the death of Chaucer and Froissart, and the enthroning of Henry the Fourth, and what an amount of incident, of change and improvement, has been crowded into the space! The rise of national literatures, the softening of feudalism, the decline of Church power,—these—illustrated by Dante and Chaucer, by the alteration in the art of war, and above all, perhaps, by the translation of the Bible into the vulgar tongue—were not only the fruits gained for the present, but the promise of greater things to come There will be occasional backslidings after this time, but the onward progress is steady and irresistible: the regressions are but the reflux waves in an advancing tide, caused by the very force and vitality of the great sea beyond. And after this view of some of the main features of the century, we shall take a very cursory glance at some of the principal events on which the portraiture is founded.

It is a bad sign of the early part of this period that our great landmarks are still battles and invasions.

After Courtrai in 1302, where the nobility rushed blindfold into a natural ditch, we come upon Bannockburn in
A.D. 1314. 1314, where Edward the Second, not comprehending the aim of his more politic father,—whose object was to counterpoise the growing power of the French monarchy by consolidating his influence at home,—had marched rather to revenge his outraged dignity than to establish his denied authority, and was signally defeated by Robert Bruce. Is it not possible that the stratagem by which the English chivalry suffered so much by means of the pits dug for their reception in the space in front of the Scottish lines was borrowed from Courtrai,—art supplying in that dry plain near Stirling what nature had furnished to the marshy Brabant? However this may be, the same fatal result ensued. Pennon and standard, waving plume and flashing sword, disappeared in those yawning gulfs, and at the present hour very rusty spurs and fragments of broken helmets are dug from beneath the soil to mark the greatness and the quality of the slaughter. Meantime, in compact phalanx—protected by the knights and gentlemen on the flanks, but left to its own free action—the Scottish array bore on. Strong spear and sharp sword did the rest, and the English army, shorn of its cavalry, disheartened by the loss of its leaders, and finally deserted by its pusillanimous king, retreated in confusion, and all hope of retaining the country by the right of conquest was forever laid aside. Poor Edward had, in appalling consciousness of his own imperfections, applied to the Pope for permission to rub himself with an ointment that would make him brave. Either the Pope refused his consent or the ointment failed of its purpose. Nothing could rouse a brave thought in the heart of the fallen Plantagenet. Sir Giles de Argentine might have been more effectual than all the unguents in the world. He led the king by the bridle till he saw

him in a place of safety. He then stopped his horse and said, "It has never been my custom to fly, and here I must take my fortune." Saying this, he put spurs to his horse, and, crying out, "An Argentine!" charged the squadron of Edward Bruce, and was borne down by the force of the Scottish spears. The fugitive king galloped in terror to the castle of Dunbar, and shipped off by sea to Berwick.

The next battle is so strongly corroborative of the failing supremacy of heavy armour, and the rising importance of the well-trained citizens, that it is worth mention, although at first sight it seems to controvert both these statements; for it was a fight in which certain courageous burghers were mercilessly exterminated by gorgeously-caparisoned knights. The townsmen of Bruges and Ypres had grown so proud and pugnacious

A.D. 1328. that in 1328 they advanced to Cassel to do battle with the young King of France, Philip of Valois, at the head of all his chivalry. There was a vast amount of mutual contempt in the two armies. The leader of the bold Flemings, who was known as Little Jack, entered the enemy's camp in disguise, and found young lords in splendid gowns proceeding from point to point, gossiping, visiting, and interchanging their invitations. Making his way back, he ordered a charge at once. The rush was nearly successful, and was only checked within a few yards of the royal tent. But the check was tremendous. The bloated burghers, filled with pride and gorged with wealth, had thought proper to ensconce their unwieldy persons in cuirasses as brilliant and embarrassing as the armour of the knights. The knights, however, were on horseback, and the embattled townsfolk were on foot. Great was the slaughter, useless the attempt to escape, and thirteen thousand were overborne and smothered. Ten thousand more were executed by some form of law, and the Bourgeoisie taught to rely for its safety on its agility and compactness, and not on "helm or hauberk's twisted mail."

The crop of battles grows rich and plentiful, for Edward the Third and Philip of Valois are rival kings and warriors, and may be taken as the representatives of the two states of society which were brought at this time face to face. For Edward, though as true a knight as Amadis himself in his own person, in policy was a favourer of the new ideas. When the war broke out, Philip behaved as if no change had taken place in the seat of power and the world had still continued divided between the lords and their armed retainers. He threw himself for support on the military service of his tenants and the aristocratic spirit of his nobles. Edward, wiser but less romantic, turned for assistance to the Commons of England,—bought over their good will and copious contributions by privileges granted to their trades,—invited skilled workmen over from Flanders, which, with the freest spirit in Europe, was under the least improved of the feudal governments,—and established woollen-works at York, fustian-works at Norwich, serges at Colchester, and kerseys in Devonshire. Mills were whirling round in all the counties, and ships coming in untaxed at every harbour. Fortunately, as is always the case in this country, it was seen that the success of one class of the people was beneficial to every other class. The baron got more rent for his land and better cloth for his apparel by the prosperity of his manufacturing neighbours. Money was voted readily in support of a king who entered into alliance with their best customers, the men of Ghent and Bruges; and at the head of all the levies which the parliament's liberality enabled him to raise were the knights and gentlemen of England, totally freed now from any bias towards the French or prejudice

against the Saxon; for they spoke the English tongue, dressed in English broadcloth, sang English ballads, and astonished the men of Gascony and Guienne with the vehemence of their unmistakably English oaths. Yet some of them held lands in feudal subjection to the French king. Flanders itself confessed the same sovereignty; and men of delicate consciences might feel uneasy if they lifted the sword against their liege lord. To soothe their scruples, James Van Arteveldt, the Brewer of Ghent, suggested to Edward the propriety of his assuming the title of King of France. The rebellious freeholders would then be in their duty in supporting their liege's claims. So Edward, founding upon the birth of his mother, the daughter of the last King, Philip le Bel,—who was excluded by the Salic law, or at least by French custom, from the throne,—made claim to the crown of St. Louis, and transmitted the barren title to all his successors till the reign of George the Fourth. As if in right of his property on both sides of the Channel, Edward converted it into his exclusive domain. He so entirely exterminated the navy of France, and
A.D. 1340. impressed that chivalrous nation with the danger of the seas by the victory of Helvoet Sluys, that for several centuries the command of the strait was left undisputed to England. Philip had endeavoured to obtain the mastery of it with a fleet of a hundred and fifty ships, mounted by forty thousand men. The Genoese had furnished an auxiliary squadron, and also a commander-in-chief, of the name of Barbavara. But the French admiral was a civilian of the name of Bahuchet, who thought the safest plan was the best, and kept his whole force huddled up in the commodious harbour. Edward collected a fleet of scarcely inferior strength, and fell upon the enemy as they lay within the port. It was in fact a fight on the land, for they ranged so close that they almost touched each other, and the gallant

Bahuchet preserved himself from sea-sickness at the expense of all their lives. For the English archers made an incredible havoc on their crowded decks, and the pike-men boarded with irresistible power. Twenty thousand were slain in that fearful *mêlée;* and Edward, to show how sincere he was in his claim upon the throne of France, hanged the unfortunate Bahuchet as a traitor. The man deserved his fate as a coward: so we need not waste much sympathy on the manner of his death. This success with his ships was soon followed by the better-known victory of Crecy, 1346, and the capture of Calais.

A.D. 1356. In ten years afterwards, the crowning triumph of Poictiers completed the destruction of the military power of France, by a slaughter nearly as great as that at Sluys and Crecy. In addition to the loss of lives in these three engagements, amounting to upwards of ninety thousand men, we are to consider the impoverishment of the country by the exorbitant ransoms claimed for the release of prisoners. John, the French king, was valued at three million crowns of gold,—an immense sum, which it would have exhausted the kingdom to raise; and, in addition to those destructive fights and crushing exactions, France was further weakened by the insurrection of the peasantry and the frightful massacres by which it was put down. If to these causes of weakness we add the depopulation produced by the unequalled pestilence, called the Plague of Florence, which spread all over the world, and in the space of a year carried off nearly a third of the inhabitants of Europe, we shall be justified in believing that France was reduced to the lowest condition she has ever reached, and that only the dotage of Edward, the death of the Black Prince, and the accession of a king like Richard II., saved that noble country from being, for a while at least, tributary and subordinate to her island-conqueror.

FIFTEENTH CENTURY.

Emperors of Germany.

A.D.

1400. Rupert.

1410. Jossus.

1410. Sigismund.

House of Austria.

1438. Albert II.

1440. Frederick IV.

1493. Maximilian I.

Kings of England.

1399. Henry IV.

1413. Henry V.

1422. Henry VI.

1461. Edward IV.

1483. Edward V.

1483. Richard III.

1485. Henry VII.

Kings of Scotland.

Robert III.—(*cont.*)

1406. James I.

1437. James II.

1460. James III.

1488. James IV.

Emperors of the East.

A.D.

Manuel Palæologus.—(*cont.*)

1425. John Palæologus II.

1448. Constantine XIII., (Palæologus.)

1453. Capture of Constantinople by the Turks, and close of the Eastern Empire.

Sultans of Turkey.

1451. Mohammed II.

1481. Bajazet II.

Kings of France.

Charles VI.—(*cont.*)

1422. Charles VII.

1461. Louis XI.

1483. Charles VIII.

1498. Louis XII.

Kings of Spain.

1479. Union of the Kingdom under Ferdinand and Isabella.

1452. Invention of Printing.

1455. Wars of the Roses begin.

1483. Luther born. 1492. Discovery of America.

Eminent Men.

John Huss, (1370–1415,) Ximines.

THE FIFTEENTH CENTURY

DECLINE OF FEUDALISM—AGINCOURT—JOAN OF ARC—THE PRINTING-PRESS—DISCOVERY OF AMERICA.

THE whole period from the twelfth to the fifteenth century has generally been considered so unvarying in its details, one century so like another, that it has been thought sufficient to class them all under the general name of the Middle Ages. Old Monteil, indeed, the author of "The French People of Various Conditions," declines to individualize any age during that lengthened epoch, for "feudalism," he says, "is as little capable of change as the castles with which it studded the land." But a closer inspection does by no means justify this declaration. From time to time we have seen what great changes have taken place. The external walls of the baronial residence may continue the same, but vast alterations have occurred within. The rooms have got a more modern air; the moat has begun to be dried up, and turned into a bowling-green; the tilt-yard is occasionally converted into a garden; and, in short, in all the civilized countries of Europe the life of society has accumulated at the heart. Power is diffused from the courts of kings; and instead of the spirit of independence and opposition to the royal authority which characterized former centuries, we find the courtiers' arts more prevalent now than the pride of local grandeur. The great vassals of the Crown are no longer the rivals of their nominal superior, but submissively receive his awards, or endeavour to obtain the sanction of his name to exactions which they would formerly have practised in their own. Monarchy, in fact, becomes the spirit of the age, and nobility sinks willingly into the subordinate rank. This itself was a great blow to the feudal system, for the essence of that organized society was equality among its members, united to subordination of conventional rank,—a strange and beautiful style of feeling between the highest and the lowest of that manly brotherhood, which made the simple chevalier equal to the king as touching their common knighthood,—of which we have at the present time the modernized form in the feeling which makes the loftiest in the land recognise an equal and a friend in the person of an untitled gentleman. But this latter was to be the result of the equalizing effect of education and character. In the fifteenth century, feudalism, represented by the great proprietors, was about to expire, as it had already perished in the decay of its armed and mailed representatives in the field of battle. By no lower hand than its own could the nobility be overthrown either in France or England. The accident of a feeble king in both countries was the occasion of an internecine struggle,—not, as it would have been in the tenth century, for the possession of the crown, but for the custody of the wearer of it. The insanity of Charles VI. almost exterminated the lords of France; the weakness of Henry VI. and the Wars of the Roses produced the same result in England. It seemed as if in both countries an epidemic madness had burst out among the nobility, which drove them to their destruction. Wildly contending with each other, neglecting and oppressing the common people, the lords and barons were unconscious of the silent advances of a power which was about to overshadow them all. And, as if to drive away from them the sympathy which their fathers had known how to excite among the lower classes by their kindness and protection, they seemed determined to obliterate every vestige of respect which might cling to their ancient possessions and historic names, by the most unheard-of cruelty and falsehood in their treatment of each other.

The leader of one of the parties which divided France was John, son of Philip the Hardy, prince of the blood royal and Duke of Burgundy. The leader of the other party was Louis of Orleans, brother of the demented king, and the gayest cavalier and most accomplished gentleman of his time. The Burgundian had many advantages in his contest for the reins of government. The wealth and population of the Low Countries made him as powerful as any of the princes of Europe, and he could at all times secure the alliance of England to the most nefarious of his schemes by the bribe of a treaty of trade and navigation. He accordingly brought his great possessions in Flanders to the aid of his French ambition, and secured the almost equally important assistance of the University of Paris, by giving in his adhesion to the Pope it had chosen and denying the authority of the Pope of his rival Orleans. Orleans had also offended the irritable population of Paris by making his vows, on some solemn occasion, by the bones of St. Denis which adorned the shrine of the town called after his name,—whereas it was well known to every Parisian that the real bones of the patron of France were those which were so religiously preserved in the treasury of Notre Dame. The clergy of the two altars took up the quarrel, and as much hostility was created by the rival relics of St. Denis and Paris as by the rival pontiffs of Avignon and Rome. Thus the Church, which in earlier times had been a bond of unity, was one of the chief causes of dissension; and the result in a few years was seen in the attempt made by France to shake off, as much as possible, the supremacy of both the divided Popes, as it managed to shake off entirely the yoke of the divided nobility.

Quarrels and reconciliations among the princes, feasts and festivals among the peerage, and the most relentless treatment of the citizens, were the distinguishing marks of the opening of this century. Isabella of Bavaria, the shameless wife of the hapless Charles, added a great feature of infamy to the state of manners at the time, by the openness of her profligacy, and her neglect of all the duties of wife and queen. Rioting with the thoughtless Orleans, while her husband was left to the misery of his situation, unwashed, unshorn, and clothed in rags and filth, the abandoned woman roused every manly heart in all the land against the cause she aided. Relying on this national disgust, the wily Burgundian waited his opportunity, and revenged his private wrongs by what he afterwards called the patriotic dagger of an assassin. On the night of the 23d of December,
A.D. 1407. 1407, the gay and handsome Louis was lured by a false message from the queen's quarters to a distant part of the town, and was walking in his satin mantle, twirling his glove in his hand, and humming the burden of a song, when he was set on by ten or twelve of the adherents of his enemy, stabbed, and beaten long after he lay dead on the pavement, and was then left motionless and uncared-for under the shade of the high house-walls of the Vieille Rue du Temple.

Public conscience was not very acute at that time; and, although no man for a moment doubted the hand that had guided the blow, the Duke of Burgundy was allowed to attend the funeral of his murdered cousin, and to hold the pall in the procession, and to weep louder than any as the coffin was lowered into the vault But the common feelings of humanity were roused at last. People remembered the handsome, kindly, merry-hearted Orleans thus suddenly struck low, and the ominous looks of the Parisians warned the powerful Burgundy that it was time to take his hypocrisy and his tears out of the sight of honest men. He slipped out of the city, and betook himself to his Flemish states. But the helm was now without a steersman; and, while all were looking for a guide out of the confusion into which the appalling incident had brought the realm, the guilty duke himself, armed *cap-à-pie,* and surrounded by a body-guard which silenced all opposition, made his solemn entry into the town, and fixed on the door of his hotel the emblematic ornament of two spears, one sharp at the point as if for immediate battle, and one blunted and guarded as if for a friendly joust. Eloquence is never long absent when power is in want of an oration. A great meeting was held, in which, by many brilliant arguments and incontrovertible examples from holy writ and other histories, John Petit proved, to the entire satisfaction of everybody who did not wish to be slaughtered on the spot, that the doing to death of the Duke of Orleans was a good deed, and that the doer was entitled to the thanks of a grateful country. The thanks were accordingly given, and the murderer was at the height of his ambition. As a warning to the worthy citizens of what they had to expect if they rebelled against his authority, he took the opportunity of hurrying northward to his states, where the men of Liege were in revolt, and, having broken their ill-formed squares, committed such slaughter upon them as only the madness of fear and hatred could have suggested. Dripping with the blood of twenty-four thousand artisans, he returned to Paris, where the citizens were hushed into silence, and perhaps admiration, by the terrors of his appearance. They called him John the Fearless,—a noble title, most inadequately acquired; but, in spite of their flattery and their submission, he did not feel secure without the presence of his faithful subjects. He therefore summoned his Flemings and Burgundians to share his triumphs, and a loose was given to all their desires. They pillaged, burned, and destroyed as if in an enemy's country, encamping outside the walls, and giving evident indications of an intention to force their way into the streets. But the sight of gore, though terrifying at first, sets the tamest of animals wild. The Parisians smelt the bloody odour and made ready for the fray. The formidable incorporation of the Butchers rose knife in hand, and at the command of their governor prepared to preserve the peace of the city. Burgundians and Orleanists were equally to be feared, and by a curious coincidence both those parties were at the gate; for the Count of Armagnac, father-in-law of the orphan Duke of Orleans, had assumed the leadership of the party, and had come up to Paris at the head of his infuriated Gascons and the men of Languedoc. North and South were again ranged in hostile ranks, and inside the walls there was a reign of terror and an amount of misery never equalled till that second reign of terror which is still the darkest spot in the memory of old men yet alive. No man could put faith in his neighbour. The murder of the Duke of Orleans had dissolved all confidence in the word of princes. One half of France was ready to draw against the other. Each half was anxious for support, from whatever quarter it came, and to gain the destruction of their rivals would sacrifice the interests of the nation.

But the same spirit of disunion and extirpation of

ancient landmarks was at work in England. The accession of Henry the Fourth was not effected without the opposition of the adherents of the former king and of the supporters, on general principles, of the legitimate line. There were treasons, and plots, and pitiless executions. The feudal chiefs were no longer the compact body which could give laws both to King and Parliament, but ranged themselves in opposite camps and waited for the spoils of the vanquished side. The clergy unanimously came to the aid of the usurper on his faithful promise to exempt them from taxation; and, by thus throwing their own proportion of the public burdens on the body of the people, they sundered the alliance which had always hitherto subsisted between the Church and the lower class. Another bribe was held out to the clerical order for its support to the unlineal crown by the surrender to their vengeance of any heretics they could discover. In the second year of this reign, accordingly, we find a law enabling the priests to burn, "on some high and conspicuous piece of ground," any who dissented from their faith. This is the first legal sanction in England to the logic of flame and fagot. How dreadfully this permission was used, we shall see ere many years elapse. In the mean time, it is worth while to remark that in proportion as the Church lost in popularity and affection it gained in legal privilege. While it was strong it did not need to be cruel; and if it had continued its care of the poor and helpless, it would have been able to leave Wickliff to his dissertations on its doctrinal errors undisturbed. A Church which is found to be nationally beneficial, and which endears itself to its adherents by the practical graces of Christianity, will never be overthrown, or even weakened, by any theoretical defects in its creeds or formularies. It was perhaps, therefore, a

A.D. 1401.

fortunate circumstance that the Church of Rome had departed as much by this time from the path of honesty and usefulness as from the simplicity of gospel truth. The Bible might have been looked at in vain, even in Wickliff's translation, if its meanings had not been rendered plain by the lives and principles of the clergy. Henry the Fifth, feeling the same necessity of clerical support which had thrown his father into the hands of the Church, left nothing untried to attach it to his cause. All the opposition which had been offered to its claims had hitherto been confined to men of low rank, and generally to members of its own body. Wickliff himself had been but a country vicar, and had been unnoticed and despised in his small parsonage at Lutterworth. But three-and-twenty years after he was dead, his name was celebrated far and wide as the enemy of constituted authority and a heretic of the most dangerous kind. His guilt consisted in nothing whatever but in having translated the Bible into English; but the fact of his having done so was patent to all. No witnesses were required. The bones of the old man were dug up from their resting-place in the quiet churchyard in Leicestershire, carried ignominiously to Oxford, and burned amid the howls and acclamations of an infuriated mob of priests and doctors. This was in 1409. But, in his character of heretic and unbeliever, Wickliff had high associates in this same year; for the General Council sitting at Pisa declared the two Popes—of Avignon and Rome—who still continued to divide the Christian world, to be "heretics, perjurers, and schismatics."

Europe, indeed, was ripe for change in almost all the relations both of Church and State. There would seem no close connection between Bohemia and England; yet in a very short time the doctrines of Wickliff penetrated to Prague. There Huss and Jerome preached against the enormities and contradictions of the Romish system, and bitterly paid for their presumption in the fires of Constance before many years had passed. But in England the effects of the new revelation of the hidden gospel had been stronger than even at Prague. Public opinion, however, divided itself into two very different channels; and while the whole nation listened with open ear to the denunciations rising everywhere against the corruption, pride, and sensuality of the priesthood, it rushed at the same time into the wildest excesses of cruelty against the opponents of any of the doctrinal errors or superstitious beliefs in which it had been brought up. In the same year in which several persons were burnt in Smithfield as supporters of Wickliff and the Bible, the Parliament sent up addresses to the Crown, advising the king to seize the temporalities of the Church, and to apply the riches wasted on luxurious monks and nuns to the payment of his soldiers. Henry the Fifth adroitly availed himself of the double direction in which the popular feeling ran. He gained over the priesthood by exterminating the opponents of their ceremonies and faith, and rewarded himself by occasionally confiscating the revenues of a dozen or two of the more notorious monasteries. In 1417 a heavier sacrifice was demanded of him than his mere presence at the burning of a plebeian heretic like John Badby, whose execution he had attended at Smithfield in 1410. He was required to give up into the hands of the Church the great and noble Oldcastle, Lord Cobham. The Church, as if to mark its triumph, did not examine the accused on any point connected with civil or political affairs. It questioned him solely on his religious beliefs; and as it found him unconvinced of the necessity of confession to a priest, of pilgrimages to the shrines of saints, of the worship of images, and of the doctrine of transubstantiation, it delivered him over to the secular arm, and the stout old soldier was taken to St. Giles's-in-the-Fields, and suspended, by an iron chain round his body, above a fire, to die by the slowest and most painful of deaths. But, in this yielding up of a nobleman to the vengeance of the priesthood, Henry had a double motive: he terrified the proudest of the barons, and attached to himself the other bodies in the State. The people were still profoundly ignorant, and looked on the innovators as the enemies both of God and man. And nothing but this can account for the astonishing spectacle presented by Europe at this date. The Church torn by contending factions—three Popes at one time—and council arrayed against council; every nation disgusted with its own priesthood, and enthusiasm bursting out in the general confusion into the wildest excesses of fanaticism and vice,—and yet a total incapacity in any country of devising means of amendment. Great efforts were made, by wise and holy men within the Church itself, to shake off the impediments to its development and increase. Reclamations were made, more in sorrow than in anger, against the universal depravation of morals and beliefs. The Popes were not unmoved with these complaints, and gave credence to the forebodings of evil which rose from every heart. Yet the network of custom, the authority of tradition, and the unchangeableness of Roman policy marred every effort at self-reformation. An opening was apparently made for the introduction of improvement, by the declaration of the supremacy of general councils, and the cessation of the great schism of the West on the nomination of Martin the Fifth to the undisputed chair. But the force of circumstances was irresistible. Cardinals who approved of the declaration while members of the council repu-

A.D. 1429.

diated its acts when, by good fortune, they succeeded to the tiara; and one of them even ventured the astounding statement that in his character of Æneas Sylvius, and approver of the decree of Basle, he was guilty of damnable sin, but was possessed of immaculate virtue in the character of Paul the Second. It was obvious that this unnatural state of things could not last. An establishment conscious of its defects, but unable to throw them off, and finally forced to the awful necessity of defending them by the foulest and most unpardonable means, might have read the inevitable result in every page of history. But worse remained behind. There sat upon the chair of St. Peter, in the year 1492, the most depraved and wicked of mankind. No earthly ruler had equalled him in profligacy and the coarser vices of cruelty and oppression since the death of the Roman Nero. This was a man of the name of Borgia, who fixed his infamous mark on the annals of the Papacy as Alexander the Sixth. While this bloodthirsty ruffian was at the summit of sacerdotal power—this poisoner of his friends, this polluter of his family circle with unimaginable crimes—as the visible representative upon earth of the Church of Christ, what hope could there be of amendment in the lower orders of the clergy, or continuance of men's belief in the popish claims? Long before this, in 1442, the falsehood of the pretended donation of Constantine, on which the Popes founded their territorial rights, was triumphantly proved by the learned Valla; and at the end of the century the reverence of mankind for the successor of the Prince of the Apostles was exposed to a trial which the authenticity of all the documents in the world could not have successfully stood, in the personal conduct of the Pope and his familiars.

While this was the general state of Europe in the

fifteenth century as regards the position of the clergy, high and low, the Church, in all countries, threw itself on the protection of the kings. By the middle, or towards the end, of this period, there was no other patronage to which they could have recourse. The nobility in France and England were practically eradicated. All confidence between baron and baron was at an end, and all belief in knightly faith and honour in the other classes of the people. As if the time for a new state of society was arrived, and instruments were required to clear the way for the approaching form, the nobility and gentry of England first were effectual in overthrowing their noble brethren in France, and then, with infuriate bitterness, turned their swords upon each other. The most rememberable general characteristic of this century is the consolidation of royal power. The king becomes despotic because the great nobility is overthrown and the Church stripped of its authority. Tired of hoping for aid from their ancient protector, the lowest classes cast their eyes of helplessness to the throne instead of to the crozier. They see in the reigning sovereign an ideal of personified Power. All other ideals with which the masses of the people have deluded themselves have passed away. The Church is stripped of the charm which its lofty claims and former kindness gave it. It is detected for the thing it is,—a corporation for the grinding of the poor and the support of tyranny and wrong. The nobility is stripped also of the glitter which covered its harsh outlines with the glow of Christian qualifications. It is found to be selfish, faithless, untrustworthy, and divided against itself. To the king, then, as the last refuge of the unfortunate, as the embodied State, a combination, in his own person, of the manly virtues of the knight with the Christian tenderness of the priest, the public transfers all the romantic confidence it had lavished on the other two. And, as if to prove that this idea came to its completeness without reference to the actual holder of sovereign authority, we find that in France the first really despotic king was Louis the Eleventh, and in England the first king by divine right was Henry the Seventh. Two more unchivalrous personages never disgraced the three-legged stool of a scrivener. Yet they sat almost simultaneously on two of earth's proudest thrones.

No century had ever witnessed so great a change in manners and position as this. In others we have seen a gradual widening-out of thought and tendencies, all, however, subdued by the universal shadow in which every thing was carried on. But in this the progress was by a sudden leap from darkness into light. In ancient times Europe was held together by certain communities of interest and feeling, of which the chief undoubtedly was the centralization of the spiritual power in Rome. At the Papal Court all the nations were represented, and Stockholm and Saragossa were brought into contact by their common dependence on the successor of St. Peter. The courtly festivals which invited a knight of Scotland to cross blunted spears in a glittering tournament with a knight of Sicily in the court of an emperor of Germany was another bond of union between remotest regions; and in the fourteenth century the indefatigable Froissart, as we remarked, conveyed a knowledge of one nation to another in the entertaining chapters with which he delighted the listeners in the different palaces where he set up his rest. But all these lights, it will be observed, illumined only the hill-tops, and left the valleys still obscure. Ambitious Churchmen encountered their brethren of all kindreds and tongues in the court of the Vatican; tiltings were only for the high-born and rich, and Froissart himself poured forth his treasures only for the delight of lords and ladies. The ballads of the common people, on the other hand, had had a strongly disuniting effect. The songs which charmed the peasant were directed against the exacting priest and oppressive noble. In England they were generally pointed against the Norman baron, with whose harshness and pride were contrasted the kindness and liberality of Robin Hood and his peers. The French ballads were hostile to the English invader; the Scottish poems were commemorative of the heroism of Wallace and the cruelties of the Southern hordes. Literatures were thus condemned to be hostile, because they were not lofty enough to overlook the boundaries of the narrow circles in which they moved. By slow and toilsome process books were multiplied,—carefully copied in legible hand, and then chained up, like inestimable jewels, in monastery or palace, as too valuable to be left at large. A king's library was talked of as a wonder when it contained six or seven hundred volumes. The writings of controversialists were passed from hand to hand, and the publication of a volume was generally achieved by its being read aloud at the refectory-table of the college and then discussed, in angry disputations, in the University Hall. Not one man in five hundred could read, if the book had been written in the plainest text; and at length the running hand was so indistinct as to be not much plainer than hieroglyphics. The discoveries, therefore, of one age had all to be discovered over again in the next. Roger Bacon, the English monk, in the eleventh century, was acquainted with gunpowder, and had clear intimations of many of the other inventions of more recent times. But what was the use of all his genius? He could only write down his triumph in a book; the book was carefully arranged on the shelf of his monastery;

clever men of his own society may have carried the report of his doings to the neighbouring establishments; but time passed on, those clever men died out, the book on the monastery-shelf was gradually covered with dust, and Roger Bacon became a conjurer in popular estimation, who foretold future events and took counsel from a supernatural brazen head. But in this century the art of printing was discovered and perfected. A thousand copies now darted off in all directions, cheap enough to be bought by the classes below the highest; portable enough to be carried about the person to the most distant lands, and in a type so large and clear that a very little instruction would enable the most illiterate to master its contents. Here was the lever that lifted the century at its first appearance into the light of modern civilization. And it came at the very nick of time. Men's minds were disturbed on many subjects; for old unreasoning obedience to authority had passed away. Who was to guide them in their future voyage? Isolated works would no longer be of any use. Great scholars and acute dialecticians had been tried and found wanting. They only acted on the highly-educated class; and now it was the people in mass—the worker, the shopkeeper, the farmer, the merchant—who were anxious to be informed; and what could a monk in a cell, or even Chaucer with his harp in hand, do for the edification of such a countless host? People would no longer be fed on the dry crust of Aristotelianism or be satisfied with the intellectual jugglery of the Schoolmen. Rome had lost its guiding hand, and its restraining sword was also found of no avail. Some rest was to be found for the minds which had felt the old foundation slip away from them; and in this century, thus pining for light, thus thrusting forward eager hands to be warmed at the first ray of a new-risen sun, there were terrible displays of the aberrations of zeal without knowledge.

Almost within hearing of the first motion of the press, incalculable numbers of enthusiasts revived the exploded sect of the Flagellants of former centuries, and perambulated Europe, plying the whip upon their naked backs and declaring that the whole of religion consisted in the use of the scourge. Others, more crazy still, pronounced the use of clothes to be evidence of an unconverted nature, and returned to the nakedness of our first parents as proof of their restoration to a state of innocence. Mortality lost all its terrors in this earnest search for something more than the ordinary ministrations of the faith could bestow; and in France and England the hideous spectacles called the Dance of Death were frequent. In these, under the banner of a grinning skeleton, the population danced with frantic violence, shouting, shrieking, in the exultation of the time,—a scene where the joyous appearance of the occupation contrasted shockingly with the awful place in which the orgies were held, for the catacombs of Paris, filled with the bones and carcasses of many generations, were the chosen site for these frightful exhibitions. Like the unnatural gayety that reigned in the same city when the guillotine had filled every family with terror or grief, they were but an abnormal development of the sentiment of despair. People danced the Dance of Death, because life had lost its charm. Life had lost its security in the two most powerful nations of the time. England was shaken with contending factions, and France exhausted and hopeless of restoration. The
A.D. 1451. peasantry in both were trampled on without remorse. Jack Cade led up his famishing thousands to lay their sufferings before the throne. They asked for nothing but a slight relaxation of the burdens

that oppressed them, and were condemned without mercy to the sword and gallows. The French "Jacques Bonhomme" was even in a worse condition. There was no controlling power on the throne to guard him from the tyrannies of a hundred petty superiors. The Church of his country was as much conquered by the Church of England as its soil by the English arms. A cardinal, bloated and bloody, dominated both London and Paris, and sent his commands from the Palace at Winchester, which were obeyed by both nations. And all this on
the very eve of the introduction of the per-
A.D. 1452. fected printing-press, the birth of Luther, and
A.D. 1483. the discovery of America! From the beginning
A.D. 1492. of the century till government became assured
by the accession of Henry VII. and Louis XI., the whole of Europe was unsettled and apparently on the verge of dissolution. In the absence of the controlling power of the Sovereign, each little baron asserted his own right and privileges, and aimed perhaps at the restoration of his feudal independence, when the spirit of feudalism had passed away. The nobility, even if it had been united, was not now numerous enough to present a ruling body to the State. It became despised as soon as it was seen to be powerless; and at last, in sheer exhaustion, the people, the churches, and the peerage of the two proudest nations in the world lay down helpless and unresisting at the footstool of the only authority likely to protect them from each other or themselves. When we think of the fifteenth century, let us remember it as the period when mankind grew tired of the establishments of all former ages, when feudalism resigned its sword into the hands of monarchy, and when the last days of the expiring state of society were distinguished by the withdrawal of the death-grasp by France and England from each other's throats, and the esta-

blishment of respectful if not friendly sentiments between them. By the year 1451, there was not one of all the conquests of the Edwards and Henrys left to the English except Calais. If that miserable relic had also been restored, it would have prevented many a heart-burning between the nations, and advanced, perhaps by centuries, the happy time when each can look across the narrow channel which divides them without a wish save for the glory and prosperity of the other.

It is like going back to the time of the Crusades to turn our eyes from the end of this century to the beginning, so great and essential is the change that has taken place. Yet it is necessary, having given the general view of the condition of affairs, to descend to certain particulars by which the progress of the history may be more vividly defined. And of these the principal are the battle of Agincourt, the relief of Orleans, the invention of Guttenberg, and the achievement of Columbus. These are fixed on, not for their own intrinsic merits, but for the great results they produced. Agincourt unfeudalized France; Joan of Arc restored man's faith in human virtue and divine superintendence; printing preserved forever the conquests of the human intellect; and the discovery of America opened a new world to the energies of mankind.

We must return to the state of France when the Duke of Orleans was so treacherously slain by the ferocious Duke of Burgundy in 1407. For a time the crime was successful in establishing the murderer's power, and the Burgundians were strengthened by obtaining the custody of the imbecile king, Charles the Sixth, and the support of his infamous consort, Isabeau of Bavaria. But authority so obtained could not be kept without plunging into greater excesses. So the populace were let loose, and no man's life was safe. In self-defence—burning with hatred of the slayer of his son-in-law and betrayer of his country—the Count of Armagnac denounced the

A.D. 1411. dominant party. Burgundy threw himself into the arms of England, and was only outbidden in his offers of submission by the Armagnacs in the following year. Each party in turn promised to support the English king in all his claims, and before he set foot in France he already found himself in possession of the

A.D. 1413. kingdom. Many strong places in the South were surrendered to him as pledges of the fidelity of his supporters. The whole land was the prey of faction and party hate. The Church had repudiated both Pope and Council; the towns were in insurrection in every street; and Henry the Fifth was only twenty-six years of age, full of courage and ambition, supported by the love and gratitude of the national Church, and anxious to glorify the usurpation of his family by a restoration of the triumphs of Cressy and Poictiers. He therefore sent an embassy to France, demanding his recognition by all the States as king, though he modestly waived the royal title till its present holder should be no more. He declared also that he would not be content without the hand of Catharine, the French king's daughter, with Normandy and other counties for her dowry; and when these reasonable conditions, as he had anticipated, were rejected, and all his preparations were completed, he threw off the mask of negotiation, and sailed from Southampton with an army of six thousand men-at-arms and twenty-four thousand archers. A beautiful sight it must have been that day in September, 1415, when the enormous convoy sailed or rowed down the placid Southampton water. Sails of various colours, and streamers waving from every mast, must have given it the appearance of an immense regatta; and while all France was on the watch for the point of attack, and Calais was universally regarded as the natural landing-place for an English army, the great flotilla pursued its course past the Isle of Wight, and struck out for the opposite coast, filling up the mouth of the Seine with innumerable vessels, and casting anchor off the town of Harfleur. Prayers for its success ascended from every parish in England; for the clergy looked on the youthful king as their champion against all their enemies,—against the Pope, who claimed their tithes, against the itinerant monks, who denied and resisted their authority, and against the nobles, who envied them their wealth and territories. And no wonder; for at this time the ecclesiastical possessions included more than the half of England. Of fifty-three thousand knightly holdings on the national register, twenty-eight thousand belonged to mother Church! Prayers also for its success were uttered in the workshops and markets. People were tired of the long inaction of Richard the Second's time, and longed for the stirring incidents they had heard their fathers speak of when the Black Prince was making the "Mounseers" fly. For by this time a stout feeling of mutual hatred had given vigour to the quarrel between the nations. Parliament had voted unexampled supplies, and "all the youth of England was afire."

Meantime the siege of Harfleur dragged its slow length along. Succours were expected by the gallant garrison, but succour never came. Proclamations had indeed been issued, summoning the *ban* and *arrière ban* of France, and knights were assembling from all quarters to take part in the unavoidable engagement. But the counsels at head-quarters were divided. The masses of the people were not hearty in the cause, and the men of Harfleur, at the end of the fifth week of their resistance, sent to say they would surrender "if they were not relieved by a great army in two days." "Take four," said Henry, wishing nothing more than a decisive action under the very walls. But the time rapidly passed, and Harfleur was once more an English town. Henry might look round and triumph in the possession of streets and houses; but that was all, for his usual barbarity had banished the inhabitants. The richer citizens were put to ransom; all the rest were driven from the place,—not quite naked, nor quite penniless, for one petticoat was left to each woman, and one farthing in ready money. Generosity to the vulgar vanquished was not yet understood, either as a Christian duty or a stroke of policy. But courage, not unmixed with braggadocio, was still the character of the time. The English had lost many men from sickness during the siege. No blow had been boldly struck in open field, and a war without a battle, however successful in its results, would have been thought no better than a tournament. All the remaining chivalry of France was now collected under its chiefs and princes, and Henry determined to try what mettle they were of. He published a proclamation that he and his English would march across the country from Harfleur to Calais in spite of all opposition; and, as the expedition would occupy eight days at least, he felt sure that some attempt would be made to revenge so cutting an insult. He might easily have sent his forces, in detachments, by sea, for there was not a French flag upon all the Channel; but trumpets were sounded one day, swords drawn, cheers no doubt heartily uttered, by an enthusiastic array of fifteen thousand men, and the dangerous march began. It was the month of October, the time of the vintage: there was plenty of wine; and a French author makes the characteristic remark, "with plenty of wine the English soldier could go to the end of the world."

When the English soldier, on this occasion, had got through the eight days' provisions with which he started, instead of finding himself at Calais, he was only advanced as far as Amiens, with the worst part of the journey before him. The fords of the Somme were said to be guarded; spies came over in the disguise of deserters, and told the king that all the land was up in arms, that the princes were all united, and that two hundred thousand men were hemming them hopelessly round. In the midst of these bad news, however, a ray of light broke in. A villager pointed out a marsh, by crossing which they could reach a ford in the stream. They traversed the marsh without hesitation, waded with difficulty through morass and water, and, behold! they were safe on the other side. The road was now clear, they thought, for Calais; and they pushed cheerily on. But, more dangerous than the marsh, more impassable than the river, the vast army of France blocked up their way. Closing across a narrow valley which lay between the castle of Agincourt and the village of Tramecourt, sixty thousand knights, gentlemen, and men-at-arms stood like a wall of steel. There were all the great names there of all the provinces,—Dukes of Lorraine, and Bar, and Bourbon, Princes of Orleans and Berri, and many more. Henry by this time had but twelve thousand men. He found he had miscalculated his movements, and was unwilling to sacrifice his army to the point of honour. He offered to resign the title of King of France and to surrender his recent conquest at Harfleur. But the princes were resolved not to negotiate, but to revenge. Henry then said to the prisoners he was leading in his train, "Gentlemen, go till this affair is settled. If your captors survive, present yourselves at Calais." His forces were soon arranged. Archers had ceased to be the mere appendages to a line of battle: they now constituted almost all the English army. All the night before they had been busy in preparation. They had furbished up their arms, and put new cords to their bows, and sharpened the stakes they carried to ward off the attack of cavalry. At early dawn they had confessed to the priest; and all the time no noise had been heard. Henry had ordered silence throughout the camp on pain of the severest penalties, A.D. 1415. —loss of his horse to a gentleman, and of his right ear to a common soldier. The 23d of October was the great, the important day. Henry put a noble helmet on his head, surmounted by a golden crown, sprang on his little gray hackney, encouraged his men with a few manly words, reminding them of Old England and how constantly they had conquered the French, and led them to a field where the grass was still green, and which the rains had not converted into mud; for the weather had long been unpropitious. And here the heroic little army expected the attack. But the enemy were in no condition to make an advance. Seated all night on their enormous war-horses, the heavy-armed cavaliers had sunk the unfortunate animals up to their knees in the adhesive soil. Old Thomas of Erpingham, seeing the decisive moment, completed the marshalling of the English as soon as possible, and, throwing his baton in the air, cried, "Now, Strike!" A great hurrah was the answer to this order; but still the French line continued unmoved. If it had been turned into stone it could not have been more inactive. Ranged thirty-two deep, and fixed to the spot they stood on, buried up in armour, and crowded in the narrow space, the knights could offer no resistance to the attack of their nimble and lightly-armed foes. A flight of ten thousand arrows poured upon the vast mass, and saddles became empty without a blow. There came, indeed, two great charges of horse from the flank of the French array; but the inevitable shaft found entrance through their coats of mail, and very few survived. Of these the greater part rushed, blind and wounded, back among their own men, crashing upon the still spell-bound line and throwing it into inextricable confusion. Horse and man rolled over in the dirt, struggling and shrieking in an undistinguishable mass. Meanwhile the archers, throwing aside their stakes and seizing the hatchets hanging round their necks, advanced at a run,—poured blows without cessation on casque and shield, completing the destruction among the crowded multitudes which their own disorder had begun; and, as the same cause which hindered their advance prevented their retreat, they sat the hopeless victims of a false position, and were slaughtered without an attempt made to resist or fly. The fate of the second line was nearly the same. Henry, forcing his way with sword and axe through the living barrier of horse and cavalier, led his compact array to the glittering body beyond. There the *mélée* became more animated, and prowess was shown upon either side. But the rear-guard, warned by previous experience, took flight before the middle lines were pierced, and Henry saw himself victor with very trifling loss, and only encumbered with the number of the slain, and still more with the multitude of prisoners. Almost all the surviving noblemen had surrendered their swords. They knew too well the fate of wounded or disarmed gentlemen even among their countrymen, and trusted rather to the generosity of the conqueror than the mercy of their own people. Alas that we must again confess that Henry was ignorant of the name of generosity! Alarmed for a moment at the threatening aspect of some of the fugitives who had resumed their ranks, he gave the pitiless word that every prisoner was to be slain. Not a soldier would lift his hand against his captive,—from the double motive of tenderness and cupidity. To tell an "archer good" to murder a great baron, the captive of his bow and spear, was to tell him to resign a ransom which would make him rich for life. But Henry was not to be balked. He appointed two hundred men to be executioners of his command; and thousands of the young and gay were slaughtered in cold blood. Was it hideous policy which thus led Henry to weaken his enemy's cause by diminishing the number of its knightly defenders, or was it really the result of the fear of being overcome? Whichever it was, the effect was the same. Ten thousand of the gentlemen of France were the sufferers on that day,—a whole generation of the rich and high-born swept away at one blow! It would have taken a long time in the course of nature to supply their place; but nature was not allowed to have her way. Wars and dissensions interfered with her restorative efforts. Six-and-thirty years were yet to be spent in mutual destruction, or in struggles against the English name; and when France was again left free from foreign occupation, when French chivalry again wished to assume the chief rule in human affairs, it was found that chivalry was out of place; a new state of things had arisen in Europe; the greatest exploit which had been known in their national annals had been performed by a woman; and knighthood had so lost its manliness that, when prosperity and population had again made France a powerful kingdom, the silk-clad courtiers of an unwarlike monarch thought it good taste to sneer at the relief of Orleans and the mission of Joan of Arc!

Six years after Agincourt, the English conqueror and the wretched phantom of kingship called Charles the

A.D. 1421. Sixth descended to their graves. Military honour and patriotism seemed utterly at an end among the French population, and our Henry the Sixth, the son of the man of Agincourt, succeeded in the great object of English ambition and was recognised from the Channel to the Loire as King of France. In the Southern provinces a spark of the old French gallantry was still unextinguished, but it showed itself in the gay unconcern with which the Dauphin, now Charles the Seventh, bore all the reverses of fortune, and consoled himself for the loss of the noblest crown in Europe by the enjoyments of love and festivity. Perhaps he saw that the whirligig of time would bring about its revenges, and that the curse of envious faction would vex the councils of the conquerors as it had ruined the fortunes of the subdued. The warriors of Henry still remained, but, without the controlling hand, they could direct their efforts to no common object. The uncles of the youthful king speedily quarrelled. The gallant Bedford was opposed by the treacherous Glo'ster, and both were dominated and supplanted by the haughty prelate, the Cardinal Bishop of Winchester. Offence was soon taken at the presumption of the English soldiery. Religious animosities supervened. The Churches of England and France had both made successful endeavours to establish a considerable amount of national independence, and the French bishops, who had withdrawn themselves from the absolutism of Rome, were little inclined to become subordinate to Winchester and Canterbury. A court gradually gathered round the Dauphin, which inspired him with more manly thoughts. His feasts and tournaments were suspended, and, with his hand on the hilt of his sword, he watched the proceedings of the English. These proceedings were uniformly successful when restricted to the operations of war.

They defeated the men of Gascony and the reinforcements sent over by the Scotch. They held a firm grasp of Paris and all the strong places of the North, and cast down the gauntlet to the rest of France by laying
A.D. 1428. siege to the beautiful city of Orleans in the winter of 1428. Once in possession of the Loire, they would be able at their leisure to extend their conquests southward; and all the loyal throughout the country took up the challenge and resolved on the defence of the beleaguered town. The English must have begun by this time to despise their enemy; for, in spite of the greatness of the stake, they undertook the siege with a force of less than three thousand men. To make up for the deficiency in numbers, they raised twelve large bastions all round the walls, exhausting the troops by the labour and finding it impossible to garrison them adequately when they were finished. It seems that Sebastopol was not the first occasion on which our soldiers were overworked. To surround a city of several thousand inhabitants, strongly garrisoned, and with an open country at its back for the supply of provisions, would have required a large and well-directed force. But the moral effects of Agincourt, and even of Cressy and Poictiers, were not yet obliterated. Public spirit was dead, and very few entertained a hope of saving the doomed place. Statesmen, politicians, and warriors, all calculated the chances of success and decided against the cause of France. But in the true heart of the common people far better feelings survived. They were neither statesmen, nor politicians, nor warriors; but they were loyal and devoted Frenchmen, and put their trust in God.

A peasant-girl, eighteen years of age, born and bred in a little village called Domremy, in Lorraine, was famous for her religious faith and simplicity of character. Her name was Joan d'Arc,—a dreamy enthusiast, believing with full heart all the legends of saints and miracles with which the neighbourhood was full. She rested, also, with a sort of romantic interest on the personal fortunes of the young discrowned king, who had been unjustly excluded by foreigners from his rights and was now about to lose the best of his remaining possessions. She walked in the woods and heard voices telling her to be up and doing. She went to pray in the dim old church, and had glorious visions of angels who smiled upon her. One time she saw a presence with a countenance like the sun, and wings upon his shoulders, who said, "Go, Joan, to the help of the King of France." But she answered, "My lord, I cannot ride, nor command men-at-arms." The voice replied, "Go to M. de Baudricourt at Vaucouleurs: he will take thee to the king. Saint Catharine and Saint Marguerite will come to thy assistance." There was no voluntary deception here. The girl lived in a world of her own, and peopled it out of the fulness of her heart. She went to Vaucouleurs: she saw M. de Baudricourt. He took her to Poictiers, where the Dauphin resided, and when she was led into the glittering ring an attempt was made to deceive her by representing another as the prince; but she went straight up to the Dauphin and said to him, "Gentle Dauphin, my name is Joan the Maid. The King of Heaven sends to you, through me, that you shall be anointed and crowned at Rheims, and you shall be lieutenant of the King of Heaven, who is King of France." All the court was moved,—the more pure-minded, with sympathy for the girl, the more experienced, with the use that might be made of her enthusiasm to rouse the nation. Both parties conspired to aid Joan in her design; and, clothed in white armour, mounted on a war-horse, holding the banner of France in her hand, and waited on by knights and pages, she set forth on her way to Orleans. It was like a religious procession all the way. She prayed at all the shrines, and was blest by the clergy, and held on her path undismayed with all the dangers that occurred at every step. At length, on the 30th of April, she made her entry into Orleans. Her coming had long been expected; and, now that it had really happened, people looked back at the difficulties of the route and thought the whole march a miracle. Meantime Joan knelt and gave thanks in the great church, and the true defence of Orleans began. Into the hard-pressed city had gathered all the surviving chivalry of France,—Dunois, the bastard of Orleans, La Hire, Saintrailles, rough and dissolute soldiers, yet all held in awe by the purity and innocence of the Maid. With Joan at the head of the column of assault, the English intrenchments fell one after another. In spite of wounds and hardships, the peasant-girl pushed fearlessly on; the knights and gentlemen could not decline to follow where she led the way; and ten days after her arrival old Talbot and Falstaff gathered up the fragments of their troops and made a precipitate retreat from the scene of their discomfiture. But there was not yet rest for the dreamer of Domremy. She hurried off to the Dauphin. "Gentle Dauphin," she said, "till you are crowned with the old crown and bedewed with the holy oil, you can never be King of France. Come with me to Rheims. There shall no enemy hurt you on the way." The country through which they had to pass was bristling with English castles and swarming with wandering troops. Yet the counsel which appeared so hardy was in fact the wisest that could be given. The faith in the sanctity of coronations was still strong. Whoever was first crowned would in the eye of faith be true king. Win-

chester was bringing over the English claimant. All France would be startled at the news that the descendant of St. Louis was beforehand with his rival; and the march was successfully made. "Gentle king,"
July 17, said Joan, kneeling after the ceremony, and
1429. calling him for the first time King,—"Gentle King, Orleans is saved, the true king is crowned. My task is done. Farewell." But they would not let her leave them so soon. The people crowded round her and blest her wherever she appeared. "Oh, the good people of Rheims!" she cried: "when I die I should like to be buried here." "When do you think you shall die?" inquired the archbishop,—perhaps with a sneer upon his lips. "That I know not," she replied: "whenever it pleases God. But, for my own part, I wish to go back and keep the sheep with my sister and brothers. They will be so glad to see me again!" But this was not to be.

If Talbot and Suffolk had been foiled and vanquished by Dunois and La Hire, they would have accepted their defeat as one of the mischances of war. A knightly hand ennobles the blow it gives. But to be humbled by a woman, a peasant, a prophetess, an impostor,—this was too much for the proud stomachs of our steel-clad countrymen. But far worse was it in the eyes of our stole-clad ecclesiastics. Apparitions of saints and angels vouchsafed to the recalcitrant Church of France!—voices heard from heaven denouncing the claims of the English king!—visible glories hanging round the head of a simple shepherdess! It was evident to every clergyman and monk and bishop in England that the woman was a witch or a deceiver. And almost all the clergymen in France thought the same; and after a while, when the exploit was looked back upon with calmness, almost all the soldiers on both sides were of the same opinion. Nobody could believe in the exaltation of a pure and enthusiastic mind, making its own visions, and performing its own miracles, without a tincture of deceit. It was easier and more orthodox to believe in the liquefaction of the holy oil and the wonders wrought by the bones of St. Denis: so, with a nearly universal assent of both the parties, the humbled English and delivered French, the most heroic and most feminine of women was handed over to the Church tribunals, and Joan's fate was sealed. Unmanly priests, whose law prevented them from having wives, unloving bishops, whose law prevented them from having daughters,—how were they to judge of the loving heart and trusting tenderness of a girl not twenty years of age, standing before them, with modesty not shown in blushes but in unabated simplicity of behaviour, telling the tale of all her actions as if she were pouring it into the ears of father and mother in her own old cottage at home, unconscious, or at least regardless, of scowling looks, and misleading questions, directed to her by those predetermined murderers? No one tried to save her. Charles the Seventh, with the oil of Rheims scarcely dried upon his head, made no attempt to get her from the hands of her enemies. The process took place at Rouen. Magic and heresy were the crimes laid to her charge; and as generosity was magic in the eyes of those narrow-souled inquisitors, and trust in God was heresy, there was no defence possible. Her whole life was a confession. First, she was condemned to perpetual imprisonment, and to resume the dress of her sex. Then she was exposed to every obloquy and insult which hatred and superstition could pour upon her. A gallant "Lord" accompanied the Count de Ligny in a visit to her cell. She was chained to a plank by both feet, and kept in this attitude night and day. The noble Englishman did honour to his rank and country. When Joan said, "I know the English will procure my death, in hopes of getting the realm of France; but they could not do it, no, if they had a hundred thousand *Goddams* more than they have to-day;" the gallant visitor was so enraged by those depreciating remarks, and perhaps at the nickname thus early indicative of the national oath, that he drew his dagger, and would have struck her, if he had not been hindered by Lord Warwick. Another gentleman, on being admitted to her prison, insulted her by the grossness of his behaviour, and then overwhelmed her with blows. It was time for Joan to escape her tormentors. She put on once more the male apparel which she had thrown off, and sentence of death was passed. On the 30th of May, 1431, in the old fishmarket of Rouen, the great crime was consummated. The flames mounted very slowly; and when at last they enveloped her from the crowd, she was still heard calling on Jesus, and declaring, "The voices I heard were of God!—the voices I heard were of God!" The age of chivalry was indeed past, and the age of Church-domination was also about to expire. The peasant-girl of Domremy wrote the dishonoured epitaph of the first in the flame of Rouen, and a citizen of Mentz was about to give the other its death-blow with the printing-press.

A.D. 1431.

This is one of the inventions apparently unimportant, by which incalculable results have been produced. At first it was intended merely to simplify the process of copying the books which were already well known. And, if we may trust some of the stories told of the earliest specimens of the art, we shall see that there was some slight portion of dishonesty mingled with the talent of the Fathers of printing. These were Guttenberg of Mentz, and his apprentice or partner Faust. The

first of their productions was a Latin Bible; and the
A.D. 1455. letters of this impression were such an exact imitation of the works of the amanuensis that they passed it off as an exquisite specimen of the copyist's art. Faust sold a copy to the King of France for seven hundred crowns, and another to the Archbishop of Paris for four hundred. The prelate, enchanted with his bargain, (for the usual price was several hundred crowns above what he had given,) showed it in triumph to the king. The king compared the two, and was filled with astonishment. They were identical in every stroke and dot. How was it possible for any two scribes, or even for the same scribe, to produce so undeniable a facsimile of his work? The capital letters of the edition were of red ink. They inquired still further, and found that many other copies had been sold, all precisely alike in form and pressure. They came to the conclusion that Faust was a wizard and had sold himself to the devil, and that the initials were of blood. The Church and State, in this case united in the persons of king and archbishop, had the magician apprehended. To save himself from the flames, the unhappy Faust had to confess the deceit, and also to discover the secret of the art. The whole mystery consisted in cutting letters upon movable metal types, and, after rubbing them with ink when they were correctly set, imprinting them upon paper by means of a screw. A simple expedient, as it appeared to everybody when the secret was spread abroad; for there had been seals stamping impressions on wax for many generations. Medals and coins had been poured forth from the dies of every nation from the dawn of history. In England, playing-cards had been produced for several years, with the figures impressed on them from wooden blocks; and in 1423 a stamped book, with wood engravings, had made its appearance,

which now, with many treasures of typography, is in the library of Lord Spencer. Even in Nineveh, we learn from recent discovery, the dried bricks, while in a soft state, had been stamped with those curious-looking inscriptions, by a board in which the unsightly letters were set in high relief. Wooden letters had also long been known; and yet it was not till 1440 that Guttenberg bethought him of the process of printing, and only after ten or twelve years' labour that he brought his experiments to perfection and with one crush of the completed press opened new hopes and prospects to the whole family of mankind. But things apparently unconnected are brought together for good when the great turning-points of human history are attained. There are always pebbles of the brook within reach when the warrior-shepherd has taken the sling in his hand. Shortly before the invention of printing, a discovery was made without which Guttenberg's skill would have been of no avail. This was the applicability of linen rags to the manufacture of paper. Parchment, and preparations of straw and papyrus, had sufficed for the transcriber and author of those unliterary times, but would have been inadequate to supply the demand of the new process; and therefore we may say that, as gunpowder was essential to the use of artillery, and steam-power for the railway-train, linen paper was indispensable to the development of the press. And tha: development was rapid beyond all imagination. In the remaining portion of the century, eight thousand five hundred and nine books were published, of which the English Caxton and his followers supplied one hundred and forty-two,—a small contribution in actual numbers, but valuable for the insight it gives us into the favourite literature of the time. Among those volumes there are

"Songs of war for gallant knight,
Lays of love for lady bright;"

"The Tale of Troy divine," for scholars; "Tullie, of old age," and "of Friendship," and "Virgil's Æneid," for the classical; "Lives of Our Ladie and divers Saints," for the religious; and "The Consolation of Boethius," for the afflicted. But several editions prove the popularity of the Father of English poetry; and we find the "Tales of Cauntyrburrie," and the "Book of Fame," and "Troylus and Cresyde, made by Geoffrey Chaucer," the great and fitting representatives of the native English muse.

We ought to remember, in judging of the paucity of books produced in England, that the Wars of the Roses broke out at the very time when Guttenberg's labours began. In such a season of struggle and unrest as the thirty years of civil strife—for though Mr. Knight, in his very interesting sketch of this date,* has shown that the period of actual and open war was very short, the state of uneasiness and expectation must have endured the whole time—there was small encouragement to the peaceful triumphs of art or literature. And, moreover, the pride of station was revolted by the prospect of the spread of information among the classes to whom it had not yet reached. The noble could afford to acknowledge his inferiority in learning and research to the priest or monk, for it was their trade to be wise and learned, and their scholarship was even considered a badge of the lowness of their birth, which had given them the primer and psalter instead of the horse and sword. But those high-hearted cavaliers could ill brook the notion of educated clowns and peasants. And, strange to say, the sentiment was shared and exaggerated by the peasants

* Popular History—Henry VI.

and clowns themselves. Jack Cade is represented, by an anachronism of date but with perfect truth of character, as profoundly irritated at the invention of printing, and the building of a paper-mill, and the introduction of such heathenish words as nominatives and adverbs: so that the press began its career opposed by the two greatest parties of the State. Yet truth is mighty and will prevail. No nobility in Europe gives such contributions to the general stock of high and healthy thought as the descendants of the men of Towton and Bosworth, and no peasantry values more deeply, or would defend more gallantly, the gifts poured upon it by a free and sympathizing press. Warwick the King-maker, if he had lived just now, would have made speeches in Parliament and had them reported in the *Times,* and Jack Cade would have been sent to the reformatory and taught to read and write.

But, with the peerages of Europe greatly thinned, with mounted feudalism overthrown, with the press rejoicing as a giant to run its course, something also was needed in order to make a wider theatre for the introduction of the new life of men. Another world lay beyond the great waters of the Atlantic. Whispers had been going round the circle of earnest inquirers, which gradually grew louder and louder till they reached the ears of kings, that great things lay hidden in the awful and mysterious solitudes of the ocean; that westward, to balance the preponderance of our used-up continent, must be solid land, equal in weight and size, so that the uninterrupted waters would conduct the adventurous mariner to the farther India by a nearer route than

A.D. 1487. Bartholomew Diaz, the Portuguese, had just discovered. This man sailed to the southern extremity of Africa, passed round to the east without being aware of his achievement, and penetrated as far as Lagoa Bay. But the crew became discontented, and the navigator retraced his steps. Alarmed at the commotion of the vast waves of the Southern Ocean pouring its floods against the Table Mountain, he had retired from further research, and called the southern point of his pilgrimage the Cape of Storms. It is now known to us by a happier augury as the Cape of Good Hope. But, whether perpetually haunted by tempests or not, the truth was discovered that the land ceased at that promontory and left an unexplored sea beyond. This was cherished in many a heart; for in this century maritime discovery kept pace with the other triumphs of mental power. Wherever ship could swim man could venture. The Azores had been discovered in 1439 and colonized by the Portuguese in 1440. Already in possession of Cape Verd, Madeira, and the Canaries, Portugal looked forward to greater discoveries, for these were the nurseries of gallant and skilful mariners. But the glory was left for another nation,—though, by a strange caprice of fortune, the chance of it had been offered to nearly all.

The life of Columbus is more wonderful than a romance. He hawked about his notion of the way to India at all the courts of Europe. By birth a Genoese, he considered the great ocean the patrimony of any person able to seize it. When his services, therefore, were rejected by his own country, he offered them successively to Portugal, to Spain, and to England. Henry the Seventh was inclined to venture a small sum in the lottery of chances; but, while still in negotiation with the brother of Columbus, the Spanish monarchs, Ferdinand and Isabella, closed with the navigator's terms, and on the 3d of August, 1492, the squadron of discovery, consisting of a vessel of some size, and two small pinnaces, with a crew at most of a hundred persons in all the three, sailed from the port of Palos, in Andalusia.

Three weeks' constant progress to the westward took them far beyond all previous navigation. The men became disheartened, discontented, and finally rebellious. Against all, Columbus bore up with the self-relying energy of a great mind, but was driven to the compromise of promising, if they confided in him for three days longer, he would return, if the object of his voyage was yet unattained. But by this time his sagacious observation had assured him of success. Strange appearances began to be perceived from the ship's decks. A carved piece of wood floated past, then a reed newly cut, and, best sign of all, a branch with red berries still fresh. "From all these symptoms, Columbus was so confident of being near land, that on the evening of the 11th of October, after public prayers for success, he ordered the sails to be furled, and the ships to lie to, keeping strict watch, lest they should be driven ashore in the night. During this interval of suspense and expectation no man shut his eyes: all kept upon deck, gazing intently towards that quarter where they expected to discover the land, which had been so long the object of their wishes. About two hours before midnight, Columbus, standing on the forecastle, observed a light at a distance, and privately pointed it out to Pedro Guttierez, a page of the queen's wardrobe. Guttierez perceiving it, and calling to Salcedo, comptroller of the fleet, all three saw it in motion, as if it were carried from place to place. A little after midnight the joyful sound of '*Land! land!*' was heard from the Pinta, which kept always ahead of the other ships. But, having been so often deceived by fallacious appearances, every man was now become slow of belief, and waited in all the anguish of uncertainty and impatience for the return of day. As soon as morning dawned, all doubts and fears were dispelled. From every ship an island was seen about two leagues to the north, whose flat and verdant fields, well stored with wood, and watered with many rivulets, presented the aspect of a delightful country. The crew of the Pinta instantly began the *Te Deum* as a hymn of thanksgiving to God, and were joined by those of the other ships, with tears of joy and transports of congratulation. This office of gratitude to Heaven was followed by an act of justice to their commander. They threw themselves at the feet of Columbus, with feelings of self-condemnation mingled with reverence. They implored him to pardon their ignorance, incredulity, and insolence, which had created him so much unceasing disquiet and had so often obstructed the prosecution of his well-concerted plan; and, passing in the warmth of their admiration from one extreme to another, they now pronounced the man whom they had so lately reviled and threatened to be a person inspired by Heaven with sagacity and fortitude more than human, in order to accomplish a design so far beyond the ideas and conception of all former ages."

Many excellent writers have described this wondrous incident, but none so well as the historian of America, Dr. Robertson, whose eloquent account is borrowed in the preceding lines. The great event occurred on Friday, the 12th of October, 1492, and the connection between the two worlds began. The place he first landed at was San Salvador, one of the Bahamas; and after attaching Cuba and Hispaniola to the Spanish crown, and going through imminent perils by land and sea, he achieved his glorious return to Palos on the 15th of March, 1493. He brought with him some of the natives of the different islands he had discovered, and their strange appearance and manners were vouchers for the facts he stated. The whole town, when he came into the harbour, was in an uproar of delight. "The bells were rung, the cannon fired, Columbus was received at landing with royal honours, and all the people, in solemn procession, accompanied him and his crew to the church, where they returned thanks to Heaven, which had so wonderfully conducted, and crowned with success, a voyage of greater length, and of more importance, than had been attempted in any former age."*

---

* Dr. Robertson.

SIXTEENTH CENTURY.

Emperors of Germany.

A.D.

MAXIMILIAN I.—(*cont.*)

1519. CHARLES V., (1st of Spain.)

1558. FERDINAND I.

1564. MAXIMILIAN II.

1576. RODOLPH II.

Kings of England.

HENRY VII.—(*cont.*)

1509. HENRY VIII.

1547. EDWARD VI.

1553. MARY.

1558. ELIZABETH.

Kings of Scotland.

JAMES IV.—(*cont.*)

1513. JAMES V.

1542. MARY.

1567. JAMES VI.

Kings of France.

A.D.

LOUIS XII.—(*cont.*)

1515. FRANCIS I.

1547. HENRY II.

1559. FRANCIS II.

1560. CHARLES IX.

1574. HENRY III.

(*The Bourbons.*)

1589. HENRY IV.

Kings of Spain.

1512. FERDINAND V., (the Catholic.)

1516. CHARLES I., (Emperor of Germany.)

1556. PHILIP II.

1598. PHILIP III.

Distinguished Men.

LEONARDO DA VINCI, MICHAEL ANGELO, RAFFAELLE, CORREGGIO, TITIAN, (Painters,) SIR PHILIP SYDNEY, RALEIGH, SPENSER, SHAKSPEARE, (1564–1616,) ARIOSTO, TASSO, LOPE DE VEGA, CALDERON, CERVANTES, SCALIGER, (1484–1558,) COPERNICUS, (1473–1543,) KNOX, (1505–1572,) CALVIN, (1509–1564,) BEZA, (1519–1605,) BELLARMINE, (1542–1621,) TYCHO BRAHE, (1546–1601.)

THE SIXTEENTH CENTURY.

THE REFORMATION—THE JESUITS—POLICY OF ELIZABETH

In the last two years of the preceding century the course of maritime discovery had been accelerated by fresh success. To balance the glories of Columbus in the West, the "regions of the rising sun" had been explored by Vasco da Gama, a Portuguese. This great navigator sailed back into the harbour of Lisbon on the 16th of September, 1499, with the astonishing news that he had doubled the Cape of Storms, which had so alarmed Bartholomew Diaz, and established relations of amity and commerce with the vast continent of India, having traded with a civilized and industrious people at Calicut, a great city on the coast of Malabar. Under these reiterated widenings of men's knowledge of the globe, the human mind itself expanded. Familiar names meet us from henceforth in the most distant quarters of the world. All national or domestic history becomes mixed up with elements hitherto unknown. The balance of power, which is the new constitution of the European States, depends on circumstances and places of the most heterogeneous character. A treaty between France and Spain, or between England and either, is regulated by events occurring on the Amazon or Ganges. The whole world gets more closely connected than ever it was before, and we can look back on the proceedings of previous ages as filling a very narrow theatre, and regulated by very contracted interests, when compared with the universal policies on which public affairs have now to rest. At first, however, the great results of these stupendous discoveries were naturally not observed. Contemporaries are justly accused of magnifying the small affairs of life of which they are witnesses; but this observation does not hold good with respect to the really momentous incidents of human history. A man who saw Columbus return from his voyage, or Guttenberg pulling at his press, could not rise to the contemplation of the prodigious consequences of these two events. He thought, perhaps, a quarrel between two neighbouring potentates, or a battle between France and Spain, the greatest incident of his time. His son forgot all about the quarrel; his grandson had no recollection of the battle; but widening in a still increasing circle, expanding into still more wonderful proportions, were the Discovery of America and the Art of Printing, —showing themselves in combinations of events and changes of circumstances where they were never expected to appear,—the one threatening to overthrow the freedom of every State in Europe by the supremacy of the Spanish crown, the other in reality preventing the chance of that consummation by raising up the indomitable spirit of spiritual liberty. For there now came to the aid of national independence the far more elevating feelings of religious emancipation. Protestantism was not limited in this century to denial of the spiritual authority of popes, but embodied itself also in resistance to the political ambition of kings. America might have enabled Charles the Fifth to conquer all Europe, if the Reformation had not strengthened men's minds with a determination to stand up against oppression.

But the commencement of this century gave no intimation of its tempestuous course. The first few years saw the peaceable accession to the thrones of Spain and

France and England of the three sovereigns whose contemporaneous reigns, and also whose personal characters, had the most preponderating influence on the succeeding current of events. We have left Spain for a long time out of these general views of a century's condition and special notices of individual incidents which affected the condition of the world; for Spain for a long time lay obscurely between the ocean and the Pyrenees and carried on wars and policies which were limited by its territorial bounds. But, if we take a hurried retrospect of the last few years, we shall see that the different nations contained in the Peninsula had amalgamated into one mighty and strongly-cemented State. Ferdinand of Aragon, by marriage with Isabella of Castile, united the various nationalities under one homogeneous government, and by wisdom and magnanimity—the wisdom being the man's and the magnanimity the woman's—had rendered forever famous the joint reign of husband and wife, had reconciled the jarring factions of their respective subjects, and seen with the triumphant faith of believers and the satisfaction of sagacious rulers the reunion of the last Mohammedan State to the dominion of the Cross and of the crown. They watched the long, slow march of the Moorish king and his cavaliers as they took their way in poverty and despair from the towers and meadows of Granada, which a possession of seven hundred years had failed to make their own. This—the conquest of Granada—took place in 1491; and 1516 saw the supreme power over all united Spain descend on the head of the grandson of Ferdinand and Isabella,—inheriting, along with their royal dignity, the cautious wisdom of the one and the wider intelligence of the other. In three years from that time—it will be easy to remember that Charles's age is the same as the cen-

A.D. 1497.

tury's—he was elected to the Imperial crown, so that the greatest dominion ever held by one man since the days of Charlemagne now fell to the rule of a youth of nineteen years of age. Germany, the Netherlands, Naples, Sicily, and Spain, more than equalled the extent and power of Charlemagne's empire. But ere Charles was a year older, vaster dominions than Charlemagne had ever dreamt of acknowledged his royal sway; for A.D. 1520. Montezuma, the Emperor of Mexico, whose realm was without appreciable limit either in size or wealth, professed himself the subject and servant of the Spanish king.

Henry the Eighth of England had also succeeded at an early age, being but eighteen in 1509, when the death of his father, the politic and successful founder of the Tudor dynasty, left him with a people silent if not quite satisfied, and an exchequer overflowing with what would now amount to ten or twelve millions of gold. This treasure had been accumulated by the infamous exactions of the late sovereign, who was aided in the ignoble service by two men of the names of Empson and Dudley. These were spies and informers, not, as in other climes and countries, about the religious or political sentiments of the people, but about their titles to their estates, the fines they were disposed to pay, or the bribes they would advance to the royal extortioner to avoid litigation and injustice. Henry had an admirable opportunity of showing his hatred of these practices, and availed himself of it at once. Before he had been four months on the throne, Empson and Dudley were ignominiously hanged; and with safe conscience, after this sacrifice at the shrine of legality, he entered into possession of the pilfered store. The people applauded the rapid decision of his character in both these instances, and scarcely grudged him the money when the subordinates were given up to their revenge. They could not, indeed, grudge their young king any thing; his manners were so open and sincere, his laugh so ready, and his teeth so white; for we are not to forget, in compliment to what is facetiously called the dignity of history, the immense advantages a ruler gains by the fact of being good-looking. Nobody feels inclined to find fault with a lad of eighteen, if moderately endowed with health and features; but when that lad is eminently handsome, rioting in strength and spirits, open in disposition, and, above all, a king, you need not wonder at the universal inclination to overlook his faults, to exaggerate his virtues, and even, after an interval of two hundred and fifty years, to hear the greatest tyrant of our history, and the worst man perhaps of his time, talked of by the ordinary title of Bluff King Hal. If he had been as ugly and humpbacked as his grand-uncle Richard the Third, he would have been detested from the first.

But in the neighbouring land of France there reigned at the same time a prince almost as handsome as Henry, and nearly as popular with his people, with as little real cause. In 1515, Francis the First was twenty years of age, a perfect specimen of manly strength,—accomplished in all knightly exercises,—generous and magnificent in his intercourse with his nobility,—and the greatest *roué* and debauchee in all the kingdom of France. Here, then, at the beginning of the age we have now to examine, were the three mightiest sovereigns of Europe, all arriving at their crowns before attaining their majority; and with so many years before them, and such powerful nations obeying their commands, great prospects for good or evil were opening on the world. But in the early years of the century no human eye perceived in what direction the future was going to pursue its course. People were all watching for the first indication of what was to come, and kept their eyes on the courts of Paris and London and Madrid; but nobody suspected that the real champions of the time were already marshalling their forces in far different situations. There was a thoughtful monk in a convent in Germany, and a Spanish soldier before the walls of Pampeluna. These were the true movers of men's minds, of the great thoughts by which events are created; and their names were soon to sound louder than those of Henry or Charles or Francis; for one was Martin Luther, the hero of the Reformation, and the other was Ignatius Loyola, the founder of the Jesuits. Take note of them here as mere accessories to the march of general history: we shall return to them again as characteristics of the century on which they placed their indelible mark. At this time, in the gay young days of the three crowned striplings, these future combatants are totally unknown. Brother Martin is singing charming hymns to the Virgin, in a voice which it was delightful to hear; and Don Ignacio is also singing to his guitar the praises of one of the beautiful maidens of his native land. Public opinion was still stagnant with regard to home-affairs, in spite of the efforts of the infant press. People, bowed down by the claims of implicit obedience exacted from them by the Church, accepted with wondering submission the pontificate of such an atrocious murderer as Alexander the Sixth; and some even ingeniously founded an argument of the divine institution of the Papacy upon its having survived the eleven years' desecration of that monster of cruelty and unbelief. Yet now it happened by a strange coincidence that the chair of St. Peter was to be filled by a gayer and more accomplished ruler than any of the earthly thrones we have mentioned. In 1513, Leo the Tenth, the most celebrated of the family of the Medicis of Florence, put on the tiara at the age of thirty-six, a period of life which was considered as youthful for the father of Christendom as even the boyish years of the temporal kings. And Leo did not belie the promise of his juvenility. None of the dulness of age, or even the caution of maturity, was perceived in his public or private conduct. He was a patron of arts and sciences, and buffoonery, and infidelity; and it is curious to observe how the pretensions of Rome were more shaken by the frivolous magnificence of a good-hearted, graceful voluptuary than they had been by the crimes of his two immediate predecessors, the truculent Borgia and the warlike Julius the Second.

This latter pontiff was intended by nature for a leader of Free Lances, to live forever in "the joy of battle," and must have felt a little out of his element as the head of the Christian Church. However, he rapidly discovered that he was a secular prince as well as a spiritual teacher, and cast his eyes in the former capacity with ominous ill will on the industrious Republic of Venice. The fishermen and fugitives of many centuries before, who had settled among the Adriatic lagoons, had risen into the position of princes and treasurers of Europe. By their possessions in the East, and their trading-factories established along the whole route from India to the Mediterranean, they had made themselves the intermediaries between the barbaric pearls and gold, the silks and spices, of the Oriental regions, and the requirements of the West. Their galleys were daily bringing them the commodities of the Levant, which they distributed at an exorbitant profit among the nations beyond the Straits of Gibraltar. Mercantile wealth and maritime enterprise elevated the taste and confidence of those Venetian traffickers, till their whole territory, amid the lifeless waters of their canals, was covered with stately palaces, and their fleets assumed the dominion of the inland seas. On the mainland they had stretched their power over Dalmatia and Trieste, and in their own peninsula over Rimini and Ferrara and a great part of the Romagna. Two ruling passions agitated the soul of Julius the Second: one was to recover whatever territory or influence had once belonged to the Holy See; the other was to expel the hated barbarian, whether Frenchman, or Swiss, or Austrian, from the soil of Italy. To achieve this last object he would sacrifice any thing except the first; and to unite the two was difficult. He made his approaches to Venice in a gentle manner at first. He asked her to restore the lands she had lately won, which he claimed as appendages of his chair, because they had been torn unjustly from the original holders by Cæsar Borgia, the son of Alexander the Infamous; and if she had agreed to this he would no doubt have proceeded with his further scheme of banishing all ultramontane invaders. But as the commercial council of the great emporium hesitated at giving up what they had entered in their books as fairly their own, he altered his note in a moment, put on the insignia of his holy office, and, denouncing the astonished republic as rebellious and ungrateful to Mother Church, he called in the aid of the very French whom he was so anxious to get quit of, to execute his judgment upon the offending State. Venice was rich, and France at that time was poor and at all times is greedy. So preparations were made for an assault with the readiness and glee with which a party of freebooters would make a descent on the Bank of England. The temptation also was too great to be resisted by other kings and princes, who were as hungry for spoil and as attached to religion as the French. So in an incredibly short space of time the league of Cambrai was joined by Maximilian, the Emperor of Germany, and Ferdinand of Spain, and dukes and marquesses of less note. There were few of the Southern potentates, indeed, who had not some cause of complaint against the haughty Venetians. A.D. 1508. Some (as the German Maximilian) they had humbled by defeat; others they had insulted by their purse-proud insolence; others, again, by superiority in commercial skill; and all, by the fact of being wealthy and, as they fancied, weak.

Louis the Twelfth of France was first in the field. He conquered at Agnadello, and, forcing his way to the shore, alarmed the marble halls of the Venetians with the sound of his harmless cannonade. The Pope was next, and took possession of the towns he wanted. The Duke of Ferrara laid hold of some loose articles in the confusion, and the Marquis of Mantua got back some villages which his grandfather had lost. Maximilian was disconsolate at not being in time for the general pillage, and had to content himself with Padua and Vicenza and Verona. Maximilian was a gentleman in difficulties, who has the misfortune to be known in history as Max the Penniless. The Venetians sent to tell him they were ready to acknowledge his suzerainty as emperor, and to pay him a tribute of fifty thousand ducats. The man would have forgiven them a hundred times their offences for half the money, and was anxious to close with their offer. But they had made no similar proposition to the French king, nor to Ferdinand, nor even of a ten-pound note to the Mantuan Marquis or the Magnifico of Ferrara. Wherefore they all began to hate the emperor. Louis declined to give him any more assistance. Julius sent a secret message to the Venetians that Holy Church was not inexorable; and Venice, relying on the placability of Rome, hung out her flag against her secular foes in prouder defiance than ever. She knelt at the feet of the Pope, and allowed him to retain his acquisitions in Romagna and elsewhere; and as his first object, the enrichment of his domain, was accomplished, he lost no time in carrying out the second. By the fortunate possession of an unlimited

A.D. 1510. power of loosing mankind from unpleasant oaths and obligations, he astonished his late confederates by publishing a sentence releasing the Venetians from the censures of the Church and the Allies from the covenants of the Treaty of Cambrai. He then joined the pontifical forces to the troops of Venice, and in hot haste made a rush upon the French. He bought over Ferdinand of Spain to the cause by giving him the investiture of Naples, hired a multitude of Swiss mercenaries, and, drawing the sword like a stout man-at-arms as he was, he laid siege to Mirandola. In spite of his great age,—he was now past seventy,—he performed all the offices of an active general, visited the trenches, encouraged his army, and after a two months' bombardment disdained to enter the city by the opened gate, but was triumphantly carried in military pomp through a breach in the shattered wall. His perfidy as a statesman and audacity as a soldier were too much for the

A.D. 1511. Emperor and the King of France. They collected as many troops as they could, and threatened to summon a general council; for what excommunication as an instrument of offence was to the popes, a general council was to the civil power. The French clergy met at Tours, and supported the Crown against Julius. The German emperor was still more indignant. He published a paper of accusations, in which the bitterness of his penniless condition is not concealed. "The enormous sums daily extracted from Germany," he says, "are perverted to the purposes of luxury or worldly views, instead of being employed for the service of God or against the Infidels. So extensive a territory has been alienated for the benefit of the Pope that scarcely a florin of revenue remains to the Emperor in Italy." Louis and the French appeared triumphant in the field; but their triumphs threw them into dismay, for their protean adversary, when defeated as temporal prince, thundered against them as successor of St. Peter, and taught them that their victories were impiety and their acquisitions sacrilege. A hard case for Louis, where if he retreated his territories were seized, and if he advanced his soul was in danger. The war, which had begun as a combination against Venice, was now converted into a holy league in defence of Rome. Spaniards came to the rescue; and Henry, the youthful champion of England, and all who either thought they loved religion or who really hated France, were inspired as if for a crusade. And Maximilian himself, A.D. 1512. poor and friendless,—how was it possible for him to continue obstinately to reject the overtures of the Pope, the purse of the Venetians, or the far more tempting whisperings of Ferdinand of Aragon, who said to him, "Julius is very old. Would it not be possible to win over the cardinals to make your majesty his successor?" Such a golden dream had never suggested itself to the pauperized emperor before. He swallowed the bait at once. He determined to bribe the Sacred College, and, to raise the necessary funds, pawned the archducal mantle of Austria to the rich merchants, the Fuggers of Antwerp, for a large sum, and wrote to his daughter Margaret, "To-morrow I shall send a bishop to the Pope, to conclude an agreement with him that I may be appointed his coadjutor and on his death succeed to the Papacy, that you may be bound to worship me,—

of which I shall be very proud." This may appear a rather jocular announcement of so serious a design; but there is no doubt that the project was entertained. Matters, however, advanced at too rapid a pace for the slow calculations of politicians. The French, by a noble victory at Ravenna, established their fame as warriors, and roused the fear of all the other powers. Maximilian grasped at last the Venetian ducats which had been offered him so long before, and turned suddenly against his ally. Ferdinand and Henry pressed forward on France itself on the side of the Pyrenees. Foot by foot the land of Italy was set free from the French invaders, and Julius the Second, dying before the emperor's plans were matured, left the tangled web of European politics to be unravelled by a younger hand.

We have dwelt on this strange contest, where many sovereign states combined to overthrow a colony of traders, and failed in all their attempts, because it is the last great appearance that Venice has made in the general history of the world. From this time her power rapidly decayed. Her galleys lay rotting at their wharves, and the marriage of her Doge to the Sea was a symbol without a meaning. The discovery of a passage to India by the Cape, which we saw announced to Europe by Vasco da Gama in the last year of the late century, was a sentence of death to the carriers of the Adriatic. Commerce sought other channels and enriched other lands. Wherever the merchant-vessels crowded the harbour, whether with the commodities of the East or West, the war-ship was sure to follow, and the treasures gained in traffic to be guarded by a navy. All the ports of Spain became rallying-places of wealth and power in this century. Portugal covered every sea with her guns and galleons; Holland rose to dignity and freedom by her heavy-armed marine; and England began the career of enterprise and liberty which is still typified and assured by the preponderance of her commercial and royal fleets. Questions are asked—which the younger among us, who may live to see the answer, may amuse themselves by considering—as to the chance of Venice recovering her ancient commerce if the pathway of Eastern trade be again traced down the Mediterranean, when the Isthmus of Suez shall be cut through by a canal or curtailed by a railway. In former times the whole civilized world lay like a golden fringe round the shores of that one sea, and the nation which predominated there, either in wealth or arms, was mistress of the globe. But the case is altered now. If the Gates of Hercules were permanently closed, the commerce of the world would still go on; and, so far from a Mediterranean supremacy indicating a universal pre-eminence, it is perhaps worthy of remark that the only Mediterranean nations which have in later times been recognised as of first-rate rank in Europe have had their principal ports upon the Atlantic and in the Channel.

There is a circumstance which we may observe as characteristic of many of the European states at this time,—the desire of combination and consolidation at home even more than of foreign conquest. In Spain the cessation of the oligarchy of kingships had established a national crown. The hopes of recasting the separated and mutilated limbs of ancient Latium into a gigantic Italy were rife in that sunny land of high resolves and futile acts. In Germany, the official supremacy of the emperor was insufficient to prevent the strong definement of the corporate nationalities. Holland secured its individuality by unheard-of efforts; and in England the great thought took possession of the political mind of a union of the whole island. Visions already floated before the statesmen on both sides of the Tweed of a Great Britain freed from intestine disturbance and guarded by undisputed seas. But the general intelligence was not yet sufficiently far advanced. The Scotch were too Scotch and the English too English to sink their national differences; and we can only pay homage to the wisdom which by a marriage between the royal houses—James the Fourth, and Margaret of England—planted the promise which came afterwards to maturity in the junction of the crowns in 1603, and the indissoluble union of the countries in 1707.

A.D. 1502.

Meantime, the wooing was of the harshest. The last great battle, Flodden, that marked the enmity of the kingdoms, was decided in this century, and has left a deep and sorrowful impression even to our own times. There is not a cottage in Scotland where "The Fight of Flodden" is not remembered yet. And its effects were so desolating and dispiriting that it may be considered the death-bed to the feeling of equality which had hitherto ennobled the weaker nation. From this time England held the position of a virtual superior, regulating her conduct without much regard to the dignity or self-respect of her neighbour, and employing the arts of diplomacy, and the meaner tricks of bribery and corruption, only because they were more easy and less expensive than the open method of invasion and conquest. "Scotland's shield" was indeed broken at Flodden, but her character for courage and honour remained. It was the treachery of Solway Moss, and the venality of most of the surviving nobility, that were the real causes of her weakness, and of the subordinate place which at this time she held in Europe.

Thus the object which in other nations had been

gained by a union of crowns was attained also in our island by the absence of opposition between the peoples. Flodden and Pinkie may therefore be looked upon with kindlier eyes if they are regarded as steps to the formation of so great a realm. No nation retained its feudal organization so long as Scotland, or so completely departed from the original spirit of feudalism. Instead of being leaders and protectors of their dependants, and attached vassals of the kings, the barons of the North were an oligarchy of armed conspirators both against the crown and the people. Few of the earlier Stuarts died in peaceful bed; for even those of them who escaped the dagger of the assassin were hunted to death by the opposition and falsehood of the chiefs. Perpetually engaged in plots against the throne or forays against each other, the Scottish nobility weakened their country both at home and abroad. Law could have no authority where mailed warriors settled every thing by the sword, and no resistance could be offered to a foreign enemy by men so divided among themselves. Down to a period when the other nations of Europe were under the rule of legal tribunals, the High Street of Edinburgh was the scene of violence and bloodshed between rival lords who were too powerful for control by the civil authority. A succession of foolishly rash or unwisely lenient sovereigns left this ferocity and independence unchecked; and though poetry and patriotism now combine to cast a melancholy grace on the defeat at Flodden, from the Roman spirit with which the intelligence was received by the population of the capital, the unbiassed inquirer must confess that, with the exception of the single virtue of personal courage, the Scottish array was ennobled by no quality which would have justified its success. It was ill commanded, ill disciplined, and ill combined. The nobility, as usual, were disaffected to the king and averse to the war. But the crown-tenants and commonalty of the Lowlands were always ready for an affray with England; and James the Fourth, the most chivalrous of that line of chivalrous and unfortunate princes, merrily crossed the Border and prepared for feats of arms as if at a tournament. The cautious Earl of Surrey, the leader of the English army, availed himself of the knightly prepossessions of his enemy, and sent a herald, in all the frippery of tabard and cross, to challenge him to battle on a set day, when Lord Thomas Howard would run a tilt with him at the head of the English van. James fell into the snare, and regulated his movements, in fact, by the direction of his opponent. When, in a momentary glimpse of common sense, he established his quarters on the side of a hill, from which it would have been impossible to dislodge him, Surrey relied on the absurd generosity of his character, and sent a message to complain that he had placed himself on ground "more like a fortress or a camp than an ordinary battle-field." James pretended to despise the taunt, and even to refuse admission to the herald; but it worked on his susceptible and fearless nature; for we find that he allowed the English to pass through difficult and narrow ways, which were commanded by his guns, and when they were fairly marshalled on level ground he set fire to his tents and actually descended the hill to place himself on equal terms with the foe. Such a beginning had the only possible close. Strong arms and sharp swords are excellent supports of generalship, but cannot always be a substitute for it. Never did the love of fight so inherent in the Scottish character display itself more gallantly than on this day. Again and again the Scottish earls dashed forward against the English squares. These were composed of the steadiest of the pikemen,

A.D. 1513.

flanked by the wondrous archers who had turned so many a tide of battle. Fain would the veteran warriors have kept their men in check; fain would the commanders of the French auxiliaries have restrained the Scottish advance. But the Northern blood was up. Onward they went, in spite of generalship and all the rules of discipline, and with a great crash burst upon the wall of steel. It was magnificent, as the Frenchmen said at Balaklava, but it was not war. Repelled by the recoil of their own impetuous charge, they fell into fragments and encumbered the gory plain. Very few fled, very few had the opportunity of flying; for the cloth-yard shaft never missed its aim. There was no crying for quarter or sparing of the flashing blade. Both sides were irritated to madness. James pushed on, shouting and waving his bloody sword, and was wounded by an arrow and gashed with a ponderous battle-axe when he had forced himself within a few paces of Surrey. Darkness was now closing in. The king's death was rapidly known, but still the struggle went on. At length the wearied armies ceased to kill. The Scotch retreated, and in the dawn of the next morning a compact body of them was seen still threatening on the side of a distant hill. But the day was lost and won. The chivalry of Scotland received a blow from which it never recovered. What Courtrai had been to the French, and Granson and Nanci to the Burgundians, and Towton and Tewkesbury to the English, the 9th of September, 1513, was to the peerage of the North. Thirteen earls were killed, fifteen barons, and chiefs and members of all the gentle houses in the land. Some were stripped utterly desolate by this appalling slaughter; and from many a hall, as well as from humble shieling, rose the burden of the tearful ballad, "The flowers o' the forest are a' wedd awa'." There were ten thousand slain in the field, the gallant James cut off in the prime of strength and manhood, and the sceptre which required the grasp of an Edward the First left to be the prize of an unprincipled queen-mother, or any ambitious cabal which could conspire to seize it. James the Fifth was but a year or two old, and the country discouraged and demoralized.

But Henry the Eighth was destined to some other triumphs in this fortunate year. First there was the victory which his forces won at Guinegate, near Calais, where the French chivalry fled in the most ignominious manner, and struck their rowels into their horses' flanks, without remembering that they carried swords in their hands. This is known in history as the second Battle of the Spurs,—not, as at Courtrai, for the number of those knightly emblems taken off the heels of the dead, but for the amazing activity they displayed on the heels of the living. And, secondly, he could boast that the foremost man in Christendom wore his livery and pocketed his pay; for Maximilian the Penniless, successor of Charlemagne and Constantine and Augustus, enlisted and did good service as an English trooper at a hundred crowns a day. Let Henry rejoice in these achievements while he may; for the time is drawing near when the old sovereigns of Europe are to be moved out of the way and France and Spain are to be governed by younger men and more ambitious politicians than himself. Evil times indeed were at hand, when it required the strength of youth and wisdom of policy to guide the bark not only of separate states, but of settled law and Christian civilization. For, however pleasant it may be to trace Henry through his home-career and Francis and Charles in their national rivalries, we are not to forget that the real interest of this century is that it is the century of the Reformation,—a movement before whose overwhelming importance the efforts of the greatest individuals sink into insignificance,—an upheaving of hidden powers and principles, which in truth so altered all former relations between man and man that it found the most influential personage in Europe, not in the Apostolic Emperor, or the Christian King, or the Defender of the Faith, but in a burly friar at Wittenberg, whose name had never been heard before.

Let us see what was the general condition of the Romish Chair before the outburst of its enemies at this time. One thing is very observable: that its claims to supremacy and obedience were, ostensibly at least, almost universally acquiesced in. From Norway to Calabria the theory of a Universal Church, divinely founded and divinely sustained, in possession of superhuman power and uncommunicated knowledge, governed by an infallible chief, and administered by an uninterrupted line of priests and bishops, who had given up the vanities of the world, satisfier of doubts, and sole instrument of salvation,—this seemed so perfect and so natural an organization that it had been accepted from time immemorial as incapable of denial. If a voice was heard here and there in an Alpine valley or in a scholastic debating-room impugning these arrangements or asking proof from history or revelation, the civil power was let loose upon the gainsayer, with the general consent of orthodox men, and the Vaudois were murdered with sword and spear and the inquiring student chained in his monkish cell. The theory and organization of the Universal Church were, in fact, never so well defined as at the moment when its reign was drawing to a close. Nobody doubted that a general Father, clothed in infallible wisdom, and armed with powers directly committed to him for the guidance or punishment of mankind, was the Heaven-sent arbiter of differences, the rewarder of faithful kings, the corrector of unruly nations; and yet the spectacle was presented, to the believers in this ideal, of a series of wicked and abandoned rulers sitting in Peter's chair, and only imitating the apostle in his furiousness and his denial; cardinals depraved and worldly beyond the example of temporal princes; a priesthood steeped, for the most part, in ignorance and vice, and monks and nuns the *opprobria* of all nations where they were found. Never were claims and performances brought into such startling contrast before. The Pope was the representative upon earth of the Saviour of men; and he poisoned his guests, like Borgia, slew his opponents, like Julius, or led the life of an intellectual epicure, like Leo the Tenth. In former times the contrariety between doctrine and practice would have been slightly known or easily reconciled. Few comparatively visited Rome; cardinals were seldom seen; priests were not more ignorant than their parishioners, and monks not more wicked than their admirers. All believed in the miraculous efficacy of the wares in which even the lower order of the clergy dealt, and their rule in country places was so lax, their penances so easily performed or commuted, their relations with their people so friendly and on such equal terms, that in the rural districts the voice of complaint was either unheard or neglected. In Italy, the headquarters of the faith, the excesses of priestly rule were the most glaring and wide-spread. Rome itself was always the seat of turbulence and disaffection. The lives of professedly holy men were known, and the vices of popes and prelates pressed heavily on the people, who were the first victims of their avarice or cruelty. But the utmost extent of their indignation never reached to a questioning of the foundation of the power from which they suffered. An Italian crushed to the earth by the extortion of his Church, irritated perhaps by the personal wickedness of his director, sought no escape from such inflictions in disbelieving either the temporal or spiritual authority of his oppressor. Rather he would have looked with savage satisfaction on the fagot-fire of any one who hinted that the principles of his Church required the slightest amendment; that the absolution of his sensual confessor was not altogether indispensable; that the image he bowed down to was common wood, or that the relics he worshipped were merely dead men's bones. Perhaps, indeed, in those luxurious regions, a bare and unadorned worship would not seem to be worship at all. With his impassioned mind and glowing fancy, the Spaniard or Italian must pour out his whole being on the object of his adoration. He loves his patron saint with the warmth of an earthly affection, and thinks he undervalues her virtues or her claims if he does not heap her shrine with his offerings and address her image with rapture. He must make external demonstration of his inward feelings, or nobody will believe in their existence. The crouchings and kneelings, therefore, which our colder natures stigmatize as idolatry, are to him nothing more than the outward manifestation of affection and thankfulness. He does the same to his master or his benefactor without degradation in the eyes of his countrymen. Without these bowings and genuflections his conduct would be thought ungrateful and disrespectful. That this amount of warm-hearted sincerity is wasted upon such unworthy objects as his saints and relics is greatly to be deplored; but wide allowances must be made for peculiarities of situation and disposition; and we should remember that whereas in the North a religion of forms and ceremonies would be a body without a soul, because there would be no inward exaltation answering to the outward manifestation, the Southern heart sees a meaning where there is none to us, is conscious of a sense of trust and reverence where we only see slavishness and imposture, and a feeling of divine consolation and hope in services which to us are histrionic and absurd. Religious belief, in the sense of a true and undivided faith in the doctrines of Christianity, had no recognised existence at the period we have reached. But this absence of religious belief was combined, however strange the statement may appear, with a most implicit trust in the directions and authority of the Church. Sunny skies might have shone forever over the political abasement and slightly Christianized paganism of the inhabitants of the two peninsulas and the Southeast of Europe, but a cloud was about to rise in the North which dimmed them for a time, but which, after it burst in purifying thunder, has refreshed and cleared the atmosphere of the whole world.

The first book that Guttenberg published in 1451 was the Holy Bible,—in the Latin language, to be sure, and after the Vulgate edition, but still containing, to those who could gather it, the manna of the Word. Two years after that, in 1453, the capture of Constantinople by the Turks had scattered the learning of the Greeks among all the nations of the West. The universities were soon supplied with professors, who displayed the hitherto-unexplored treasures of the language of Pericles and Demosthenes. Everywhere a spirit of inquiry began to reawaken, but limited as yet to subjects of philosophy and antiquity. Christianity, indeed, had so lost its hold on the minds of scholars that it was not considered worth inquiring into. It was looked on as a fable, and only profitable as an instrument of policy. Erasmus was alarmed at the state of feeling in 1516, and expressed his belief that, if those Grecian studies were pursued, the ancient deities would resume their sway. But the Bible was already reaping its appointed harvest. Its voice, lost in the din of speculative philosophies and the dissipation of courts, was heard in obscure places, where it never had penetrated before. In 1505, Luther was twenty-two years of age. He had made himself a scholar by attendance at schools where his poverty almost debarred him from appearing. At Eisenach he gained his bread by singing at the richer inhabitants' doors. Afterwards he had gone to Erfurt, and, tired or afraid of the world, anxious for opportunities of self-examination, and dissatisfied with his spiritual state, he entered the convent of the Augustines, and in two years more, in 1507, became priest and monk. There was an amazing amount of goodness and simplicity of life among the brotherhood of this community. Learning and devout meditation were encouraged, holy ascetic lives were led, the body was kept under with fastings and stripes. A Bible was open to them all, but chained to its place in the chapel, and only to be studied by standing before the desk on which it lay. All these things were insufficient, and Brother Martin was miserable. His companions pitied and respected him. Staupitz, a man of great rank in the Church, a sort of inspector-general of a large district, visited the convent, and in a moment was attracted by the youthful monk. He conversed with him, soothed his agitated mind, not with anodynes from the pharmacopœia of the Church, but from the fountain-head of the faith. He painted God as the forgiver of sinners, the Father of all men; and Luther took some comfort. But, on going away, the kind-hearted Staupitz gave the young man a Bible, —a Bible all to himself, his own property, to carry in his bosom, to study in his cell. His vocation was at once fixed. The Reformer felt his future all before him, like Achilles when he grasped the sword and rejected the feminine toys. The books he had taken with him into the monastery were Plautus and Virgil; but he studied plays and epics no more. Augustin and the Bible supplied their place. Hungering for better things than the works of the law,—abstinence, prayer-repetitions, scourgings, and all the wearisome routine of mechanical devotion,—he dashed boldly into the other extreme, and preached free grace,—grace without merit, the great doctrine which is called, theologically, "justification by faith alone." This had been the main theme of his master Augustin, and Luther now gave it practical shape. In 1510 he was sent on some business of his convent to Rome,—to Rome, the head-quarters of the Church, the earthly residence of the infallible! How holy will be its dwellings, how gracious the words of its inhabitants! The German monk saw nothing but sin and infidelity. In high places as in low, the taint of corruption was polluting all the air. In terror and dismay, he left the city of iniquity within a fortnight of his arrival, and hurried back to the peacefulness of his convent. "I would not for a hundred thousand florins have missed seeing Rome," he said, long afterwards. "I should always have felt an uneasy doubt whether I was not, after all, doing injustice to the Pope. As it is, I am quite satisfied on the point." The Pope was Julius the Second, whose career we followed in the League of Cambrai; and we may enter into the surprise of Luther at seeing the Father of the Faithful breathing blood and ruin to his rival neighbours. But the force of early education was still unimpaired. The Pope was Pope, and the devout German thought of him on his knees. But in the year 1517 a man of the name of Tetzel, a Dominican of the rudest manners and most brazen audacity, appeared in the market-place of Wittenberg, ringing a bell, and hawking indulgences from the Holy See to be sold to all the faithful. A new Pope was on the throne,—the voluptuous Leo the Tenth. He had resolved to carry on the building of the great Church of St. Peter, and, having exhausted his funds in riotous living, he sent round his emissaries to collect fresh treasures by the sale of these pardons for human sin. "Pour in your money," cried Tetzel, "and whatever crimes you have committed, or may commit, are forgiven! Pour in your coin, and the souls of your friends and relations will fly out of purgatory the moment they hear the chink of your dollars at the bottom of the box." Luther was Doctor of Divinity, Professor in the University, and pastoral visitor of two provinces of the empire. He felt it was his duty to interfere. He learned for the first time himself how far indulgences were supposed to go, and shuddered at the profanity of the notion of their being of any value whatever. On the festival of All Saints, in November, 1517, he read a series of propositions against them in the great church, and startled all Germany like a thunderbolt with a printed sermon on the same subject. The press began its work, and people no longer fought in darkness. Nationalities were at an end when so wide-embracing a subject was treated by so universal an agent. The monk's voice was heard in all lands, even in the walls of Rome, and crossed the sea, and came in due time to England. "Tush, tush! 'tis a quarrel of monks," said Leo the Tenth; and, with an affectation of candour, he remarked, "This Luther writes well: he is a man of fine genius."

Gallant young Henry the Eighth thought it a good opportunity to show his talent, and meditated an assault on the heretic,—a curious duel between a pale recluse and the gayest prince in Christendom. But the recluse was none the worse when the book was published, and the prince earned from the gratitude of the Pope the name "Defender of the Faith," which is still one of the titles of the English crown. Penniless Maximilian looked on well pleased, and wrote to a Saxon counsellor, "All the popes I have had any thing to do with have been rogues and cheats. The game with the priests is beginning. What your monk is doing is not to be despised: take care of him. It may happen that we shall have need of him." Luther's own prince, the Elector of Saxony, was his firm friend, and on one side or other all Europe was on the gaze. Leo at last perceived the danger, and summoned the monk to Rome. He might as well have yielded in the struggle at once, for from Rome he never could have returned alive. He consented, however, to appear before the Legate at Augsburg, attended by a strong body-guard furnished by the Elector, and held his ground against the threats and promises of the Cardinal of Cajeta. But Maximilian carried his poverty and disappointment to the grave in 1519; and when Leo saw the safe accession of his successor Charles the Fifth, the faithful servant of St. Peter, he pushed matters with a higher hand against the daring innovator. Brother Martin, however, was unmoved. He would not retreat; he even advanced in his course, and wrote to the Pope himself an account of the iniquities of Rome. "You have three or four cardinals," he says, "of learning and faith; but what are these three or four in so vast a crowd of infidels and reprobates? The days of Rome are numbered, and the anger of God has been breathed forth upon her. She hates councils, she dreads reforms, and will not hear of a check being placed on her desperate impiety." This was a dangerous man to meet with such devices as

bulls and interdicts. Charles determined to try harsher measures, and summoned him to appear at a Diet of the States held in Worms. The emperor was now twenty-one years old. His sceptre stretched over the half of Europe, and across the great sea to the golden realm of Mexico. Martin begged a new gown from the not very lavish Elector, and went in a sort of chariot to the appointed city,—serene and confident, for he had a safe-conduct from the emperor and various princes, and trusted in the goodness of his cause. Such
A.D. 1521.
a scene never occurred in any age of the world as was presented when the assemblage met. All the peers and potentates of the German Empire, presided over by the most powerful ruler that ever had been known in Europe, were gathered to hear the trial and condemnation of a thin, wan-visaged young man, dressed in a monk's gown and hood and worn with the fatigues and hazards of his recent life. "Yet prophet-like that lone one stood, with dauntless words and high," and answered all questions with force and modesty. But answers were not what the Diet required, and retractation was far from Luther's mind. So the Chancellor of Treves came to him and said, "Martin, thou art disobedient to his Imperial Majesty: wherefore depart hence under the safe-conduct he has given thee." And the monk departed. As he was nearing his destination, and was passing through a wood alone, some horsemen seized his person, dressed him in military garb, and put on him a false beard. They then mounted him on a led horse and rode rapidly away. His friends were anxious about his fate, for a dreadful sentence had been uttered against him by the emperor on the day when his safe-conduct expired, forbidding any one to sustain or shelter him, and ordering all persons to arrest and bring him into prison to await the judgment he deserved.

People thought he had been waylaid and killed, or at all events sent into a dungeon. Meantime he was living peaceably and comfortably in the castle of Wartburg, to which he had been conveyed in this mysterious manner by his friend the Elector,—safe from the machinations of his enemies, and busily engaged in his immortal translation of the Bible.

The movement thus communicated by Luther knew no pause nor end. It soon ceased to be a merely national excitement caused by local circumstances, and became the one great overwhelming question of the time. Every thing was brought into its vortex: however distant might be its starting-point, to this great central idea it was sure to attach itself at last. Involuntarily, unconsciously, unwillingly, every government found that the Reformation formed part of its scheme and policy. One nation, and one only, had the clear eye and firm hand to make it ostensibly, and of its deliberate choice, the guide and landmark in its dangerous and finally triumphant career. This was England,—not when under the degrading domination of its Henry or the heavy hand of its Mary, but under the skilful piloting of the great Elizabeth, the first of rulers who seems to have perceived that submission to a foreign priest is a political error on the part both of kings and subjects, and that occupation by a foreign army is not more subversive of freedom and independence than the supremacy of a foreign Church. Hitherto England had been nearly divided from the whole world, and was merely one of the distant satellites that revolved on the outside of the European system, the centre of which was Rome. She was now to burn with light of her own. The Continent, indeed, at the commencement of the Reformation, seemed almost in a state of dissolution. In 1529 disunion had attained such a pitch in the

Empire that the different princes were ranged on hostile sides. At the Diet of Spires, in this year, the name of Protestant had been assumed by the opponents of the excesses and errors of the Church of Rome. At the same time that the religious unity was thus finally thrown off, the Turks were thundering at the Eastern gates of Europe, and Solyman of Constantinople laid siege to Vienna. France was exhausted with her internal troubles. Spain came to the rescue of the outraged faith, and made heresy punishable with death throughout all her dominions. While the Netherlands, against which this was directed, was groaning under this new infliction, disorder seemed to extend over the solid earth itself. There were earthquakes and great storms in many lands. Lisbon was shaken into ruins, with a loss of thirty thousand inhabitants; and the dykes of Holland were overwhelmed by a prodigious rising of the sea, and four hundred thousand people were drowned.

Preparations were made in all quarters for a great and momentous struggle: nobody could tell where it would break forth or where it would end. And ever and anon Luther's rallying-cry was heard in answer to the furious denunciations of cardinals and popes. Interests get parcelled out in so many separate portions that it is impossible to unravel the state of affairs with any clearness. We shall only notice that, in 1531, the famous league of Smalcalde first embodied Protestantism in its national and lay constitution by the banding together of nine of the sovereign princes of Germany, and eleven free cities, in armed defence, if needed, of their religious belief. Where is the fiery Henry of England, with his pen or sword? A very changed man from what we saw him only thirteen years ago. He has no pen now, and his sword is kept for his discontented subjects at home. In 1534, King and Lords and Commons, in Parliament assembled, threw off the supremacy of Rome, and Henry is at last a king, for his courts hold cognizance of all causes within the realm, whether ecclesiastical or civil. Everybody knows the steps by which this embodied selfishness achieved his emancipation from a dominant Church. It little concerns us now, except as a question of historic curiosity, what his motives were. Judging from the analogy of all his other actions, we should say they were bad; but by some means or other the evil deeds of this man were generally productive of benefit to his country. He cast off the Pope that he might be freed from a disagreeable wife; but as the Pope whom he rejected was the servant of Charles, (the nephew of the repudiated queen,) he found that he had freed his kingdom at the same time from its degrading vassalage to the puppet of a rival monarch. He dissolved the monasteries in England for the purpose of grasping their wealth; but the country found he had at the same time delivered it from a swarm of idle and mischievous corporations, which in no long time would have swallowed up the land. Their revenues were immense, and the extent of their domains almost incredible. Before people had recovered from their disgust at the hateful motives of their tyrant's behaviour, the results of it became apparent in the elevation of the finest class of the English population; for the "bold peasantry, their country's pride," began to establish their independent holdings on the parcelled-out territories of the monks and nuns. Vast tracts of ground were thrown open to the competition of lay proprietors. Even the poorest was not without hope of becoming an owner of the soil; nay, the released estates were so plentiful that in Elizabeth's reign an act was passed making it illegal for a man to build a cottage "unless he laid four acres of land thereto." The cottager, therefore, became a small farmer; and small farmers were the defence of England; and the defence of England was the safety of freedom and religion throughout the world. There were some hundred thousands of those landed cottagers and smaller gentry and great proprietors established by this most respectable sacrilege of Henry the Eighth, and for the sake of these excellent consequences we forgive him his pride and cruelty and all his faults. But Henry's work was done, and in January, 1547, he died. The rivals with whom he started on the race of life were still alive; but life was getting dark and dreary with both of them. Francis was no longer the hero of "The Field of the Cloth-of-Gold," conqueror of Marignano, the gallant captive of Pavia, or the winner of all hearts. He was worn out with a life of great vicissitudes, and heard with ominous foreboding the news of Henry's death. A fate seemed to unite them in all those years of revelry and hate and friendship, and in a few weeks the most chivalrous and generous of the Valois followed the most tyrannical of the Tudors to the tomb. A year before this, the Monk of Wittenberg, now the renowned and married Dr. Martin Luther, had left a place vacant which no man could fill; and now of all those combatants Charles was the sole survivor. Selfish as Henry, dissolute as Francis, obstinate as Martin, his race also was drawing to a close. But the play was played out before these chief performers withdrew All Europe had changed its aspect. The England, the France, the Empire, of five-and-twenty years before had utterly passed away. New objects were filling men's minds, new principles of policy were regulating states. Protestantism was an established fact, and the Treaty of Passau in 1552 gave liberty and equality to

March 11, 1547.

the professors of the new faith. Charles was sagacious though heartless as a ruler, but an unredeemed bigot as an individual man. The necessities of his condition, by which he was forced to give toleration to the enemies of the Church, weighed upon his heart. A younger hand and bloodier disposition, he thought, were needed to regain the ground he had been obliged to yield; and in Philip his son he perceived all these requirements fulfilled. When he looked round, he saw nothing to give him comfort in his declining years. War was going on in Hungary against the still advancing Turks; war was raging in Lorraine between his forces and the French; Italy, the land of volcanoes, was on the eve of outbreak and anarchy; and, thundering out defiance of the Imperial power and the Christian Cross, the guns of the Ottoman fleet were heard around the shores of Sicily and up to the Bay of Naples. The emperor was faint and weary: his armies were scattered and dispirited; his fleets were unequal to their enemy: so in 1556 he resigned his pompous title of monarch of Spain and the Indies, with all their dependencies, to his son, and the empire to his brother Ferdinand, who was already King of Hungary and Bohemia and hereditary Duke of Austria; and then, with the appearance of resignation, but his soul embittered by anger and disappointment, he retired to the Convent of St. Just, where he gorged himself into insanity with gluttonies which would have disgraced Vitellius, and amused himself by interfering in state affairs which he had forsworn, and making watches which he could not regulate, and going through the revolting farce of a rehearsal of his funeral, with his body in the coffin and the monks of the monastery for mourners. Those theatrical lamentations were probably as sincere as those which followed his real demise in 1558; for when he surrendered the power which made him respected he gave evidence only of the qualities which made him disliked.

The Reformation, you remember, is the characteristic of this century. We have traced it in Germany to its recognition as a separate and liberated faith. In England we are going to see Protestantism established and triumphant. But not yet; for we have first to notice a period when Protestantism seems at its last hour, when Mary, wife of the bigot Philip, and true and honourable daughter of the Church, is determined to restore her nation to the Romish chair, or die in the holy attempt. We are not going into the minutiæ of this dreadful time, or to excite your feelings with the accounts of the burnings and torturings of the dissenters from the queen's belief. None of us are ignorant of the cruelty of those proceedings, or have read unmoved the sad recital of the martyrdom of the bishops and of such men as the joyous and innocent Rowland Taylor of Hadleigh. Men's hearts did not become hardened by these sights. Rather they melted with compassion towards the dauntless sufferers; and, though the hush of terror kept the masses of the people silent, great thoughts were rising in the general mind, and toleration ripened even under the heat of the Smithfield fires. Attempts have been made to blacken Mary beyond her demerits and to whiten her beyond her deservings. Protestants have denied her the virtues she unquestionably possessed,—truthfulness, firmness, conscientiousness, and unimpeachable morals. Her panegyrists take higher ground, and claim for her the noblest qualifications both as queen and woman,—patriotism, love of her people, fulfilment of all her duties, and exquisite tenderness of disposition. It will be sufficient for us to look at her actions, and we will leave her secret sentiments alone. We shall only say that it is very doubtful whether the plea of conscientiousness is admissible in such a case. If perverted reasoning or previous education has made a Thug feel it a point of conscience to put his throttling instrument under a quiet traveller's throat, the conscientious belief of the performer that his act is for the good of the sufferer's soul will scarcely save him from the gallows. On the contrary, a conscientious persistence in what is manifestly wrong should be an aggravation of the crime, for it gives an appearance of respectability to atrocity, and, when punishment overtakes the wrong-doers, makes the Thug an honoured martyr to his opinions, instead of a convicted felon for his misdeeds. Let us hope that the rights of conscience will never be pleaded in defence of cruelty or persecution.

The restoration of England to the obedience of the Church, the marriage of Mary, the warmest partisan of Popery, with Philip, the fanatical oppressor of
A.D. 1554. the reformed,—these must have raised the hopes of Rome to an extraordinary pitch. But greater as a support, and more reliable than queens or kings, was the Society of the Jesuits, which at this time demonstrated its attachment to the Holy See, and devoted itself blindly, remorselessly, unquestioning, to the defence of the old faith. Having sketched the rise of Luther, a companion-picture is required of the fortunes of Ignatius Loyola. We hinted that a Biscayan soldier, wounded at the siege of Pampeluna in Spain, divided the notice of Europe with the poor Austin Friar of Wittenberg. Enthusiasm, rising almost into madness, was no bar, in the case of this wonderful Spaniard, to the possession of faculties for government and organization which have never been surpassed. Shut out by the lameness resulting from his wound from the struggles of worldly and soldierly ambition, he gave full way to the mystic exaltation of his Southern disposition. He

devoted himself as knight and champion to the Virgin, heard with contempt and horror of the efforts made to deny the omnipotence of the Chair of Rome, and swore to be its defender. Others of similar sentiments joined him in his crusade against innovation. A company of self-denying, self-sacrificing men began, and, adding to the previous laws of their order a vow of unqualified submission to the Pope, they were recognised by a bull,
A.D. 1540. and the Society of Jesus became the strongest and most remarkable institution of modern times. Through all varieties of fortune, in exile and imprisonment, and even in dissolution, their oath of uninquiring, unhesitating obedience to the papal command has never been broken. With Protean variety of appearance, but unvarying identity of intention, these soldiers of St. Peter are as relentless to others, and as regardless of themselves, as the body-guard of the old Assassins. No degradation is too servile, no place too distant, no action too revolting, for these unreasoning instruments of power. Wilfully surrendering the right of judgment and the feelings of conscience into the hands of their superior, there is no method by law or argument of regulating their conduct. The one principle of submission has swallowed up all the rest, and fulfilment of that duty ennobles the iniquitous deeds by which it is shown. Other societies put a clause, either by words or implication, in their promise of obedience, limiting it to things which are just and proper. This limit is ostentatiously abrogated by the followers of Loyola. The merit of obeying an order to slay an enemy of the Church more than compensates for the guilt of the murder. In other orders a homicide is looked upon with horror; in this, a Jesuit who kills a heretical king by command of his chiefs is venerated as a saint. Against practices and feelings like these you

can neither reason nor be on your guard. In all kingdoms, accordingly, at some time or other, the existence of the order has been found inconsistent with the safety of the State, and it has been dissolved by the civil power. The moment, however, the Church regains its hold, the Jesuits are sure to be restored. The alliance, indeed, is indispensable, and the mutual aid of the Order and of the Papacy a necessity of their existence. Incorporated in 1540, the brothers of the Company of Jesus considered the defections of the Reformation in a fair way of being compensated when the death of our little, cold-hearted, self-willed Edward the Sixth—a Henry the Eighth in the bud—left the throne in 1553 to Mary, a Henry the Eighth full blown. When nearly five years of conscientious truculence had shown the earnestness of this unhappy woman's belief, the accession

A.D. 1558.

of Elizabeth inaugurated a new system in this country, from which it has never departed since without a perceptible loss both of happiness and power. A strictly home and national policy was immediately established by this most remarkable of our sovereigns, and pursued through good report and evil report, sometimes at the expense of her feelings—if she was so little of a Tudor as to have any—of tenderness and compassion, sometimes at the expense—and here she was Tudor enough to have very acute sensations indeed—of her personal and official dignity, but always with the one object of establishing a great united and irresistible bulwark against foreign oppression and domestic disunion. It shows how powerful was her impression upon the course of European history, that her character is as fiercely canvassed at this day as in the speech of her contemporaries. Nobody feels as if Elizabeth was a personage removed from us by three hundred years We discuss her actions, and even argue about her looks and manners, as if she had lived in our own time. And this is the reason why such divergent judgments are pronounced on a person who, more than any other ruler, united the opinions of her subjects during the whole of her long and agitated life. Her acts remain, but her judges are different. If we could throw ourselves with the reality of circumstance as well as the vividness of feeling into the period in which she moved and governed, we should come to truer decisions on the points submitted to our view. But if we look with the refinements of the present time, and the speculative niceties permissible in questions which have no direct bearing on our prosperity and safety, we shall see much to disapprove of, which escaped the notice, or even excited the admiration, of the people who saw what tremendous arbitraments were on the scale. If we were told that a cold-blooded individual had placed on one occasion some murderous weapons on a height, and then requested a number of his friends to stand before them, while some unsuspecting persons came up in that direction, and then, suddenly telling his companions to stand on one side, had sent bullets hissing and crashing through the gentlemen advancing to him, you would shudder with disgust at such atrocious cruelty, till you were told that the cold-blooded individual was the Duke of Wellington, and the advancing gentlemen the French Old Guard at Waterloo. And in the same way, if we read of Elizabeth interfering in Scotland, domineering at home, and bellicose abroad, let us inquire, before we condemn, whether she was in her duty during those operations,—whether, in fact, she was resisting an assault, or capriciously and unjustifiably opening her batteries on the innocent and unprepared. Fiery-hearted, strong-handed Scotchmen are ready to fight at this time for the immaculate purity and sinless martyrdom of their beautiful Mary, and sturdy Englishmen start up with as bold a countenance in defence of good Queen Bess. It is not to be doubted that a roll-call as numerous as that of Bannockburn or Flodden could be mustered on this quarrel of three centuries ago; but the fight is needless. The points of view are so different that a verdict can never be given on the merits of the two personages principally engaged; but we think an unprejudiced examination of the course of Elizabeth's policy in Scotland, and her treatment of her rival, will establish certain facts which neither party can gainsay.

1st. From this it will result, that, to keep reformed England secure, it was indispensable to have reformed Scotland on her side.

2d. That, in order to have Scotland either reformed or on her side, it was indispensable to render powerless a popish queen,—a queen who was supported as legitimate inheritor of England by the Pope and Philip of Spain, and the King and princes of France.

3d. That Elizabeth had a right, by all the laws of self-preservation, to sustain by every legal and peaceable means that party in Scotland which was *de facto* the government of the country, and which promised to be most useful to the objects she had in view. Those objects have already been named,—peace and security for the Protestant religion, and the honour and independence of the whole British realm.

To gain these ends, who denies that she bribed and bullied and deceived?—that she degraded the Scottish nobles by alternate promises and threats, and weakened the Scottish crown by encouraging its enemies, both ecclesiastical and civil? In prudishly finding fault with these proceedings, we forget the Scotch, French, Spanish, popish, emissaries who were let loose upon England; the plots at home, the scowling messages from abroad; the excommunications uttered from Rome; the massacre of the Protestants gloried in in France, and the vast navies and immense armies gathering against the devoted Isle from all the coasts and provinces of Spain.

In 1568, after the defeat of the queen's party at Langside, Mary threw herself on the pity and protection of Elizabeth, and was kept in honourable safety for many years. She did not allow her to collect partisans for the recovery of her kingdom, nor to cabal against the government which had expelled her. To do so would not have been to shelter a fugitive, but to declare war on Scotland. In 1848, Louis Philippe, chased by the revolutionists of Paris, came over to England. He was kept in honourable retirement. He was not allowed to cabal against his former subjects, nor to threaten their policy. To do so would not have been to shelter a fugitive, but to declare war on France. Even in the case of the earlier Bourbons, we permitted no gatherings of forces on their behalf, and did not encourage their followers to molest the settled government,—no, not when the throne of France was filled by an enemy and we were at deadly war with Napoleon. But Mary was put to death. A sad story, and very melancholy to read in quiet drawing-rooms with Britannia ruling the waves and keeping all danger from our coasts. But in 1804, if Louis the Eighteenth or Charles the Tenth, instead of eating the bread of charity in peace, had been detected in conspiracy with our enemies, in corresponding with foreign emissaries, when a thousand flat-bottomed boats were marshalling for our invasion at Boulogne, and Brest and Cherbourg and Toulon were crowded with ships and sailors to protect the flotilla, it needs no great knowledge of character to pronounce that English William Pitt and Scottish Harry Dundas would have had the royal Bourbon's head on a block, or his body on Tyburn-tree, in spite of all the romance and eloquence in the world.

Mary's guilt or innocence of the charges brought against her in her relations with Darnley and Bothwell has nothing to do with the treatment she received from Elizabeth. She was not amenable to English law for any thing she did in Scotland, nor was she condemned for any thing but treasonable practices which it was impossible to deny. She certainly owed submission and allegiance to the English crown while she lived under its protection. Let us indulge our chivalrous generosity, and enjoy delightful poems in defence of an unfortunate and beautiful sovereign, by believing that the blots upon her fame were the aspersions of malignity and political baseness: the great fact remains, that it was an indispensable incident to the security of both the kingdoms that she should be deprived of authority, and finally, as the storm darkened, and derived all its perils from her conspiracies against the State and breaches of the law, that she should be deprived of life. Far more sweeping measures were pursued and defended by the enemies of Elizabeth abroad. Present forever, like a skeleton at a feast, must have been the massacre of St. Bartholomew in the thoughts of every Protestant in Europe, and most vividly of all in those of the English queen. That great blow was meant to be a warning to heretics wherever they were found, and in olden times and more revengeful dispositions might have been an excuse for similar atrocity on the other side. The Bartholomew massacre and the Armada are the two great features of the latter part of this century; and they are both so well known that it will be sufficient to recall them in a very few words.

This massacre was no chance-sprung event, like an ordinary popular rising, but had been matured for many years. The Council of Trent, which met in 1545 and continued its sittings till 1563, had devoted those eighteen years to codifying the laws of the Catholic Church. A definite, clear, consistent system was established, and acknowledged as the religious and ecclesiastical faith of Christendom. Men were not now left to a painful gathering of the sentiments and rescripts of popes and doctors out of varying and scattered writings. Here were the statutes at large, minutely indexed and easy of reference. From these many texts could be gathered which justified any method of diffusing the true belief or exterminating the false. And accordingly, a short time after the close of the Council, an interview took place between two personages, of very sinister augury for the Protestant cause. Catherine de Medicis and the Duke of Alva met at Bayonne in 1565. In this consultation great things were discussed; and it was decided by the wickedest woman and harshest man in Europe that government could not be safe nor religion honoured unless by the introduction of the Inquisition and a general massacre of heretics in every land. A few months later saw the ferocious Alva beginning his bloodthirsty career in the Netherlands, in which he boasted he had put eighteen thousand Hollanders to death on the scaffold in five years. Catherine also pondered his lessons in her heart, and when seven years had passed, and the Huguenots were still unsubdued, she persuaded her son Charles the Ninth that the time was come to establish his kingdom in righteousness by the indiscriminate murder of all the Protestants. An occasion was found in 1572, when the marriage of Henry of Navarre, afterwards the best-loved king of France, with the Princess Margaret de Valois, held out a prospect of soothing the religious troubles, and also (which suited her designs better) of attracting all the heads of the Huguenot cause to Paris. Every thing turned out as she hoped. There had been feasts and gayeties, and suspicion had been thoroughly disarmed. Suddenly the tocsin was sounded, and the murderers let loose over all the town. No plea was received in extenuation of the deadly crime of favouring the new opinions. Hospitality, friendship, relationship, youth, sex, all were disregarded. The streets were red with blood, and the river choked with mutilated bodies. Upwards of seventy thousand were butchered in Paris alone, and the metropolitan example was followed in other places. The deed was so awful that for a while it silenced the whole of Europe. Some doubted, some shuddered; but Rome sprang up with a shout of joy when the news was confirmed, and uttered prayers of thanksgiving for so great a victory. If it could have been possible to put every gainsayer to death everywhere, the triumph would have been complete; but there were countries where Catherine's dagger could not reach; and whenever her name was heard, and the terrible details of the massacre were known, undying hatred of the Church which encouraged such iniquity mingled with the feelings of pity and alarm. For no one henceforth could feel safe. The Huguenots were under the highest protection known to the heart of man. They were guests, and they were taken unawares in the midst of the rejoicings of a marriage. Rome lost more by the massacre than the Protestants. People looked round and saw the butcheries in the Netherlands, the slaughters in Paris, the tortures in the Inquisition, and over all, rioting in hopes of recovered dominion, supported by his priests and Dominicans, a Pope who plainly threatened a repetition of such scenes wherever his power was acknowledged. Germany, the Netherlands, England, Scotland, and the Northern nations, were lost to the Church of Rome more surely by the scaffold and crimes which professed to bring her aid, than by any other cause. Elizabeth was now the accepted champion and leader of the Protestants, and on her all the malice of the baffled Romanists was turned. To weaken, to dethrone or murder the English heretic was the praiseworthiest of deeds.

But one great means of distracting England from her onward course was now removed. In former days Scotland would have been let loose upon her unguarded flanks; but by this time the genius of Knox, running parallel with the efforts of the Southern reformers, had raised a religious feeling which responded to the English call. Scotland, freed from an oppressive priesthood, did manful battle at the side of her former enemy. Elizabeth was kept safe by the joint hatred the nations entertained to Rome, and, as regarded foreigners, the Union had already taken place. On one sure ground, however, those foreigners could still build their hopes. Mary, conscientious in her religion, and embittered in her dislike, was still alive, to be the rallying-point for every discontented cry and to represent the old causes,—the legitimate descent and the true faith. The greatest circumspection would have been required to keep her conduct from suspicion in these embarrassing circumstances. But she was still as thoughtless as in her happier days, and exposed herself to legal inquiries by the unguardedness of her behaviour. The wise counsellors of Elizabeth saw but one way to put an end to all those fears and expectations; and Mary, after due trial,
A.D. 1587. was condemned and executed. Hope was now at an end; but revenge remained, and the great Colossus of the Papacy bestirred himself to punish the sacrilegious usurper. Philip the Second was still the most Catholic of kings. More stern and bigoted than when he had tried to restrain the burning zeal of Mary

of England, he was resolved to restore by force a revolted people to the Chair of St. Peter and exact vengeance for the slights and scorns which had rankled in his heart from the date of his ill-omened visit. He prepared all his forces for the glorious attempt. Nothing could have been devised more calculated to bring all English hearts more closely to their queen. Every report of a fresh squadron joining the fleets already assembled for the invasion called forth more zeal in behalf of the reformed Church and the undaunted Elizabeth. Scotland also held some vessels ready to assist her sister in this great extremity, and lined her shores with Presbyterian spearmen. Community of danger showed more clearly than ever that safety lay in combination. Chains, we know, were brought over in those missionary galleys, and all the apparatus of torture, with smiths to set them to work. But the smiths and the chains never made good their landing on British ground. The ships covered all the narrow sea; but the wind blew, and they were scattered. It was perhaps better, as a warning and a lesson, that the principal cause of the Spaniard's disaster was a storm. If it had been fairly inflicted on them in open battle, the superior seamanship or numbers or discipline of the enemy might have been pleaded. But there must have mingled something more depressing than the mere sorrow of defeat when Philip received his discomfited admiral with the words, "We cannot blame you for what has happened: we cannot struggle against the will of God."

SEVENTEENTH CENTURY.

Kings of France.

A.D.

HENRY IV.—(*cont.*)

1610. LOUIS XIII.

1643. LOUIS XIV.

Emperors of Germany.

RODOLPH II.—(*cont.*)

1612. MATTHIAS.

1619. FERDINAND II.

1637. FERDINAND III.

1658. LEOPOLD I.

Kings of England and Scotland.

A.D.

ELIZABETH.—(*cont.*)

(*House of Stuart.*)

1603. JAMES I.

1625. CHARLES I.

1649. Commonwealth.

1660. CHARLES II.

1685. JAMES II.

1689. WILLIAM III. and MARY.

Kings of Spain.

PHILIP III.—(*cont.*)

1621. PHILIP IV.

1665. CHARLES II.

Distinguished Men.

BACON, MILTON, LOCKE, CORNEILLE, RACINE, MOLIERE, KEPLER, (1571–1630,) BOYLE, (1627–1691,) BOSSUET, (1627–1704,) NEWTON, (1642–1727,) BURNET, (1643–1715,) BAYLE, (1647–1706,) CONDÉ, TURENNE, (1611–1675,) MARLBOROUGH, (1650–1722.)

THE SEVENTEENTH CENTURY.

ENGLISH REBELLION AND REVOLUTION—DESPOTISM OF LOUIS THE FOURTEENTH.

We are apt to suppose that progress and innovation are so peculiarly the features of these latter times that it is only in them that a man of more than ordinary length of life has witnessed any remarkable change. We meet with men still alive who were acquainted with Franklin and Voltaire, who have been presented at the court of Louis the Sixteenth and have visited President Pierce at the White House. But the period we have now to examine is quite as varied in the contrasts presented by the duration of a lifetime as in any other age of the world. Of this we shall take a French chronicler as an example,—a man who was as greedy of news, and as garrulous in relating it, as Froissart himself, but who must take a very inferior rank to that prose minstrel of "gentle blood," as he limited his researches principally to the scandals which characterized his time. We mean the truth-speaking libeller Brantôme. This
A.D. 1616. man died within a year or two of Shakspeare, and yet had accompanied Mary to Scotland, and given that poetical account of the voyage from Calais, when she sat in the stern of the vessel with her eyes fixed on the receding shore, and said, "Adieu, France, adieu! I shall never see you more;" and again, on the following morning, bending her looks across the water when land was no longer to be seen, and exclaiming, "Adieu, France! I shall never see you more." The

mere comparison of these two things—the return of Mary to her native kingdom, torn at that time with all the struggles of anarchy and distress, and the death of the greatest of earth's poets, rich and honoured, in his well-built house at Stratford-on-Avon—suggests a strange contrast between the beginning of Brantôme's literary career and its close: the events filling up the interval are like the scarcely-discernible heavings in a dark and tumultuous sea,—a storm perpetually raging, and waves breaking upon every shore. In his own country, cruelty and demoralization had infected all orders in the State, till murder, and the wildest profligacy of manners, were looked on without a shudder. Brantôme attended the scanty and unregretted funeral of Henry the Third, the last of the house of Valois, who was stabbed by the monk Jacques Clement for faltering in his allegiance to the Church. A sentence had been pronounced at Rome against the miserable king, and the fanatic's dagger was ready. Sixtus the Fifth, in full consistory, declared that the regicide was "comparable, as regards the salvation of the world, to the incarnation and the resurrection, and that the courage of the youthful Jacobin surpassed that of Eleazar and Judith." "That Pope," says Chateaubriand, the Catholic historian of France, "had too little political conviction, and too much genius, to be sincere in these sacrilegious comparisons; but it was of importance to him to encourage the fanatics who were ready to murder kings in the name of the papal power." Brantôme had seen the issuing of a bull containing the same penalties against Elizabeth, the death of Mary on the scaffold, and the failure of the Armada. After the horrors of the religious wars, from the conspiracy of Amboise in 1560 to the publication of the edict of toleration given at Nantes in 1598, he had seen the comparatively peaceful days of Henry the Fourth, till fanaticism again awoke a suspicion of a return to his original Protestant leanings, as shown in his opposition to the house of Austria, and Ravaillac renewed the meritorious work of Clement in 1610. Last of all, the spectator of all these changes saw England and Scotland forever united under one crown, and the first rise of the master of the modern policy of Europe, for in the year of Brantôme's death a young priest was appointed Secretary of State in France, whom men soon gazed on with fear and wonder as the great Cardinal Richelieu.

In England the alterations were as great and striking. After the troubled years from Elizabeth's accession to the Armada, a period of rest and progress came. Interests became spread over the whole nation, and did not depend so exclusively on the throne. Wisdom and good feeling made Elizabeth's crown, in fact, what laws and compacts have made her successors',—a constitutional sovereign's. She ascertained the sentiments of her people almost without the intervention of Parliament, and was more a carrier-through of the national will than the originator of absolute decrees. The moral battles of a nation in pursuit of some momentous object like religious or political freedom bring forth great future crops, as fields are enriched on which mighty armies have been engaged. The fertilizing influence extends in every direction, far and near. If, therefore, the intellectual harvest that followed the final rejection of the Pope and crowning defeat of the Spaniard included Shakspeare and Bacon, and a host of lesser but still majestic names, we may venture also to remark, on the duller and more prosaic side of the question, that in the first year of the seventeenth century a patent was issued by which a commercial speculation attained a substantive existence, for the East India

Company was founded, with a stock of seventy-two thousand pounds, and a fleet of four vessels took their way from the English harbours, on their first voyage to the realm where hereafter their employers, who thus began as merchant adventurers, were to rule as kings. The example set by these enterprising men was followed by high and low. During the previous century people had been too busy with their domestic and religious disputes to pay much attention to foreign exploration. They were occupied with securing their liberties from the tyranny of Henry the Eighth and their lives from the truculence of Mary. Then the plots perpetually formed against Elizabeth, by domestic treason and foreign levy, kept their attention exclusively on home-affairs. But when the State was settled and religion secure, the long-pent-up activity of the national mind found vent in distant expeditions. A chivalrous contempt of danger, and poetic longing for new adventure, mingled with the baser attractions of those maritime wanderings. The families of gentle blood in England, instead of sending their sons to waste their lives in pursuit of knightly fame in the service of foreign states, equipped them for far higher enterprises, and sent them forth to gather the riches of unknown lands beyond the sea. Romantic rumours were rife in every manor-house of the strange sights and inexhaustible wealth to be gained by undaunted seamanship and judicious treatment of the natives of yet-unexplored dominions. Spain and Portugal had their kingdoms, but the extent of America was great enough for all. Islands were everywhere to be found untouched as yet by the foot of European; and many a winter's night was spent in talking over the possible results of sailing up some of the vast rivers that came down like bursting oceans from the far-inland regions to which nobody had as yet ascended,—the people and cities that lay upon their banks, the gold and jewels that paved the common soil. Towards the end of Elizabeth's reign, these imaginings had grown into sufficing motives of action, and gentlemen were ready from all the ports of the kingdom to sail on their adventurous voyages. In addition to the chance those gallant mariners had of realizing their day-dreams by the tedious methods of discovery and exploration, there was always the prospect of making prize of a galleon of Spain; for at all times, however friendly the nations might be in the European waters, a war was carried on beyond the Azores. Not altogether lost, therefore, was the old knightly spirit of peril-seeking and adventure in those commercial and geographical speculations. There were articles of merchandise in the hold, gaudy-coloured cloths, and bead ornaments, and wretched looking-glasses, besides brass and iron; but all round the captain's cabin were arranged swords and pistols, boarding-pikes, and other implements of fight. Guns also of larger size peeped out of the port-holes, and the crew were chosen as much with a view to warlike operations as to the ordinary duties of the ship. The Spaniards had made their way into the Pacific, and had established large settlements on the shores of Chili and Peru. Scenes which have been reacted at the diggings in modern times took place where the Europeans fixed their seat, and ships loaded with the precious metals found their way home, exposed to all the perils of storm and war. Drake had pounced upon several of their galleys and despoiled them of their precious cargo. Cavendish, a gentleman of good estate in Suffolk, had followed in his wake, and, after forcing his way through the Straits of Magellan, had reached the shores of California itself and there captured a Spanish vessel freighted with a vast amount of gold.

All these adventures of the expiring sixteenth century became traditions and ballads of the young seventeenth. Raleigh, the most accomplished gentleman of his time, gave the glory of his example to the maritime career, and all the oceans were alive with British ships. While Raleigh and others of the upper class were carrying on a sort of cultivated crusade against the monopoly of the Spaniards, others of a less aristocratic position were busied in the more regular paths of commerce. We have seen the formation of the India Company in 1600. Our competitors, the Dutch, fitted out fleets on a larger scale, and established relations of trade and friendship with the natives of Polynesia and New Holland, and even of Java and India. But the zeal of the public in trading-speculations was not only shown in those well-conducted expeditions to lands easily accessible and already known: a company was established for the purpose of opening out the African trade, and a commercial voyage was undertaken to no less a place than Timbuctoo by a gallant pair of seamen of the names of Thomson and Jobson. It was not long before these efforts at honest international communication, and even the exploits of the Drakes and Cavendishes, who acted under commissions from the queen, degenerated into lawless piracy and the golden age of the Buccaneers. The policy of Spain was complete monopoly in her own hands, and a refusal of foreign intercourse worthy of the potentates of China and Japan. All access was prohibited to the flags of foreign nations, and the natural result followed. Adventurous voyagers made their appearance with no flag at all, or with the hideous emblem of a death's head emblazoned on their standard, determined to trade peaceably if possible, but to trade whether peaceably or not. The Spanish colonists were not indisposed to exchange their commodities with those of the new-comers, but the law was imperative. The Buccaneers, therefore, proceeded to help themselves to what they wanted by force, and at length came to consider themselves an organized estate, governed by their own laws, and qualified to make treaties like any other established and recognised power. Cuba had been nearly depopulated by the cruelties and fanaticism of its Spanish masters, and was seized on by the Buccaneers. From this rich and beautiful island the pirate-barks dashed out upon any Spanish sail which might be leaving the mainland. Commanding the Gulf of Mexico, and with the power of crossing the Isthmus of Panama by a rapid march, those redoubtable bandits held the treasure-lands of the Spaniards in terrible subjection. And up to the commencement even of the eighteenth century the frightful spectacle was presented of a powerful confederacy of the wildest and most dissolute villains in Europe domineering over the most frequented seas in the world, and filling peaceful voyagers, and even well-armed men-of-war, with alarm by their unsparing cruelty, and atrocities which it curdles the blood to think of.

Eastward as far as China, westward to the islands and shores of the great Pacific, up the rivers of Africa, and even among the forests of New Holland and Tasmania, the swarms of European adventurers succeeded each other without cessation. The marvel is, that, with such ceaseless activity, any islands, however remote or small, were left for the discovery of after-times. But the tide of English emigration rolled towards the mainland of North America with a steadier flow than to any other quarter. The idea of a northwest passage to India had taken possession of men's minds, and hardy seamen had already braved the horrors of a polar winter, and set examples of fortitude and patience which their successors, from Behrens to Kane, have so nobly followed. But the fertile plains of Virginia, and the navigable streams of the eastern shore, were more alluring to the peaceful and unenterprising settlers, whose object was to find a new home and carry on a lucrative trade with the native Indians. In 1607, a colony, properly so called,—for it had made provision for permanent settlement, and consisted of a hundred and ten persons, male and female,—arrived at the mouth of the Chesapeake. The river Powhatan was eagerly explored; and at a point sufficiently far up to be secure from sudden attack from the sea, and on an isthmus easily defended from native assault, they pitched their tents on a spot which was hereafter known as Jamestown and is still honoured as the earliest of the American settlements. Our neighbour Holland was not behindhand either in trade or colonization, and equally with England was excited to fresh efforts by its recovered liberty and independence. In all directions of intellectual and physical employment those two States went boundingly forward at the head of the movement. The absolute monarchies lay lazily by, and relied on the inertness of their mass for their defence against those active competitors; and Spain, an unwieldy bulk, showed the intimate connection there will always exist between liberal institutions at home and active progress abroad. The sun never set on the dominions of the Spanish crown, but the life of the people was crushed out of them by the weight of the Inquisition and despotism. The United Provinces and combined Great Britain had shaken off both those petrifying institutions, and Englishmen, Scotchmen, and Dutchmen were ploughing up every sea, presenting themselves at the courts of strange-coloured potentates, in regions whose existence had been unknown a few years before, and gradually accustoming the wealth and commerce of the world to find their way to London and Amsterdam.

To go from these views of hardihood and enterprise, from the wild heaving of unruly vigour which animated the traffickers and tyrants of the main, to the peaceful and pedantic domestic reign of James the First, shows the two extremes of European character at this time. The English people were not more than four millions in number, but they were the happiest and most favoured of all the nations. This was indeed the time,

> "Ere England's woes began,
> When every rood of land maintain'd its man;"

for we have seen how the division of the great monastic properties had created a new order in the State. All accounts concur in describing the opening of this century as the period of the greatest physical prosperity of the body of the people. A great deal of dulness and unrefinement there must still have been in the boroughs, where such sage officials as Dogberry displayed their pomp and ignorance,—a great deal of clownishness and coarseness in country-places, where Audreys and Autolycuses were to be found; but among townsmen and peasantry there was none of the grinding poverty which a more unequal distribution of national wealth creates. There were great Whitsun ales, and dancings round the Maypole; feasts on village greens, and a spirit of rude and personal independence, which became mellowed into manly self-respect when treated with deference by the higher ranks, the old hereditary gentry and the retired statesmen of Queen Bess, but bristled up in insolence and rebellion when the governing power thwarted its wishes, or fanaticism soured it with the bitter waters of polemic strife. The sturdy Englishman who doffed his hat to the squire, and joined his young lord in sports upon the green, in the beginning of James's reign, was the same stout-hearted, strong-willed individual who stiffened into Puritanism and contempt of all earthly authorities in the unlovely, unloving days of the Rump and Cromwell. Nor should we miss the great truth which lies hidden under the rigid forms of that period,—that the same noble qualities which characterized the happy yeoman and jocund squire of 1620—their earnestness, energy, and intensity of home affections—were no less existent in their ascetic short-haired descendants of 1650. The brimfulness of life which overflowed into expeditions against the Spaniards in Peru, and unravellings of the tangled rivers of Africa, and trackings of the wild bears among the ice-floes of Hudson's Bay, took a new direction when the century reached the middle of its course, and developed itself in the stormy discussions of the contending sects and the blood and misery of so many battle-fields. How was this great change worked on the English mind? How was it that the long-surviving soldier, courtier, landholder, of Queen Elizabeth saw his grandson grow up into the hard-featured, heavy-browed, keen-sworded Ironside of Oliver? A squire who ruined himself in loyal entertainments to King James on his larder-and-cellar-emptying journey from Edinburgh to London in 1603 may have lived to see his son, and son's son, rejoicing with unholy triumph over the victory of Naseby in 1644 and the death of Charles in 1649.

Great causes must have been at work to produce this astonishing change, and some of them it will not be difficult to point out. Perhaps, indeed, the prosperity we have described may itself have contributed to the alteration in the English ways of thought. While the nation was trampled on by Henry the Eighth, with property and life insecure and poverty universally diffused, or even while it was guided by the strong hand of Elizabeth, it had neither power nor inclination to examine into its rights. The rights of a starving and oppressed population are not very great, even in its own eyes. It is the well-fed, law-protected, enterprising citizen who sees the value of just and settled government, because the blessings he enjoys depend upon its continuance. The mind of the nation had been pauperized along with its body by the life of charitable dependence it had led at the doors of church and monastery in the olden time. It little mattered to a gaping crowd expecting the accustomed dole whether the great man in London was a tyrannical king or not. They did not care whether he dismissed his Parliaments or cut off the heads of his nobility. They still found their "bit and sup," and saw the King, and Parliament, and nobility, united in obedience to the Church. But when this debasing charity was discontinued, independence came on. The idle hanger-on of the religious house became a cottager, and worked on his own land; by industry he got capital enough to take some additional acres; and the man of the next generation had forgotten the low condition he sprang from, and had so sharpened his mind by the theological quarrels of the time that he began to be able to comprehend the question of general politics. He saw, as every population and potentate in Europe saw with equal clearness, that the question of civil freedom was indissolubly connected with the relation between Church and State; he perceived that the extent of divergence from the old faith regulated in a great measure the spirit, and even the constitution, of government where it took place,—that adhesion to Rome meant absolutism and dependence, that Calvinism had a strong bias towards the republican form, and that the Church he had helped to establish was calculated to fill up the ground between those two extremes, and be the religious representative of a State as liberal as Geneva by its attention to the interests of all, and as monarchical as Spain by its loyalty to an hereditary crown. Now, the middle ground in great and agitating affairs is always the most difficult to maintain. Both sides make it their battle-field, and try to win it to themselves; and according as one assailant seems on the point of carrying his object, the defender of that disputed territory has to lean towards the other. Both parties are offended at the apparent inconsistency; and we are therefore not to be surprised if we find the Church accused of looking to both the hostile camps in turn.

James was a fatal personage to every cause he undertook to defend. He had neither the strength of will of Henry, nor the proud consistency of Elizabeth; but he had the arrogance and presumption of both. Questions which the wise queen was afraid to touch, and left to the ripening influence of time, this blustering arguer dragged into premature discussion, stripped them of all their dignity by the frivolousness of the treatment he gave them, and disgusted all parties by the harshness and rapidity of his partial decisions. Every step he took in the quelling of religious dissension by declarations in favour of proscription and authority which would have endeared him to Gregory the Seventh, he accompanied with some frightful display of his absolutist tendencies in civil affairs. The same man who roared down the modest claims of a thousand of the clergy who wished some further modification of the Book of Common Prayer threw recusant members of Parliament into prison, persecuted personal enemies to death, with scarcely a form of law, punished refractory towns with loss of franchises and privileges, and made open declaration of his unlimited power over the lives and properties of all his subjects. People saw this unvarying alliance between his polemics and his politics, and began to consider seriously whether the comforts their trade and industry had given them could be safe under a Church calling itself reformed, but protected by such a king. If he was only suspected in England, in his own country he was fully known. Dearer to James would have been a hundred bishops and cardinals seated in conclave in Holyrood than a Presbyterian Synod praying against his policy in the High Kirk. He had even written to the Pope with offers of accommodation and reconcilement, and made no secret of his individual and official disgust at the levelling ideas of those grave followers of Knox and Calvin. Those grave followers of Knox and Calvin, however, were not unknown on the south side of the Tweed. The intercourse between the countries was not limited to the hungry gentry who followed James on his accession. A community of interest and feeling united the more serious of the Reformers, and visits and correspondence were common between them. But, while a regard for their personal freedom and the security of their wealth attracted the attention of the English middle class to the proceedings of King James, events were going on in foreign lands which had an immense effect on the development of the anti-monarchic, anti-episcopal spirit at home. These events have not been sufficiently considered in this relation, and we have been too much in the habit of looking at our English doings in those momentous years,—from the end of James's reign to the Restoration,—as if Britain had continued as isolated from her Continental neighbours as before the Norman Conquest. But a careful comparison of dates and actions will show how intimate the connection had become between the European States, and how instantaneously the striking of a chord at Prague or Vienna thrilled through the general heart in Edinburgh and London.

The Reformation, after achieving its independence and equality at the Treaty of Augsburg in 1555, had made great though silent progress. Broken off in Germany into two parties, the Lutheran and the Calvinist, who hated each other, as usual, in exact proportion to the smallness of their difference, the union was still kept up between them as regarded their antagonism to the Papists. With all three denominations, the religious part of the question had fallen into terrible abeyance. It was now looked on by the leaders entirely as a matter of personal advancement and political rule. In this pursuit the fanaticism which is generally limited to theology took the direction of men's political conduct; and there were enthusiasts among all the sects, who saw visions, and dreamed dreams, about the succession to thrones and the raising of armies, as used to happen in more ancient times about the bones of martyrs and the beatification of saints. The great object of Protestants and Catholics was to obtain a majority in the college of the Prince Electors by whom the Empire was bestowed. This consisted of the seven chief potentates of Germany, of whom four were secular,—the King of Bohemia, the Count Palatine of the Rhine, the Duke of Saxony, and the Marquis of Brandenburg; and three ecclesiastic,—the Archbishops of Mentz, Trêves, and Cologne. The majority was naturally secured to the Romanists by the official adhesion of these last. But it chanced that the Elector of Cologne fell violently in love with Agnes of Mansfeldt, a canoness of Gerrestein; and having of course studied the history of our Henry the Eighth and Anne Boleyn, he determined to follow his example, and offered the fair canoness his hand. He was unwilling, however, to offer his hand without the Electoral crozier, and, by the advice of his friends, and with the promised support of many of the Protestant rulers, he retained his ecclesiastical dignity and made the beautiful Agnes his wife. This would not have been of much consequence in a lower rank, for many of the cathedral dignitaries in Cologne and other places had retained their offices after changing their faith; but all Germany was awake to the momentous nature of this transaction, for it would have conveyed a majority of the Electoral voices to the Protestants and opened the throne of the empire itself to a Protestant prince. Such, however, was the strength at that time of the opposition to Rome, that all the efforts of the Catholics would have been ineffectual to prevent this ruinous arrangement but for a circumstance which threw division into the Protestant camp. Gebhard had adhered to the Calvinistic branch of the Reformation, and the Lutherans hated him with a deadlier hatred than the Pope himself. With delight they saw him outlawed by the Emperor and excommunicated by Rome, his place supplied by a Prince of Bavaria, who was elected by the Chapter of Cologne to protect them from their apostate archbishop, and the head of the house of Austria strengthened by the consolidation of his Electoral allies and the unappeasable dissensions of his enemies. While petty interests and the narrowest quarrels of sectarianism divided the Protestants, and while the Electors and other princes who had adopted their theological opinions were doubtful of the political results of religious freedom, and many had waxed cold, and others were discontented with the small extent of the liberation from ancient trammels they had yet obtained, a very different spectacle was presented on the other side. Popes and Jesuits were heartily and unhesitatingly at work. "No cold, faint-hearted doubtings teased them." Their object was incommoded by no refinements or verbal differences; they were determined to assert their old supremacy,—to trample out every vestige of resistance to their power; and they entered upon the task without scruple or remorse. Ferdinand the Emperor, the prop and champion of the Romish cause, was as sincere and as unpitying as Dominic. When he had been nominated King Elect of Bohemia, in 1598, while yet in his twentieth year, his first thought was the future use he might make of his authority in the extermination of the Protestant faith. The Jesuits, by whom he was trained from his earliest years, never turned out a more hopeful pupil. His ambition would have been, if he had had it in his power, to become a follower of Loyola himself; but, as he was condemned by fate to the lower office of the first of secular princes, he determined to employ all its power at the dictation of his teachers. He went a pilgrimage to Loretto, and, bowing before the miraculous image of the Virgin, promised to reinstate the true Church in its unquestioned supremacy, and bent all his thoughts to the fulfilment of his vow. Two-thirds of his subjects in his hereditary states were Protestant, but he risked all to attain his object. He displaced their clergy, and banished all who would not conform. He introduced Catholics from foreign countries to supply the waste of population, and sent armed men to destroy the newly-erected schools and churches of the hateful heretics. This man was crowned King of Bohemia in 1618, and Emperor of Germany in the following year.

The attention of the British public had been particularly directed to German interests for the six years preceding this date, by the marriage of Frederick, Elector Palatine of the Rhine, with Elizabeth, the graceful and accomplished daughter of King James. Frederick was

young and ambitious, and was endeared to the English people as leader of the Protestant cause against the overweening pretensions of the house of Austria. That house was still the most powerful in Europe; for though the Spanish monarchy was held by another branch, for all the purposes of despotism and religion its weight was thrown into the same scale. Spanish soldiers, and all the treasures of America, were still at the command of the Empire; and perhaps Catholicism was rather strengthened than weakened by the adherence of two of the greatest sovereigns in the world, instead of having the personal influence of only one, as in the reign of Charles the Fifth. All the Elector's movements were followed with affectionate interest by the subjects of his father-in-law; but James himself disapproved of opposition being offered to the wildest excesses of royal prerogative either in himself or any other anointed ruler. Besides this, he was particularly hostile to the young champion's religious principles, for the latter was attached to the Calvinistic or unepiscopal party. James declined to give him any aid in maintaining his right to the crown of Bohemia, to which he was elected by the Protestant majority of that kingdom on the accession
A.D. 1619. of Ferdinand to the Empire, and managed to show his feelings in the most offensive manner, by oppressing such of Frederick's co-religionists as he found in any part of his dominions. The advocates of peace at any price have praised the behaviour of the king in this emergency; but it may be doubted whether an energetic display of English power at this time might not have prevented the great and cruel reaction against freedom and Protestantism which the victory of the bigoted Ferdinand over his neglected competitor introduced. A riot, accompanied with violence against the Catholic authorities, was the beginning of the

troubles in Bohemia; and Ferdinand, as if to explain his conduct to the satisfaction of James, published a manifesto, which might almost be believed to have been the production of that Solomon of the North. "If sovereign power," he says, "emanates from God, these atrocious deeds must proceed from the devil, and therefore must draw down divine punishment." This logic was unanswerable at Whitehall, and the work of extermination went on. Feeble efforts were forced upon the unwilling father-in-law; for all the chivalry of England was wild with sympathy and admiration of the Bohemian queen. Hundreds of gallant gentlemen passed over to swell the Protestant ranks; and when they returned and told the tale of all the horrors they had seen, the remorseless vengeance of the triumphant Church, and all the threatenings with which Rome and the Empire endeavoured to terrify the nations which had rebelled against their yoke, Puritanism, or resistance to the slightest approach towards Popery either in essentials or externals, became patriotism and self-defence; and at this very time, while men's minds were inflamed with the descriptions of the torturings and executions which followed the battle of Prague in 1620, and the devastation and depopulation of Bohemia, James took the opportunity of forcing the Episcopal form of government on the Scottish Presbyterians.

"The greatest matter," he says, in an address to the prelates of the reluctant dioceses,—"the greatest matter the Puritans had to object against the Church government was, that your proceedings were warranted by no law, which now by this last Parliament is cutted short. The sword is now put in your hands. Go on, therefore, to use it, and let it rest no longer till ye have perfected the service trusted to you; or otherwise we must use it both against you and them." While the people of both nations were willing to sink their polemic differences of Calvinist and Anglican in one great attempt to deliver the Protestants in Germany from the power of the house of Austria,—while for this purpose they would have voted taxes and raised armies with the heartiest good will,—the king's whole attention was bestowed on a set of manœuvres for the obtaining a Spanish-Austrian bride for his son. To gain this he would have humbled himself to the lowest acts. At a whisper from Madrid, he interfered with the German war, to the detriment of his own daughter; and England perceived that his ineradicable love of power and hatred of freedom had blinded him to national interests and natural affections. If we follow the whole career of James, and a great portion of his successor's, we shall see the same remarkable coincidence between the events in England and abroad,—unpopularity of the king, produced by his apparent lukewarmness in the general Protestant cause as much as by his arbitrary acts at home. Whatever the nation desired, the king opposed. When Gustavus Adolphus, the Lion of the North, began his triumphant career in 1630, and re-established the fallen fortunes of Protestantism, Charles concluded a dishonourable peace with Spain, without a single provision in favour of the Protestants of the German States, and allowed the Popish Cardinal Richelieu first to consolidate his forces by an unsparing oppression of the Huguenots in France, and then to almost compensate for his harshness by a gallant support of the Swedish hero in his struggle against the Austrian power.

There was no longer the same content and happiness in the towns and country districts as there had been at the commencement of the century. Men had looked with contempt and dislike on the proceedings of James's court,—his coarse buffoonery, and disgraceful patronage of a succession of worthless favourites; and they continued to look, not indeed with contempt, but with increased dislike and suspicion, on the far purer court and dignified manners of his unfortunate son. A French princess, though the daughter of Henry the Fourth, was regarded as an evil omen for the continuance of good government or religious progress. Her attendants, lay and clerical, were not unjustly considered spies, and advisers with interests hostile to the popular tendencies. And all this time went on the unlucky coincidences which distinguished this reign,—of Catholic cruelties in foreign lands, and approaches to the Catholic ceremonial in the reformed Church. While Tilly, the remorseless general of the Emperor, was letting loose the most ferocious army which ever served under a national standard upon the inhabitants of Magdeburg, heaping into the history of that miserable assault all the sufferings that "horror e'er conceived or fancy feigned,"—and while the echo of that awful butchery, which has not yet died out of the German heart, was making sorrowful every fireside in what was once merry England,—the king's advisers pursued their blind way, torturing their opponents with knife and burning-brand upon the pillory, flogging gentlemen nearly to death upon the streets, and consecrating churches with an array of surplice, and censer, and processions, and organ-blowings, which would have done honour to St. Peter's at Rome. People saw a lamentable connection between the excesses of Catholic cruelty and the tendency in our sober establishment to Catholic traditions, and became fanatical in their detestation of the simplest forms.

In ordinary times the wise man considers mere forms as almost below his notice; but there are periods when the emblem is of as much importance as the thing it typifies. Church ceremonies, and gorgeous robes, and magnificent worship, were accepted by both parties as the touchstone of their political and religious opinions. Laud pushed aside the Archbishop of Glasgow, who stood at Charles's right hand on his visit to Scotland in 1633, on the express ground that he had not the orthodox fringe upon his habit,—a ridiculous ground for so open an insult, if it had not had an inner sense. The Archbishop of Glasgow professed himself a moderate Churchman by the plainness of his dress, and Laud accepted it as a defiance. Meanwhile the essential insignificance of the symbol threw an air of ridicule over the importance attached to it. Dull-minded men, who had not the faculty of seeing how deep a question may lie in a simple exposition of it, or frivolous men, who could not rise to the real earnestness which enveloped those discussions, were scandalized at the persistency of Laud in enforcing his fancies, and the obstinacy of a great portion of the clergy and people in resisting them. But the Puritans, with clearer eyes, saw that a dance, according to proclamation, on the village green on Sunday, meant not a mere desecration of the Sabbath, but a crusade against the rights of conscience and an assertion of arbitrary power. Altars instead of communion-tables in churches meant not merely a restoration of the Popish belief in the real sacrifice of the mass, but a placing of the king above the law, and the abrogation of all liberty. They could not at this time persuade the nation of these things. The nation, for the most part, saw nothing more than met their bodily eyes; and, in despair of escaping the slavery which they saw the success of Ferdinand in Germany was likely to spread over Europe, they began the long train of voyages to the Western World, which times of suffering and uncertainty have continued at intervals to the present day.

It is said that a vessel was stopped by royal warrant when it was on the point of sailing from the Thames with emigrants to America in 1637. On board were various persons whose names would probably never have been heard of if they had been allowed in peace and safety to pursue their way to Boston, but with which in a few years "all England rang from side to side." They were Oliver Cromwell, and Hampden, and Haselrig, Lord Brook, and Lord Saye.

Affairs had now reached such a crisis that they could no longer continue undecided. A Parliament was called in 1640, after an unexampled interval of eleven years, and, after a few days' session, was angrily dissolved. Another, however, was indispensable in the same year, and on the 3d of November the Long Parliament met. The long-repressed indignation of the Commons broke forth at once. Laud and Wentworth, the principal advisers of the king, were tried and executed, and precautions taken, by stringent acts, to prevent a recurrence of arbitrary government. Everywhere there seemed a rally in favour of the Protestant or liberal cause. The death of Richelieu, the destroyer of French freedom, opened a prospect of recovered independence to the Huguenots; the victories of Torstenson the Swede, worthy successor of Gustavus Adolphus, brought down the pride of the Austrian Catholics; and Puritans, Independents, and other outraged sects and parties, by the restoration of the Parliament, got a terrible instrument of vengeance against their oppressors. A dreadful time, when on both sides the forms of law were perverted to the most lawless purposes; when peacefully-inclined citizens must have been tormented with sad misgivings by the contending claims of Parliament and King,—a Parliament correctly constituted and in the exercise of its recognised authority, a King with no flaw to his title, and professing his willingness to limit himself to the undoubted prerogatives of his place. It was probably a relief to the undecided when A.D. 1642. the arbitrament was removed from the court of argument to the field of battle. All the time of that miserable civil war, the other states of Europe were in nearly as great confusion as ourselves. France was torn to pieces by factions which contended for the mantle of the departed cardinal; Germany was traversed from end to end by alternately retreating and advancing armies. But still the simultaneousness of events abroad and at home is worthy of remark. The great fights which decided the quarrel in England were answered by victories of the Protestant arms in Germany and the apparent triumph of the discontented in France. The young king, Louis the Fourteenth, carried from town to town, and disputed between the parties, gave little augury of the despotism and injustice of his future throne. There were barricades in Paris, and insurrections all over the land. But at last, and at the same time, all the combatants in England, and France, and Germany—Huguenot, Puritan, Calvinist, Protestant, and Papist—were tired out with the length and bitterness of the struggle. So in 1648 the long Thirty Years' War was brought to a close by the Peace of Westphalia. Kingly power in France was curtailed, the house of Austria was humbled; and Charles was carried prisoner to Windsor. The Protestants of Germany, by the terms of the peace, were replaced in their ancient possessions. They had freedom of worship and equality of civil rights secured. A general law preserved them from the injustice or aggressions of their local masters; and the compromise guaranteed by so many divergent interests, and guarded by such equally-divided numbers, has endured to the present time. The

English conquerors would be contented with no less than their foreign friends had obtained. But the blot upon their conduct, the blood of the misguided and humbled Charles, hindered the result of their wisest deliberations. Moderate men were revolted by the violence of the act, and old English loyalty, delivered from the fear of foreign or domestic oppression, was awakened by the sad end of a crowned and anointed King. Nothing compensates in an old hereditary monarchy for the want of high descent in its ruler. Not all Cromwell's vigour and genius, his glory abroad and energetic government at home, attracted the veneration of English squires, whose forefathers had fought at Crecy, to the grandson of a city knight, or, at most, to the descendant of a minister of Henry the Eighth. Charles the Second rose before them with the transmitted dignity of a hundred kings. He counted back to Scottish monarchs before the Norman Conquest, and traced by his mother's side his lineal ancestry up to Charlemagne and Clovis. English history presents no instance of the intrusion of an unroyal usurper in her list of sovereigns. Cromwell stands forth the solitary instance of a man of the people virtually seizing the crown; and the ballads and pamphlets of the time show how the comparative humility of his birth excited the scorn of his contemporaries. And this feeling was not limited to ancient lords and belted cavaliers: it permeated the common mind. There was something ennobling for the humblest peasant to die for King and Cause; but, however our traditions and the lapse of two hundred years may have elevated the conqueror at Worcester and Dunbar, we are not to forget that, in the estimation of those who had drunk his beer at Huntingdon or listened to his tedious harangues in Parliament, there would be neither patriotism nor honour in

A.D. 1649.

dying for bluff Old Noll. But there were more dangerous enemies to bluff Old Noll than the newness of his name. The same cause which had made the nation dissatisfied with the arbitrary pretensions of James and Charles was at work in making it intolerant of the rule of the usurpers.

The great soldier and politician, who had overthrown an ancient dynasty and crushed the seditions of the sects, had increased the commercial prosperity of the three kingdoms. Wealth poured in at all the ports, and was rapidly diffused over the land; internal improvements kept pace with foreign enterprise; and the England which long ago had been too rich to be arbitrarily governed was now again too rich to be kept in durance by the sour-faced hypocrisies of the Puritans. Those lank-haired gentlemen, whose conduct had not quite answered to the self-denying proclamations with which they had begun, were no longer able to persuade the well-to-do citizen, and the high-waged mechanic, and the prosperous farmer, that religion consisted in speaking through the nose and forswearing all innocent enjoyment. The great battle had been fought, and the fruits of it, they thought, were secure. Were people to be debarred from social meetings and merry-makings at Christmas, and junketings at fairs, by act of Parliament? Acts of Parliament would first have been required strong enough to do away with youth and health, and the power of admiring beauty, and the hopes of
A.D. 1641 marriage. The troubles had lasted seven or
-49. eight years; and all through that period, and for some time before, while the thick cloud was gathering, all gayety had disappeared from the land. But by the middle of Cromwell's time there was a new generation, in the first flush of youth,—lads and lasses who had been too young to know any thing of the dark

days of Laud and Wentworth. They were twenty years of age now. Were they to have no cakes and ale because their elders were so prodigiously virtuous? They had many years of weary restraint and formalism to make up for, and in 1660 the accumulated tide of joyousness and delight burst all barriers. A flood of dancing and revelry, and utter abandonment to happiness, spread over the whole country; and merriest of the dancers, loudest of the revellers, happiest of the emancipated, was the young and brilliant king. Never since the old times of the Feasts of Fools and the gaudy processions of the Carnival had there been such a riotous jubilee as inaugurated the Restoration. The reaction against Puritanism carried the nation almost beyond Christianity and landed it in heathenism again. The saturnalia of Rome were renewed in the banquetings of St. James's. Nothing in those first days of relaxation seemed real. King and courtiers and cavaliers in courtly palaces, and enthusiastic townsfolk and madly loyal husbandmen, seemed like mummers at a play; and it was not till the candles were burned out, and the scenes grew dingy, and daylight poured upon that ghastly imitation of enjoyment, that England came to its sober senses again. Then it saw how false was the parody it had been playing. It had not been happy; it had only been drunk; and already, while Charles was in the gloss of his recovered crown, the second reaction began. Cromwell became respectable by comparison with the sensual debauchee who sold the dignity of his country for a little present enjoyment and soothed the reproaches of his people with a joke. Give us a Man to rule over us, the English said, and not a sayer of witty sayings and a juggler with such sleight of hand. And yet the example of the court was so contagious, and the fashion of enjoyment so wide-spread, that on the surface every thing appeared prosperous and happy. The stern realities of the first recusants had been so travestied by the exaggerated imitation of their successors that no faith was placed in the serious earnestness of man or woman. Frivolity was therefore adopted as a mark of sense; and if the popular literature of a period is to be accepted as a mirror held up to show the time its image, the old English character had undergone a perfect change. Thousands flocked every day to the playhouses to listen to dialogues, and watch the evolvement of plots, where all the laws of decency and honour were held up to ridicule. Comus and his crew, which long ago had held their poetic festival in the pure pages of Milton, were let loose, without the purity or the poetry, in every family circle. And the worst and most disgusting feature of the picture is that those wassailers who were thus the missionaries of vice were persecutors for religion. While one royal brother was leading the revels at Whitehall, surrounded by luxury and immorality as by an atmosphere without which he could not live, the other, as luxurious, but more moodily depraved, listened to the groans of tortured Covenanters at Holyrood House. Charles and James were like the two executioners of Louis the Eleventh: one laughed, and the other groaned, but both were pitilessly cruel. A recurrence to the dark days of the Sects, the godly wrestlings in prayer of illiterate horsemen, and the sincere fanaticism of the Fifth-Monarchy men, would have been a change for the better from the filth and foulness of the reign of the Merry Monarch and the blood and misery of that of the gloomy bigot.

But happier times were almost within view, though still hid behind the glare of those orgies of the unclean. From 1660 to 1688 does not seem a very long time in the annals of a nation, nor even in the life of one of ourselves. Twenty-eight years have elapsed since the Revolution in Paris which placed Louis Philippe upon the throne; and the young man of twenty at that time is not very old yet. But when men or nations are cheated in the object of their hopes, it does not take long to turn disappointment into hatred. The Restoration of 1660 was to bring back the golden age of the first years of James,—the prosperity without the tyranny, the old hereditary rule without its high pretensions, the manliness of the English yeoman without his tendency to fanatical innovation. And instead of this Arcadia there was nothing to be seen but a kingdom without dignity, a king without honesty, and a people without independence. England was no longer the arbiter of European differences, as in the earlier reigns, nor dominator of all the nations, as when the heavy sword of Cromwell was uneasy in its sheath. It was not even a second-rate power: its capital had been insulted by the Dutch; its monarch was pensioned by the French; its religion was threatened by the Pope; the old animosities between England and Scotland were unarranged; and the point to be remembered in your review of the Seventeenth Century is that in the years from the Restoration to the Revolution we had touched the basest string of humility. We were neither united at home nor respected abroad. We had few ships, little commerce, and no public spirit. France revenged Crecy and Poictiers and Agincourt, by dressing our kings in her livery; and the degraded monarchs pocketed their wages without feeling their humiliation. Therefore, as the highest point we have hitherto stood upon was when Elizabeth saw the destruction of the Armada, the lowest was undoubtedly that when we submitted to the buffoonery of Charles and the bloodthirstiness of James.

But far more remarkable, as a characteristic of this century, than the lowering of the rank of England in relation to foreign states, is the rise, for the first time in Europe, of a figure hitherto unknown,—a true, unshackled, and absolute king, and that in the least likely of all positions and in the person of the least likely man. This was the appearance on the throne of France of Louis the Fourteenth. Other monarchs, both in England and France, had attained supreme power,—supreme, but not independent. No one had hitherto been irresponsible to some other portions of the State. The strongest of the feudal kings was held in check by his nobility,—the greatest of the Tudors by Parliament and people. Declarations, indeed, had frequently been made that God's anointed were answerable to God alone. But of the two loudest of these declaimers, John, who said,—

> "What earthly power to interrogatory
> Can tax the free breath of a Christian king?"

had shortly after this magnificent oration surrendered his crown to the Pope; and James the First, who blustered more fiercely (if possible) about his superiority to human law, was glad to bend before his Lords and Commons in anticipation of a subsidy, and eat his leek in peace.

But this phenomenon of a king above all other authority occurred, we have observed, in the most unlikely country to present so strange a sight; for nowhere was a European throne so weak and unstable as the throne of the house of Bourbon after the murder of Henry the Fourth. The moment that strong hand was withdrawn from the government, all classes broke loose. The nobles conspired against the queen, Marie de Medicis, who relied upon foreign favourites and irritated the nation to madness. Paris rose in insurrection, and tore the wretched Concini, her counsellor, whom she had created Marshal D'Ancre, to pieces; and, to glut their vengeance still more, the judges condemned his innocent wife to be burned as a sorceress. Louis the Thirteenth, the unworthy son of the great Henry, rejoiced in these atrocities, which he thought freed him from all restraint. But he found it impossible to quell the wild passions by which he profited for a while. Civil war raged between the court and country factions, and soon became embittered into religious animosities. A.D. 1622. The sight of a king marching at the head of a Catholic army against a portion of his Reformed subjects was looked upon by the rapidly-increasing malcontents in England with anxious curiosity. For year by year the strange spectacle was unrolled before their eyes of what might yet be their fate at home. Perhaps, indeed, the success of the royal arms, and the policy of strength and firmness introduced by Cardinal Richelieu, may have contributed in no slight degree to the measures pursued by Wentworth and Laud in their treatment of the English recusants. With an anticipative interest in our Hull and Exeter, the Puritans of England looked on the resistance made by Rochelle; and we can therefore easily imagine with what feelings the future soldiers of Marston Moor received the tidings that the Popish cardinal had humbled the capital of the Huguenots by the help of fleets furnished to them by Holland and England! Richelieu, indeed, knew how to make his enemies weaken each other throughout his whole career. A.D. 1627. Those enemies were the nobility of France, the house of Austria, and the Reformed Faith. When Rochelle was attacked the second time, and England pretended to arm for its defence, he contrived to win Buckingham, the chief of the expedition, to his cause, and procured a letter from King Charles, placing the fleet, which apparently went to the support of the Huguenots, at the service of the King of France! After a year's siege, and the most heroic resistance, Rochelle fell at last, in 1628. And, now that the Huguenots were destroyed as a dangerous party, the eyes of the great minister were turned against his other foes. He divided the nobles into hostile ranks, degraded them by petty annoyances, terrified them by unpitying executions of the chiefs of the oldest families, showed their weakness by arresting marshals at the head of their armies, and during the remaining years of his authority monopolized all the powers of the state. To weaken Spain and Austria, we have seen how he assisted the Protestants in the Thirty Years' War; to weaken England, which was only great when it assumed its place as bulwark and champion of the Protestant faith, he encouraged the court in its suicidal policy and the oppressed population in resistance. Ever stirring up trouble abroad, and ever busy in repressing liberty at home, the ministry of Richelieu is the triumph of unprincipled skill. But when he died, in 1643, there was no man left to lift up the burden he threw off. The king himself, Louis the Thirteenth, as much a puppet as the old descendants of Clovis under their Mayors of the Palace, left the throne he had nominally filled, vacant in the same year; and the heir to the dishonoured crown and exhausted country was a boy of five years of age, under the tutelage of an unprincipled mother, and with the old hereditary counsellors and props of his throne decimated by the scaffold or impoverished by confiscation. The tyranny of Richelieu had at least attained something noble by the high-handed insolence of all his acts. If people were to be trampled on, it was a kind of consolation to them that their oppressor was feared by others as well as themselves.

But the oppression of the doomed French nation was to be continued by a more ignoble hand. The Cardinal Mazarin brought every thing into greater confusion than ever. In twenty millions of men there will always be great and overmastering spirits, if only an opportunity is found for their development; but civil commotion is not the element in which greatness lives. All sense of honour disappears when conduct is regulated
A.D. 1648 -1654. by the shifting motives of party politics. The dissensions of the Fronde, accordingly, produced no champion to whom either side could look with unmingled respect. The Great Condé and the famous Turenne showed military talent of the highest order, but a want of principle and a flighty frivolity of character counterbalanced all their virtues. The scenes of those six years are like a series of dissolving views, or the changing combinations of a kaleidoscope: Condé and Turenne, always on opposite sides,—for each changed his party as often as the other; battles prepared for by masquerades and theatricals, and celebrated on both sides with epigrams and songs; the wildest excesses of debauchery and vice practised by both sexes and all ranks in the State; archbishops fighting like gladiators and intriguing like the vulgarest conspirators; princes imprisoned with a jest, and executions attended with cheers and laughter; and over all an Italian ecclesiastic, grinning with satisfaction at the increase of his wealth, —caballing, cheating, and lying, but keeping a firm grasp of power:—no country was ever so split into faction or so denuded of great men.

It seemed, indeed, like a demoniacal caricature of our British troubles: no sternness, no reality; love-letters and witty verses supplying the place of the Biblical language and awful earnestness of the words and deeds of the Covenanters and Independents; the gentlemen of

France utterly debased and frivolized; religion ridiculed; nothing left of the old landmarks; and no Cromwell possible. But, while all these elements of confusion were heaving and tumbling in what seemed an inextricable chaos, Mazarin, the vainest and most selfish of charlatans, died, and the young king, whom he had kept in distressing dependence and the profoundest political inactivity, found himself delivered from a master and free to choose his path. This was in 1661. Charles and Louis were equally on their recovered thrones; for what exile had been to the one, Mazarin
A.D. 1641 had been to the other. Charles had had the
–1660. experience of nineteen years and of various fortunes to guide him. He had seen many men and cities, and he deceived every expectation. Louis had been studiously brought up by his mother and her Italian favourite in the abasement of every lofty aspiration. He was only encouraged in luxury and vice, and kept in such painful vassalage that his shyness and awkwardness revealed the absence of self-respect to the very pages of his court; and he, no less than Charles, deceived all the expectations that had been formed of his career. He found out, as if by intuition, how brightly the monarchical principle still burned in the heart of all the French. Even in their fights and quarrellings there was a deep reverence entertained for the ideal of the throne. The King's name was a tower of strength; and when the nation, in the course of the miserable years from 1610 to 1661, saw the extinction of nobility, religion, law, and almost of civilized society, it caught the first sound that told it it still had a king, as an echo from the past assuring it of its future. It forgot Louis the Thirteenth and Anne of Austria, and only remembered that its monarch was the grandson of Henry the Fourth. Nobody remembered that circum-

stance so vividly as Louis himself; but he remembered also that his line went upwards from the Bourbons, and included the Saint Louis of the thirteenth century and the renewer of the Roman Empire of the ninth. He let the world know, therefore, that his title was Most Christian King as well as foremost of European powers. He forced Spain to yield him precedence, and, for the first time in history, exacted a humiliating apology from the Pope. The world is always apt to take a man at his own valuation. Louis, swelling with pride, ambitious of fame, and madly fond of power, declared himself the greatest, wisest, and most magnificent of men; and everybody believed him. Every thing was soon changed throughout the land. Ministers had been more powerful than the crown, and had held unlimited authority in right of their appointment. A minister was nothing more to Louis than a *valet-de-chambre*. He gave him certain work to do, and rewarded him if he did it; if he neglected it, he discharged him. At first the few relics of the historic names of France, the descendants of the great vassals, who carried their heads as lofty as the Capets or Valois, looked on with surprise at the new arrangements in camp and court. But the people were too happy to escape the oligarchic confederacy of those hereditary oppressors to encourage them in their haughty disaffection. Before Louis had been three years on the unovershadowed throne, the struggle had been fairly entered on by all the orders of the State, which should be most slavish in its submission. Rank, talent, beauty, science, and military fame all vied with each other in their devotion to the king. He would have been more than mortal if he had retained his senses unimpaired amid the intoxicating fumes of such incense. Success in more important affairs came to the support of his personal assumptions. Victories followed his standards everywhere. Generals, engineers, and administrators, of abilities hitherto unmatched in Europe, sprang up whenever his requirements called them forth. Colbert doubled his income without increasing the burdens on his people. Turenne, Condé, Luxembourg, and twenty others, led his armies. Vauban strengthened his fortifications or conducted his sieges, and the dockyards of Toulon and Brest filled the Mediterranean and the Atlantic with his fleets. Poets like Molière, Corneille, and Racine ennobled his stage; while the genius of Bossuet and Fénélon inaugurated the restoration of religion. For eight-and-twenty years his fortunes knew no ebb. He was the object of all men's hopes and fears, and almost of their prayers. Nothing was too great or too minute for his decision. He was called on to arbitrate (with the authority of a master) between sovereign States, and to regulate a point of precedence between the duchesses of his court. Oh, the weary days and nights of that uneasy splendour at Versailles! when his steps were watched by hungry courtiers, and his bed itself surrounded by applicants for place and favour. No galley-slave ever toiled harder at his oar than this monarch of all he surveyed at the management of his unruly family. It was the day of etiquette and form. The rights of princesses to arm-chairs or chairs with only a back were contested with a vigour which might have settled the succession to a throne. The rank which entitled to a seat in the king's coach or an invitation to Marly was disputed almost with bloodshed, and certainly with scandal and bitterness. The depth of the bows exacted by a prince of the blood, the number of attendants necessary for a legitimated son of La Vallière or Montespan, put the whole court into a turmoil of angry parties; and all these important points, and fifty more of equal magnitude, were formally submitted to the king and decided with a gravity befitting a weightier cause. Nothing is more remarkable in the midst of these absurd inanities than the great fund of good common sense that is found in all the king's judgments. He meditates, and temporizes, and reasons; and only on great occasions, such as a quarrel about dignity between the wife of the dauphin and the Duchess of Maine, does he put on the terrors of his kingly frown and interpose his irresistible command. It would have been some consolation to the foreign potentates he bullied or protected—the Austrian and Spaniard, or Charles in Whitehall—if they had known what a wretched and undignified life their enslaver and insulter lived at home. It was whispered, indeed, that he was tremendously hen-pecked by Madame de Maintenon, whom he married without having the courage to elevate her to the throne; but none of them knew the pettinesses, the degradations, and the miseries of his inner circle. They thought, perhaps, he was planning some innovation in the order of affairs in Europe,—the destruction of a kingdom, or the change of a dynasty. He was devoting his deepest cogitations to the arrangement of a quarrel between his sons and his daughters-in-law, the invitations to a little supper-party in his private room, or the number of steps it was necessary to advance at the reception of a petty Italian sovereign. The quarrels between his children became more bitter; the little supper-parties became more dull. Death came into the gilded chambers, and he was growing old and desolate. Still the torturing wheel of ceremony went round, and the father, with breaking heart, had to leave the chamber of his deceased son, and act the part of a great king, and go through the same tedious forms of grandeur and routine which he had done before the calamity came. Fancy has never drawn a personage

more truly pitiable than Louis growing feeble and friendless in the midst of all that magnificence and all that heartless crowd. You pardon him for retiring for consolation and sympathy to the quiet apartment where Madame de Maintenon received him without formality and continued her needlework or her reading while he was engaged in council with his ministers. He must have known that to all but her he was an Office and not a Man. He yearned for somebody that he could trust in and consult with, as entering into his thoughts and interests; and that calm-blooded, meek-mannered, narrow-hearted woman persuaded him that in her he had found all that his heart thirsted for in the desert of his royalty. But in that little apartment he was now to find refuge from more serious calamities than the falsehood of courtiers or the quarrels of women. Even French loyalty was worn out at last. Victories had glorified the monarch, but brought poverty and loss to the population. Complaints arose in all parts of the country of the excess of taxation, the grasping dishonesty of the collectors, the extravagance of the court, and even—but this was not openly whispered—the selfishness of the king. He had lavished ten millions sterling on the palace and gardens of Versailles; he had enriched his sycophants with pensions on the Treasury; he had gratified the Church with gorgeous donations, and with the far more fatal gift of vengeance upon its opponents. The Huguenots were in the peaceful enjoyment of the rights secured to them by the Edict of Nantes, granted by Henry the Fourth in 1598. But those rights included the right of worshipping God in a different manner from the Church, and denying the distinguishing doctrines of the Holy Catholic faith. The Edict of
A.D. 1685. Toleration was repealed as a blot on the purity of the throne of the Most Christian King.

Thousands of the best workmen in France were banished by this impolitic proceeding, and Louis thought he had shown his attachment to his religion by sending the ingenuity and wealth, and glowing animosity, of the most valuable portion of his subjects into other lands. Germany calculated that the depopulation caused by his wars was more than compensated by the immigration. England could forgive him his contemptuous behaviour to her king and Parliament when she saw the silk-mills of Spitalfields supplied by the skilled workmen of Lyons. Eight hundred thousand people left their homes in consequence of this proscription of their religion, and Germany and Switzerland grew rich with the stream of fugitives. It is said that only five thousand found their way to this country,—enough to set the example of peaceful industry and to introduce new methods of manufacture.

But the full benefit of the measures of Louis and Maintenon was denied us, by the distrust with which the Protestant exiles looked on the accession to our throne of a narrower despot and more bigoted persecutor than Louis; for in this same year James the Second succeeded Charles. Relying on each other's support, and gratified with the formal approval of the repeal of the Edict of Nantes pronounced by the Pope, the two champions of Christendom pursued their way,—dismissals from office, exclusion from promotion, proscription from worship in France, and assaults on the Church, and bloody assizes, in England,—till all the nations felt that a great crisis was reached in the fortunes both of England and France, and Protestant and Romanist alike looked on in expectation of the winding-up of so strange a history. Judicial blindness was equally on the eyes of the two potentates chiefly interested. James remained inactive while William Prince of Orange, the

avowed chief of the new opinions, was getting ready his ships and army, and congratulated himself on the silence of his people, which he thought was the sign of their acquiescence instead of the hush of expectation. All the other powers—the Papal Chair included—were not sorry to see a counterpoise to the predominance of France; and when William appeared in England as the
A.D. 1688. deliverer from Popery and oppression, the battle was decided without a blow. James was a fugitive in his turn, and found his way to Versailles. It is difficult to believe that any of the blood of Scotland or Navarre flowed in the veins of the pusillanimous king. He begged his protector, through whose councils he had lost his kingdom, to give it him back again; and the opportunity of a theatrical display of grandeur and magnanimity was too tempting to be thrown away. Louis promised to restore him his crown, as if it were a broken toy. It was a strange sight, during the remainder of their lives, to see those two monarchs keeping up the dignity of their rank by exaggerations of their former state. No mimic stage ever presented a more piteous spectacle of poverty and tinsel than the royal pair. Punctilios were observed at their meetings and separations, as if a bow more or less were of as much consequence as the bestowal or recovery of Great Britain; and in the estimation of those professors of manners and deportment a breach of etiquette would have been more serious than La Hogue or the Boyne. In that wondrous palace of Versailles all things had long ceased to be real. Speeches were made for effect, and dresses and decorations had become a part of the art of governing, and for some years the system seemed to succeed. When the king required to show that he was still a conqueror like Alexander the Great, preparations were made for his reception at the seat of war,

and a pre-arranged victory was attached to his arrival, as Cleopatra wished to fix a broiled fish to Anthony's hook. He entered the town of Mons in triumph when Luxembourg had secured its fall. He appeared also with unbounded applause at the first siege of Namur, and carried in person the news of his achievement to Versailles. Every day came couriers hot and tired with intelligence of fresh successes. Luxembourg conquered at Fleurus, 1690; Catinat conquered Savoy, 1691; Luxembourg again, in 1692, had gained the great day of Steinkirk, and Nerwinde in 1693. But the tide now turned. William the Third was the representative at that time of the stubbornness of his new subjects' character, who have always found it difficult to see that they were defeated. He was generally forced to retire after a vigorously-contested fight; but he was always ready to fight again next day, always calm and determined, and as confident as ever in the firmness of his men. Reports very different from the glorious bulletins of the earlier years of the Great Monarch now came pouring in. Namur was retaken, Dieppe and Havre bombarded, all the French establishments in India seized by the Dutch, their colony at St. Domingo captured by the English, Luxembourg dead, and the whole land again, for the second time, exhausted of men and money. It was another opportunity for the display of his absolute power. France prayed him to grant peace to Europe, and the earthly divinity granted France's prayer. Europe itself, which had rebelled against him, accepted the pacification it had won by its battles and combinations, as if it were a gift from a superior being. He surrendered his conquests with such grandeur, and looked so dignified while he withdrew his pretensions, acknowledging the Prince of Orange to be King of England, and the King of England to have no claim on the crown he had promised to restore to him, that it took some time to perceive that the terms of the Peace of Ryswick were proofs of weakness and not of magnanimity. But the object of his life had been gained. He had abased every order in the State for the aggrandizement of the Crown, and, for the first time since the termination of the Roman Empire, had concentrated the whole power of a nation into the will of an individual. And this strange spectacle of a possessor of unlimited authority over the lives and fortunes of all his subjects was presented in an age that had seen Charles the First of England brought to the block and James the Second driven into exile! The chance of France's peacefully rising again from this state of depression into liberty would have been greater if Louis, in displacing the other authorities, had not disgraced them. He dissolved his Parliament, not with a file of soldiers, like Cromwell or Napoleon, but with a riding-whip in his hand. He degraded the nobility by making them the satellites of his throne and creatures of his favour. He humbled the Church by secularizing its leaders; so that Bossuet, bishop and orator as he was, was proud to undertake the office of peacemaker between him and Madame de Montespan in one of their lovers' quarrels. And the Frenchmen of the next century looked in vain for some rallying-point from which to begin their forward course towards constitutional improvement. They found nothing but parliaments contemned, nobles dishonoured, and priests unchristianized.

A.D. 1697.

EIGHTEENTH CENTURY.

Kings of France.

A.D.
Louis XIV.—(*cont.*)
1715. Louis XV.
1774. Louis XVI.
1793. Louis XVII.

Emperors of Germany.

Leopold I.—(*cont.*)
1705. Joseph I.
1711. Charles VI.
1740. Maria-Theresa.
1742. Charles VII.
1745. Francis I.
1765. Joseph II.
1790. Leopold II.
1792. Francis II.

Kings of England and Scotland.

A.D.
William III. and Mary.—(*cont.*)
1702. Anne.
(*Great Britain*, 1707.)
1714. George I. } House of Hanover.
1727. George II. }
1760. George III. }

Kings of Spain.

1700. Philip V.
1724. Louis I.
1724. Philip V. again.
1745. Ferdinand VI.
1759. Charles III.
1788. Charles IV.

Distinguished Men.

Addison, Steele, Swift, Pope, Robertson, Hume, Gibbon, Voltaire, Rousseau, Lesage, Marmontel, Montesquieu, Franklin, (1706–1790,) Johnson, (1709–1784,) Goldsmith, (1728–1774,) Wolfe, (1726–1759,) Washington, (1732–1799.)

THE EIGHTEENTH CENTURY.

INDIA—AMERICA—FRANCE.

THE characteristic feature of this period is constant change on the greatest scale. Hitherto changes have occurred in the internal government of nations: the monarchic or popular feeling has found its expression in the alternate elevation of the Kingly or Parliamentary power. But in this most momentous of the centuries, nations themselves come into being or disappear. Russia and Prussia for the first time play conspicuous parts in the great drama of human affairs. France, which begins the century with the despotic Louis the Fourteenth at its head, leaves it as a vigorous Republic, with Napoleon Buonaparte as its First Consul. The foundations of a British empire were laid in India, which before the end of the period more than compensated for the loss of that other empire in the West, which is now the United States of America. It was the century of the breaking of old traditions, and of the introduction of new systems in life and government,—more complete in its transformations than the splitting up into hitherto unheard-of nationalities of the old Roman world had been; for what Goth and Vandal, and Frank and Lombard, were to the political geography of Europe in the earlier time, new modes of thought, both religious and political, were to the moral constitution of that later date. The barbarous invasions of the early centuries were the overflowing of rivers by the breaking down of the embankments; the revolutionary madness of France was the sudden detachment of an avalanche which had been growing unobserved, but which at last a voice or a footstep was sufficient to set in motion. In all nations it was a period of doubt and uneasiness. Something was about to happen, but nobody could say what. The political sleight-of-hand men, who considered the safety of the world to depend on the balance of power, where a weight must be cast into one scale, exactly sufficient, and not more than sufficient, to keep the other in equilibrio, were never so much puzzled since the science of balancing began. A vast country, hitherto omitted from their calculations, or only considered as a make-weight against Sweden or Denmark, suddenly came forward to be a check, and sometimes an over-weight, to half the states in Europe. Something had therefore to be found to be a counterpoise to the twenty millions of men and illimitable dominions of the Russian Czars. This was close at the conjurer's hand in Prussia and her Austrian neighbour. Counties were added,—populations fitted in,—Silesia given to the one, Gallicia added to the other; and at last the whole of Poland, which had ceased to be of any importance in its separate existence, was cut up into such portions as might be required, with here a fragment and there a fragment, till the scales stood pretty even, and the three contiguous kingdoms were satisfied with their respective shares of infamy and plunder. If you hear, therefore, of robberies upon a gigantic scale,—no longer the buccaneering exploits of a few isolated adventurers in the Western seas, but of kingdoms deliberately stolen, or imperiously taken hold of by the right of the strong hand; of the same Titanic magnitude distinguishing almost all other transactions; colonies throwing off their allegiance, and swelling out into hostile empires, instead of the usual discontent and occasional quarrellings between the mother-country and her children; of whole nations breaking forth into anarchy, instead of the former local efforts at reformation ending in temporary civil strife; of commercial speculations reaching the sublime of swindling and credulity, and involving whole populations in ruin; and of commercial establishments, on the other hand, vaster even in their territorial acquisitions than all the conquests of Alexander,—you are to remember that these things can only have happened in the Eighteenth Century; the century when the trammels of all former experiences were thrown off, and when wealth, power, energy, and mental aspirations were pushed to an unexampled excess. This exaggerated action of the age is shown in the one great statement which nearly comprehends all the rest. The Debt of this country, which at the beginning of this century was sixteen millions and a half and tormented our forefathers with fears of bankruptcy, had risen at the end of it, in the heroic madness of conquest and national pride, to the sum of three hundred and eighty millions, without a doubt of our perfect competency to sustain the burden.

If the tendency of affairs on the other side of our encircling sea was to pull down, to destroy, to modify, and to redistribute, the tendency at home was to build up and consolidate; so that in almost exact proportion to the wild experiments and frantic strugglings of other nations after something new—new principles of government, new theories of society—there arose in this country a dogged spirit of resistance to all alterations, and a persistence in old paths and old opinions. The charms which constitution-mongers saw in untried novelties and philosophic systems existed for John Bull only in what had stood the wear and tear of hundreds of years. The Prussians, Austrians, Americans, and finally the French, were groping after vague abstractions; and Frederick the Soldier, and Joseph the Philanthropist, and Citizen Franklin, and Lafayette and Mirabeau, were each in their own way carried away with the delusion of a golden age; but the English statesmen clung rigidly to the realities of life,—declared the universal fraternity of nations to be a cry of knaves or hypocrites,—and answered all exclamations about the dignity of humanity and the sovereignty of the people with "Rule Britannia," and "God save the King." How deeply this sentiment of loyalty and traditionary Toryism is seated in the national mind is proved by nothing so much as by the dreadful ordeal it had to go through in the days of the first two Georges. It certainly was a faith altogether independent of external circumstances, which saw the divinity that hedges kings in such vulgar, gossiping, and undignified individuals. And yet through all the troubled years of their reigns the great British heart beat true with loyalty to the throne, though it was grieved with the proceedings of the sovereigns; and when the third George gave it a man to rally round—as truly native-born as the most indigenous of the people, as stubborn, as strong-willed, and as determined to resist innovation as the most consistent of the squires and most anti-foreign of the citizens—the nation attained a point of union which had never been known in all their previous history, and looked across the Channel, at the insanity of the perplexed populations and the threats of their furious leaders, with a growl of contempt and hatred which warned their democrats and incendiaries of the fate that awaited them here. There are times in all national annals when the narrowest prejudices have an amazing resemblance to the noblest virtues. When Hannibal was encamped at the gates of Rome, the bigoted old

Patricians in the forum carried on their courts of law as usual, and would not deduct a farthing from the value of the lands they set up for sale, though the besieger was encamped upon them. When a king of Sicily offered a great army and fleet for the defence of Greece against the Persians, the Athenian ambassador said, "Heaven forefend that a man of Athens should serve under a foreign admiral!" The Lacedemonian ambassador said the Spartans would put him to death if he proposed any man but a Spartan to command their troops; and those very prejudiced and narrow-minded patriots were reduced to the necessity of exterminating the invaders by themselves. Great Britain, in the year 1800, was also of opinion that she was equal to all the world,—that she could hold her own whatever powers might be gathered against her,—and would not have exchanged her Hood, and Jervis, and Nelson, for the assistance of all the fleets of Europe.

Nothing seems to die out so rapidly as the memory of martial achievements. The military glory of this country is a thing of fits and starts. Cressy and Poictiers left us at a pitch of reputation which you might have supposed would have lasted for a long time. But in a very few years after those victories the English name was a byword of reproach. All the conquests of the Edwards were wrenched away, and it needed only the short period of the reign of Richard the Second to sink the recollection of the imperturbable line and inevitable shaft. Henry the Fifth and Agincourt for a moment brought the previous triumphs into very vivid remembrance. But civil dissensions between York and Lancaster blunted the English sword upon kindred helmets, and peaceful Henry the Seventh loaded the subject with intolerable taxes, and his son wasted his treasures in feasts and tournaments. The long reigns of Elizabeth and James were undistinguished by British armies performing any separate achievements on the Continent; and again civil war lavished on domestic fields an amount of courage and conduct which would have eclipsed all previous actions if exhibited on a wider scene. We need not, therefore, be surprised, if, after the astonishing course of Louis the Fourteenth's arms, the discomfiture of his adversaries, the constant repulses of the English contingent which fought under William in Flanders, and at last the quiet, looking so like exhaustion, which ushered in the Eighteenth Century, the British forces were despised, and we were confessed, in the ludicrous cant which at intervals becomes fashionable still, to be not a military nation. How this astounding proposition agrees with the fact that we have met in battle every single nation, and tribe, and kindred, and tongue, on the face of the whole earth, in Europe, Asia, Africa, and America, and have beaten them all; how it further agrees with the fact that no civilized power was ever engaged in such constant and multitudinous wars, so that there is no month or week in the history of the last two hundred years in which it can be said we were not interchanging shot or sabre-stroke somewhere or other on the surface of the globe; how, further still, the statement is to be reconciled with the fact, perceptible to all mankind, that the result of these engagements is an unexampled growth of influence and empire,—the acquisition of kingdoms defended by millions of warriors in Hindostan, of colonies ten times the extent of the conqueror's realm, defended by Montcalm and the armies of France,—we must leave to the individuals who make it: the truth being that the British people is not only the most military nation the world has ever seen, not excepting the Roman, but the most warlike. It is impossible to say when these pages may meet the reader's eye; but, at whatever time it may be, he has only to look at the "Times" newspaper of that morning, and he will see that either in the East or the West, in China or the Cape, or the Persian Gulf, or on the Indus, or the Irrawaddy, the meteor flag is waved in bloody advance. And this seems an indispensable part of the British position. She is so ludicrously small upon the map, and so absorbed in speculation, so padded with cotton, and so sunk in coal-pits, that it is only constant experience of her prowess that keeps the world aware of her power.. The other great nations can repose upon their size, and their armies of six or seven hundred thousand men. Nobody would think France or Russia weak because they were inactive. But with us the case is different: we must fight or fall.

Twice in the century we are now engaged on, we rose to be first of the military states in Europe, and twice, by mere inaction, we sank to the rank of Portugal or Naples.

Charles the Second of Spain died in November, 1700,—a person so feeble in health and intellect that in a lower state of life he would have been put in charge of guardians and debarred from the management of his affairs. As he was a king, these duties were performed on his behalf by the priests, and the wretched young man—he succeeded at three years old—was nothing but the slave and plaything of his confessor. Yet, though his existence was of no importance, his decease set all Europe in turmoil. By his testament, obtained from him on his death-bed, he appointed the grandson of Louis the Fourteenth his heir. A previous will had nominated Charles of Austria. A previous treaty between Louis and William of England and the States of Holland had arranged a partition of the Spanish monarchy for the benefit of the contracting parties and the maintenance of the balance of power. But now, when a choice was to be made between the wills and the treaty, between the balance of power and his personal ambition, the temptation was too great for the cupidity of the Grand Monarque. He accepted the throne of Spain and the Indies for his grandson Philip of Anjou, and sent him over the Pyrenees to take possession of his dignity. The stroke was so sudden that people were silent from surprise. A French prince at Madrid, at Milan, and Naples, was only the lieutenant in those capitals for the French king. The preponderance of the house of Bourbon was dangerous to the liberties of Europe, and when the house of Bourbon was represented by the haughtiest, and vainest, and most insulting of men, the dignity of the remaining sovereigns was offended by his ostentatious superiority; and the house of Austria, which in the previous century had been the terror of statesmen and princes, was turned to as a shelter from its successful rival, and all the world prepared to defend the cause of the Austrian Charles. The affairs of Europe, which were disturbed by the death of an imbecile king in Spain, were further complicated by the death of a still more imbecile king at St. Germain's. James the Second brought his strange life to a close in 1701; and, though the advisers of Louis pointed out the consequence of offending England at that particular time by recognising the Prince of Wales as inheritor of the English crown, the vanity of the old man who could not forego the luxury of having a crowned king among his attendants prevailed over his better knowledge, and one day, to the amazement of courtiers and council, he gave the royal reception to James the Third, and threw down the gauntlet to William and England, which they were not slow to take up. William of Orange was not popular among his new subjects, and was always looked on as a foreigner. Perhaps the memory of Ruyter and Van Tromp was still fresh enough to make him additionally disliked because he was a Dutchman. But when it was known over the country that the bigoted and insulting despot in Paris had nominated a King of England, while the man the nation had chosen was still alive in Whitehall, the indignation of all classes was roused, and found its expression in loyalty and attachment to their deliverer from Popery and persecution. Great exertions were made to conduct the war on a scale befitting the importance of the interests at stake. Addresses poured in, with declarations of devotion to the throne; troops were raised, and taxes voted; and in the midst of these preparations, the King, prematurely old, in the fifty-third year of his age, died of a fall from his horse at Kensington, in March, 1702, and the powers of Europe felt that the best soldier they possessed was lost to the cause. Rather it was a fortunate thing for the confederated princes that William died at this time; for he never rose to the rank of a first-rate commander, and was so ambitious of glory and power that he would not have left the way clear for a greater than himself.

This was found in Marlborough. Military science was the characteristic of this illustrious general; and no one before his time had ever possessed in an equal degree the power of attaching an army to its chief, or of regulating his strategic movements by the higher consideration of policy and statesmanship. For the first time, in English history at least, a march was equivalent to a battle. A change of his camp, or even a temporary retreat, was as effectual as a victory; and it was seen by the clearer observers of the time that a campaign was a game of skill, and not of the mere dash and intrepidity which appeal to the vulgar passions of our nature. Not so, however, the general public: their idea of war was a succession of hard knocks, with enormous lists of the killed and wounded. A manœuvre, without a charge of bayonets at the end of it, was little better than cowardice; and complaints were loud and common against the inactivity of a man who, by dint of long-prepared combinations, compelled the enemy to retreat by a mere shift of position and cleared the Low Countries of its invaders without requiring to strike a blow. "Let them see how we can fight," cried all the corporations in the realm: "anybody can march and pitch his camp." And it is not impossible that the foreign populations who had never seen the red-coats, or, at most, who had only known them acting as auxiliaries to the Dutch and often compelled to retire before the numbers and impetuosity of the French, had no expectation of success when they should be fairly brought opposite their former antagonists. Friends and foes alike were prepared for a renewal of the days of Luxembourg and Turenne. In this they were not disappointed; for a pupil of Turenne renewed, in a very remarkable manner, the glories of his master. Marlborough had served under that great commander, and profited by his lessons. He had fifty thousand British soldiers under his undivided command; and, to please the grumblers at home and the doubters abroad, he made the reign of Anne the most glorious in the English military annals by thick-coming fights, still unforgotten, though dimmed by the exploits of the more illustrious Wellington. The first of these was Blenheim, against the French and Bavarians, in 1704. How different this was from the hand-to-hand thrust and parry of ancient times is shown by the fate of a strong body of French, who were so posted on this occasion that the duke saw they were in his power without requiring to fire a gun. He sent his aid-de-camp, Lord Orkney, to them to point out the hopelessness of their position; and when he rode up, accompanied by a French officer, to act, perhaps, as his interpreter, a shout of gratulation broke from the unsuspecting Frenchmen. "Is it a prisoner you have brought us?" they asked their countryman. "Alas! no," he replies: "Lord Orkney has come from Marlborough to tell you you are his prisoners. His lordship offers you your lives." A glance at the contending armies confirmed the truth of this appalling communication, and the brigade laid down its arms. The tide of victory, once begun, knew no ebb till the grandeur of Louis the Fourteenth was overwhelmed. Disgraces followed quickly one upon the other,—marshals beaten, towns taken, conquests lost, his wealth exhausted, his people discontented, and the bravest of his generals hopeless of success. Prince Eugene of Savoy, equal to Marlborough in military genius, was more embittered against the French monarch, to whom he had offered his services, and who had had the folly to reject them. France, on the side of Germany and the Low Countries, was pressed upon by the triumphant invaders. In Spain, the affairs of the new king were more desperate still. Gibraltar was taken in 1704. Lord Peterborough, a wiser Quixote, of whose victories it is difficult to say whether they were the result of madness or skill, marched through the kingdom at the head of six or seven thousand English and conquered wherever he went.

When the war had lasted eight or nine years, the reputation of Marlborough and the British arms was at its height. Our fleets were masters of the sea, and the Grand Monarque sent humble petitions to the opposing powers for peace upon any terms. People tell us that Marlborough rejected all overtures which might have deprived him of the immense emoluments he received for carrying on the war. Perhaps, also, he was inspired

by the love of fame; but, whether meanness or ambition was his motive, his warlike propensities were finally
A.D. 1711. overcome,—for his wife, the imperious duchess, quarrelled with Queen Anne,—the ministry was changed, and the jealousies of Whitehall interfered with the campaigns in Flanders. Marlborough was displaced, and a peace patched up, which, under the name of the
A.D. 1713. Peace of Utrecht, is quoted as showing what small fruits British diplomacy sometimes derives from British valour. Louis the Fourteenth, conquered at all points, his kingdom exhausted, and all his reputation gone, saw his grandson in possession of the crown which had been the original cause of the war, and Great Britain rewarded for all her struggles by the empty glory of filling up the harbour of Dunkirk, and the scarcely more substantial advantage, as many considered it at the time, of retaining Gibraltar, a barren rock, and Minorca, a useless island. After this, we find a long period of inaction on the continent produce its usual effect. When thirty years had passed without the foreign populations having sight of the British grenadiers, they either forgot their existence altogether, or had persuaded them-
A.D. 1743. selves that the new generation had greatly de-
A.D. 1745. teriorated from the old. It needed the victory of Dettingen, and the more glorious repulse of Fontenoy, to recall the soldiers of Oudenarde and Malplaquet.

In the interval, amazing things had been going on. Even while the career of Marlborough was attended with such glory in arms, a peaceful achievement was accomplished of far more importance than all his victories. An Act of Union between the two peoples who occupied the Isle was passed by both their Parliaments in 1707, and England and Scotland disappeared in their separate nationalities, to receive the more dignified appellation of the Kingdom of Great Britain. This was a statesman's triumph; for the popular feeling on both sides of the Tweed was against it. Scotland considered herself sold; and England thought she was cheated. Clauses were introduced to preserve, as far as possible, the distinctions which each thought it for its honour to keep up. National peculiarities exaggerated themselves to prevent the chance of being obliterated; and Scotchmen were never so Scotch, nor Englishmen ever so English, as at the time when these denominations were about to cease. As neighbours, with the mere tie between them of being subjects of the same crown, they were on amicable and respectful terms. But when the alliance was proposed to be more intimate, their interests to be considered identical and the Parliaments to be merged in one, both parties took the alarm. "The preponderating number of English members would scarcely be affected by the miserable forty-five votes reserved for the Scotch representatives," said Caledonia, stern and wild. "The compact phalanx of forty-five determined Scotchmen will give them the decision of every question brought before Parliament," replied England, with equal fear,—and equal misapprehension, as it happily turned out. When eight years had elapsed after this great event in our domestic history, with just sufficient experience of the new machinery to find out some of its defects, it was put to the proof by an incident which might have been fatal to a far longer established system of government. This was a rebellion in favour of the exiled Stuarts. James the Third, whom we saw recognised by Louis the Fourteenth on the death of his father in 1701, made his appearance among the Highlanders of the North in 1714, and summoned them to support his family claims.

But the memory of his ancestors was too recent. Men of middle age remembered James the Second in

his tyrannical supremacy at Holyrood. The time was not sufficiently remote for romance to have gathered round the harsh reality and hidden its repulsive outlines. A few months showed the Pretender the hopelessness of his attempt; and the tranquillity of the country was considered to be re-established when the adherents of the losing cause were visited with the harshest penalties. The real result of these vindictive punishments was, that they added the spirit of revenge for private wrong to the spirit of loyalty to the banished line. Many circumstances concurred to favour the defeated candidate, who seemed to require to do nothing but bide his time. The throne was no longer held, even under legalized usurpation, as the discontented expressed it, by one of the ancient blood. A foreigner, old and
A.D. 1714. stupid, had come over from Hanover and claimed the Parliamentary crown, and the few remaining links of attachment which kept the high-prerogative men and the Roman Catholics inactive in the reign of Queen Anne, the daughter of their rightful king, lost all their power over them on the advent of George the First, who had to trace up through mother and grandmother till he struck into the royal pedigree in the reign of James the First. It was thought hard that descent from that champion of monarchic authority and hereditary right should be pleaded as a title to a crown dependent on the popular choice. As years passed on, the number of the discontented was of course increased. Whoever considered himself neglected by the intrusive government turned instinctively to the rival house. A courtier offended by the brutal manners of the Hanoverian rulers looked longingly across the sea to the descendant of his lineal kings. The foreign predilections, and still more foreign English, of the coarse-minded Georges, made them unpopular with the weak or inconsiderate,

who did not see that a very inelegant pronunciation might be united with a true regard for the interests of their country.

The commercial passions of the nations succeeded to the military enthusiasm of the past age, and brought their usual fruits of selfish competition and social degradation. Money became the most powerful principle of public and private life: Sir Robert Walpole, a man of perfect honesty himself, founded his ministry on the avowed disbelief of personal honesty among all classes
A.D. 1720. of the people; and there were many things which appeared to justify his incredulity. There was the South-Sea Bubble, a swindling speculation, to which our own railway-mania is the only parallel, where lords and ladies, high ecclesiastics and dignified office-bearers, the highest and the lowest, rushed into the wildest excesses of gambling and false play, and which caused a greater loss of character and moral integrity than even of money to its dupes and framers. There was the acknowledged system of rewarding a ministerial vote with notes for five hundred or a thousand pounds. There were the party libels of the time, all imputing the greatest iniquities to the object of their vituperation, and left uncontradicted except by savage proceedings at law or by similar insinuations against the other side. There were philosophers like Bolingbroke and clergymen like Swift. But let us distinguish between the performers on the great scenes of life, the place-hunter at St. James's, and the great body of the English and Scottish gentry, and their still undepraved friends and neighbours, whom it is the fashion to involve in the same condemnation of recklessness and dishonour. We are to remember that the dregs of the former society were not yet cleared away. The generation had been brought up at the feet of the professors of morality and religion as

they were practised in the days of Charles and James, with Congreve and Wycherly for their exponents on the stage and Dryden for their poet-laureate.

It seems a characteristic of literature that it becomes pure in proportion as it becomes powerful. While it is the mere vehicle for amusement or the exercise of wit and fancy, it does not care in what degrading quarters its materials are found. But when it feels that its voice is influential and its lessons attended to by a wider audience, it rises to the height of the great office to which it is called, and is dignified because it is conscious of its authority. In the incontestable amendment visible in the writings of the period of Anne and the Georges, we find a proof that the vices of the busy politicians and gambling speculators were not shared by the general public. The papers of the *Spectator* and *Tatler*, the writings of Pope and Arbuthnot, were not addressed to a depraved or sensualized people, as the works of Rochester and Sedley had been. When we talk, therefore, of the Augustan age of Anne, we are to remember that its freedom from grossness and immorality is still more remarkable than its advance in literary merit, and we are to look on the conduct of intriguing directors and bribed members of Parliament as the relics of a time about to pass away and to give place to truer ideas of commercial honesty and public duty. The country, in spite of coarseness of manners and language, was still sound at heart. The jolly squire swore at inconvenient seasons and drank beyond what was right, but he kept open house to friend and tenant, administered justice to the best of his ability, had his children Christianly and virtuously brought up, and was a connecting link in his own neighbourhood between the great nobles who affected almost a princely state, and the snug merchant in the country town, or retired citizen from London, whom he met at the weekly club. The glimpses we get of the social status of the country gentlemen of Queen Anne make us enamoured of their simple ways and patriarchal position. For the argument to be drawn from the character and friends of Sir Roger de Coverly and the delightful Lady Lizard and her daughters, is that the great British nation was still the home of the domestic affections, that the behaviour was pure though the grammar was a little faulty, and the ideas modest and becoming though the expression might be somewhat unadorned. Hence it was that, when the trial came, the heart of all the people turned to the uninviting but honest man who filled the British throne. George the Second became a hero, because the country was healthy at the core.

A son of the old Pretender, relying on the lax morality of the statesmen and the venality of the courtiers, forgot the unshaken firmness and dogged love of the right which was yet a living principle among the populations of both the nations, and landed in the North of Scotland in 1745, to recover the kingdom of his ancestors by force of arms. The kingdoms, however, had got entirely out of the habit of being recovered by any such means. The law had become so powerful, and was so guarded by forms and precedents, that Prince Charles Edward would have had a better chance of obtaining his object by an action of ejectment, or a suit of recovery, than by the aid of sword and bayonet. Everybody knows the main incidents of this romantic campaign,—the successful battles which gave the insurgents the apparent command of the Lowlands,—the advance into England,—the retreat from Derby,—the disasters of the rebel army, and its final extinction at Culloden. But, although to us it appears a very serious state of affairs,—a crown placed on the arbitrament of war, battles in open field, surprise on the part of the Hanoverians, and loud talking on the part of their rivals,—the tranquillity of all ranks and in all quarters is the most inexplicable thing in the whole proceeding. When the landing was first announced, alarm was of course felt, as at a fair when it is reported that a tiger has broken loose from the menagerie. But in a little time every thing resumed its ordinary appearance. George himself cried, "Pooh! pooh! Don't talk to me of such nonsense." His ministers, who probably knew the state of public feeling, were equally unconcerned. A few troops were brought over from the Continent, to show that force was not wanting if the application of it was required. But in other respects no one appeared to believe that the assumed fears of the disaffected, and the no less assumed exultation of the Jacobites, had any foundation in fact. Trade, law, buying and selling, writing and publishing, went on exactly as before. The march of the Pretender was little attended to, except perhaps in the political circles in London. In the great towns it passed almost unheeded. Quiet families within a few miles of the invaders' march posted or walked across to see the uncouth battalions pass. Their strange appearance furnished subjects of conversation for a month; but nowhere does there seem to have been the terror of a real state of war,—the anxious waiting for intelligence, "the pang, the agony, the doubt:" no one felt uneasy as to the result. England had determined to have no more Stuart kings, and Scotland was beginning to feel the benefit of the Union, and left the defence of the true inheritor to the uninformed, discontented, disunited inhabitants of the hills. When the tribes emerged from their mountains, they seemed to melt like their winter snows. No squadrons of stout-armed cavaliers came to join them from holt and farm, as in the days of the Great Rebellion, when the royal flag was raised at Nottingham. Puritans and Independents took no heed, and cried no cries about "the sword of the Lord and of Gideon." They had turned cutlers at Sheffield and fustian-makers at Manchester. The Prince found not only that he created no enthusiasm, but no alarm,—a most painful thing for an invading chief; and, in fact, when they had reached the great central plains of England they felt lost in the immensity of the solitude that surrounded them. If they had met enemies they would have fought; if they had found friends they would have hoped; but they positively wasted away for lack of either confederate or opponent. The expedition disappeared like a small river in sand. What was the use of going on? If they reached London itself, they would be swallowed up in the vastness of the population, and, instead of meeting an army, they would be in danger of being taken up by the police. So they reversed their steps. Donald had stolen considerably in the course of the foray, and was anxious to go and invest his fortune in his native vale. An English guinea—a coin hitherto as fabulous as the *Bodach glas*—would pay the rent of his holding for twenty years; five pounds would make him a cousin of the Laird. But Donald never got back to display the spoils of Carlisle or Derby. He loitered by the road, and was stripped of all his booty. He was imprisoned, and hanged, and starved, and beaten, and A.D. 1746. finally, after the strange tragi-comedy of his fight at Falkirk, had the good fortune, on that bare expanse of Drummossie Moor, to hide some of the ludicrous features of his retreat in the glory of a warrior's death. Justice became revenge by its severity after the insurrection was quelled. The followers of the Prince were punished as traitors; but treason means rebellion against an acknowledged government, which extends to its subjects the securities of law. These did not exist in the Highlands. All those distant populations knew of law was the edge of its sword, not the balance of its scales. They saw their chiefs depressed, they remembered the dismal massacre of Glencoe in William's time, and the legal massacres of George the First's. They spoke another language, were different in blood, and manners, and religion, and should have been treated as prisoners of war fighting under a legal banner, and not drawn and quartered as revolted subjects. It is doubtful if one man in the hundred knew the name of the king he was trying to displace, or the position of the prince who summoned him to his camp. Poor, gallant, warm-hearted, ignorant, trusting Gael! His chieftain told him to follow and slay the Saxons, and he required no further instruction. He was not cruel or bloodthirsty in his strange advance. He had no personal enmity to Scot or Englishman, and, with the simple awe of childhood, soon looked with reverence on the proofs of wealth and skill which met him in the crowded cities and cultivated plains. He was subdued by the solemn cathedrals and grand old gentlemen's seats that studded all the road, as some of his ancestors, the ancient Gauls, had been at the sight of the Roman civilization. And, for all these causes, the incursion of the Jacobites left no lasting bitterness among the British peoples. Pity began before long to take the place of opposition; and when all was quite secure, and the Highlanders were fairly subdued, and the Pretender himself was sunk in sloth and drunkenness, a sort of morbid sympathy with the gallant adventurers arose among the new generation. Tender and romantic ballads, purporting to be "Laments for Charlie," and declarations of attachment to the "Young Chevalier," were composed by comfortable ladies and gentlemen, and sung in polished drawing-rooms in Edinburgh and London with immense applause. Macaulay's "Lays of Ancient Rome," or Aytoun's "Lays of the Scottish Cavaliers," have as much right to be called the contemporary expression of the sacrifice of Virginia or the burial of Dundee as the Jacobite songs to be the living voice of the Forty-Five. Who was there in the Forty-Five, or Forty-Six, or for many years after that date, to write such charming verses? The Highlanders themselves knew not a word of English; the blue bonnets in Scotland were not addicted to the graces of poetry and music. The citizens of England were too busy, the gentlemen of England too little concerned in the rising, to immortalize the landing at Kinloch-Moidart or the procession to Holyrood. The earliest song which commemorates the Pretender's arrival, or laments his fall, was not written within twenty years of his attempt. By that time George the Third was on the safest throne in Europe, and Great Britain was mistress of the trade of India and the illimitable regions of America. It was easy to sing about having our "rightful King," when we were in undisputed possession of the Ganges and the Hudson and had just planted the British colours on Quebec and Montreal.

This rebellion of Forty-Five, therefore, is remarkable as a feature in this century, not for the greatness of the interest it excited, but for the small effect it had upon either government or people. It showed on what firm foundations the liberties and religion of the nations rested, that the appearance of armed enemies upon our soil never shook our justly-balanced state. The courts sat at Westminster, and the bells rang for church. People read Thomson's "Seasons," and wondered at Garrick in "Hamlet" at Drury Lane.

Meantime, a great contest was going on abroad, which, after being hushed for a while by the peace of 1748, broke
A.D. 1756 out with fiercer vehemence than ever in what
-1763. is called the Seven Years' War. The military

hero of this period was Frederick the Second of Prussia, by whose genius and skill the kingdom he succeeded to—a match for Saxony or Bavaria—rapidly assumed its position as a first-rate power. A combination of all the old despotisms was formed against him,—not, however, without cause; for a more unprincipled remover of his neighbour's landmarks, and despiser of generosity and justice, never appeared in history. But when he was pressed on one side by Russia and Austria, and on the other by France, and all the little German potentates were on the watch to pounce on the unprotected State and get their respective shares in the general pillage, Frederick placed his life upon the cast, and stood the hazard of the die in many tremendous combats, crushed the belligerents one by one, made forced marches which caught them unawares, and, though often defeated, conducted his retreats so that they yielded him all the fruits of victory. In his extremity he sought and found alliances in the most unlikely quarters. Though a self-willed despot in his own domains, he won the earnest support and liberal subsidies of the freedom-loving English; and though a philosopher of the most amazing powers of unbelief, he awakened the sympathy of all the religious Protestants in our land. All his faults were forgiven—his unchivalrous treatment of the heroic *King* of Hungary, Maria-Theresa, the Empress-Queen, his assaults upon her territory, and general faithlessness and ambition—on the one strong ground that he opposed Catholics and tyrants, and, though irreligious and even scoffing himself, was at the head of a true-hearted Protestant people.

It is not unlikely the instincts of a free nation led us at that time to throw our moral weight, if nothing more, into the scale against the intrusion of a new and untried power which began to take part in the conflicts of Eu-

rope; for at this period we find the ill-omened announcement that the Russians have issued from their deserts a hundred thousand strong, and made themselves masters of most of the Prussian provinces. Though defeated in
A.D. 1758. the great battle of Zorndorf, they never lost the hope of renewing the march they had made eleven years before, when thirty-five thousand of them had rested on the Rhine. But Britain was not blind either to the past or future. At the head of our affairs was a man whose fame continues as fresh at the present hour as in the day of his greatness. William Pitt had been a cornet of horse, and even in his youth had attracted the admiration and hatred of old Sir Robert Walpole by an eloquence and a character which the world has agreed in honouring with the epithet of majestic; and when war was again perplexing the nations, and Britain, as usual, had sunk to the lowest point in the military estimate of the Continent, the Great Commoner, as he was called, took the government into his hands, and the glories of the noblest periods of our annals were immediately renewed or cast into the shade. Wherever the Great Commoner pointed with his finger, success was certain. His fleets swept the seas. Howe and Hawke and Boscawen executed his plans. In the East he was answered by the congenial energy of Clive, and in the West by the heroic bravery of Wolfe. For, though the war in which we were now engaged had commenced nominally for European interests, the crash of arms between France and England extended to all quarters of the world. In India and America equally their troops and policies were opposed, and, in fact, the battle of the two nations was fought out in those distant realms. Our triumph at Plassey and on the Heights of Abraham had an immense reaction on both the peoples at home. And a very cursory glance at those regions, from the

middle of the century, will be a fitting introduction to the crowning event of the period we have now reached, —namely, the French Revolution of 1789. The rise of the British Empire in the East, no less than the loss of our dominion in the West, will be found to contribute to that grand catastrophe, of which the results for good and evil will be felt "to the last syllable of recorded time."

The first commercial adventure to India was in the bold days of Elizabeth, in 1591. In the course of a hundred years from that time various companies had been established by royal charter, and a regular trade had sprung up. In 1702 all previous charters were consolidated into one, and the East India Company began its career. Its beginning was very quiet and humble. It was a trader, and nothing more; but when it saw a convenient harbour, a favourable landing-place, and an industrious population, it bent as lowly as any Oriental slave at the footstool of the unsuspecting Rajah, and obtained permission to build a storehouse, to widen the wharf, and, finally, to erect a small tower, merely for the defence of its property from the dangerous inhabitants of the town. The storehouses became barracks, the towers became citadels; and by the year 1750 the recognised possessions of the inoffensive and unambitious merchants comprised mighty states, and were dotted at intervals along the coast from Surat and Bombay on the west to Madras and Calcutta on the east and far north. The French also had not been idle, and looked out ill pleased, from their domains at Pondicherry and Chandernagore, on the widely-diffused settlements and stealthy progress of their silent rivals. They might have made as rapid progress, and secured as extensive settlements, if they had imitated their rivals' stealthiness and silence. But power is nothing in the estimation of a Frenchman unless he can wear it like a court suit and display it to all the world. The governors, therefore, of their factories, obtained honours and ornaments from the native princes. One went so far as to forge a gift of almost regal power from the Great Mogul, and sat on a musnud, and was addressed with prostration by his countrymen and the workmen in the warerooms. Wherever the British wormed their way, the French put obstacles in their path. Whether there was peace between Paris and London or not, made no difference to the rival companies on the Coromandel shore. They were always at war, and only cloaked their national hatred under the guise of supporters of opposite pretenders to some Indian throne. Great men arose on both sides. The climate or policies of Hindostan, which weaken the native inhabitant, only call forth the energies and manly virtues of the intrusive settler. No kingdom has such a bead-roll of illustrious names as the British occupation. That one century of "work and will" has called forth more self-reliant heroism and statesmanlike sagacity than any period of three times the extent since the Norman Conquest. From Clive, the first of the line, to the Lawrences and Havelocks of the present day, there has been no pause in the patriotic and chivalrous procession. Clive came just at the proper time. A born general, though sent out in an humble mercantile situation, he retrieved the affairs of his employers and laid the foundation of a new empire for the British crown. Calcutta had been seized by a native ruler, instigated by the French, in 1756. The British residents, to the number of one hundred and forty-six, were packed in a frightful dungeon without a sufficiency of light or air, and, after a night which transcends all nights of suffering and despair, when the prison-doors were thrown open, but twenty-two of the whole number survived. But these were twenty-two living witnesses to the tyranny and cruelty of Surajah Dowlat. Clive was on his track ere many months had passed. Calcutta was recovered, other places were taken, and the battle of Plassey fought. In this unparalleled exploit, Clive, with three thousand soldiers, principally Sepoys, revenged the victims of the Black Hole, by defeating their murderer at the head of sixty thousand men. This was on the 23d of June, 1757; and when in that same year the news of the great European war between the nations came thundering up the Ganges, the victors enlarged their plans. They determined to expel the French from all their possessions in the East; and Admiral Pococke and Colonel Coote were worthy rivals of the gallant Clive. Great fleets encountered in the Indian seas, and victory was always with the British flag. Battles took place by land, and uniformly with the same result. Closer and closer the invading lines converged upon the French; and at last, in 1761, Pondicherry, the last remaining of all their establishments, was taken, after a vigorous defence, and the French influence was at an end in India. These four years, from 1757 to 1761, had been scarcely less prolific of distinguished men on the French side than our own. The last known of these was Lally Tollendal, a man of a furious courage and headstrong disposition, against whom his enemies at home had no ground of accusation except his want of success and savageness of manner. Yet when he returned, after the loss of Pondicherry and a long imprisonment in England, he was attacked with all the vehemence of personal hatred. He was tried for betraying the interests of the king, tortured, and executed. The prosecution lasted many years, and the public rage seemed rather to increase. Long after peace was concluded between France and England, A.D. 1766. the tragedy of the French expulsion from India received its final scene in the death of the unfortunate Count Lally.

Quebec and its dependencies, during the same glorious administration, were conquered and annexed by Wolfe; and already the throes of the great Revolution were felt, though the causes remained obscure. Cut off from the money-making regions of Hindostan and the patriarchal settlements of Canada, the Frenchman, oppressed at home, had no outlet either for his ambition or discontent. The feeling of his misery was further aggravated by the sight of British prosperity. The race of men called Nabobs, mercantile adventurers who had gone out to India poor and came back loaded with almost incredible wealth, brought the ostentatious habits of their Oriental experience with them to Europe, and offended French and English alike by the tasteless profusion of their expense. Money wrung by extortion from native princes was lavished without enjoyment by the denationalized *parvenu*. A French duke found himself outglittered by the equipage of the over-enriched clove-dealer, —and hated him for his presumption. The Frenchman of lower rank must have looked on him as the lucky and dishonourable rival who had usurped his place, and hated him for the opportunity he had possessed of winning all that wealth. Ground to the earth by taxes and toil, without a chance of rising in the social scale or of escaping from the ever-growing burden of his griefs, the French peasant and small farmer must have listened with indignation to the accounts of British families of their own rank emerging from a twenty years' residence in Madras or Calcutta with more riches than half the hereditary nobles. It was therefore with a feeling of unanimous satisfaction that all classes of

Frenchmen heard, in 1773, that the old English colonies in America were filled with disaffection,—that Boston had risen in insurrection, and that a spirit of resistance to the mother-country was rife in all the provinces.

The quarrel came to a crisis between the Crown and the colonies within fourteen years of the conquest of Canada. It seemed as if the British had provided themselves with a new territory to compensate for the approaching loss of the old; and bitter must have been the reflection of the French when they perceived that the loyalty of that recent acquisition remained undisturbed throughout the succeeding troubles. Taxation, the root of all strength and the cause of all weakness, had been pushed to excess, not in the amount of its exaction, but in the principle of its imposition; and the British blood had not been so colonialized as to submit to what struck the inhabitants of all the towns as an unjustifiable exercise of power. The cry at first, therefore, was, No tax without representation; but the cry waxed louder and took other forms of expression. The cry was despised, whether gentle or loud,—then listened to,—then resented. The passions of both countries became raised. America would not submit to dictation; Britain would not be silenced by threats. Feelings which would have found vent at home in angry speeches in Parliament, and riots at a new election, took a far more serious shape when existing between populations separated indeed by a wide ocean, but identical in most of their qualities and aspirations. The king has been blamed. "George the Third lost us the colonies by his obstinacy: he would not yield an inch of his royal dignity, and behold the United States our rivals and enemies,—perhaps some day our conquerors and oppressors!" Now, we should remember that the Great Britain of 1774 was a very narrow-minded, self-opinion-

ated, pig-headed Great Britain, compared to the cosmopolitan, philanthropical, and altogether disinterested Great Britain we call it now. If the king had bated his breath for a moment, or even spoken respectfully and kindly of the traitors and rebels who were firing upon his flags, he would have been the most unpopular man in his dominions. Many, no doubt, held aloof, and found excuses for the colonists' behaviour; but the influence of those meditative spirits was small; their voice was drowned in the chorus of indignation at what appeared revolt and mutiny more than resistance to injustice. And when other elements came into the question,—when the French monarch, ostensibly at peace with Britain, permitted his nobles and generals and soldiers to volunteer in the patriot cause,—the sentiments of this nation became embittered with its hereditary dislike to its ancient foe. We turned them out of India: were they going to turn us out of America? We had taken Canada: are they going to take New York? We might have offered terms to our own countrymen, made concessions, granted exemptions from imperial burdens, or even a share in imperial legislation; but with Lafayette haranguing about abstract freedom, and all the young counts and marquises of his expedi-
A.D. 1778 tion declaring against the House of Lords, the
-1780. thing was impossible. War was declared upon France, and upon Spain, and upon Holland. We fought everywhere, and lavished blood and treasure in this great quarrel. And yet the nation had gradually accustomed itself to the new view of American wrongs. The Ministry, by going so far in their efforts at accommodation, had confessed the original injustice of their cause. So we fought with a blunted sword, and hailed even our victories with misgivings as to our right to win them. But it was the season of vast changes in

the political distribution of all the world. Prussia was a foremost kingdom. Russia was a European Empire. India had risen into a compact dominion under the shield of Britain. Why should not America take a substantive place in the great family of nations, and play a part hereafter in the old game of statesmen, called the Balance of Power? In 1783 this opinion prevailed. France, Spain, and Holland sheathed their swords. The Independence of the United States was acknowledged at the Peace of Versailles, and everybody believed that the struggle against established governments was over.

France seemed elevated by the results of the American War, and Great Britain humiliated. Prophecies were frequent about our rapid fall and final extinction. Our own orators were, as usual, the loudest in confessions of our powerlessness and decay. Our institutions were held up to dislike; and if you had believed the speeches and pamphlets of discontented patriots, you would have thought we were the most spiritless and down-trodden, the most unmerciful and dishonest, nation in the world. The whole land was in a fury of self-abasement at the degradation brought upon our name and standing by the treachery and iniquities of Warren Hastings in India; our European glory was crushed by the surrender at Paris. It must be satisfactory to all lovers of their country to know that John Bull has no such satisfaction as in proving that he is utterly exhausted,—always deceived by his friends, always overreached by his enemies, always disappointed in his aims. In this self-depreciating spirit he conducts all his wars and all his treaties; yet somehow it always happens that he gets what he wanted, and the overreaching and deceiving antagonist gives it up. His power is over a sixth of the human race, and he began a hundred years ago with a population of less than fourteen millions; and all the time he has been singing the most doleful ditties of the ill success that always attends him,—of his ruinous losses and heart-breaking disappointments. The men at the head of affairs in the trying years from the Peace of Versailles to 1793 were therefore quite right not to be taken in by the querulous lamentations of the nation. We had lost three millions of colonists, and gained three million independent customers. We were trading to India, and building up and putting down the oldest dynasties of Hindostan. Ships and commerce increased in a remarkable degree; the losses of the war were compensated by the gains of those peaceful pursuits in a very few years; and we were contented to leave to Paris the reputation of the gayest city in the world, and to the French the reputation of the happiest and best-ruled people. But Paris was the wretchedest of towns, and the French the most miserable of peoples. When anybody asks us in future what was the cause of the French Revolution, we need not waste time to discuss the writings of Voltaire, or the unbelief of the clergy, or the immorality of the nobles. We must answer at once by naming the one great cause by which all revolutions are produced,—over-taxation. The French peasant, sighing for liberty, had no higher object than an escape from the intolerable burden of his payments. He cared no more for the rights of man, or the happiness of the human race, than for the quarrels of Achilles and Agamemnon. He wanted to get rid of the "taille," the "corvée," and twenty other imposts which robbed him of his last penny. If he had had a chicken in his pot, and could do as he liked with his own spade and pick-axe, he never would have troubled his head about codes and constitutions. But life had become a burden to him. Everybody had turned against him. The grand old feudal noble, who would have protected and cherished him under the shadow of his castle-wall, was a lord-chamberlain at court. The kind old priest, who would have attended to his wants and fed him, if required, at the church-door, was dancing attendance in the ante-chamber of a great lady in Paris, or singing improper songs at a jolly supper-party at Versailles. There were intendants and commissaries visiting his wretched hovel at rapidly-decreasing intervals of time, to collect his contributions to the revenue. These men farmed the taxes, and squeezed out the last farthing like a Turkish pasha. But while the small land-owner—and they were already immensely numerous—and the serf—for he was no better—were oppressed by these exactions, the gentry were exempt. The seigneur visited his castle for a month or two in the year, but it was to embitter the country-man's lot by the contrast. His property had many rights, but no duties. In ancient times in France, and at all times in England, those two qualities went together. Our upper classes lived among their tenants and dependants. They had no alleviation of burdens in consequence of their wealth, but they took care that their poorer neighbours should have alleviation in consequence of their poverty. Cottages had no window-tax. The pressure of the public burdens increased with the power to bear them. But in France the reverse was the case. Poverty paid the money, and wealth and luxury spent it. The evil was too deep-rooted to be remedied without pulling up the tree. The wretched millions were starving, toiling, despairing, and the thousands were rioting in extravagance and show. The same thing occurred in 1789 as had occurred in the last glimmer of the Roman civilization in the time of Clovis. The Roman Emperor issued edicts for the collection of his revenue. Commissioners spread over the land; the miserable Gaul saw the last sheaf of his corn torn away, and the last lamb of his flock. But when the last property of the poorest was taken away, the imperial exchequer could not remain unfilled. You remember the unhappy men called Curials,—holders of small estates in the vicinity of towns. They were also endowed with rank, and appointed to office. Their office was to make up from their own resources, or by extra severity among their neighbours, for any deficiency in the sum assessed. Peasant, land-owner, curial,—all sank into hopeless misery by the crushing of this gold-producing machinery. They looked across the Rhine to Clovis and the Franks, and hailed the ferocious warriors as their deliverers from an intolerable woe. They could not be worse off by the sword of the stranger than by the ledger of the tax-collector. In 1789 the system of the old Roman extortion was revived. The village or district was made a curial, and became responsible in its aggregate character for the individual payments. If the number of payers diminished, the increase fell upon the few who were not yet stripped. The Clovis of the present day who was to do away with their oppressors, though perhaps to immolate themselves, was a Revolution,—a levelling of all distinctions, ranks, rights, exemptions, privileges. This was the "liberty, equality, fraternity" that were to overflow the worn-out world and fertilize it as the Nile does Egypt.

Great pity has naturally been expressed for the nobility (or gentry) and clergy of France; but, properly considered, France had at that time neither a nobility nor a clergy. A nobility with no status independent of the king—with no connection with its estates beyond the reception of their rents—with no weight in the legislature; with ridiculously exaggerated rank, and ridiculously contracted influence; with no interest in local expenditure or voice in public management; a gentry, in short, debarred from active life, except as officers of the army—shut out by monarchic jealousy from interference in affairs, and by the pride of birth from the pursuits of commerce—is not a gentry at all. A clergy, in the same way, is a priesthood only in right of its belief in the doctrines it professes to hold, and the attention it bestows on its parishioners. Except in some few instances, the Christianity both of faith and practice had disappeared from France. It was time, therefore, that nobility and clergy should also disappear. The excesses of the Revolution which broke out in 1789, and reached their climax in the murder of the king in 1793, showed the excesses of the misgovernment of former years. If there had been one redeeming feature of the ancient system, it would have produced its fruits in the milder treatment of the victims of the reaction. In one or two provinces, indeed, we are told that hereditary attachment still bound the people to their superiors, and in those provinces, the philosophic chronicler of the fact informs us, the centralizing system had not completed its authority. The gentry still performed some of the duties of their station, and the priests, of their profession. Everywhere else blind hatred, unreasoning hope, and bloody revenge. The century, which began with the vainglorious egotism of Louis the Fourteenth and the war of the Spanish Succession,—which progressed through the British masterdom of India and the self-sustaining republicanism of America,—died out in the convulsive strugglings of thirty-one millions of souls on the soil of France to breathe a purer political air and shake off the trammels which had gradually been riveted upon them for three hundred years. Great Britain had preceded them by a century, and has ever since shown the bloodless and legal origin of her freedom by the bloodless and legal use she has made of it. We emerged from the darkness of 1688 with all the great landmarks of our country not only erect, but strengthened. We had king, lords, and commons, and a respect for law, and veneration for precedents, which led the great Duke of Wellington to say, in answer to some question about the chance of a British revolution, that "no man could foresee whether such a thing might occur or not, but, when it did, he was sure it would be done by Act of Parliament."

War with France began in 1793. Our military reputation was at the lowest, for Wolfe and Clive had had time to be forgotten; and even our navy was looked on without dismay, for the laurels of Howe and Boscawen were sere from age. But in the remaining years of the century great things were done, and Britannia had the trident firmly in her hand. Jervis, and Duncan, and Nelson, were answering with victories at sea the triumphs of Napoleon in Italy. And while fame was blowing the names of those champions far and wide, a blast came across also from India, where Wellesley had begun his wondrous career. Equally matched the belligerents, and equally favoured with mighty men of valour to conduct their forces, the feverish energy of the newly-emancipated France being met by the healthful vigour of the matured and self-respecting Britain, the world was uncertain how the great drama would close. But the last year of the century seemed to incline the scale to the British side. Napoleon, after a dash at Egypt, had been checked by the guns of Nelson in the great battle of the Nile. He secretly withdrew from his dispirited army, and made his appearance in Paris as much in the character of a fugitive as of a candidate for power. But all the fruits of his former battles had been torn from his

A.D. 1798.

A.D. 1799.

countrymen in his absence. Italy was delivered from their grasp; Russia was pouring her hordes into the South; confusion was reigning everywhere, and the fleets of Great Britain were blocking up every harbour in France.

Napoleon was created First Consul, and the Century went down upon the final preparations of the embittered rivals. Both parties felt now that the struggle was for life or death, and "the boldest held his breath for a time," when he thought of what awful events the Nineteenth Century would be the scene.

INDEX.

THE END.

MODERN BRITISH ESSAYISTS,

COMPRISING

The Critical & Miscellaneous Works

OF

ALISON,	**CARLYLE,**
JEFFREY,	**MACAULAY,**
MACKINTOSH,	**SYDNEY SMITH,**
STEPHEN,	**TALFOURD,**

And Prof. WILSON.

In 8 vols., large 8vo., uniform Cloth, $13. Sheep, $17. Half Calf Ext., $25.

Each Volume to be had separately.

Alison's Essays.
Miscellaneous Essays. By ARCHIBALD ALISON, F. R. S. Reprinted from the English originals, with the author's corrections for this edition. 1 large vol. 8vo. Portrait. Cloth, $1 25; sheep, $1 75.

Carlyle's Essays.
Critical and Miscellaneous Essays. By THOMAS CARLYLE. Complete in one volume. 1 large vol. 8vo. Portrait. Cloth, $2; sheep, $2 50.

Jeffrey's Essays.
Contributions to the Edinburgh Review. By FRANCIS JEFFREY. The four volumes complete in one. 1 very large vol. 8vo. Portrait. Cloth, $2; sheep, $2 50.

Macaulay's Essays.
Essays, Critical and Miscellaneous. By T. BABINGTON MACAULAY. New and Revised edition. 1 very large vol. 8vo. Portrait. Cloth, $2; sheep, $2 50.

Mackintosh's Essays.
The Miscellaneous Works of the Right Honorable Sir JAMES MACKINTOSH. The three volumes in one. 1 vol. large 8vo. Portrait. Cloth, $2; sheep, $2 50.

Sydney Smith's Works.
The Works of the Rev. SYDNEY SMITH. Three volumes complete in one. 1 large vol. 8vo. Portrait. Cloth, $1 25; sheep, $1 75.

Talfourd's and Stephen's Essays.
Critical and Miscellaneous Writings of T. NOON TALFOURD, author of "Ion," &c. Critical and Miscellaneous Essays of JAMES STEPHEN. In 1 vol. large 8vo. Portrait. Cloth, $1 25; sheep, $1 75.

Wilson's Essays.
The Recreations of CHRISTOPHER NORTH [Prof. JOHN WILSON.] Complete in 1 vol. large 8vo. Portrait. Cloth, $1 25; sheep, $1 75.